Master the Art of Unreal Engine 4 - Blueprints

Creating a 3D Point 'n Click Adventure!

Master the Art of Unreal Engine 4 - Blueprints - Creating a 3D Point 'n Click Adventure!

First Published: 10/02/2015
Production Reference: 0501032SNAKE14180

ISBN-13: 978-1506119045
ISBN-10: 1506119042

www.kitatusstudios.co.uk
Cover image by Ryan Shah (contact@kitatusstudios.co.uk)

Credits

Author

Ryan Shah

Editor

Paul Alifragis

Special Thanks

Bojan Brankovic - Thanks for the inspiration for the book and for being totally awesome. You rock!

Patreons

Daniel Green

Ray Canapini

Rob Wheeler

James Leno

Steve Ruk Jr

Diego

Andrei Bosco Bezerra Torres

Tom Keen

Cameron Carroll

Brian Huqueriza

About the Author

Ryan Shah is Project Lead / Lead Developer at Kitatus Studios. Boasting over 10 years of experience creating video-games, Ryan has worked on an assortment of different programs to create video-game experiences.

Before Kitatus Studios, Ryan was a freelance writer, who self-published works of fiction. Using his experience as a writer, Ryan turned to video-games, a life-long passion to bring the worlds of his ideas to life.

He can be found online at http://kitatusstudios.co.uk and can be contacted at contact@kitatusstudios.co.uk

Acknowledgement

A huge thank-you and a half has to go to my beautiful girlfriend Scarlett, who no matter what has always believed in me when nobody else did. Her patience is inspiring.

I'd like to thank Epic for creating such a diverse yet easy to use system with Unreal Engine 4. When people say it's a game changer, they weren't wrong!

I'd also like to thank you, the reader. I might not know you personally, but by you buying this book - You're helping to support me and helping to support the video-game industry. Who knows - Maybe this book will help you and become the stepping stone you need to make the BEST GAME OF ALL TIME. Anything is possible!

Table of Contents

Preface

Unreal Engine 4 is the latest version of the popular video-game development package; the Unreal Engine. The Unreal Engine needs no introduction; Being the powerhouse behind the previous console generation from the start. To call the Unreal Engine a powerhouse would be an understatement, the Unreal Engine is everything a developer (Indie and Commercial) would ever need in a video-game engine to create their ideal project. With it's latest iteration, Unreal Engine 4, Epic has improved Unreal Engine and propelled the engine into the next-generation, they have brought the future to the present with Unreal Engine 4 and there's literally never been a better time to begin using Unreal Engine 4 for any project, big or small, commercial or independent.

Master the Art of Unreal Engine 4 - Blueprints (Point & Click) takes a concise, clear, informative but fun approach to developing Unreal Engine 4, without touching a single line of code. By using this book, you'll be creating various small projects completely in blueprint. From this book, you'll be equipped with the know-how you'll need to create the game of your dreams. On top of mastering the Blueprints system in Unreal Engine 4, you'll also learn the secrets behind getting the most out of the beast of an engine.

What You'll Need For This Book

In order to take full advantage of this book; You'll need a Windows, Mac or Linux computer that is capable of running Unreal Engine 4. It requires a computer with the following system configuration, which doubles up at the "Minimum Requirements" for this book:

- Desktop PC or Mac
- Windows 7 64-bit or Mac OS X 10.9.2 or later
- Quad-core Intel or AMD processor, 2.5 GHz or faster

- NVIDIA GeForce 470 GTX or AMD Radeon 6870 HD series card or higher
- 8 GB RAM

Note: Believe it or not, You'll also need Unreal Engine 4 (Version 4.5 or newer).

Who this Book is For

Mastering the Art of Unreal Engine 4 - Blueprints (Point 'n Click) is designed for anyone whose dreamt of creating video-games, but didn't have the knowhow to. This book is also designed for everyone who want to harness the power of Unreal Engine 4 to take their creations to the next level and beyond and the people who want to create games without writing a single line of code.

Those who are familiar with Unreal Engine 4 will have an easier time, but everything in the book is explained clearly and with reference screenshots to make the process of mastering the blueprints system in Unreal Engine 4 a breeze. People with no prior experience to using Unreal Engine 4, or game engines in general should have no problem with following this book, but if you need additional help with anything in the book, feel free to ask on the Unreal Engine Forums (http://forums.unrealengine.com) or email me directly: contact@kitatusstudios.co.uk.

Reader Feedback

I love feedback! Good or bad, it's all welcome and I highly recommend you do so! If you loved reading or hated it, I seriously would love to know. Feedback is important in helping letting me know how I've done, what needs to be fixed and I'm just generally intrigued on how well / bad I've done. I'm a perfectionist and I strive for the best, so if there's anything I can improve on, feel free to email: contact@kitatusstudios.co.uk

Customer Support

Since you're the owner of this book, You have the opportunity to get bonus content, such as colour images and project content: Head to http://content.Kitatusstudios.co.uk to access to these files!

Piracy

I'm not going to pretend it doesn't exist; Piracy is piracy and nothing is going to stop it. If you've pirated this book; It's alright. I'm not going to curse you or anything. It's sad that you're not willing to spend money on this book, but I know times are tough and in the digital world I know that everything is free to some people.

Due to the fact I've given up the time to write this book to help teach others to harness the power of Blueprints, losing out on work hours and time I could have spent on Super Distro (My first Commercially to-be-released project), I ask that if you pirated this book and you've enjoyed this book, Please consider purchasing Super Distro or you could send a donation through my website. This means that even if you don't spend the full-price on this book, My efforts to bring these tutorials to you aren't 100% in vein.

If you've purchased this book, then I can't thank-you enough for supporting me and my work and I seriously am grateful you're experiencing the book through legitimate means.

Errata

At the time of writing, the book has no errors. However, as the engine is updated, things might change. In the unlikely event some of the code no longer works, please email me immediately: contact@kitatusstudios.co.uk - By doing this, you not only secure the integrity of the book, but you also help others by not coming across errors and this leads to a stress-free experience with this book. Who knows, you might also be credited in later book revisions!

Downloading DLC (Downloadable Content)

You can download colour variations of the images in this book, as well as UE4 project files from http://content.kitatusstudios.co.uk.

Questions

If you have any questions, email me at contact@kitatusstudios.co.uk. The line is open, so please don't be afraid to get in touch.

IMPORTANT NOTICE:

This book was originally created as a continuation of the "Master the Art of Blueprints" series but during development became a re-imagining of the series, incorporating elements of the previous books to save you the time of having to read between the books.

This book, as well as containing the information on how to create a Point and Click adventure game, also contains the information that was previously available in some form in previous books: *Book #1* and *UMG / HUD Basics*.

I have tried to write in a style that is aimed at new readers as well as readers of these previous books. Even if there's a part in this book that has been covered previously, please do not skip these parts - There is new, crucial information contained within that will only improve your skills for your future adventures!

Also, PLEASE NOTE that this book has been created with the intention of use for Unreal Engine 4 version 4.6. Any future changes to the engine that change the functionality of this book will be corrected on http://www.kitatus.co.uk in the forums, so this book will never become "Outdated"!

Best of luck developers, I hope you have great fun with this book and your projects!

What Is Our Mission?

In this edition of "Master the Art of Unreal Engine 4 - Blueprints", we are going to be creating a "Point and Click" adventure game. As we want to utilize the full power of Unreal Engine 4; We'll be creating a fully 3D Point and Click style of game in the same vain of many *Telltale Games* games that are available these days such as *Sam and Max, Tales Of Monkey Island, Back To The Future* .etc

So what are we going to create today?

- Creating an interactive scene
- Manipulating the camera with Blueprints
- Creating our own controls!
- Importing files from other projects
- Basic Inventory System
- Building lighting, Navmeshes and more!
- Blueprints: How to use them and how it's almost like child's play!
- What is the difference between an Int, Float, Bool .etc
- Much… Much More!

Let's Begin the Mission!

Template to use:

Third-Person Blueprint

Time it should Take:

2 hours (Minimum) <- There's a LOT of ground to cover!

What we'll be making:

Interactive scene where players can walk around, interact with objects as well as picking up objects. We'll also touch on Matinee scenes (Cutscenes), Player-driven choices via a player conversation as well as a simple menu.

By the end of this mission, You will:

- Have a great starting point for creating your own FULL point and click adventure project!
- Have an understanding of coding through Blueprints, Where you (Hopefully!) won't need to view tutorials to create the game of your dreams!
- Feel comfortable in Unreal Engine to create your dream projects!
- Gain knowledge of working with a game engine to create video-games.
- Have a great time (I'll make sure to keep it laid-back and fun!)

Let's Begin!

Hello beautiful developers! Today, we'll be tackling something suggested by *Bojan* via email. He wrote:

" *I am interested to make a [Point and Click] adventure type of game with dialogs, some puzzle logics etc...Could you include in your future books something about that?* "

Well Bojan, I'm here to try and help solve your question!

We'll start with the very basics and we'll build upon that until we have our own 3D "Point 'n Click" adventure game!

To start things off, we're obviously going to need a new project, but we'll need some more stuff first! If you've been following the books to date *(If not, do not worry. We'll be covering all the things we have covered previously AND MORE!)* , the next few steps will be a breeze! If you're unsure how to make a new project, don't worry, here's a super-quick and simple run-through to get you started in no time!

First things first, Open up the Unreal Engine launcher, which looks something like this:

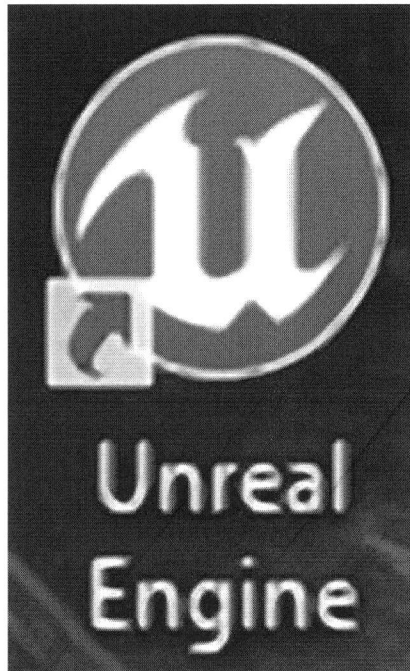

This is how it looks on the desktop, but as long as you've installed Unreal Engine 4, you should be able to find it on your computer without a problem!

Once it's been opened, you'll be greeted with something that looks similar to this (But it will no doubt change over time, but don't worry, it's super simple to navigate around!)

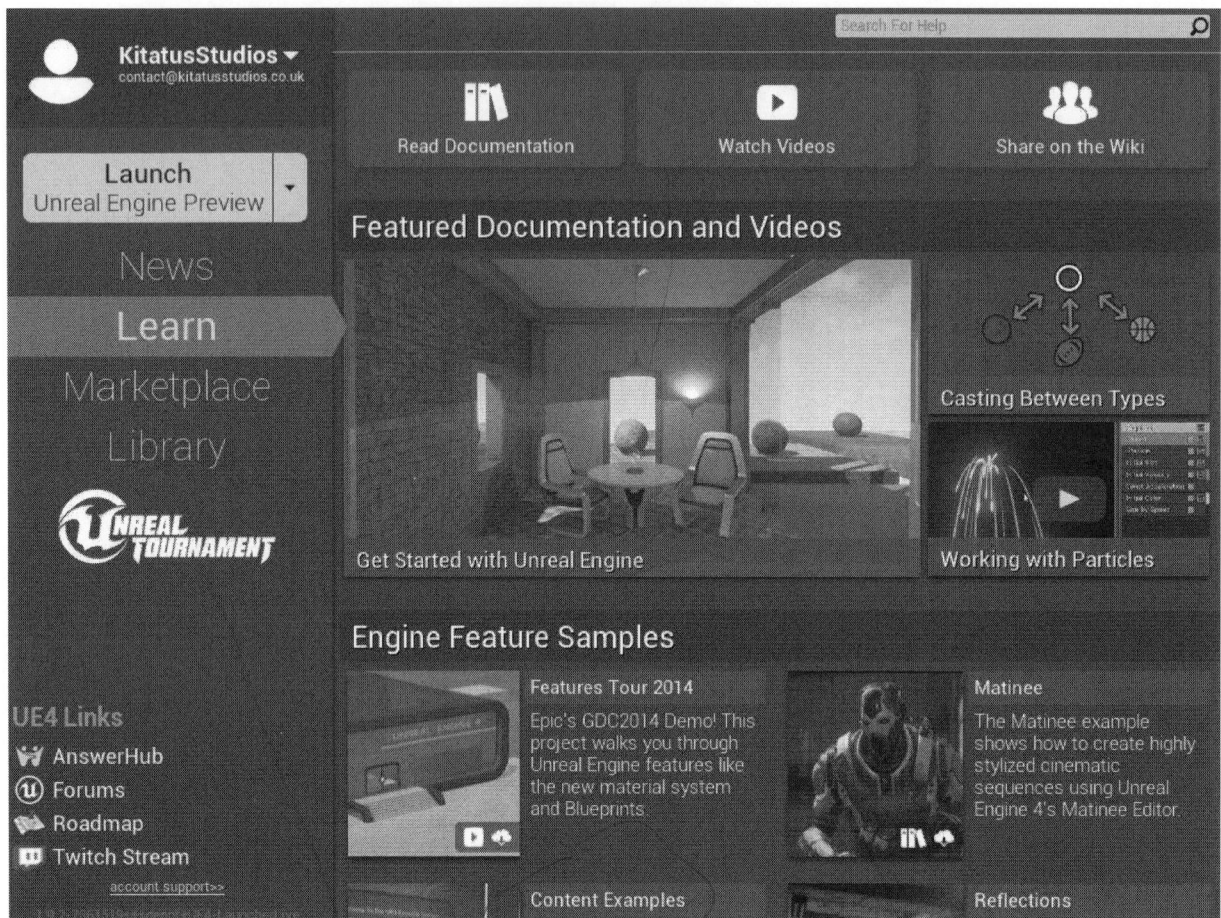

NOTE: If you're reading this and the image is hard to make out or a little blurry, you can find high-quality versions of the images available to YOU for free @ http://content.kitatusstudios.co.uk

For our project, we'll be needing a Highlight material to show the player what is currently highlighted, but don't worry - We won't be making this ourselves - It's already available to us!

In order to get hold of the Highlight material, go to the "Learn" tab in the launcher and click the "Content Examples" button to open up the download page. Select your version and select Download to download the free project provided by Epic Games to help you get to grips with the engine!

Once it has been installed; You'll notice that the "Download" button has transformed into a "Create Project" button. We want to create the project, so go ahead and click it, name it and install it!

But what if you've misplaced the "Content Examples" page and you want to install it but don't want to go via the Learn tab? No worries! Once it's installed (Or even when it's installing!) - Head over to the Library tab, which shows all your currently installed projects and files!

NOTE: The "Secrets!" part of the image above is something I have done to hide what I'm working on, your version of the engine won't have it - T'was the power of Photoshop!

While in the Library tab, if you scroll down to the "Vault" section - You'll find your "Content Examples" installation and once it's downloaded, go ahead and create a new project with it, name it and install it!

Now that it's installed, we don't actually want to go into it just yet - Because we want to migrate the highlight into our own project - We'll need to create our project first!

(Think about it, you can't give somebody a cookie if that person doesn't exist!)

On the top-left hand side of the launcher, you'll see a nice, tasty "Launch" button, click that or alternatively go into the "Library" tab and select an engine version launch (Make sure you're using 4.5 or newer!)

Now, once the engine has launched, you'll be greeted with this screen:

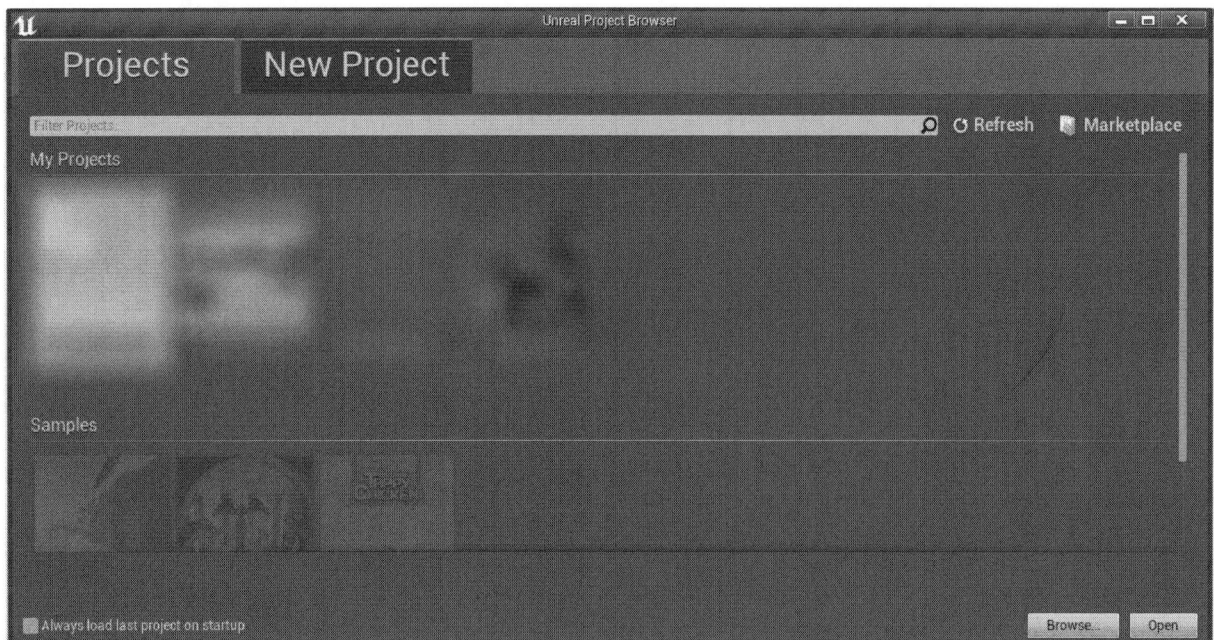

This is the "Project Browser", where you're free to create new projects or load up projects stored in your projects folder!

For our Point and Click Adventure adventure (Get it?), we need to create a new Blueprint project, so head over to the "New Project" tab by using the top two navigation buttons to enter the "New Project" window.

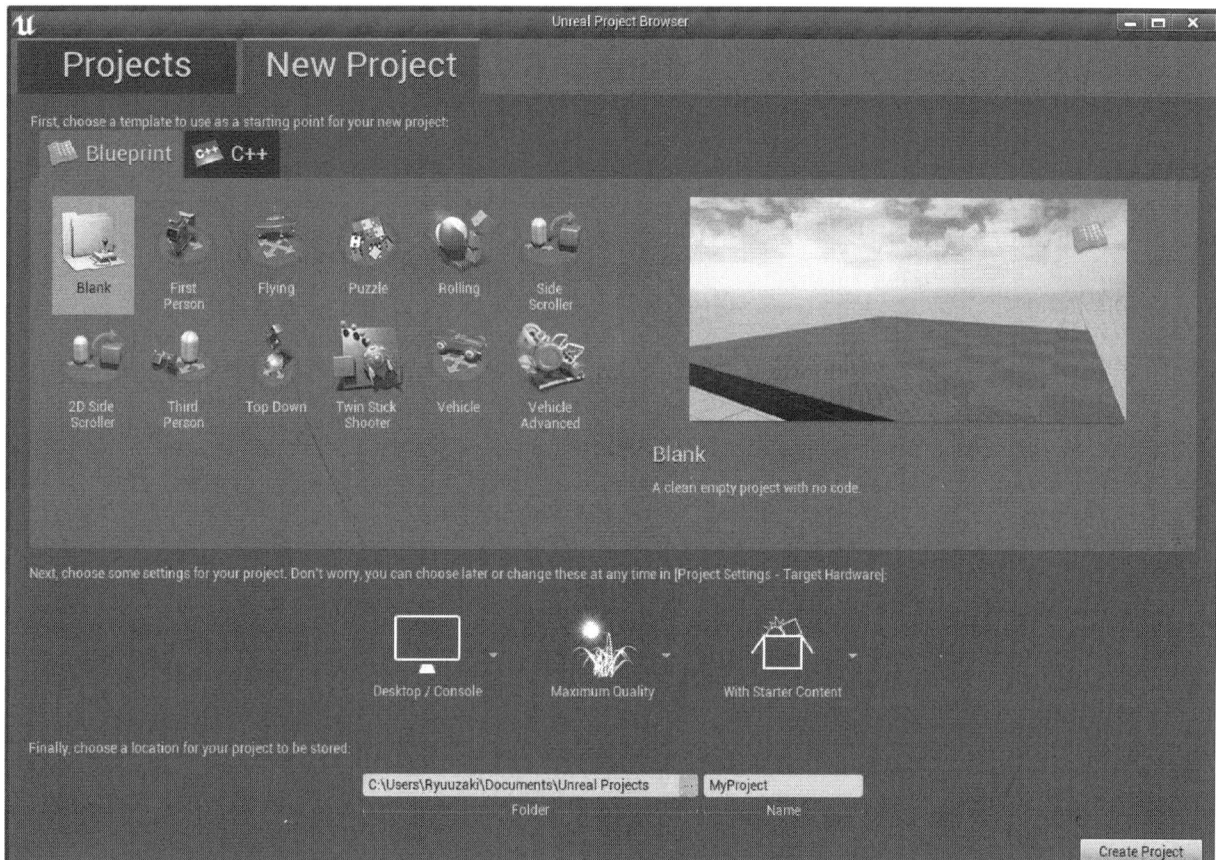

This window is pretty self-explanatory; Just under the "Projects" and "New Project" buttons on the top are two more buttons - These ones are called "Blueprint" and "C++" - These buttons will give you templates for either Blueprint projects or C++ projects.

Technically when using Unreal Engine 4, you are free to use either one as you are free to add Blueprints / C++ code to any project in Unreal Engine 4 at anytime but for the purposes of this tutorial, you'll want to make sure you're in the "Blueprint" tab.

Now underneath the "Blueprint" and "C++" buttons are a selection of Templates for you to choose from. As we're creating a Point and Click game in the style of

Telltale's games, where you can either use the mouse or a controller to move around the World, *we'll need to use the "Third Person" template*.

To use the template, simply click on it. If you can't find it, it looks like this (At least in version 4.5 it does!)

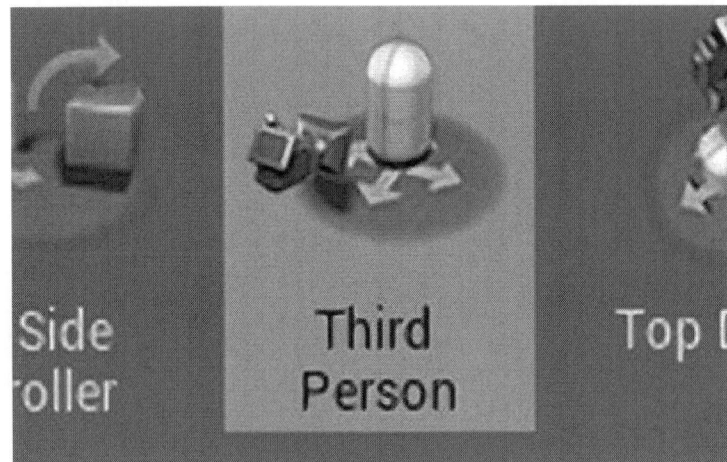

Once you've got the correct template selected ("Third Person", if you've already forgotten!), head down to the section underneath of the "Template" view, where it asks what settings you'd like to set for your project.

Normally, you can set these to your needs but for the sake of this tutorial, We'll want them set like this:

NOTE: If you can't make out the image clearly, it reads "Desktop / Console - Maximum Quality - With Starter Content"

This means that we're creating the project with computers and consoles in mind, We want the maximum quality of our project, so we can take advantage of all of

Unreal Engine 4's advanced graphical features. Lastly, we want to include the "Starter Content" in our project - This is so we can take advantage of Unreal Engine 4 objects and materials without having to provide our own!

Finally at the bottom of the window, you're asked to select the location and the name of the project. If the default location isn't suitable for you, set a new folder path (But remember where you store it!) and name the project whatever you like (For the sake of this tutorial, I will be naming the project ArtofBP_03)

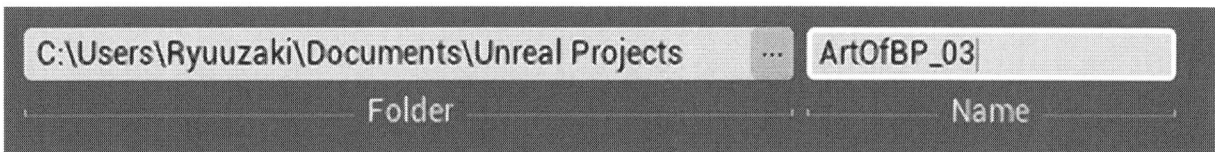

Once you're happy with all the settings, click "Create Project" and Unreal Engine 4 will get to work bringing your project to life - Give it a minute or two to set the project up for first-time use!

Once the project has loaded, you'll be greeted with a screen similar to this:

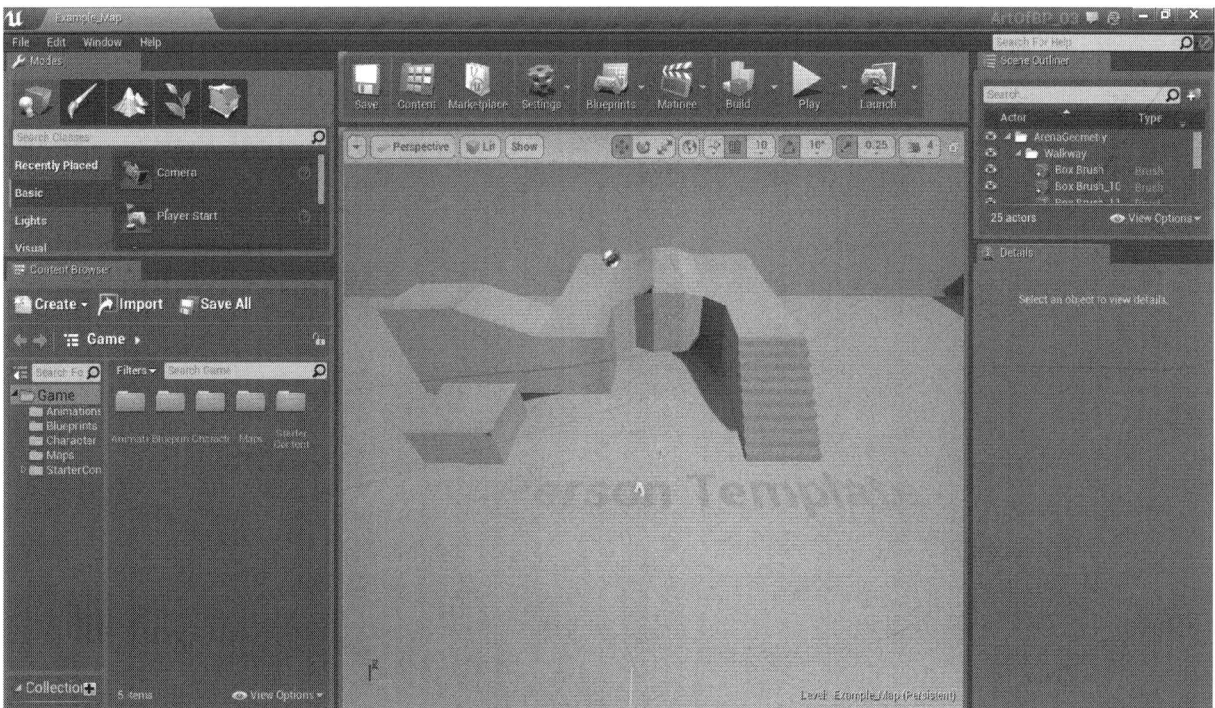

NOTE: Your screen maybe a little different as my computer's resolution will most likely be different to yours but the point still stands, This is what you should see which means that you're now able to edit the project to your heart's desire!

Now the project has loaded up, go to "File > Save All" and then once you've saved, close the project.

Why I hear you ask? - Because now the project exists, we can import the "Highlight" material from the Content Example into our project so we have it for use later!

Migrating Between Projects!

Once your new project has been saved, you can go ahead and close Unreal Engine and head back into the launcher, just like you did before.

This time, instead of creating a new project, open up the "Content Examples" project we created earlier (If you have not downloaded and installed the "Content Examples" yet, don't worry, just skim back a few pages!)

Once you've opened up the "Content Examples" project, use the "Content Browser" (Which by default is on the bottom-left of your screen) to navigate to the *"Game/ExampleContent/Blueprint_Communications/Materials"* folder (Double-click on the folders to expand them!)

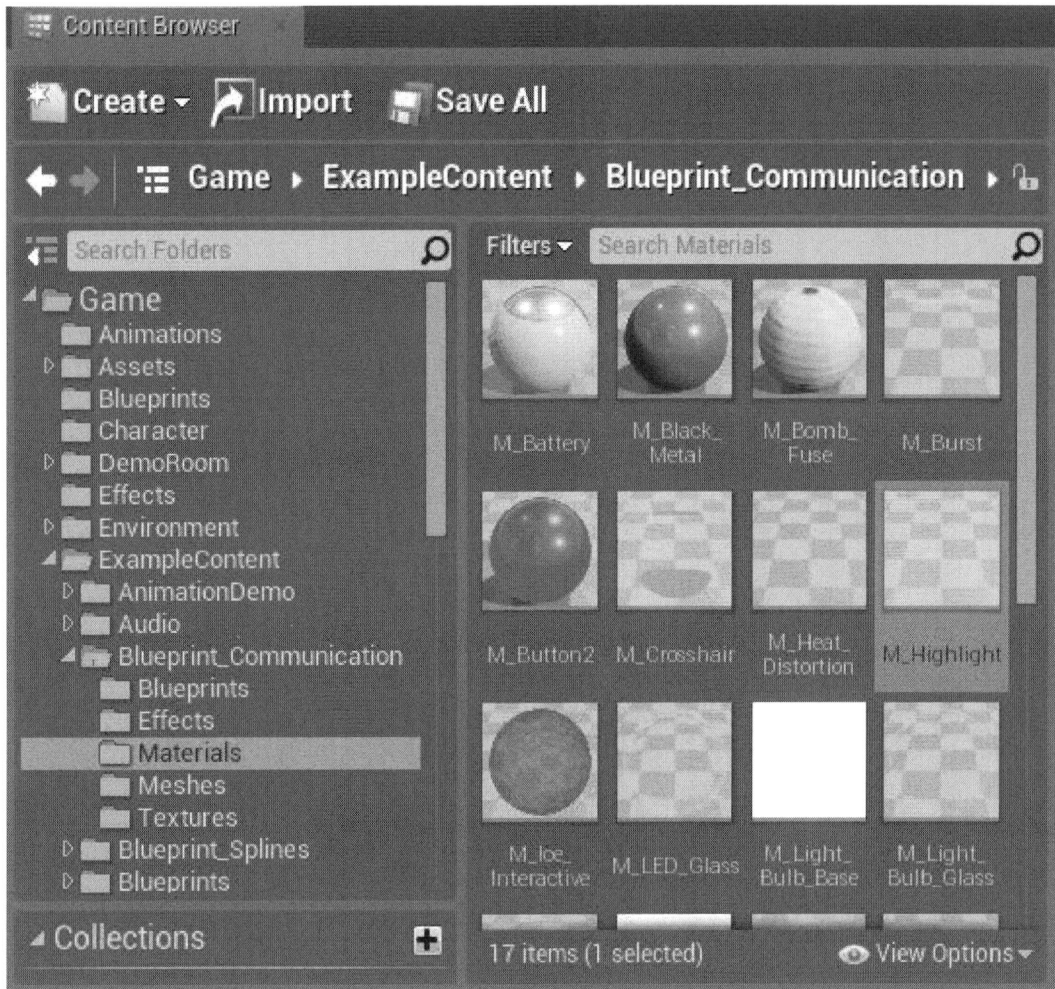

Within this folder, Find the Material "M_Highlight" (If you can't find up use the "Search Materials" searchbox just underneath the top of the "Content Browser". Once you've found M_Highlight, Right click (Ctrl + Click on a Mac) on "M_Highlight" and in the menu that pops up, select "Asset Actions" and in this menu click "Migrate".

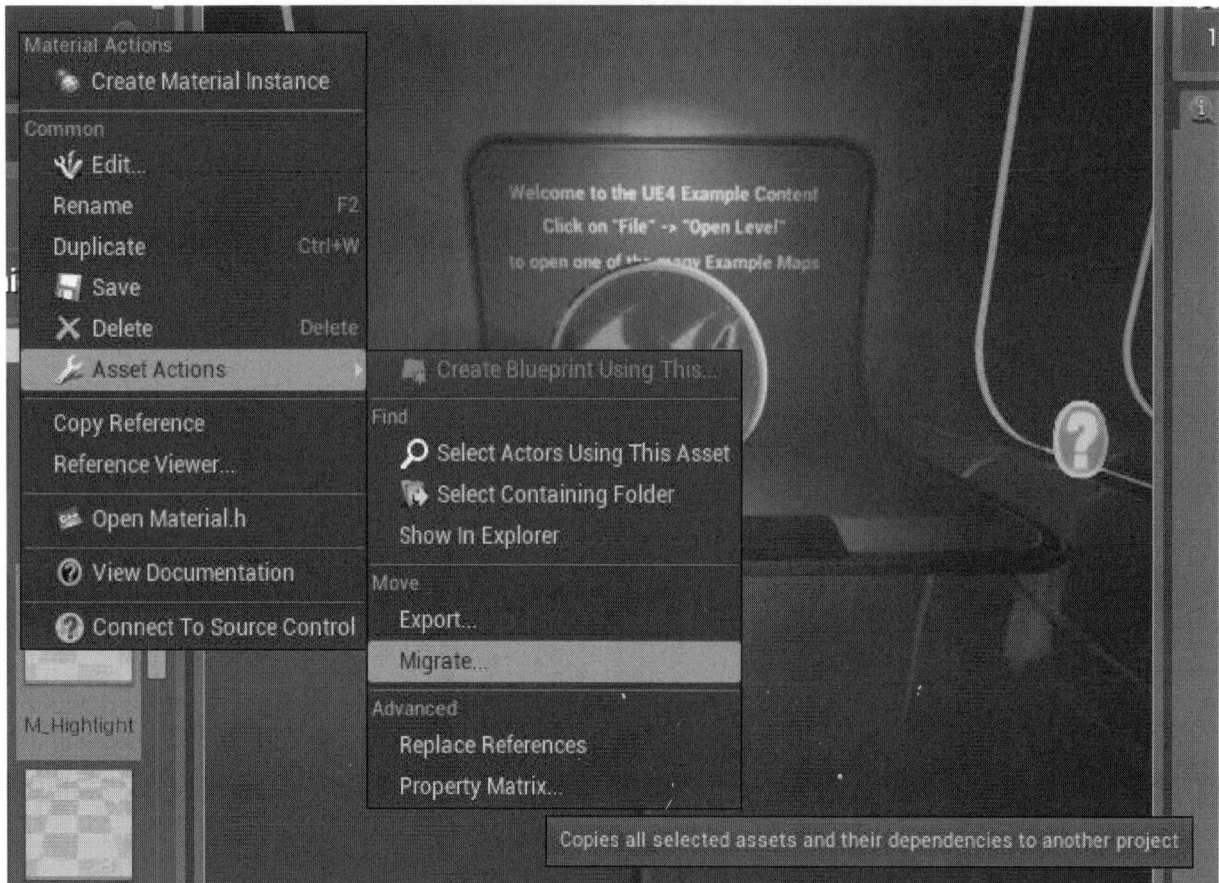

The "Asset Report" will now open up, which is a window that tells us what Assets are about to be exported and imported to the project of our choosing!

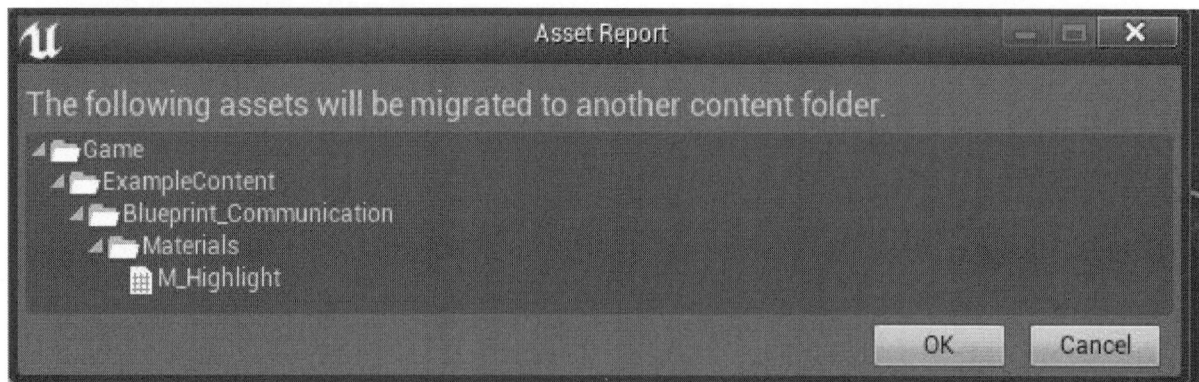

As we're only migrating the "M_Highlight" material; Everything is all good. So hit "OK" to go to the next window (In which we will select the project we want to "Migrate" to).

So now the "Browse for Folder" window opens up. There isn't a lot of description on this, but to sum it up in as little words as possible, we are looking for the "Point and Click Project" we already created. Once we've found it, we then need to go inside and find the "Content" folder (Which is the folder you see in the "Content Browser" in-engine!) and export "M_Highlight" there!

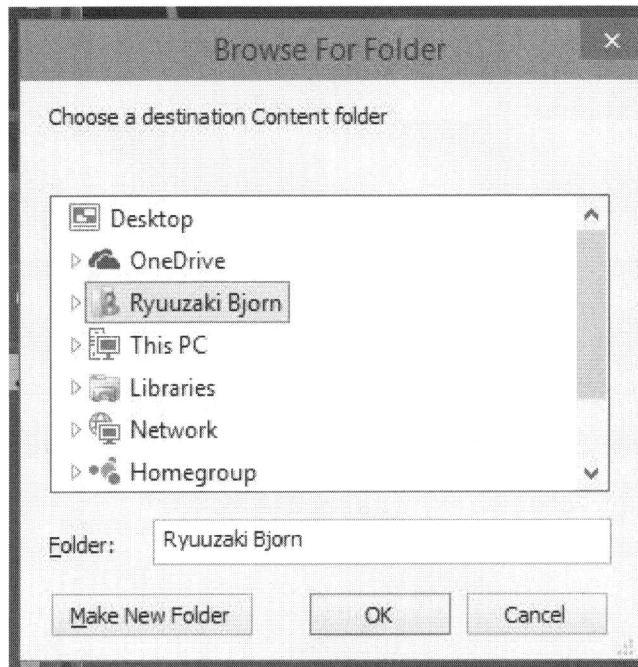

The default install path for projects is:
"C:\Users\YOURUSERNAMEHERE\Documents\Unreal Projects" (For example, my install path for Unreal Engine 4 projects is:
"C:\Users\Ryuuzaki\Documents\Unreal Projects". Naturally, if you've set it to a different directory then it will be where you've chosen.

Once you've found the directory for your Unreal Projects, double click the folder with the same project name as your "Point and Click project" to open it up!

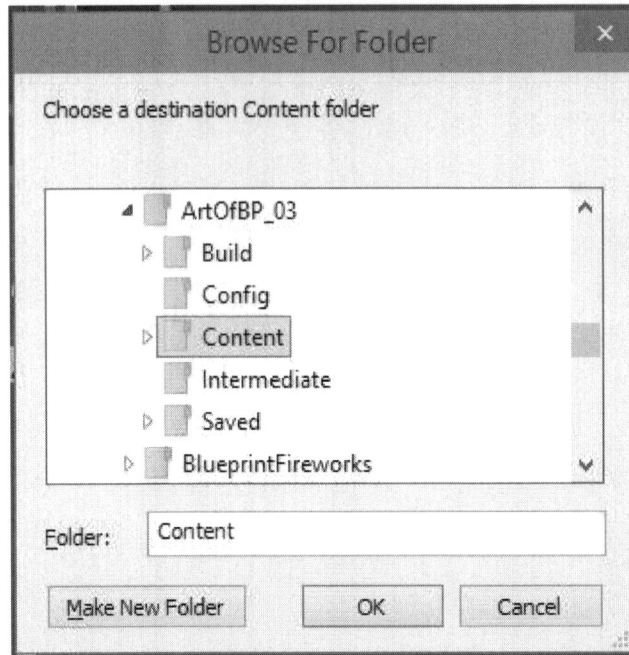

Browse For Folder

Choose a destination Content folder

▲ ArtOfBP_03
  ▷ Build
    Config
  ▷ Content
    Intermediate
  ▷ Saved
  ▷ BlueprintFireworks

Folder: Content

Make New Folder   OK   Cancel

Once you are in your "Point and Click" project folder, find the "Content" folder and click it once. Once it's open select "OK" at the bottom of the window and just like magic, the engine will duplicate the content and import it into the other project.

So why did we do this way as opposed to doing it manually by either exporting and importing or manually dragging it over? You'd think the answer would be speed but it's actually compatibility.

For some reason, manually dragging / dropping and importing / exporting doesn't actually work as intended at the moment (As of 4.5). I mean, it does import to the new project, but all the textures that are referenced .etc seem to lose their connections in Materials .etc when transferring manually, which is a real pain in the butt.

I have no doubt that this will be fixed soon but at the moment, migrating is the way forward!

And now the files are in our other project! We can close the "Content Examples" project and re-open our point and click project!

Once the project is open; Take a quick look at the Content Browser. As if by magic, there is now an "Example Content" folder! If you take a look inside, you'll find "M_Highlight" in the same folder structure as seen in the "Content Examples". Magic!

That's all we have to do with "M_Highlight" for the moment. We'll come back to it later but for now, we can forget it's there and continue on in our quest!

Preparing our Map!

Now that we've got the highlight material ready, before we can use it, we need a map. More specifically, we need a game area that can really show off our point and click game, and huge open environments don't really work in point and click games.

Don't get me wrong, some point and click games do them great but for the purpose of showcasing our "Point and Click Skills", we're going to need a small play area. So what can we do?

Seeing as it's hard to follow a "Build this, build that there", I'm simply going to give the choice of following a vague outline or downloading the map from http://content.kitatusstudios.co.uk - But don't worry, we'll only be doing minimal changes to the already present "Example_Map" to make it more suitable for our point and click adventure!

Before we continue, it's probably useful to inform you how to delete objects in a scene. It's super simple!

So first things first, make sure you're in the main view of your project. This is the view with the Content Browser in the bottom-left and the scene view in the centre screen. Your screen will look similar to this:

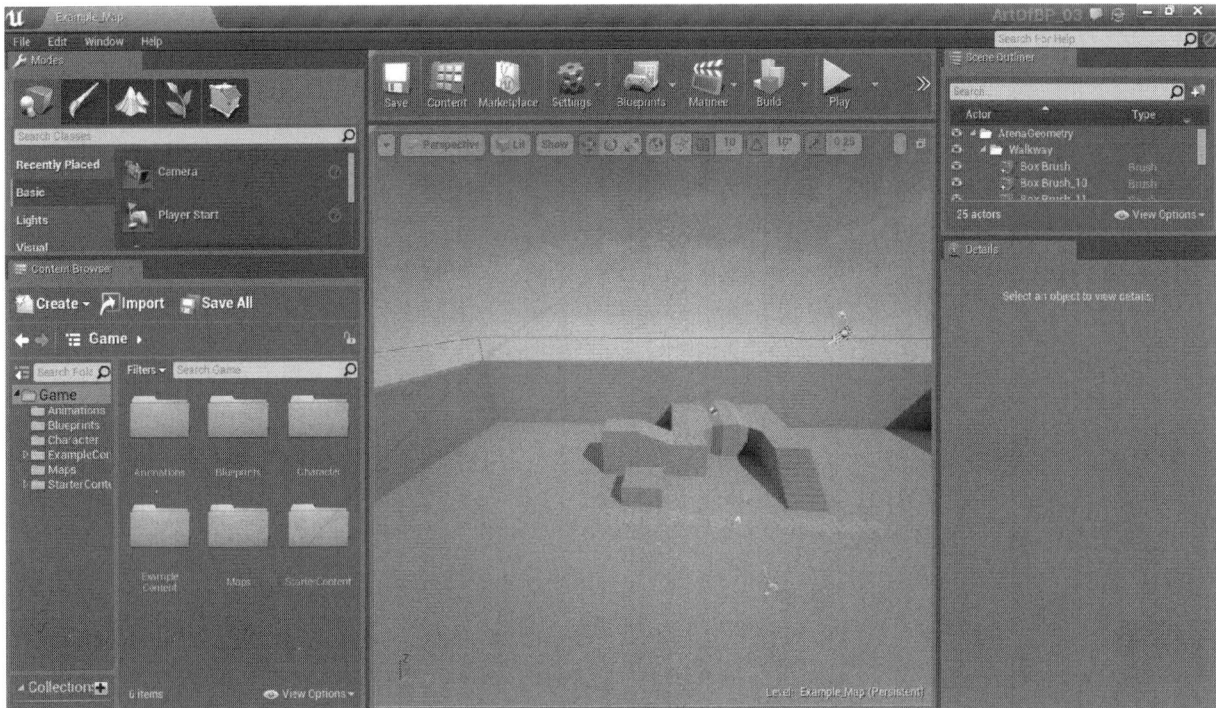

We're going to be focusing on the scene view. If you click on the stairs, you'll see that the stairs are now selected. Now if you hit the delete key on your keyboard (Or alternatively you can Right Click [Ctrl + Click] on the stairs and in the menu go to "Edit > Delete") and as if by magic - The stairs are now gone!

See how easy that was? Now I want you to repeat this and delete the geometry that was connected to the stairs apart from the back wall and the floor (Also delete the "Third Person Template" text!)

You should end up with a box-room looking map like this:

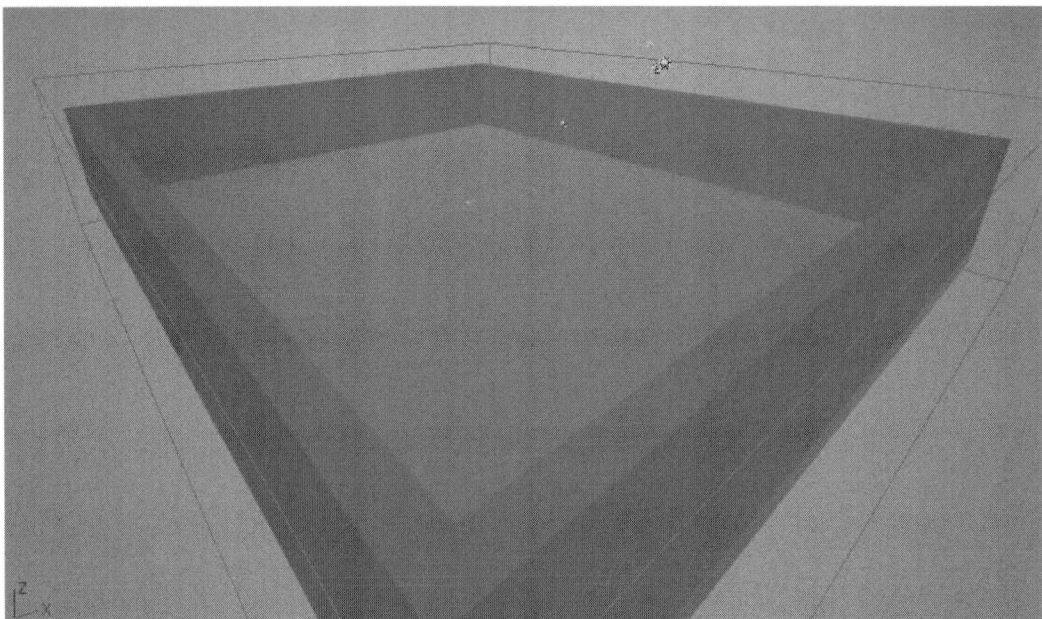

This is technically our blank slate. Now we're going to create a simple map to best show-off our point and click adventure!

USING BSPS TO CRAFT OUT MAP

To do this, head over the "Modes" toolbox (Usually in the top-left of your editor).

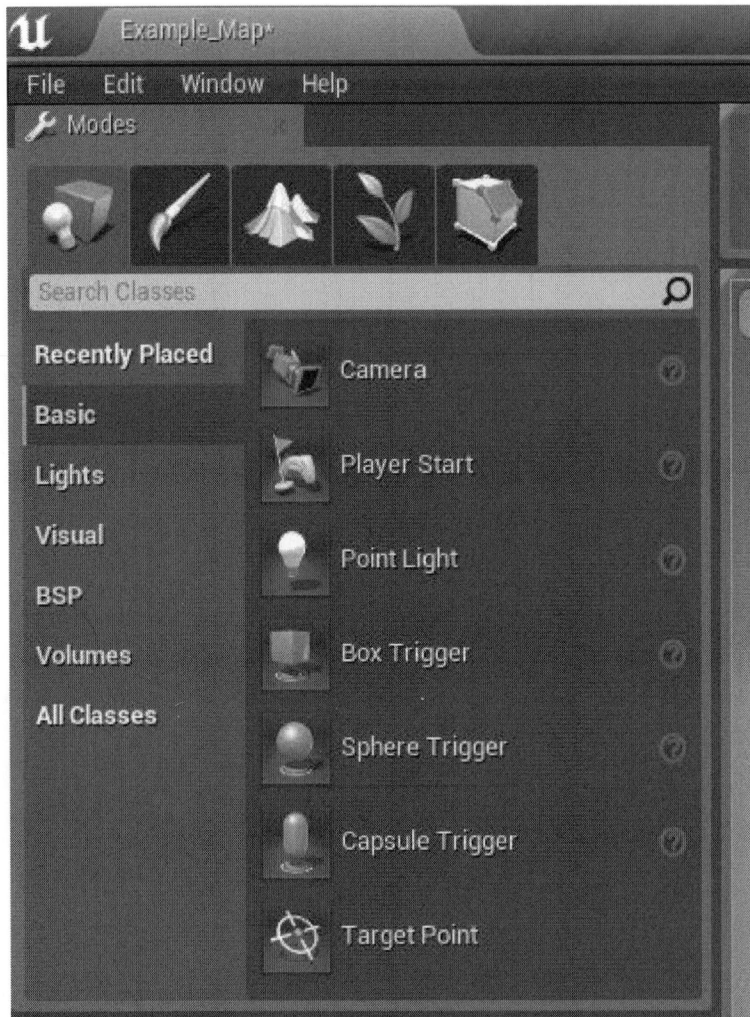

NOTE: The "Modes" toolbox likes to hide a lot of its options based on your screen resolution. Don't be afraid to pull the bottom and sides of the box to extend it so you can see all the options!

Found the "Modes" toolbox? Excellent! Now we need to create some geometry using BSP brushes. Before we do, let me quickly explain what BSPs are and what the benefits and whatnot are of using BSPs.

BSPs are piece of editable geometry you can use to "Flesh" out a level. Think of using customisable LEGOs to create your level; You can get the overall shape of the level but it's not ideal to use this legos in the final produced project. Why? Because BSPs are a resource-hog. Compared to normal static meshes, they drain a lot more memory and power to render as their primary function is to help you block out a level.

I'm sure after reading that, you must be thinking "Why use them in the first place?". Well, my friend, BSPs make it super-quick and simple to create a working level within Unreal Engine 4. Within the space of 30 seconds, you could create a block-room which is ready for you to run around in.

Better yet - You can convert any BSP (Or collection of BSPs!) into a static mesh, which you can then export into your preferred 3D modelling program and use them as a basis to create your final level. Once created, you can import the mesh back into the engine and replace the BSPS, saving you a lot of time and a lot of extra unneeded effort!

For more information on BSPs, I recommend checking out the Documentation on either the Unreal Engine website or by pressing F1 in any editor window of Unreal Engine 4!

We're now going to create two walls in our scene, to partition our big block off and give our map a little bit of depth to make it more interesting!

So what are we waiting for? Head into the "Modes" toolbox (Remember to resize the window if you can't see all the options!) and select the "BSP" category and click and drag the "Box" into the game scene.

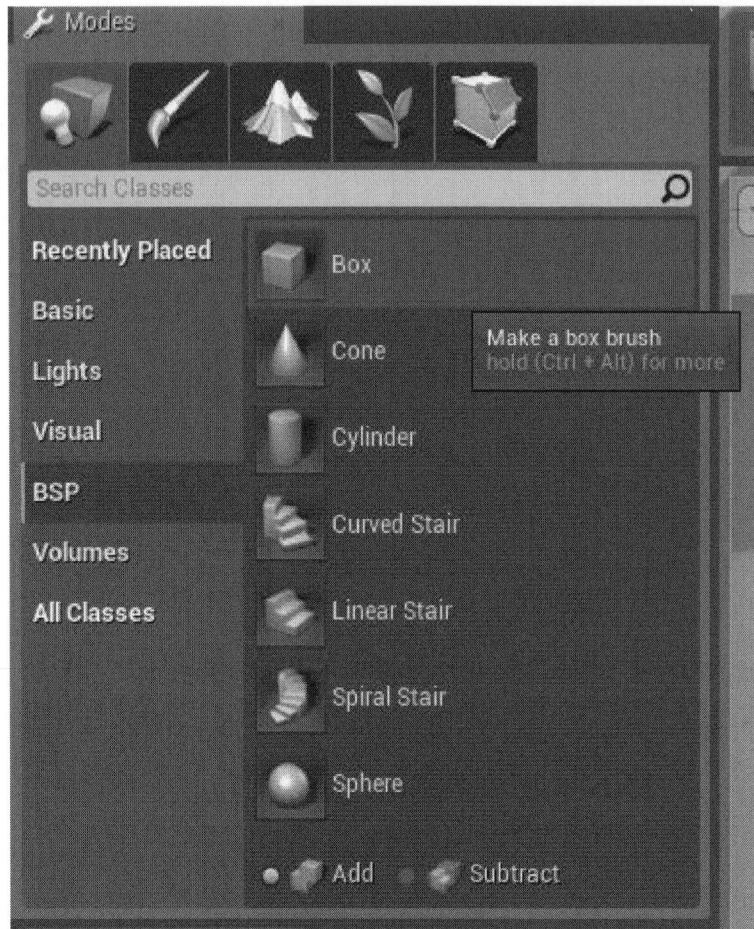

Your scene should now have a nicely sized box in it from where you spawned the BSP. Note that if your box is half-way into the floor or half-way into a wall, you can use the transform gizmo (The three arrows: Blue, Red and Green) to move it out of the floor / wall until it's sitting nicely on-top. If you can't see the transform gizmo, simply click your box within in the scene and hey presto - It'll appear!

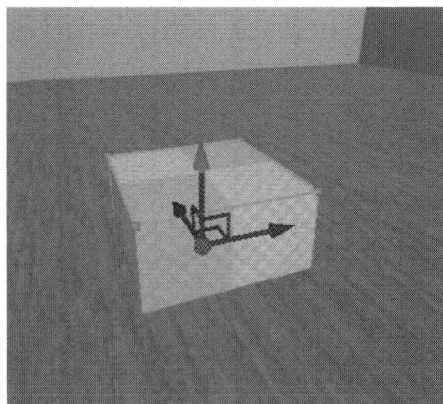

This box is nice and all, but it's hardly a wall at the moment, is it? It's a pretty easy method to turn this box into the wall but just before we do - Use the transform gizmo on the box (Remember: Simply click the box and the gizmo will appear!) and move the box into the centre of our map. You should end up with something along the lines of this:

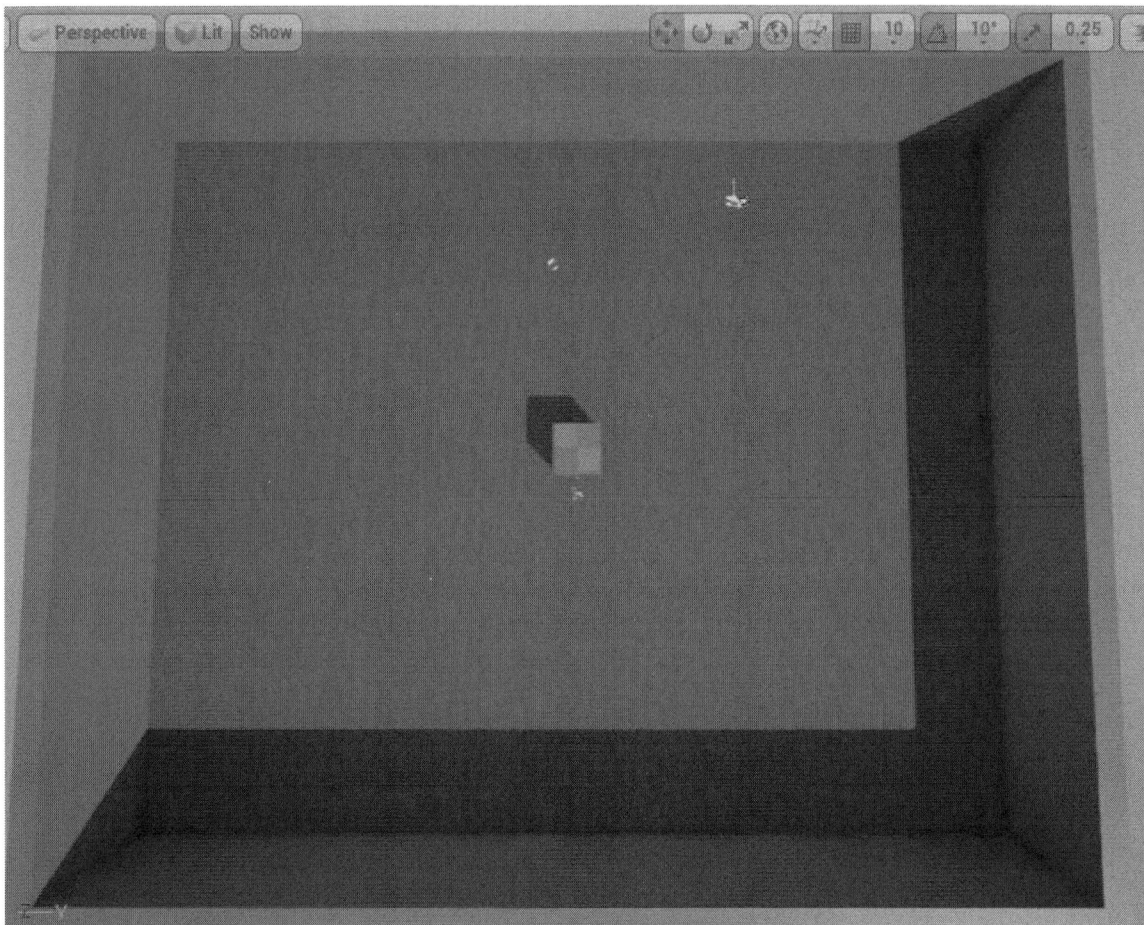

NOTE: While moving your box, you may accidently put it on top of the object in the scene that looks like a joystick & flag with a blue arrow coming out of it. This joystick is where the player will spawn and the arrow is what direction

the player will face. If this joystick is inside your box, the player will spawn inside your box and it will be a very messy situation. Bear this in mind when moving your box!

You can easily move the joystick out of the way by simply clicking it and using the transform gizmo or alternatively, you can find the "PlayerStart" in the Scene Outliner (Which is usually in the top-right area of your workspace) and click on it there to enable the gizmo to move it out of the way!

By now, your box should be centred, but it's still not quite looking like a wall just yet - Here comes the fun part!

Head over to the "Modes" toolbox again (The area in which we used to create our cube). You'll notice that on the top of the "Modes" toolbox, there's five buttons with images on them;

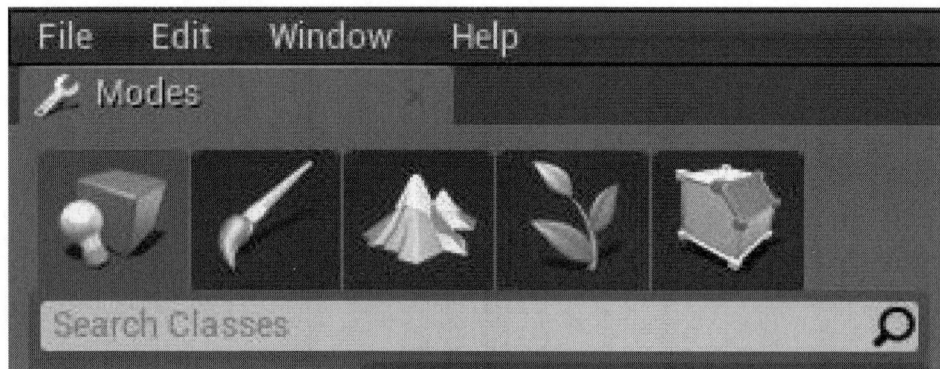

- **Image #1: "Place" Tab** - The image is a cube with a light bulb in front of it - This tab is for placing objects into the scene such as lights, BSPs, Triggers .etc
- **Image #2: "Paint" Tab** - The image on this tab is a paintbrush - This tab is for tools to paint vertex information onto Static Meshes, For example adding moss to a rock (You'd have to have the moss in the Material of the rock already, but that's a tutorial for another day!)
- **Image #3: "Landscape" Tab** - This tab's image is of some mountains with snow on them! - This tool is used for either generating landscapes (Think

something like the Far Cry editor) or importing pre-created landscapes via heightmaps.

- **Image #4: "Foliage" Tab** - The image of this tool is a sad-looking plant, with very few leafs. The point of this tool is to give you the power to place many meshes at once, such as grass or trees.
- **Image #5: "Geometry Edit" Tab** - The image on this tab is of a box with a quarter of the box sliced away - This tool allows you to edit the vertices of a BSP brush you've placed in the game. For example, you can make sides of a box bigger or smaller, you could make two corners meet .etc

We need to make our cube into more of a wall, so we'll be using tool #5 - the "Geometry Edit" tool. Simply click the tab's button and you'll notice the "Modes" toolbox's options will change.

The tool will automatically load into the default settings, which means that your "Geo Edit" tool will be in "Edit" mode. You can tell what mode you're in by simply looking at the filled in dot within the top part of the "Modes" toolbox, just underneath the images:

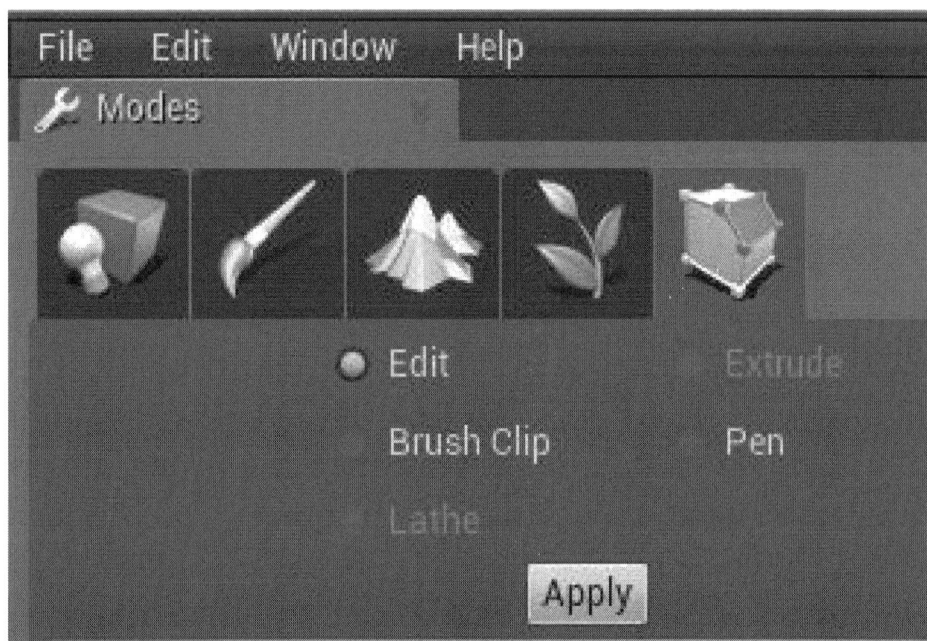

We need to use the "Edit" mode, so we don't need to alter any of these settings, but it's always good to know the options are there should you need them!

TIP: Even though it's a little confusing, simply clicking the "Geo Edit" tab activates the tool. With most tools in Unreal Engine 4, there's a clear "I'm Active!" indication beside the tool, which is usually an orange tint to the button. The "Modes" toolbox works a little different - Why am I telling you this?

Because a lot of the time, when you're trying to move a BSP, you'll accidentally pull a face and make the box huge when all you wanted to do was move the box from A to B. How do you prevent this? Easy! Simply check your "Modes" toolbox every now and again and make sure you're in the "Place" tool and not any of the other tools!

Now that the "Geo Edit" tool is selected, we need to select the BSP we want to edit. How do we do this? Simple! - Simply click the BSP in the scene view!

As we want to edit the box we created, simply click on the box. The yellow and blue highlight around the edges of the box (With blue squares on the corners) confirms that box is selected and we can now edit it.

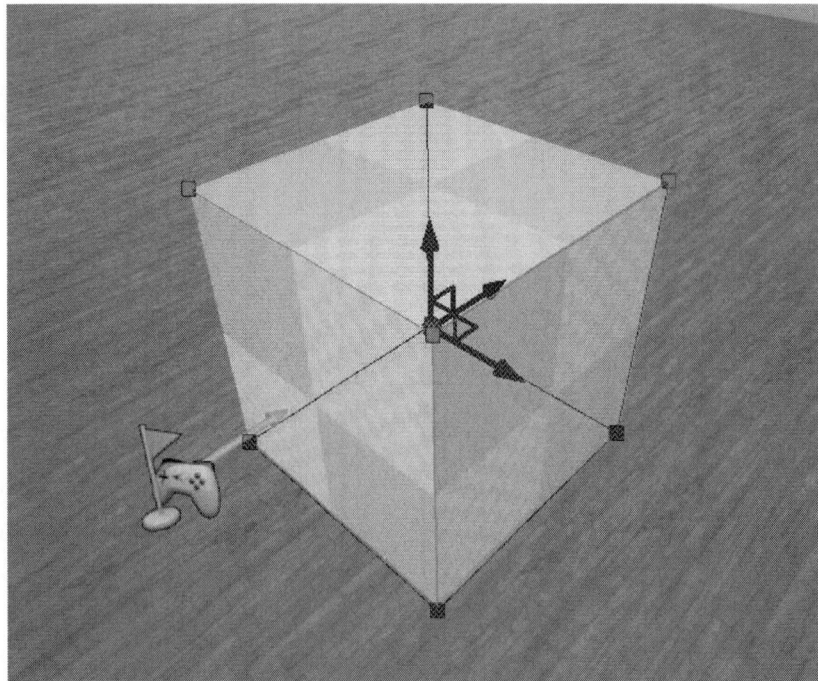

NOTE: Once you've clicked your box, Is your gizmo (The red, blue and green tool in the centre of the selected object) more of an oval shape or does the gizmo have small boxes on the end instead of arrows, then you are in the wrong "Gizmo mode".

To get into the correct "Gizmo mode", use the Gizmo Selector. Head to your scene view and (Depending on your screen size) the Gizmo Selector will either be in the centre of your screen or in the top-right of your screen.

This is the Gizmo Selector. The option which is in orange is the currently selected Gizmo. As you can see, there are three options: The left option, middle and right.

The left option is the "Transform" gizmo, which let's us move objects on the XYZ plane.

The middle option is the "Rotator" option, which allows us to rotate an object in the XYZ axis.

The right-hand option is the "Scale" Gizmo, which is a tool that allows us to scale an object either bigger or smaller.

To move our boxes faces into a wall shape with the "Geo Edit", we will need to use the left-hand Gizmo, the Transform Gizmo. If it's not currently selected,

simply click the left-hand Gizmo button to change the "Gizmo mode" into "Transform" mode.

We can now edit the box's dimensions, but how exactly do we go about doing that? Once the box is selected, selecting a face of the box allows us to edit the face on that box.

So make sure the box is already selected and click on any of the faces. You'll know when you've entered the face editing mode as the face will have an orange highlight!

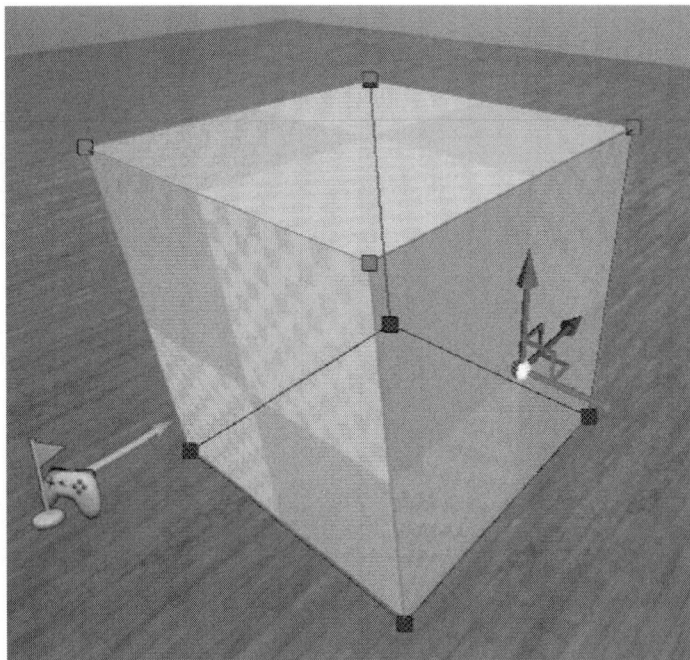

For this face; We need to thin the wall a bit. Thick walls are okay but a thinner wall is more aesthetically pleasing! So how do we thin the wall out? Simply grab the green arrow on the Transform Gizmo and pull the face in until the box is half as thick as it currently is!

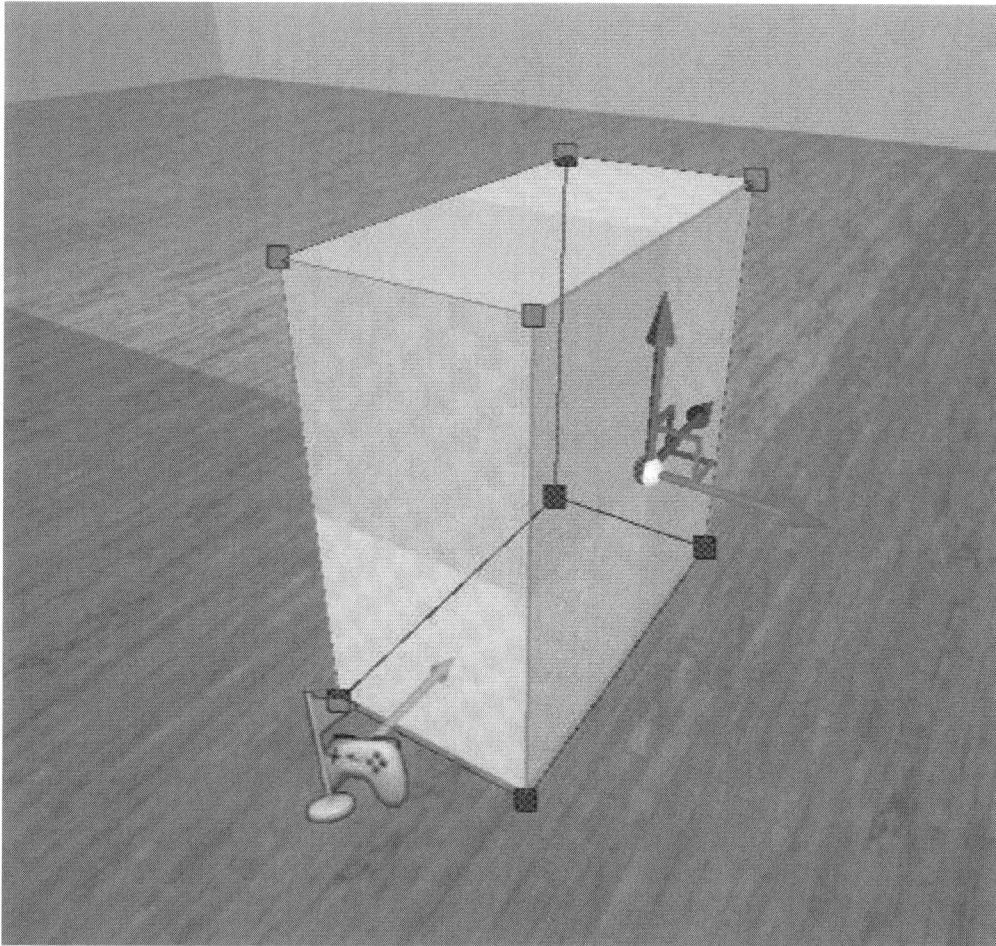

See how easy it is to deform a cube? Use this skill you've just learned to create a wall.

Click the face to the left of the face you just resized and pull it all the way to outside wall (That the project auto-generated for us when we first created the project!)

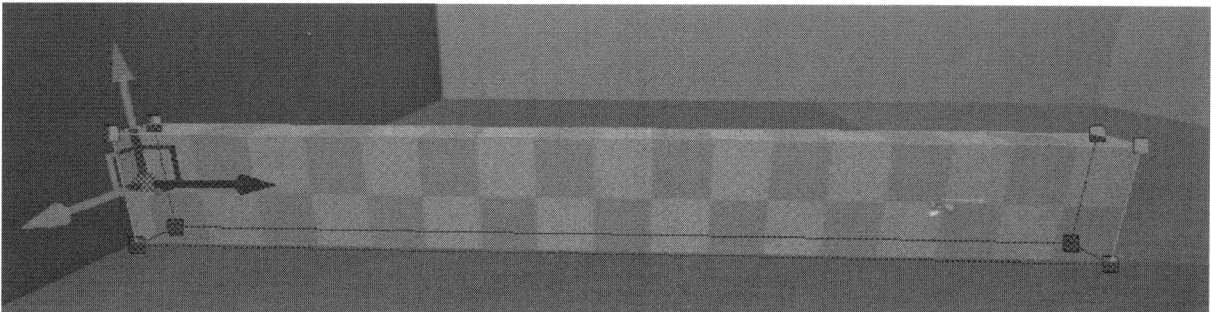

Once you've done it for one side… You guessed it! Click the face on the opposite side and drag that face to the wall on the other side. You'll end up with a wall that splits the game area in half completely. But it's quite short in it's current state…

Can you guess how we're going to make it taller? You got it! All we have to do is grab the top face and pull it up! So do just that… Pull it up so it matches the height of the walls around it.

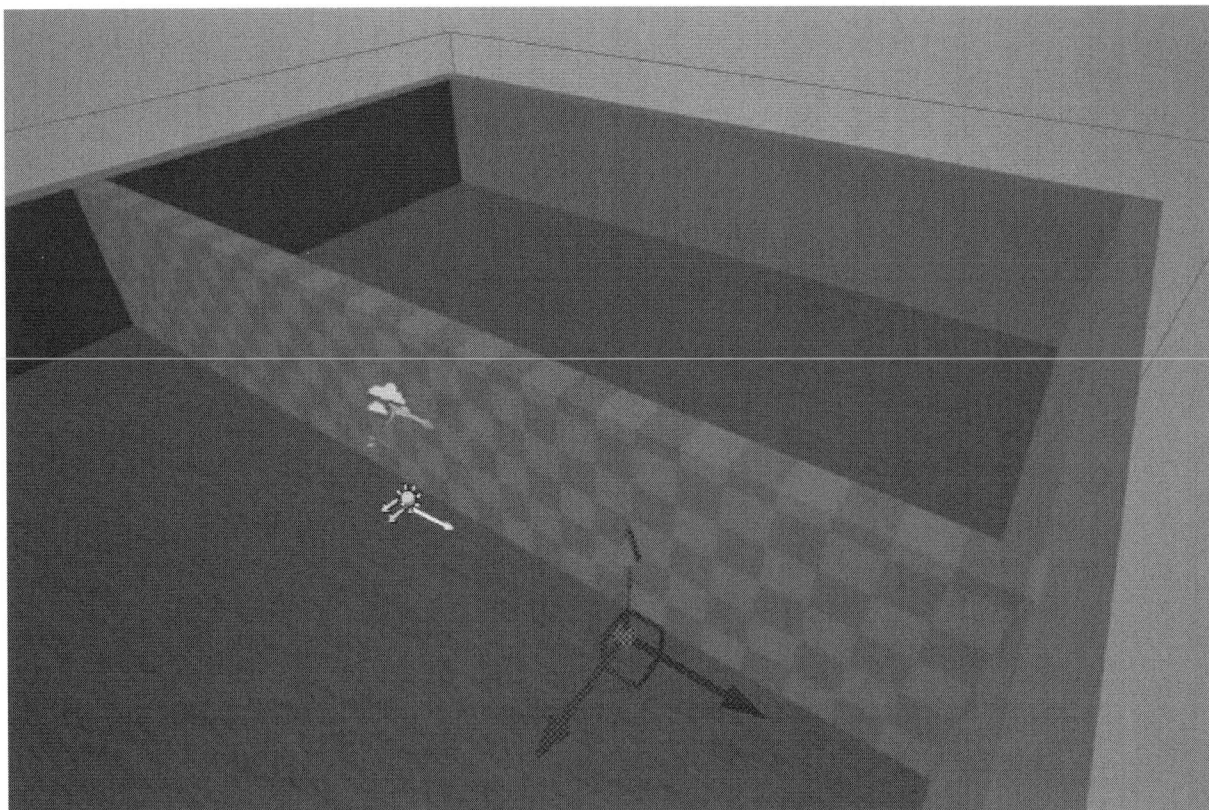

And there we have it - We've got a wall that cuts out level in half! Great work! But there's still some cool things left that we can do to our level before we can call it finished!

As we explained before, come out of "Geo Edit" mode by heading into the "Modes" toolbox and clicking the "Place" mode image (On the top of the "Modes" area, it is the image with the lightbulb with a cube behind it).

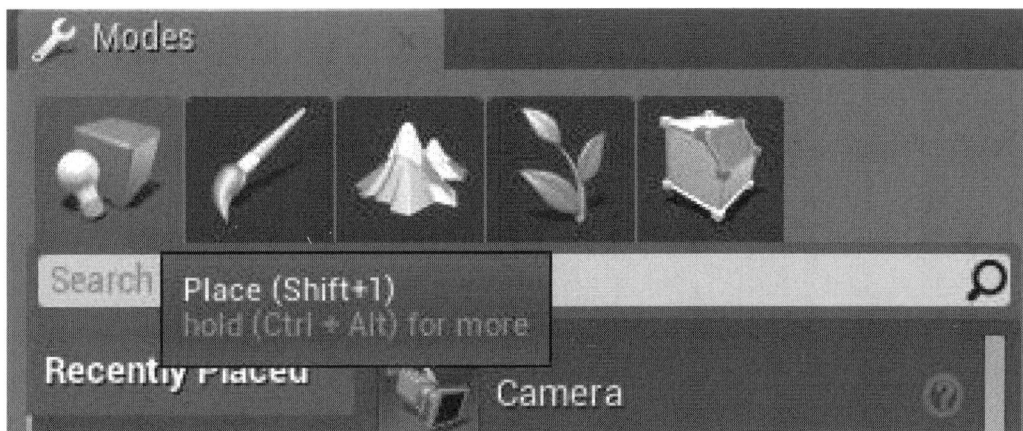

Once you're in the "Place" mode, click the wall you just created.

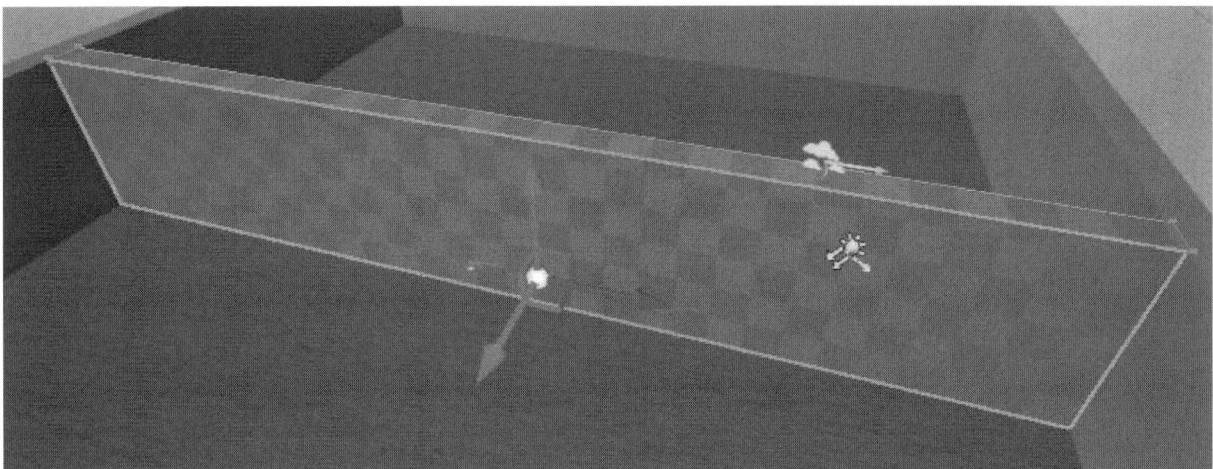

Is it now selected? Awesome! With the new wall selected, press Ctrl + C to copy the wall and Ctrl + V to paste a duplicate of the wall.

Alternatively, you can right click the wall (Ctrl + click), go to the Edit option and select "Duplicate" to make a copy of the wall.

When the wall has been duplicated, you might not be able to see it, but fret not. Head up to the top / top-right of your scene view over to the "Gizmo" selection bar (We talked about this a few pages back) and select the middle Gizmo (The "Rotator" Gizmo).

Now rotate your wall to the left or right (Using the Blue area of the Rotate Gizmo that has appeared) until you have rotated your wall 90 degrees (So the walls make a big X or + in the middle of your map).

Notice how the newly created wall just misses reaching the outer walls? Use everything you've learned up until this point and use the "Geo Edit" tool to get it to the correct size.

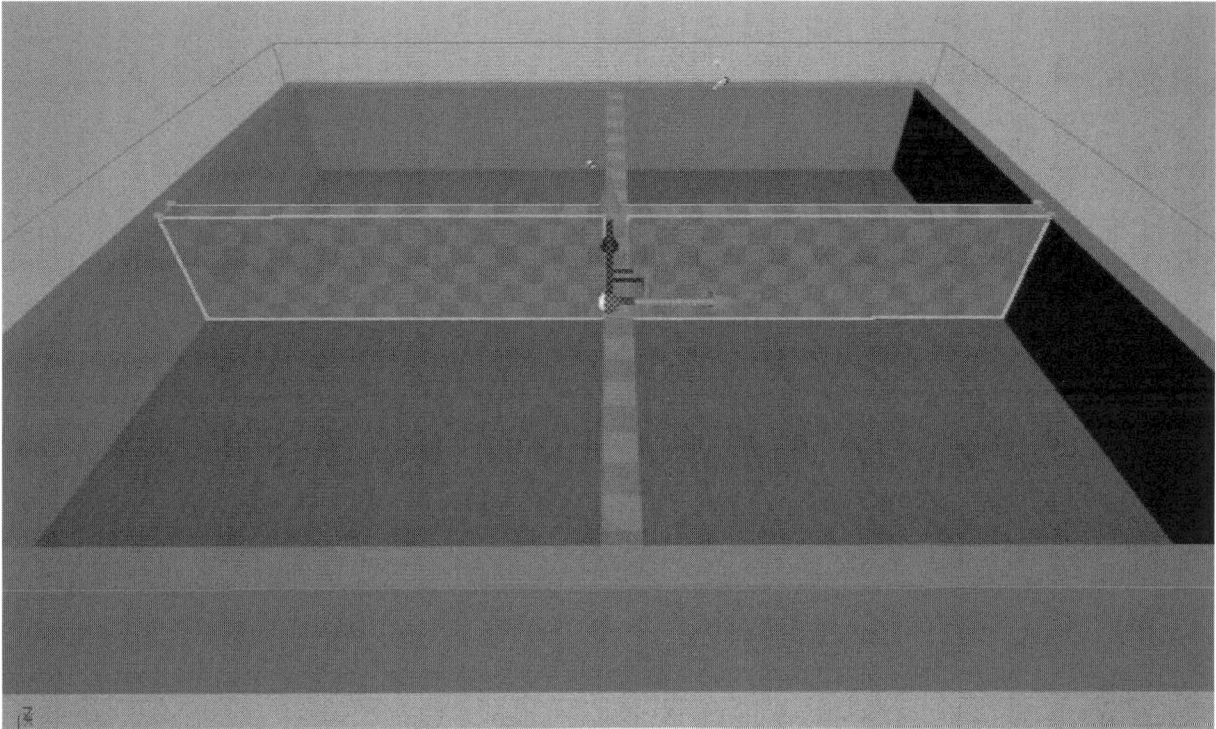

Great job! You should now have four perfectly divided "Rooms" for us to create a cool project within! But have you noticed something odd... As if something super-important is missing?

If you try out the project as it is, you'll notice that these walls don't currently let you move room to room. So let's change that!

How are we going to change that? Through subtraction volumes of course!

CREATING WITH SUBTRACTING BSPS

What are subtraction volumes? Subtraction volumes are used with BSP meshes and allow us to remove a chunk of a BSP. For example, Think of a wall with a door. To create this with BSPs, we would create a wall, and then use a Subtract BSP to cut-out a doorway. Which is, funnily enough, what we're going to do!

The process of creating a subtraction BSP isn't that much different to how we created our walls. In fact, the process is nearly identical.

First, we need to create another cube, just like before.

To do this, head over the "Modes" toolbox (Usually in the top-left of your editor).

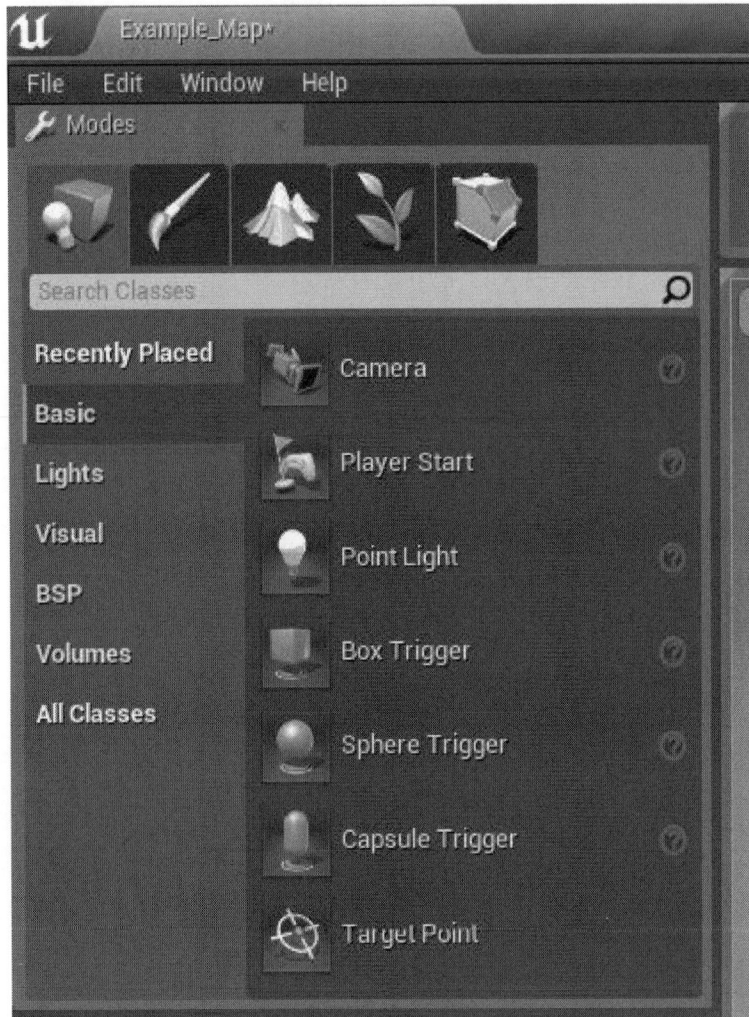

NOTE: The "Modes" toolbox likes to hide a lot of its options based on your screen resolution. Don't be afraid to pull the bottom and sides of the box to extend it so you can see all the options!

Select the "BSP" category and click and drag the "Box" into the game scene.

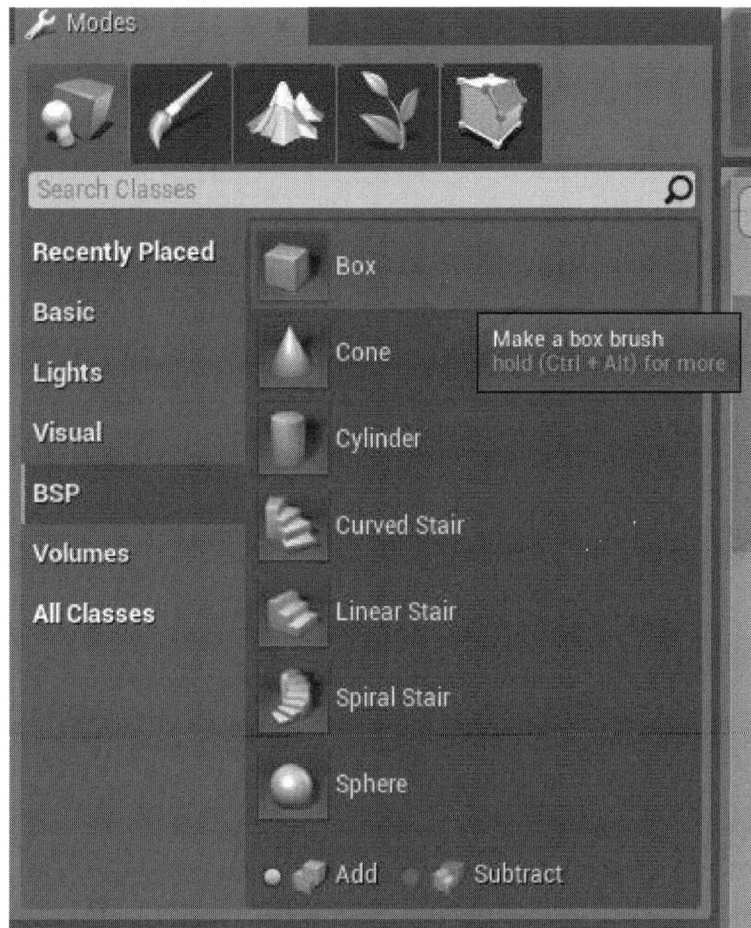

Your scene should now have a nicely sized box in it from where you spawned the BSP. Note that if your box is half-way into the floor or half-way into a wall, you can use the transform gizmo (The three arrows: Blue, Red and Green) to move it out of the floor / wall until it's sitting nicely on-top. If you can't see the transform gizmo, simply click your box within in the scene and hey presto - It'll appear!

Now, using the "Geo Edit" mode (In which we have covered a few times now!) make the box into more of a doorframe shape. For reference the template character (That comes with Unreal Engine 4) is around 190cm. Even though it's hard to get exact measurements (At the moment anyway) using the "Geo Edit" tool, try to make sure the door is at least around 200cm so that the character can easily walk through it - A good way to test this is to press "Alt+P" to run around your level and make sure the cube lines up with your character alright (Use your "ESC" button to exit Play-in-editor mode!).

But when trying "Play in Editor", you may notice that your character is either falling through the floor into the eternal abyss below or your character is in a different area of the map compared to the cube (As the map is split into four sections at the moment)

To fix this, head over to the "Scene Outliner" in the top right of your Unreal Engine 4 window.

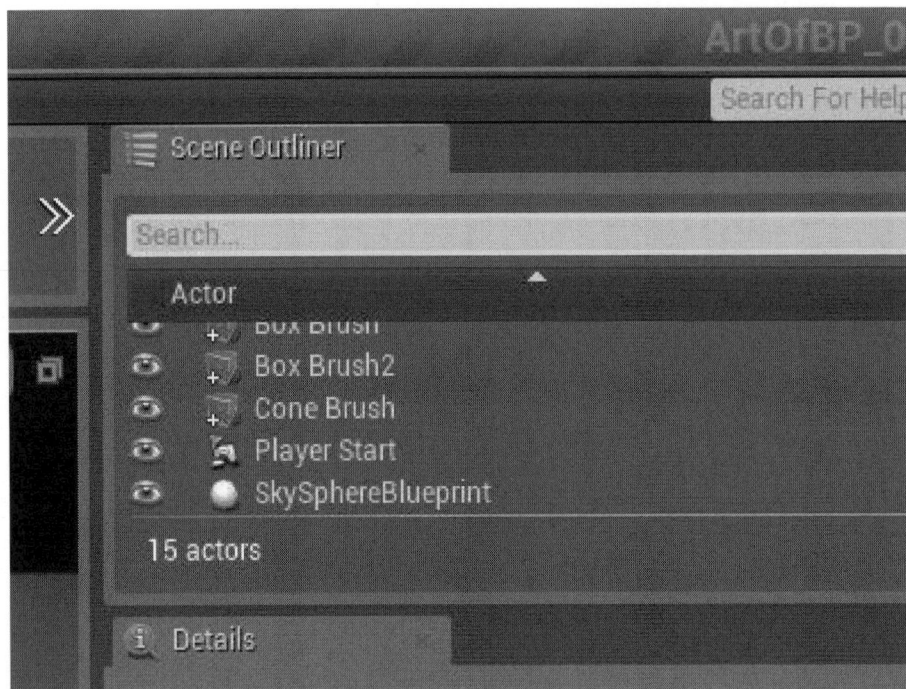

Find "Player Start" in the Scene Outliner (You might have to scroll down!) and simply click it. It'll now be selected in your scene view, and you can use the transform gizmo to move it nearer to your newly created cube.

Once you've made your cube into more of a door shape and you're happy with it - It's time to now turn it into a subtraction BSP!

Before we do, for the sake of this tutorial, we need to duplicate (Right Click [Ctrl+Click] the door, go to Edit within the menu that pops up and select Duplicate) the door four times.

This is because even though we can duplicate the door when it is a subtraction volume, they are much harder to see (As they are invisible with a red tint) and thus harder to screenshot to show you all what to do!

With the four doors we've created, it's time to position them. To get the hang of things, we'll do one at a time. I'll show you how to do the first one and it should be pretty simple from there.
Click on one of the walls and use the Gizmo that shows up to move it in the correct place, which would be halfway of the wall in the "Room".

NOTE: In the above image, I've changed the Material on the box to a grass texture. This is only so you can see it better in the screenshots!

When moving the box, you may notice that the box isn't thick enough to cover the thickness of the wall (It should come out both sides of the wall, it doesn't have to be exact but it HAS to be bigger than the thickness of the wall on both sides!)

How are we going to fix that? Well, remember the "Geo Edit" mode in the "Modes" toolbox? Use that and manipulate the faces of the door until both the front and back of the door are sticking out of the wall.

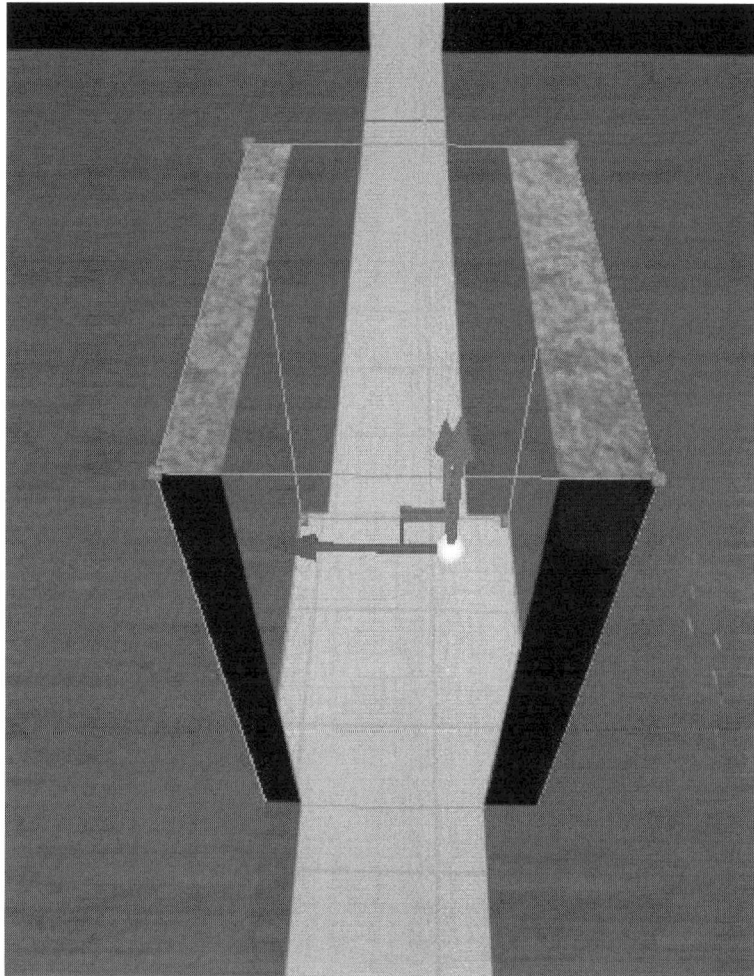

NOTE: This image was taken INSIDE the wall, which is why the floor is transparent. This is to show you how much roughly the door should "Spill over" the sides of the wall.

Once you're happy with how the door looks and its position, we're ready to turn it into a door!

With the "Door" still selected, you can view it's properties (In it's default location) on the right-hand side of the editor, underneath the "Scene Outliner". This is called the "Details" panel.

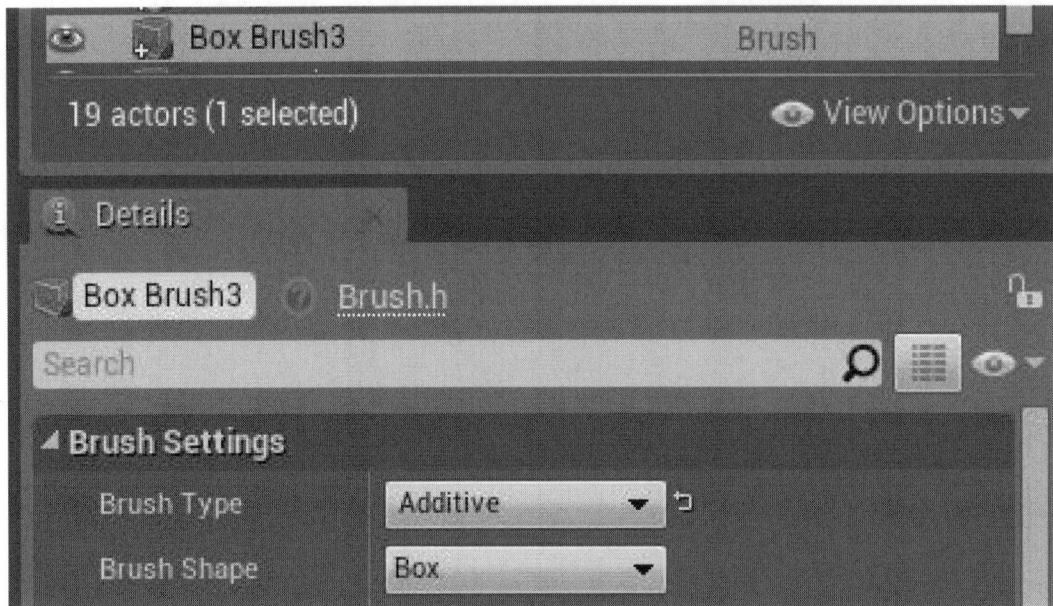

Within these settings, right at the top (Just under the "Search" box), there's a section called "Brush Settings". The first option in this settings category is "Brush Type", which is currently set to Additive.

This means that currently, this BSP is "Adding" to the world. What we want to do is take away from the world, So click the option and in the drop-down menu, select "Subtractive".

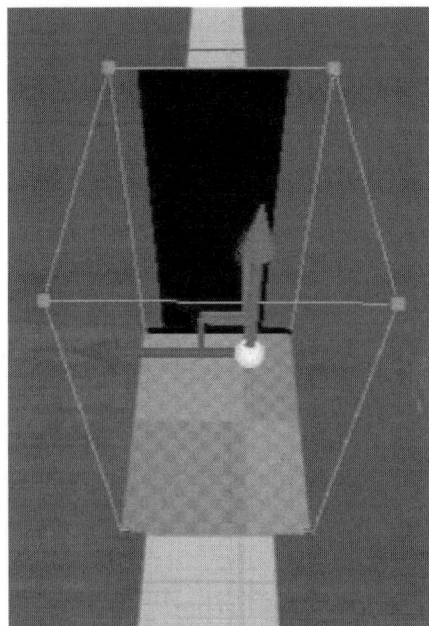

You'll now notice that the BSP we created is no longer visible. Instead of "Adding" itself to the world, it is now "Taking away" from the World, removing geometry that was inside it.

NOTE: "Subtracting" BSPs only works with BSPs. You can't do this to Static Meshes!

You may notice that our "Door" has eaten some of the floor. This isn't a problem at the moment - We'll come to fix at the end of setting these doors.

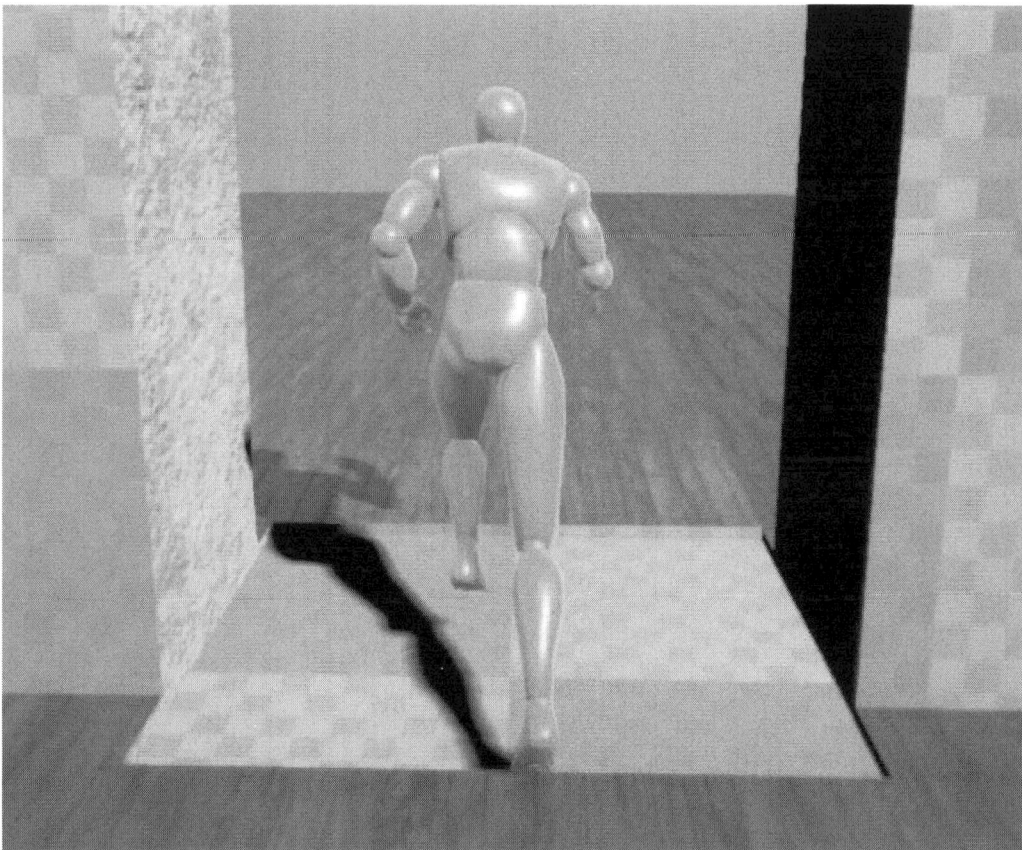

Give the level a super-quick test (Alt+P to test it and ESC once you're happy) to make sure that the character can walk through the Doorway with no problems.

Again, don't worry about the floor. We'll fix that once we've set the other doorways.

So now take your other three doors and do the same for those three; Turning them into doorways. Make sure the player can run all around your map (Put a doorway against every wall inside our play area, but not on the outside walls!) and once you're happy with their placement, test them out. Once you can run around your map from the start "Room" all the way around back to the start "Room", we can continue.

FIXING THE FLOOR

We now need to quickly fix the floor. To fix it, it's best to first describe why the holes in the floor has happened and what we can do to fix it.

The floor is a BSP and as we've already discovered, Any piece of a BSP that is inside a "Subtract BSP" while it's subtracting will be taken away from the World as opposed to being added.

I'm sure you're wondering how we can get around this; There will be times where you don't want the "Subtract BSP" to subtract every BSP; For example a hole in the floor with stairs. You wouldn't want the top of the stairs to be subtracted, but you would want the hole in the floor taken away from the World.

Solving this issue is easier than you'd think but at the same time it makes little sense. If you want a BSP to NOT be subtracted, all you have to do is… Copy it. That's right.

For some reason, duplicating a BSP and deleting the original will tell a Subtraction BSP: "Hey, I want all of this BSP to exist in the world. Don't subtract anything from this BSP!".

Why it works like this is quite bizarre but the fact that the method exists plays massively in our favour when creating our in-game worlds. It gives us an extra tool to add depth and save time when drafting up our levels while at the same time not getting in the way and happening when we don't want it to.

But there is one thing to note about this method - Only things duplicated AFTER the subtraction BSP has been created will work with this; Things duplicated before a subtraction BSP is placed will still be subtracted. Naturally, to get around this, simply duplicate the item again and it will work fine.

So let's fix the floor!

Select the floor, Press Ctrl + X and Ctrl + V (Which are Cut and Paste" respectively to get around the "Duplicate to not Subtract" issue.

Doing it this way saves a minute or two as well, as we don't need to duplicate, find the original and delete it.

BUILDING OUR LIGHTING

This would be a great chance to talk about building our lighting. Naturally, for those who aren't used to Unreal Engine (Or maybe even Game Development itself!) are most likely confused at this point; But don't worry! Building lighting is very simple, even if it's pretty important for the visual quality of your projects!

So before we jump ahead, What exactly is Building Lighting?

Lighting in Unreal Engine is done in a few different ways - "Static" lighting is baked into what is called a "Lightmap".

These lightmaps are used when you play your game to save performance by calling up images that have already been created to simulate light where you don't need to think about shadows of objects that move or any fancy lighting effects (Such as lights that move around .etc)

Dynamic lights are the opposite of this, They cost performance (As they don't use the lightmaps in the way Static lighting does) but allow for things like shadows of moving objects as well as things such as moving the light, changing it's colour .etc

The lighting in our example map has already been set-up. The map uses a directional light, which works like a sun (Lights the whole scene) and there is a Lightmass Importance Volume already wrapped around the playing field.

The lightmass importance volume is a volume that you use to tell Unreal Engine where you want your shadows to be drawn on your map from the static lighting. If you don't set one up, the engine will draw lightmaps for the whole world on your game - Even the parts with no geometry.

Why is this bad? Simply put, drawing unnecessary lightmaps wastes time as well as file size on your end user's computer. This is why we use the Lightmass Importance Volume system.

To save file size inflation, all we have to do is make sure the LIV (Lightmass Importance Volume) wraps around all the area we want the player to walk around / get to. This means that in this LIV area, the static lighting is high quality without wasting unnecessary space.

The areas outside of the LIV will not have high-quality shadows and it is not recommended to let the player outside of the area of the Lightmass Importance Volume.

Getting back to the project, our project already has a Lightmass Important Volume and the sunlight pre-setup for us. However, you'll notice that our shadows have become outdated since we've started messing around with the map and adding / removing geometry. You'll notice this when areas of the floor have inconsistent lighting such as the doorways we created.

To fix this, head up to the "Action" bar above the scene view. This is the selection of actions such as "Save, Content, Marketplace, Settings .etc"

There is a button on this action bar called "Build". This is to the right of "Matinee" (With the image of a Clapperboard) and to the left of "Play" (The image of a play icon in front of a DOS-like Window). The Build button has an image of around four buildings, with one being a dark-blue.

Clicking the building image will "Auto-Build", which means the project will build the current lighting, as well as other settings in which we'll cover in the future.

Clicking the down arrow to the right of the building image will show a drop-down menu where we can build specific things, such as lighting, A.I Navigation and more. We can also alter the settings, such as determining the lighting quality .etc

TIP: Use preview lighting until you're ready to ship. This saves time building lighting, where "Preview lighting" doesn't really look that different to "Production", which coupled with the fact that "Preview" is the fastest method of lighting makes it perfectly fine to use during development.

As we're only building lighting, all you have to do now is either click the "Build" building image or select "Build Lighting Only" from the dropdown menu.

Your project will now build the lighting. You can tell when the build has finished by checking the bottom-right of your screen.

When you see "Lighting Build Complete", the lighting has been built and we can continue!

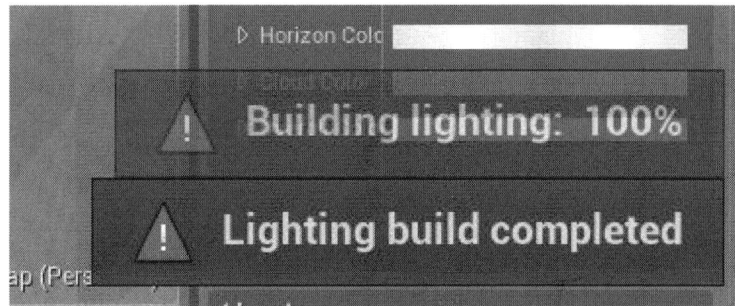

Just before we do actually continue, have a quick look at your shadows now and see how rich they look. Double-check they look correct and semi-realistic. If you're not happy, you are free to alter the settings in the "Build" dropdown menu until you get a result you're happy with.

Let's just take a moment to see what we've done - We've edited the map to our needs, learnt the basics of BSPs and touched on the basics of lighting. Not bad! But our adventure has just begun - Let's work on creating a camera system!

Creating the Camera

For this next task; We'll be using only a portion of our map. This is to make sure things don't get too confusing. Unless I state otherwise, for the foreseeable future, we will be working in the bottom right "Square" room of our map.

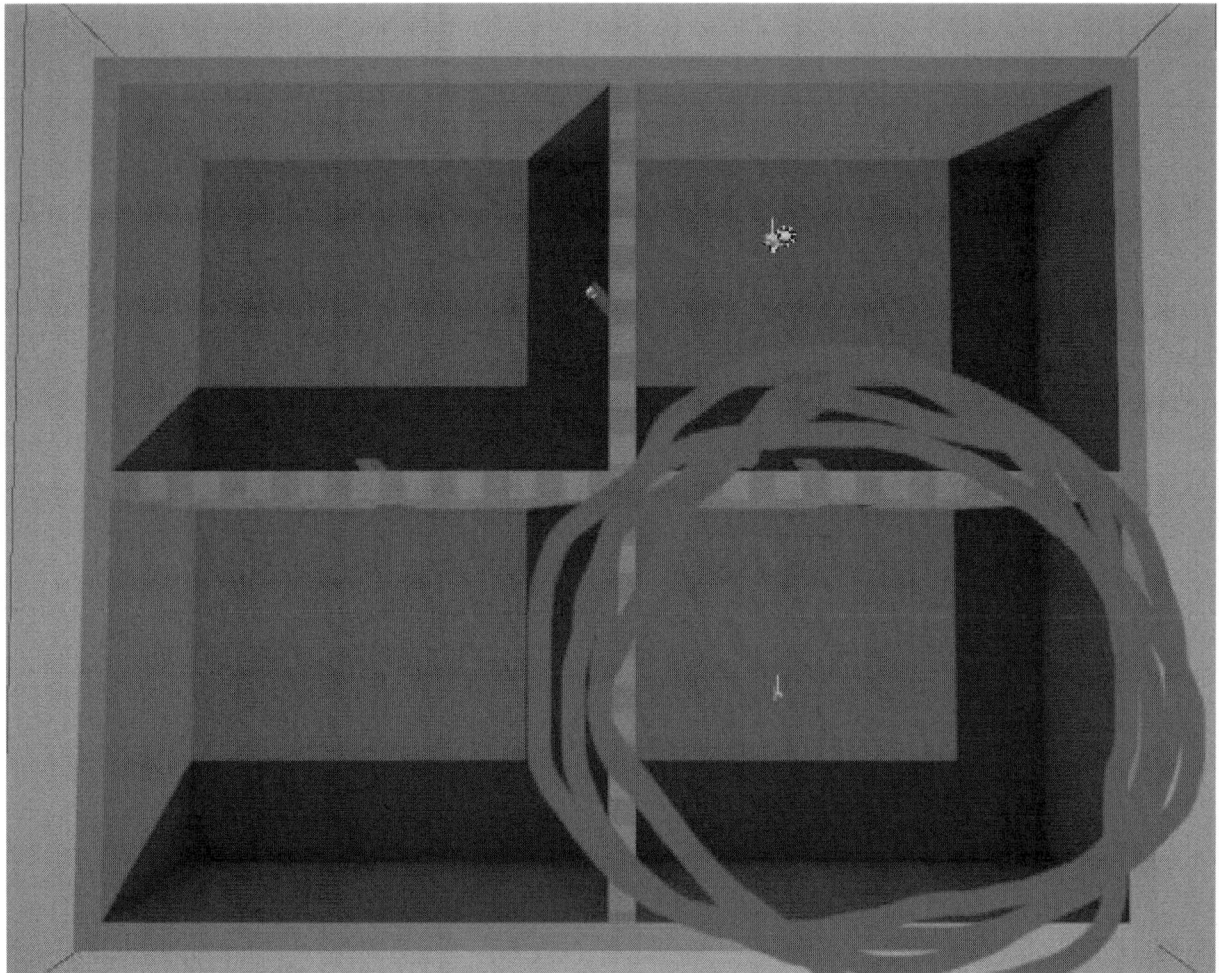

If your PlayerStart is not in this in this room already; Simply drag it into the room for the next few steps!

Ready to continue? Awesome!

We're now going to need a new Blueprint - This will be a Camera that we can place as many times as we want around the map and it will follow the player no matter where it is.

For those who don't understand what I mean, Think the Camera that you find in Telltale Point and Click Adventure games or the camera in the original Resident Evil games.

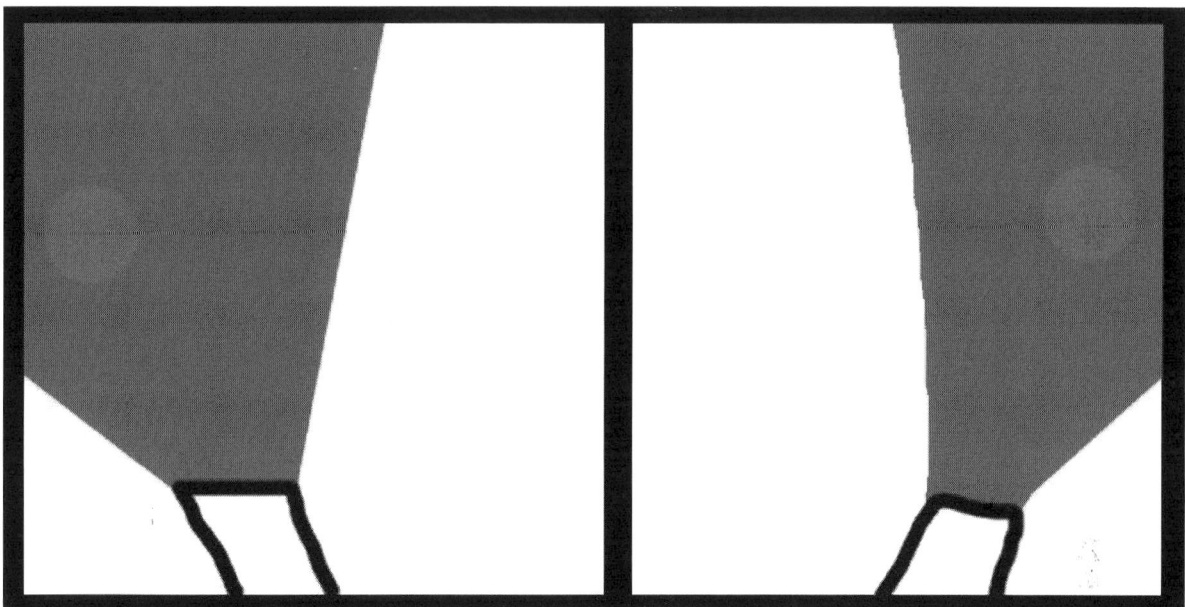

In the image above, I've used the mastery of Paint to quickly visualise what I mean - When the player is on the left-hand side of the room, the camera is facing the left and when the player is on the right - The camera faces the right.

The best way to think about this camera is to think of it as a CCTV camera that is always following the player - As if the player is a juvenile delinquent in a shop filled with tasty candy.

So let's head back into the Engine - It's time to bring our camera system to life!

Within Unreal Engine 4, Head over to the Content Browser. If you've forgotten where it is, its default location is the bottom-left of the editor.

This is where we can access all the files for our project. A simple drag and drop can place our objects into the scene; Be it Materials, Blueprints or whatever!

You can import, edit and even export files all within the Content Browser - So it's a feature that shouldn't even be overlooked!

We're now going to create a new Blueprint, but before we do, we're going to need to create a folder to store our Blueprint.

Before we carry on, make sure the "Game" folder is highlighted. This is so that when we create a new folder, it will put it in the "Game" folder and not in a subdirectory - Which would make it harder to find!

To select the "Game" folder, simply click it! When it goes Orange, that means it's selected.

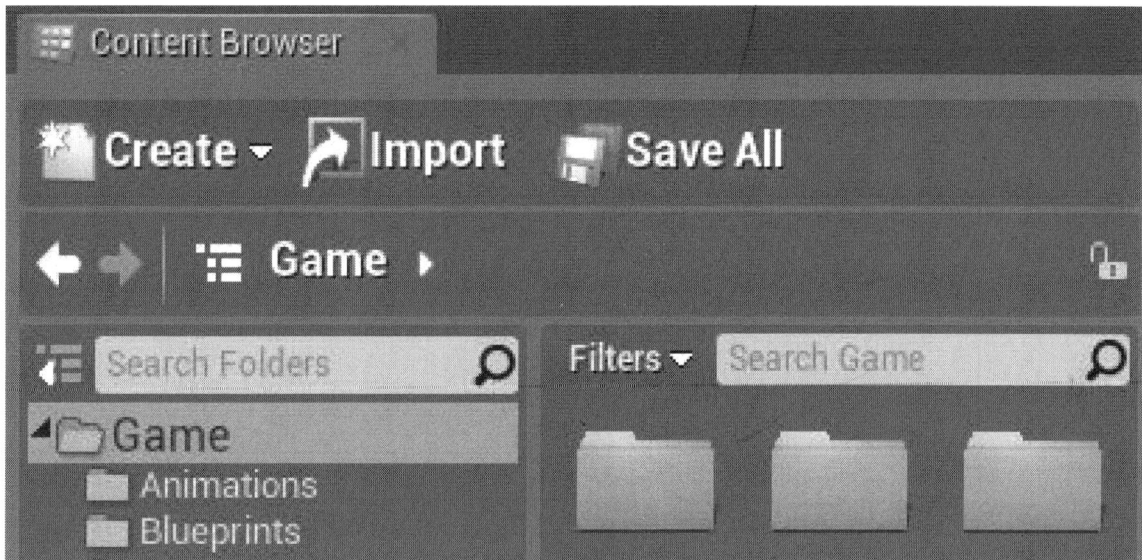

Now, with the "Game" folder selected, Press the "Create" button on the top of the "Content Browser". A dropdown menu will now appear. From here, select "Create Folder" and this will create the folder in the "/Game/" folder.

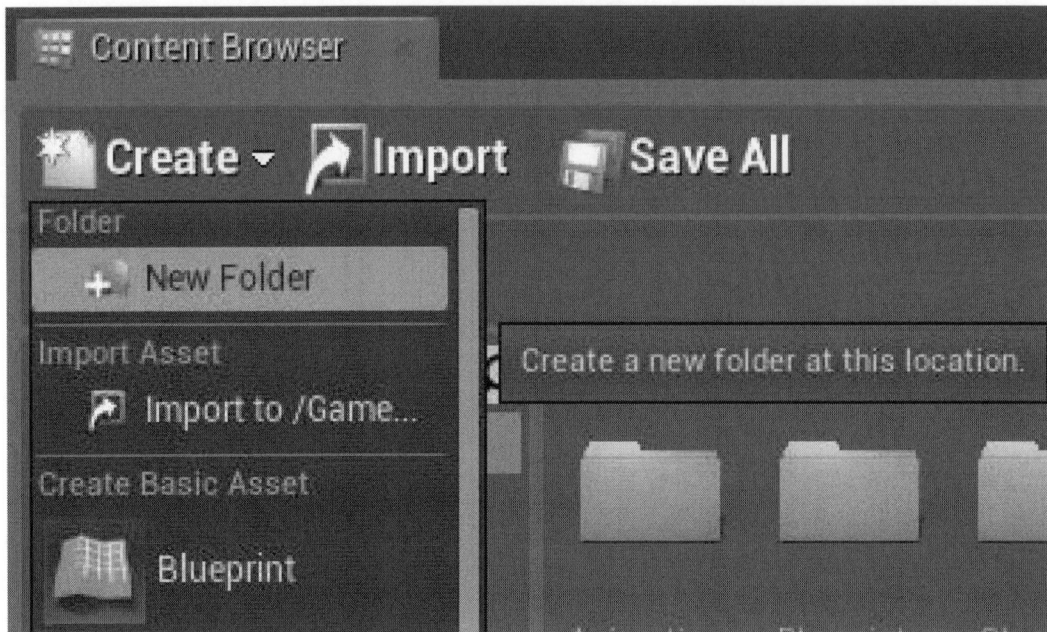

When the folder is first created, the folder will be selected and the text field will be editable. Use this moment to name the folder "ArtOfBP".

TIP: If you accidently click off of the folder and the text is no longer editable, don't worry! If you right click [Ctrl + Click] the folder and select "Rename". (Alternatively, you can select the folder and press F2)

Now that the folder has been created, double-click the folder to open it up.

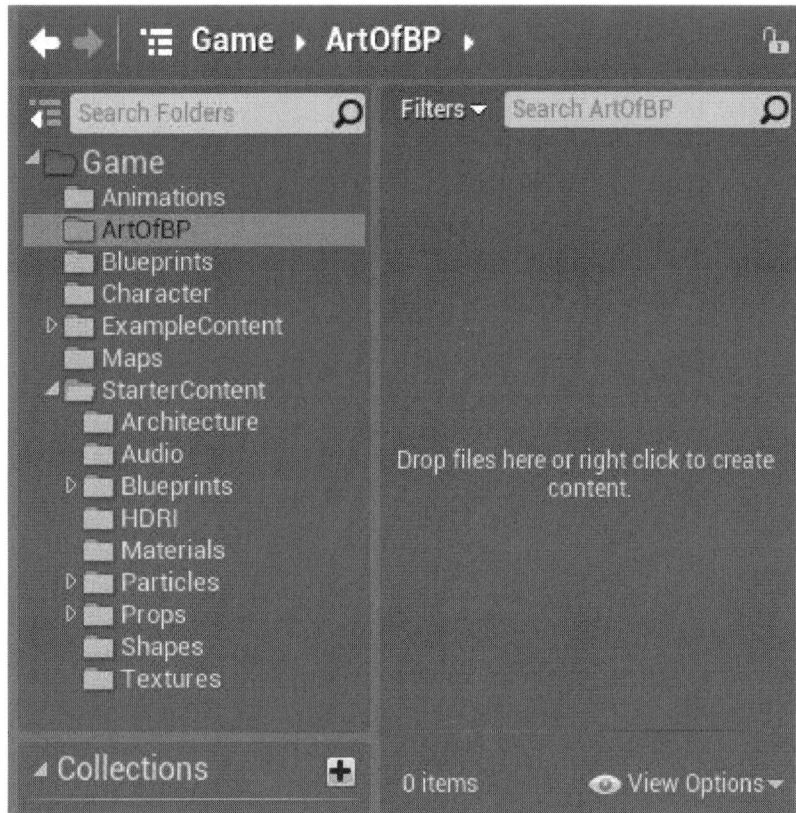

Now that we're in the folder, when we create a Blueprint using the "Create" menu, it will place the Blueprint in this folder - Saving us time and effort from moving it from folder to folder.

And that's exactly what we're going to do right now - Hit the "Create" button and select "Blueprint".

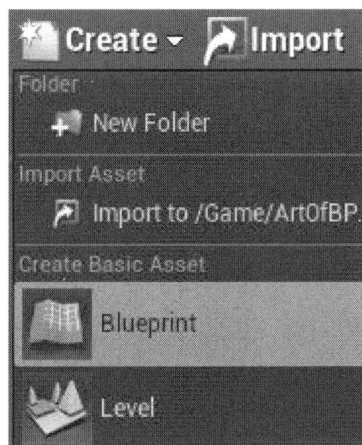

This will open up the "Pick Parent Class" window, in which we can pick a Blueprint "Style" to base our Blueprint off.

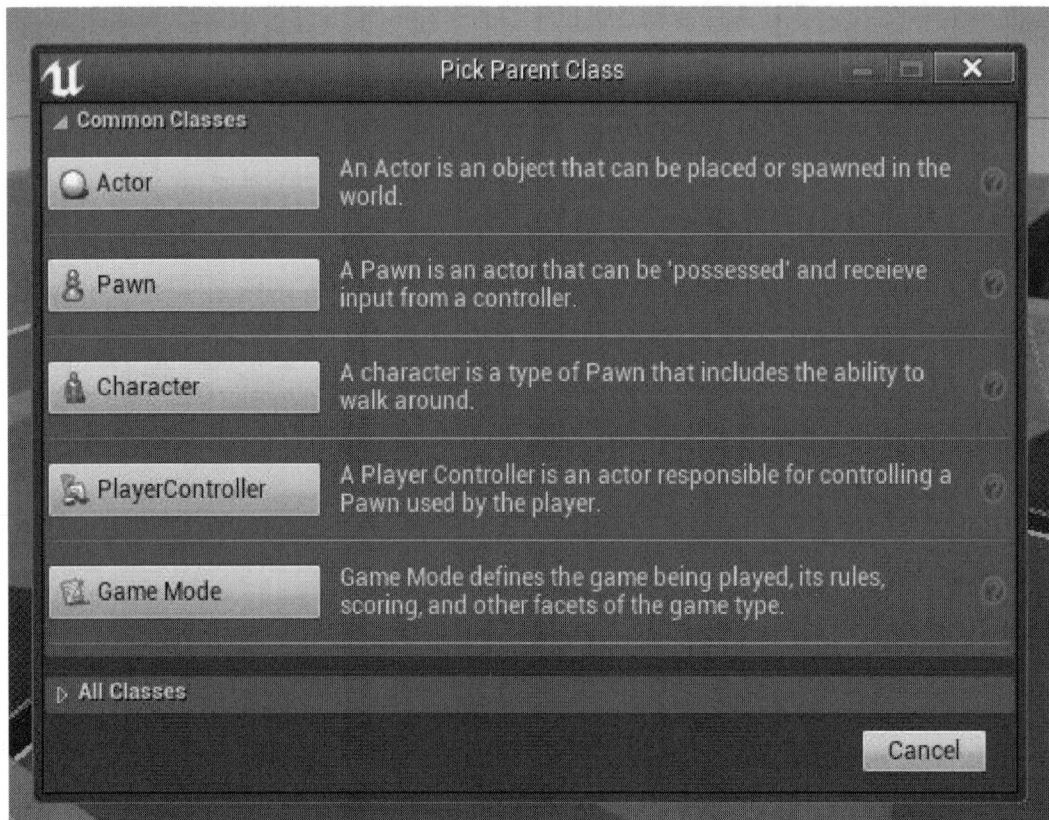

I know at first glance this can sound a little confusing but to sum it up as simply as possible, it's like saying: If you picked an Apple as a base class, a Blueprint would be created with an apple core whereas if you picked an orange, Seeds would be created instead of the apple core.

It was created with ease of use and simplicity in mind. It saves time by setting up a Blueprint in a style that you need it to be as opposed to having create it from scratch, which could take up to a whole day in some cases.

Each of the "Main" classes have a small but helpful description of what each class is and what they are created to achieve - So spend a quick minute or two to read what they are and what they do, as it'll be super-helpful in your future projects!

For our project, we need an "Actor" class Blueprint. This is because an "Actor" class blueprint is perfect for anything that lives independently in the in-game world. This is because objects in the scene (That aren't BSPs) are called "Actors" (As opposed to objects).

Select the "Actor" button and this will create the Blueprint. It will then ask for you to name the Blueprint, just like we did when we created a folder.

Call this Blueprint "BP_Camera", which stands for "Blueprint of a Camera", which is a great naming convention for finding things in the future. This is what I personally do for projects.

When I create a Material, I make sure that I use "M_" as a prefix and even with Animation Blueprints, I use "AnimBP_" as a prefix. This means whenever I am looking for something but I can't remember the name, as long as I remember the type of file I'm looking for, It should be simple to find it again using the built-in search feature of the "Content Browser".

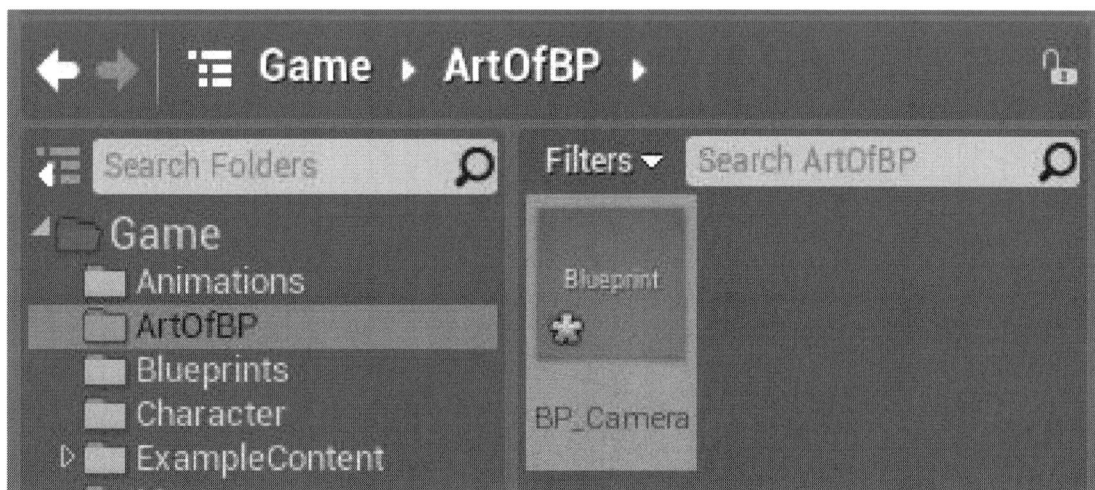

Now that we have created the Blueprint, we need to now edit it to create it into Blueprint we actually want.

To edit the Blueprint, double click the "BP_Camera" to open into the Blueprint editor.

It will now open to the "Component" view. The blueprint editor is broken into three sections: "Defaults", "Component" and "Graph". The defaults section is where you set the "Default" options of the Blueprint, the "Component" section is where we can set the objects within the Blueprint and the Graph editor is where we set the actual code for the Blueprint.

A simple way to remember all of this is "Settings - Objects - Code".

We need to make sure we're in the "Component" tab. To find out which tab we're in, check the top-right of your Blueprint window. You'll see the navigation buttons with the active one with an orangey-yellow highlight around it.

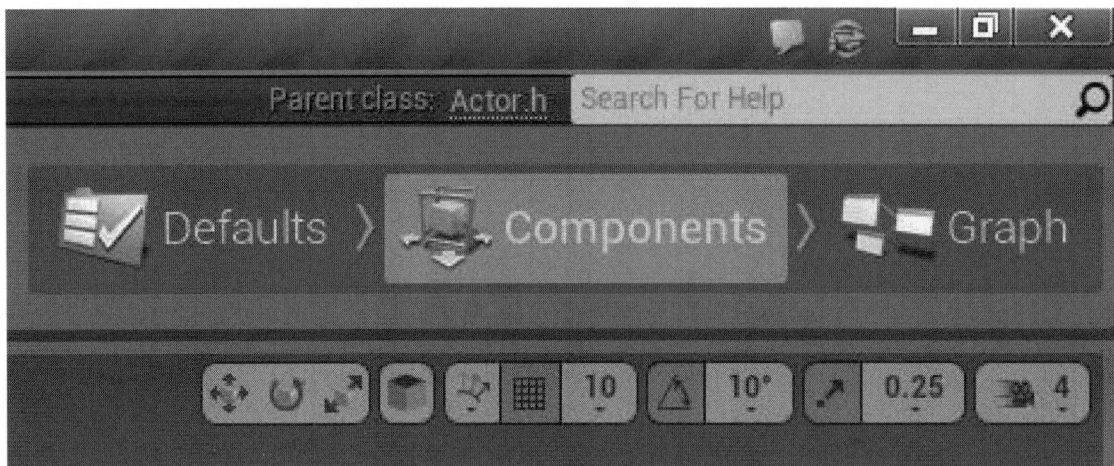

So, in the Components tab? Great! On the left of this screen, we have a view similar to the "Content Browser" intelligently called "Components". This is where we add and sort the components of this Blueprint!

Currently, the "Root" component is called "[ROOT] DefaultSceneRoot" - But what does this actually mean? The root component is basically home base.

When throwing a ball with a string attached, the "Home base" is the hand the ball comes from. But why would the string be attached to the ball in the first place? Well the string tells us where the ball is (In case it goes out of view) as well as acting as a method of getting the ball back if we want to throw it again.

Obviously, we're not dealing with a ball or string here, but the same thought process applies.

But now I'm going to throw a curveball (Pun not intended): As soon as we add a component, it will overwrite this "DefaultSceneRoot" and delete it - So we lose our "String".

I bet you're wondering now - Why the hell did you tell me this when it gets removed anyway? Simple. Even though we lose our "DefaultSceneRoot", we can add it back manually, so we can choose whether or not to have our string.

Can you guess why the system currently works like this? At first glance it seems quite complicated but when you break it down it's rather simple: When we have no components - The Blueprint gives us a "Root" so that we can code whatever we want component-less, which would work in certain situations where you don't need any components. Then, when you create a Blueprint where you need components, the Blueprint removes this "Root" and gives you a choice of whether or not you need our theoretical "String".

It's really hard to explain in a simple manner but I hope that I've managed to get the point across!

Getting back to our project, Head to the Component area and use the "Create Component" button. From the dropdown menu, search for "Scene" and select it to manually insert a "Scene" component (Which acts as our "String" for the "Ball" we're going to create).

When it asks to rename the Component, you have the choice to either rename it or leave it as it is. Once it's created you'll see [ROOT] Scene1 (Or your scene name). That means that the "Scene" component has been created successfully and we can move on to adding a Camera.

How do we add the Camera? Exactly the same way we added the "Scene". Just click "Add Component" and select "Camera".

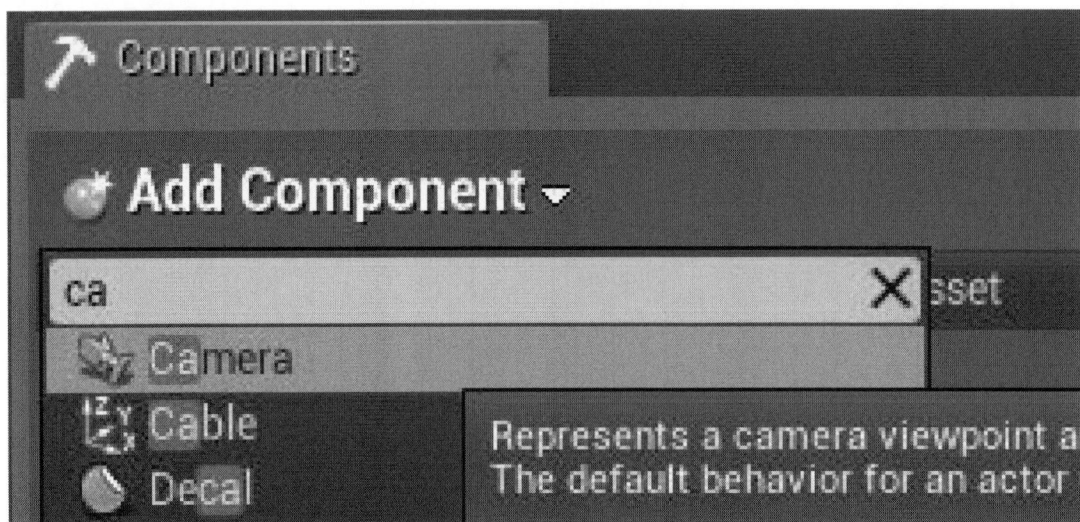

Again, you have the choice to either rename it or leave it as it is. Your Component Graph should now look something like this:

What does this mean? Well, as we discovered before, the "Root" scene acts as our "Home Base" and the Camera is the "Child" of this home base. What does a child eventually do? Yup, you guessed it - Leave home.

Just as we discussed earlier - The root acts as a string and the Camera acts as our ball. No matter where the ROOT Scene is in the in-game world, The Camera will always be same distance from the Root and the scene always knows there the Camera is and vice versa.

Now, we have the components (Or ingredients if you want to think of it like that) for our Blueprint, the next step is to code our Blueprint - That's where we tell the Blueprint what to actually do, as at the moment if we drag it into our scene, it will just sit there doing absolutely nothing.

Just like before, look back at the top-right side of the screen and use the Navigation buttons to head into the "Graph" mode.

OUR FIRST CODE

Now that we're in the Graph view, it's time to have some fun!

IMPORTANT NOTE: From here on out for this book and beyond, whenever I tell you to create a node, I am talking about using the "Compact Blueprint Library" to find and create the node (Unless otherwise stated). To bring up the CBL, Right Click (Ctrl + Click) empty space within the Blueprint graph and enter the node name into the "Search" field.

To start things off, we're going to need a "Tick" event. But let's not get ahead of ourselves, We first need to ask the questions: What is an event and what is a Tick?

What is an event? - An event in Blueprints is exactly what it says on the tin: An event that takes place. You have to go into Blueprints with the knowledge that nothing can happen without an event. Think of the big bang theory: The big bang event happened and then different actions happen because of it. That's what an event is. If something isn't connected to an Event in a Blueprint, it won't "Fire" - It won't run.

So when creating Blueprints, remember that an Event has to happen before the "Action" of that Blueprint can happen.

You can easily tell the difference between an "Event" and an "Action" node in a Blueprint as an Event only has an output pin (Which is on the right) and is red, whereas an Action node usually has an input AND an output and is blue.

So: Red = Event, Blue = Action.

What is a Tick Event? - A Tick Event is an event that fires every frame of game-time. New players to the Game Development game might be confused what this means - Especially when comparing a frame to a second - But a lot of gamers already know all about this subliminally. Every frame IS NOT every second - It's faster.

Have you ever ran a benchmark for a game or deliberately purchased a computer part to get a certain Frame per second (FPS) in a video-game? Think about it - 30 / 60 FPS is talked about a hell of a lot when people talk about games. Every single frame is when this "Tick" gets fired. So 60 Frames Per Second means 60 times this "Tick" event fires whatever is connected to it.

So now it's time to apply this to our project; We've learnt what a Tick is, so now we can use this knowledge to our advantage; We can use a "Tick" event to control our camera's position and get it to look at the player.

So where do we begin? Where every Blueprint script begins - With an event! For this case, we'll be using what we've just covered: The "Tick" event!

Just before we start our script - Make sure you're in the right "Area" of the scripting interface. You can tell which section you're in by checking just under the "Debug filter" area, You'll see two tabs: Construction Script and Event Graph.

The construction script is where you create code to set-up the blueprint - For example, setting the mesh of the blueprint, telling the BP to do a certain thing when we're messing around in the editor .etc

The Event Graph is for code which is fired by Events. These can either be fired from the BP or another BP can fire the events remotely to fire the code connected to events in the Blueprint.

For reference, 9/10 times, you'll be coding in the "Event Graph" as the "Construction Script" doesn't really interact with the world or other blueprints whereas the Event Graph can do just that.

You can tell which code mode you're in by checking which tab is lighter grey. The darker greyed out tab means that this mode is not currently a active,

In the Event Graph? Great!

As described before, we need an event. Because no code can fire if it hasn't been triggered. As we want the code we are about the create to fire every single frame, we'll be using the tick.

So go ahead and create a tick node. Just to help you remember, to create a node: Right click (Ctrl + Click) to open up the CBL ("Compact Blueprint Library") and either find it manually or use the search filter.

Simply clicking the "Event Tick" will create the node.

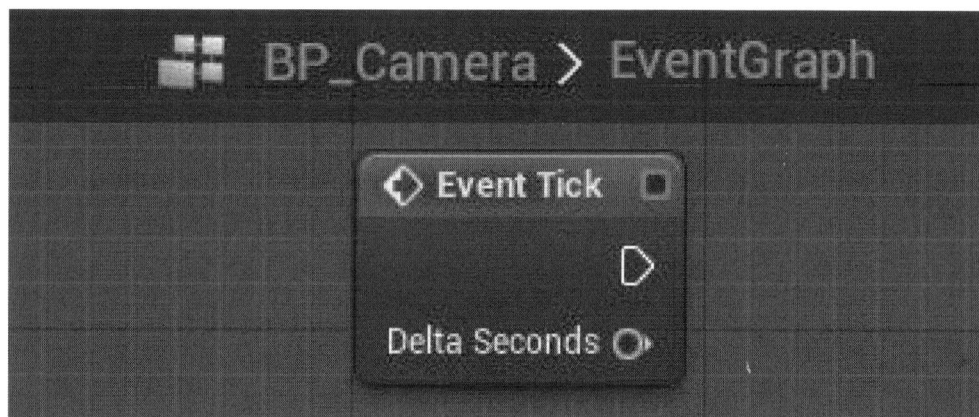

Now that the node has been created, we'll quickly run over what all of the icons on the node mean:

First thing you'll notice is that the "Event Tick" text has a red tint behind it. This tells us that this is an "Event" and not an "Action". This is confirmed by the icon to the left of the "Event Tick" text which is a see through arrow in a diamond.

The next thing you'll most likely notice is the black square to the right of the "Event Tick" text which has a bright red border. This icon is an "Output Delegate". What the heck is a delegate, I hear you ask? We'll cover this some other time (As it's stepping into more advanced territory and we don't need to cover it right now).

Below the red tint, you'll notice two icons, an empty arrow head pointing to the right and a green empty circle pointing to the right.

Before I explain what they do, notice their location. With nodes, the inputs and outputs are separated by their location in the node. If they are on the left-hand side, they are inputs and if they are on the right-hand side… You guessed it! - Right hand side icons are outputs.
This will also help you determine events from actions, Events will only ever have outputs (Icons on the right) and will never have inputs whereas actions will either have them on the left AND right or just on the left.

So to recap: Icons on the left of a node are inputs whereas icons on the right are outputs.

What do we connect to outputs? Inputs!

Say you have a USB keyboard: In order to use the USB keyboard, you have to plug the USB cable into the USB socket. When you type on the keyboard, think of that as an event. The event then fires down the cable into whatever the USB output is inputted into.

That's a pretty perfect example on how to imagine how a Blueprint works: Event > Event Output > Action Input > Action.

But there's one key thing we're missing here - Something that's essential for this Event > Action to work and that's the execution pin.

When you look at the "Event Tick", you'll notice that of the two icons below the red tint, there's a white hollow arrow head. THIS is the execution pin we're talking about.

But what is it? - An execution pin is the veins of the operation. It transfers the "Power" of the event to the next node it is connected to.

Thinking of it in an example, think that the Event node is a complete "Circuit" whereas the "Action" node isn't complete as it's missing power. You can use the execution pin output of the event to give the action power and it will work, but what if you wanted two actions?

Well, we can. Even though an action node needs the "Power" from an event node, it doesn't actually need to do anything with this "Power" - It simply uses this as validation as in "Yes, I received the signal, I can run now!", so if you were to have an Event connected to an action through their execution nodes and then connect another action to the chain by hooking it to the "Output" of that first action, they would both use that "Power" from the event node and run without problem (As none of this "Power" is lost).

This is one of those things where seeing it in practical is easier then reading the "Theory". And that's exactly what we're going to do!

We'll do this by first creating the node we're going to need. As the camera will always be facing the player, the node we are going to create is a "Set World Rotation" node.

This node alone won't do much but as we're connecting it to an "Event Tick" node it will change the camera's rotation every frame.

So before we continue, go ahead and create the "Set World Rotation" node. If you're using 4.6 or above, you'll see it in the CBL as "Set World Rotation (Camera1)" (Or the name of your Camera!).

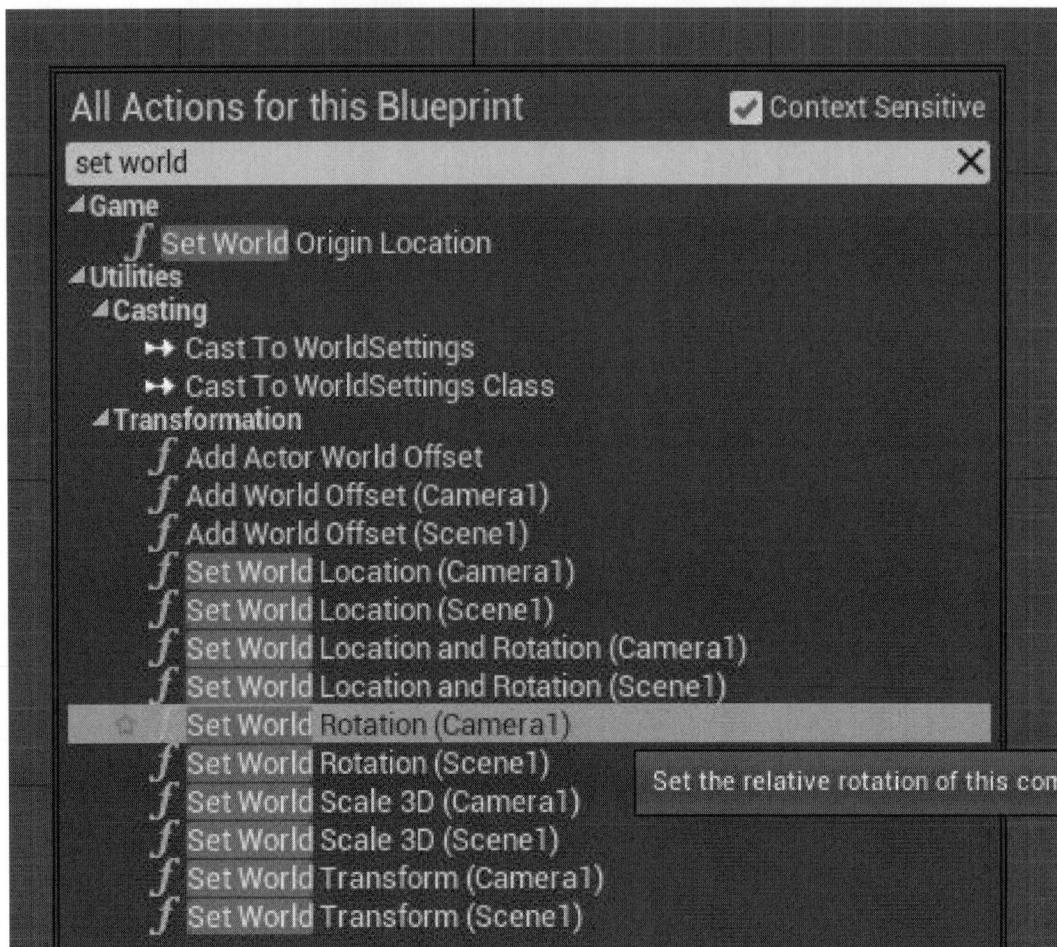

All Actions for this Blueprint ☑ Context Sensitive

set world ✕

▲ Game
   f Set World Origin Location
▲ Utilities
  ▲ Casting
    ↦ Cast To WorldSettings
    ↦ Cast To WorldSettings Class
  ▲ Transformation
    f Add Actor World Offset
    f Add World Offset (Camera1)
    f Add World Offset (Scene1)
    f Set World Location (Camera1)
    f Set World Location (Scene1)
    f Set World Location and Rotation (Camera1)
    f Set World Location and Rotation (Scene1)
      Set World Rotation (Camera1)
    f Set World Rotation (Scene1)   Set the relative rotation of this com
    f Set World Scale 3D (Camera1)
    f Set World Scale 3D (Scene1)
    f Set World Transform (Camera1)
    f Set World Transform (Scene1)

NOTE: If you're using an older version of Unreal Engine (Any version older than 4.6), you'll only see "Set World Rotation" and you'll have to manually set the "Camera1" by dragging it into the "Target" pin of the node (From the variable library on the left of the Blueprint view!) once it's created. Some older versions of the engine will force you to drag in the "Camera1" from the variable library and then drag off from the pin of that variable and then type in "Set World Rotation".

Confusing I know but all you'll need to know is that if you're using 4.6, simply right clicking (Ctrl + Clicking) will bring up the Compact Blueprint Library, where you can search for "Set World Rotation" and select "Set World Rotation (Camera1)".

Just as we explained before, the action needs to connected to the event.

Set World Rotation
Target is BP_Camera_C (Camera1)

Event Tick

Delta Seconds

Target self

New Rotation
R 0.0   P 0.0   Y 0.0

To do this, simply connect the "Output" execution arrow of the "Event Tick" to the "Input" execution arrow of the "Set World Rotation (Camera1)".

Set World Rotation
Target is BP_Camera_C (Camera1)

Event Tick

Delta Seconds

Target self

New Rotation
R 0.0   P 0.0   Y 0.0

You can tell once the connection has been made as the hollow execution pins will now be filled in with white and a line similar to cables connect the two pins together.

Now we are setting the World Rotation of the camera every frame, but if you look closely at what we've created; We're not actually setting any rotation; We're simply telling the camera to stay at the rotation "Roll = 0, Pos = 0 and Yaw = 0" - Which obviously isn't what we want to happen; We want the camera to rotate to follow the player.

So let's create the code to track the player!

Everything we're about to create will not have execution pins, which I know is almost the exact opposite to what we've been talking about. This is because what we're going to create now aren't action nodes. In fact, they're barely nodes at all - It's hard to explain exactly what I mean until you see this in action in a moment but the most important thing to remember is: These nodes will get their "Power" from the output as opposed to the "Input" as they don't use execution pins.

The best way to see this is to recap on this once we've created the next section of code, so we're going to go ahead and work on the code and then look-back and figure out how it's working.

All of this next block of code is going to be connected to the "New Rotation" of the "Set World Rotation (Camera1)", so make sure you've got quite a bit of room as your blueprint can get really ugly super-quickly if you have wires crossing everywhere.

So whenever you're ready to begin the next section of the Blueprint, head over to the Variable Library on the left and under components, find "Camera1" (Or whatever you named your camera in the Component view)

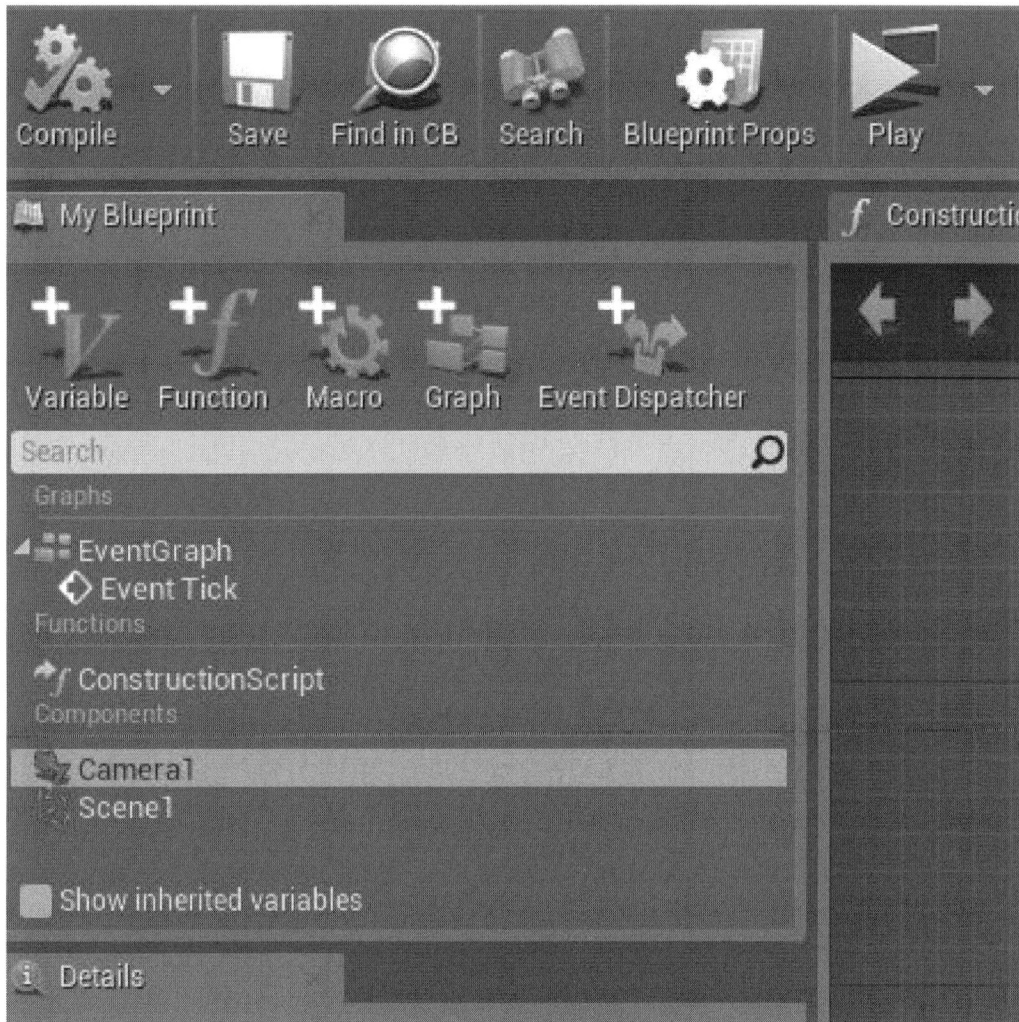

Click the "Camera1" text and drag the variable into the Blueprint. A small menu will now pop up and ask "Get" or "Set"? This is asking if we want to get the information of this variable or set the variable's core information (Which in this case would be a new camera actor), so we're going to go ahead and select "GET".

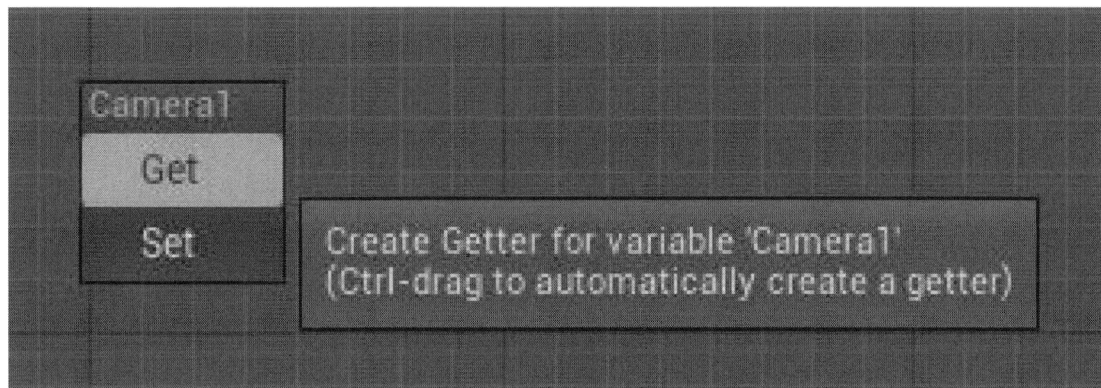

If you selected get, you'll now have a blue-ish rectangle with curved edges and a blue output pin. If you have something different, you did not select "Get" when dragging in "Camera1" from the Variable Library, so go back and make sure you did everything correctly.

Once "Camera1" is in the Blueprint, click the blue output pin of the node and drag to the right: The "Compact Blueprint Library" will now open up.

We need to get the camera's world rotation, so go ahead and type "Get World Rotation":

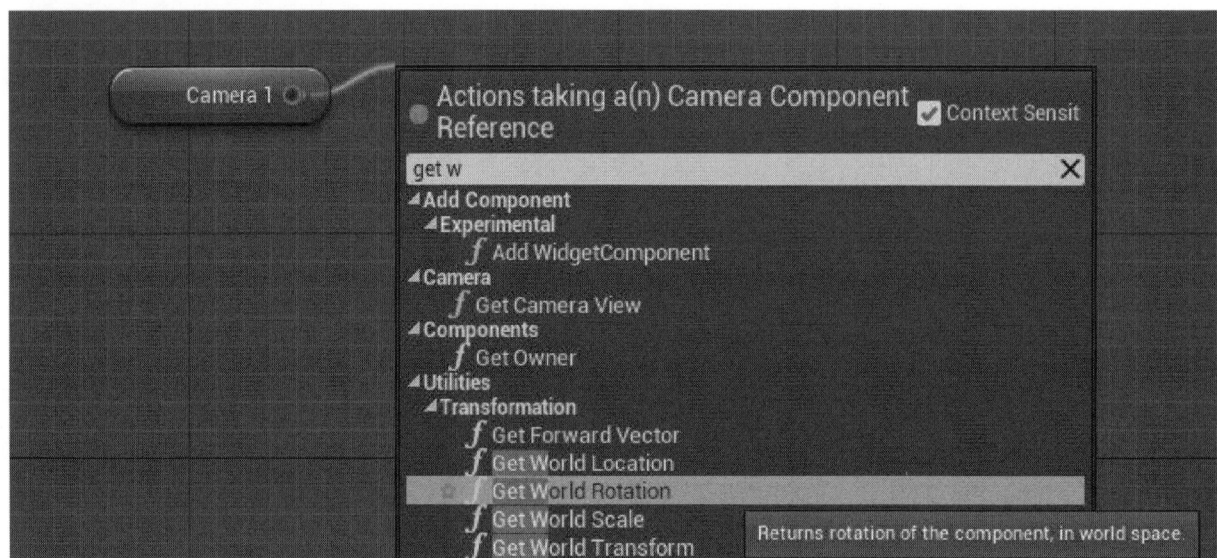

Once you've found it, go ahead and click it to create the node (Which should be pre-connected to our "Camera1". If it isn't, just go ahead and connect it. If there are any issues, you didn't drag off from the "Camera1" node, so you'll need to repeat the last few steps! But if you followed everything correctly and both the nodes we have created hook up properly, then you've done just fine!

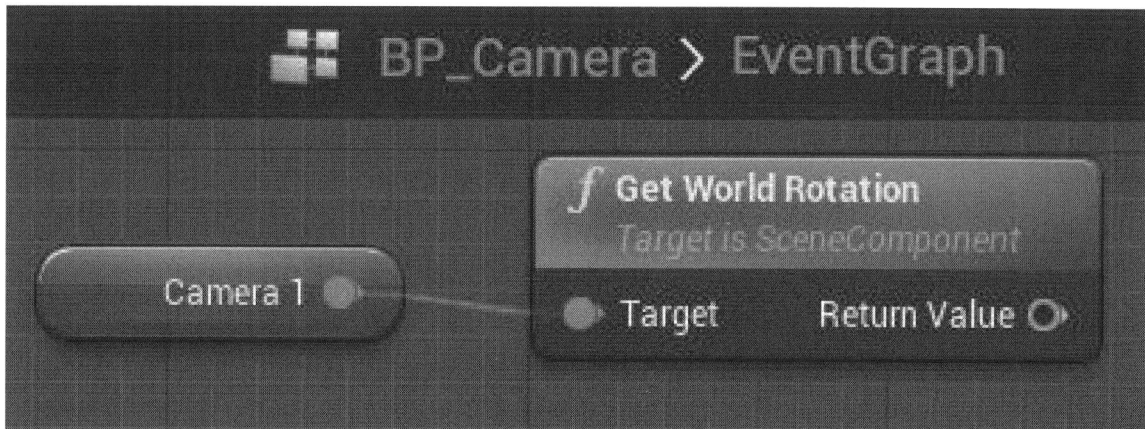

So now we're getting the rotation of the camera in the world (For example if it is looking 45 degrees X, 51 degress Y .etc, it will tell us "Hey, the camera is looking at X = 45, Y = 51 .etc") but we don't need all of this information; We need to strip down the information as all we need is the "X" vector information (Left - Right directional information) of the camera, Which will help us easily trace where / what the camera is currently looking at.

So using the CBL, create a "Get Rotation XVector" node and connect it to the rotation output pin of the "Get World Rotation" node.

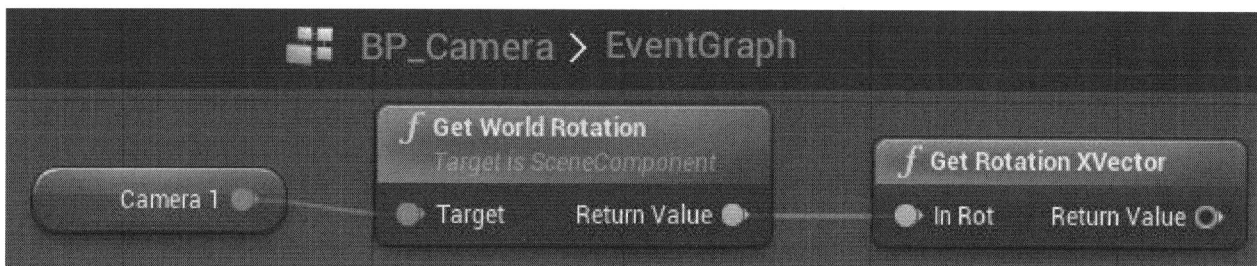

Now we're getting the information of where the camera is looking (On the left to right scale) [*Technically, we're not at the moment as this isn't connected to the*

main chain of events, but in theory if we were to connect this to the main chain of events, this would give us the left / right data of the camera] but this is only part of the code we need to get a camera that follows the player.

We're going to connect the information we've collected so far (The X vector value of the camera) to move the camera accordingly, but we want the moving of our camera to be smooth.

We're going to use a "VInterp To" node to achieve this. This node lets us create a smooth transition between two values.

So go ahead and use the Compact Blueprint Library to create a "VInterp To" node (Not "VInterp To Constant"!) and connect the output of "Get Rotation XVector" to the "Current" pin of the "VInterp To".

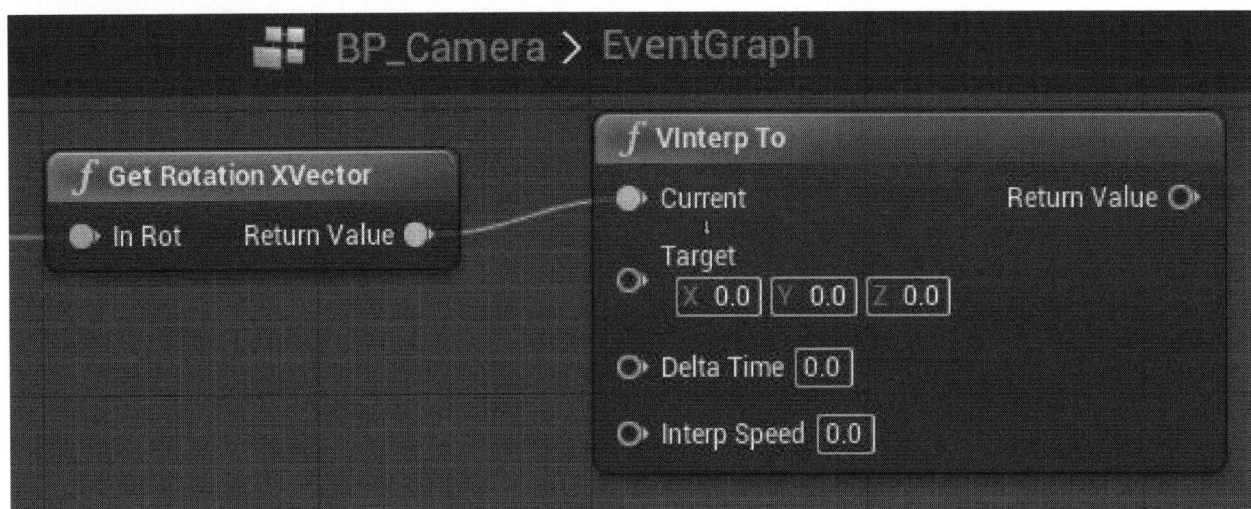

You'll notice that there are three inputs that we have to fill before we can call this node "Complete" as at the moment, the node is not doing anything at all.

We'll sort the "Target" value in a few steps time but for the moment, we're going to focus on Delta Time and Interp Speed.

We can very simply set Interp Speed to 0.01, which means every 0.01 of "Delta Time" (We'll explain what that is into two moments!), we're going to update the current rotation and set it to the target of where we want the camera to face.

So go ahead and do that right now, set the "Interp Speed" of "VInterp To" to 0.01.

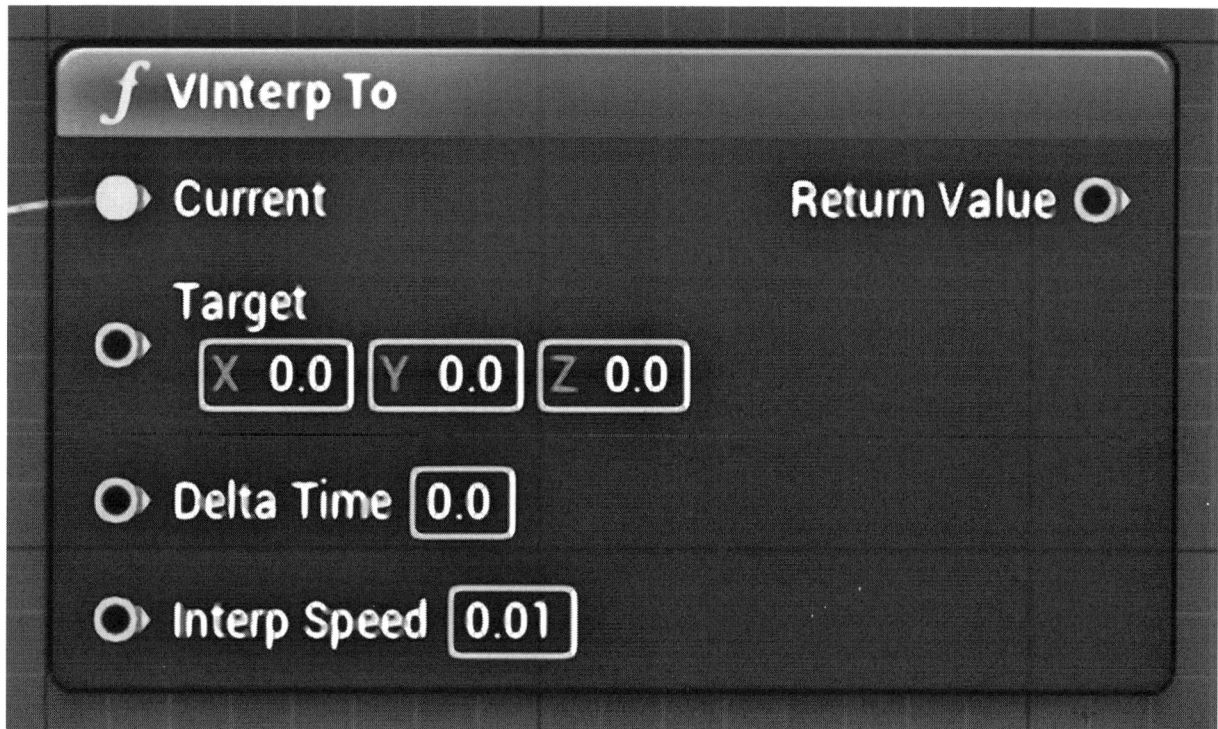

Now we'll set up the Delta Time and this involves a small part of backtracking. There's two ways of plugging this Delta time but just before we do; It'd probably be good to explain what Delta Time actually is:

What is Delta Time? - Delta Time is the time since the last tick (Or, as we learnt, the last frame)

You may have noticed that we've already seen Delta Time before... Do you remember? It was attached to the "Event Tick" automatically for us.

There's two ways we can connect the Delta Time of the "Event Tick", we can either click the output pin of "Delta Time" from Event Tick and drag it to the input of "Delta Time" of the "Vinterp To" node.

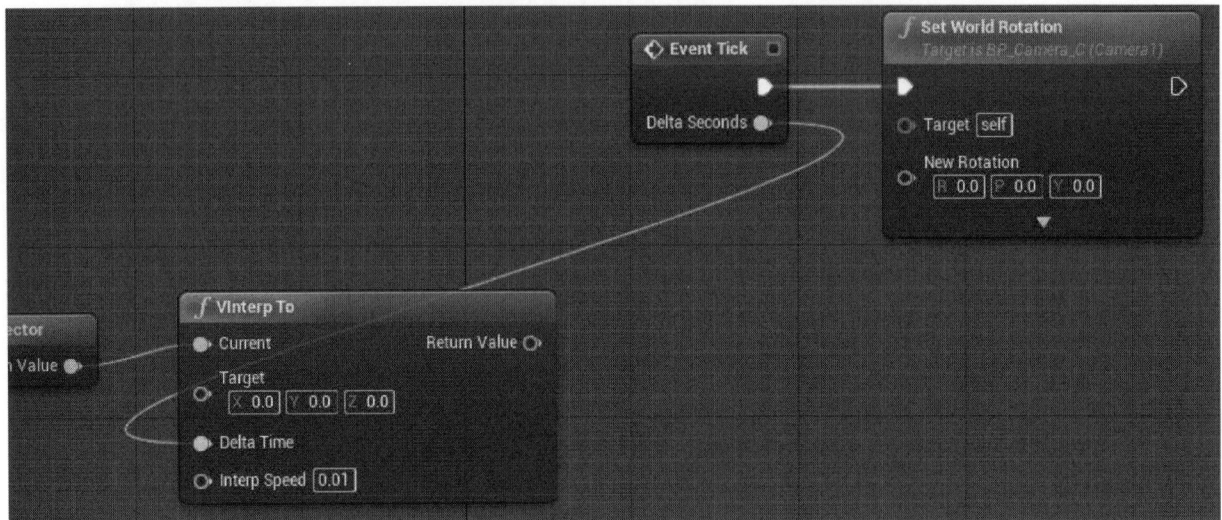

As you can tell from this screenshot though, this is an extremely messy way of doing things. While not a problem now, when we get to creating more complicated Blueprints, it will get extremely hard to figure out what is connected to what.

So we're going to save the "Delta Time" as a variable. This not only keeps a Blueprint cleaner but lets us call this "Delta Time" whenever we need it.

I know some of you will be like "There's no point, I'm just going to skip this part" but I will theoretically slap your wrist and tell you pay attention; Here is a few reasons why converting "Delta Time" to a variable is beneficial and shouldn't be overlooked:

1. Keeps Blueprints clean and easy to read / follow
2. Helps when you need to call "Delta Time" numerous times
3. Helps if you choose to collapse nodes into a separate graph (Don't worry, we'll cover this soon!)
4. A tidy Blueprint means a tidy mind!

So, if you have already connected the two Delta Time's together, it's time to break that connection. You can do this by Alt + Clicking on either pin at the end of the connection. This will break the connection and let us do things "The proper way".

Thanks to the advancements of 4.6, there is now a much simpler way to convert our "Delta Time" into a variable, which we can call whenever need it.

In 4.6 or above, head to the "Event Tick" and more specifically, head to the "Delta Time" of the "Event Tick" node. Once here, simply Right Click (Ctrl + Click) on the "Delta Time" output pin and select "Promote to Variable".

This will create a "Set New Var" node as well as created the "NewVar" variable in the Variable Library on the left of your screen.

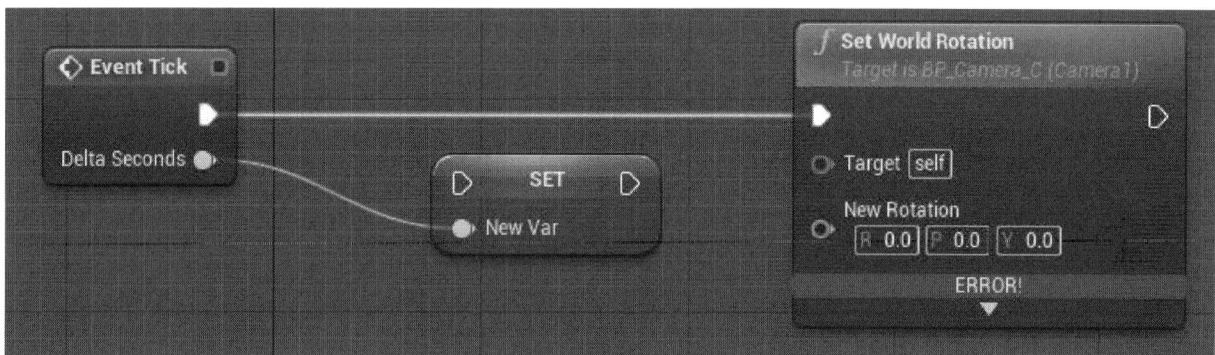

There's a few things to notice before we continue quickly: You'll notice that "Set World Rotation" now says "ERROR!". Don't worry - Nothing's wrong here. You simply need to press "Compile" on the top-left hotbar of your Blueprint view (The image of two gears with a question mark box in front of them) to re-compile the Blueprint and this fixes this issue.

Second, you'll notice that as we explained before, that the "Set NewVar" is not connected to the main chain of events (Or the "Power" line of the Blueprint).

You can fix this quite simply Alt + Clicking either execution pin (Either the output of "Event Tick" or the input of "Set World Rotation") to break the connection between them both and connecting the output execution of "Event Tick" to the input of the "Set NewVar". THEN, connect the output of "Set NewVar" to the input of "Set World Rotation".

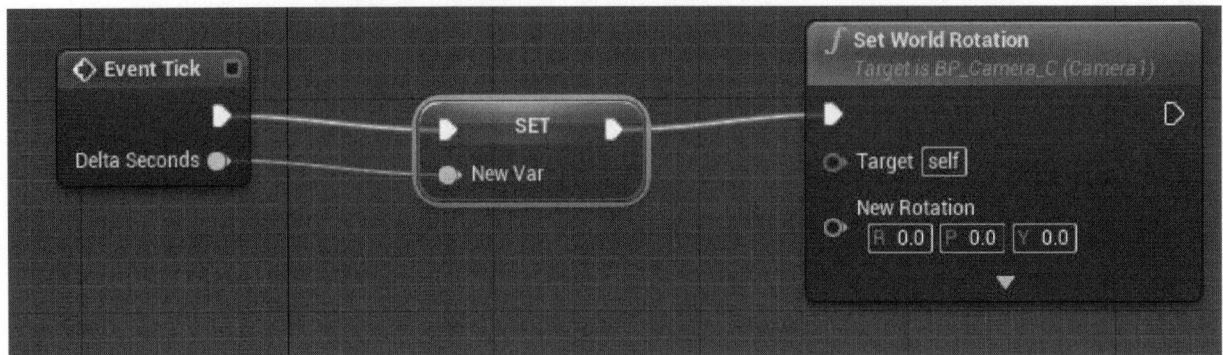

This makes sure that every frame, we are setting the Delta Seconds before doing anything else, which is crucial for calling "Delta Seconds" later as it gives us the best result as it's a time-based variable.

The last problem with this variable is the name. It's pretty easy to forget what "New Var" stands for. So, let's quickly rename it to something more memorable!

To do this, head over to the left hand side of our Blueprint view, over to the "Variable Library".

Here you'll see "New Var" has now been created. Simply click it and in the details panel, you'll see various options. One of the first properties in this "Details" panel is "Variable Name", which is currently set to "New Var".

Rename "New Var" to "DT_DeltaTime". Once you've renamed it, press Enter on your keyboard and then compile the Blueprint (Using the button on the top-left which looks like a question mark in a box with two gears behind it) and once that has been done, use the save button to the right of the "Compile" button to make sure all of these changes have been saved.

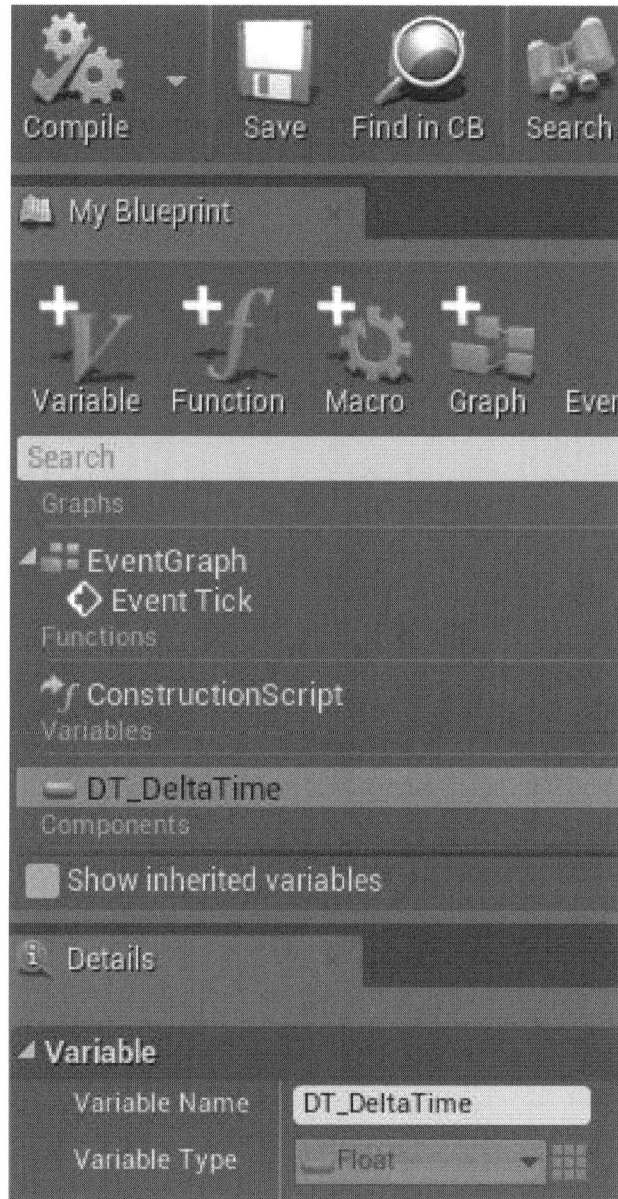

If you're using an older version of Unreal Engine 4 (Older than 4.6), you won't be able to simply use "Promote to Variable" on the "Delta Time" of "Event Tick". Instead, you'll have to manually create the Variable inside the "Variable Library", set it as a Float (We'll get to why a little bit later!) and bring it into the Blueprint and select "Set".

Once you've done that, re-follow the previous steps to hook it up to the "Execution power line" and you should be up to speed. There is one extra thing you'll have to do pre-4.6, which is you'll need to drag from the "Delta Time" pin of Event Tick and drag it into the input pin of "New Var / DT_DeltaTime" of the "Set New Var / DT_DeltaTime" - But if you're using 4.6 or newer (Or used "Promote to Variable"), then you can skip that part!

Now that we have our "DT_DeltaTime" variable, all we have to do is simply drag in "DT_DeltaTime" from our Variable Library and drop it on top of the "DeltaTime" pin of the "VInterp To". Alternatively, you can drag it into the Blueprint area and select "Get" and connect that to the "Delta Time" of "VInterp To".

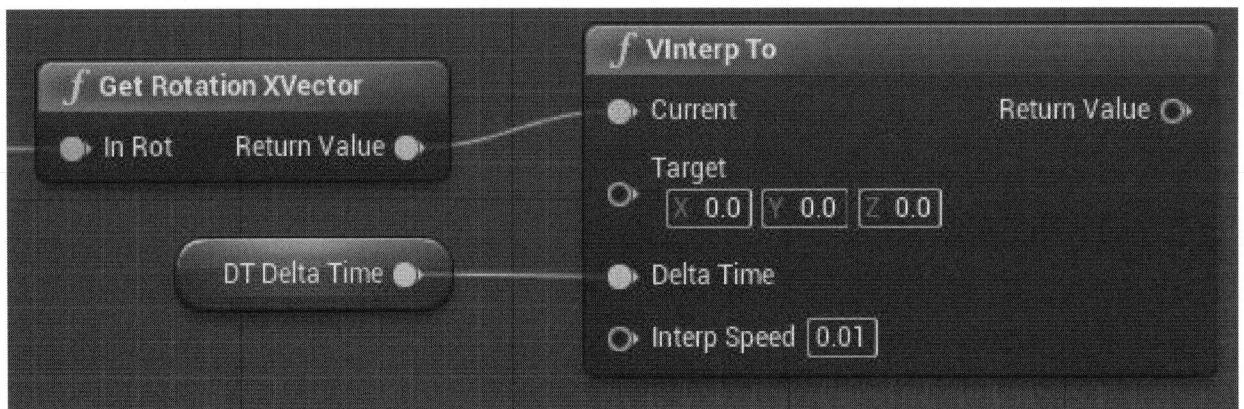

We're now going to tackle the "Target" input of "VInterp To". It's pretty obvious what this is used for but for those who are focusing too much and overlooking things; This target input is what we want to transition the "Current" input to.

Let's make a quick example to help explain: If target is 1 and Target is 5, then the VInterp will use the Delta Time and Interp Speed to blend 1 to 5. As we'll be firing this every second, this helps keep things super-smooth and not jerky.

So let's create the code needed to put in the "Target" input!

Just like we've done before, use the Variable Library to drag in "Camera1" (Or whatever you called your Camera) into the Blueprint and select "Get".

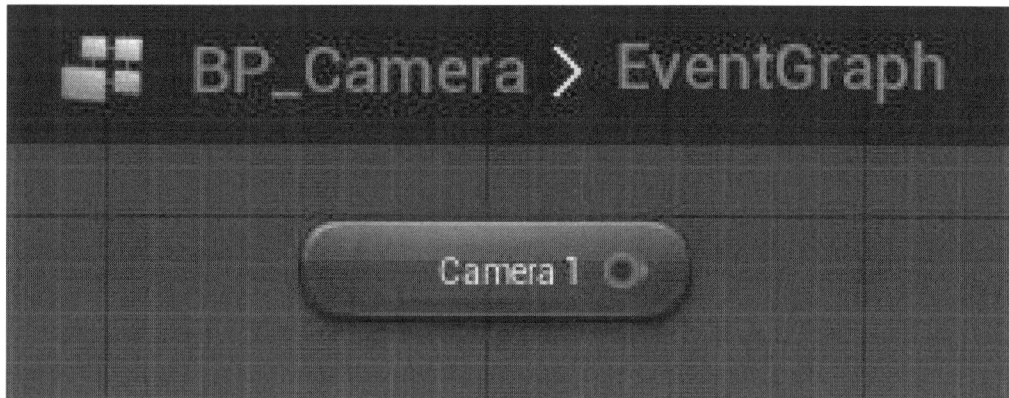

Now right click (Ctrl + Click) to open up the CBL and type in "Get Player" and select "Get Player Character".

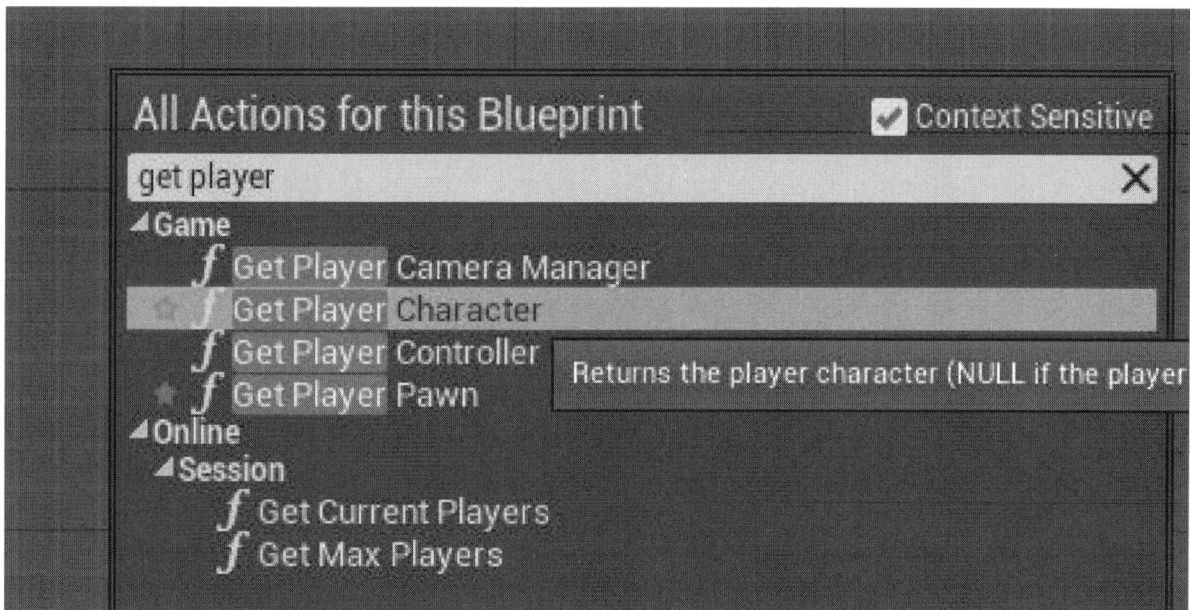

This will get a node which will get the current player (In-game) and their respective Player Blueprint (We'll touch on this a bit later)

Camera 1

∫ **Get Player Character**

Player Index 0   Return Value

We now need to get their respective locations in the world. To do this, open up the CBL and type in "Get Actor" and select "Get Actor Location". Connect the input of this node to the "Return Value" pin of "Get Player Character".

Camera 1

∫ Get Player Character

∫ **Get Actor Location**
Target is Actor

Player Index 0   Return Value   Target   Return Value

Once you've done this, Click the output pin of the "Camera1" node we created and drag to the right. Once the Compact Blueprint Library opens up, type in "Get World" and select "Get World Location".

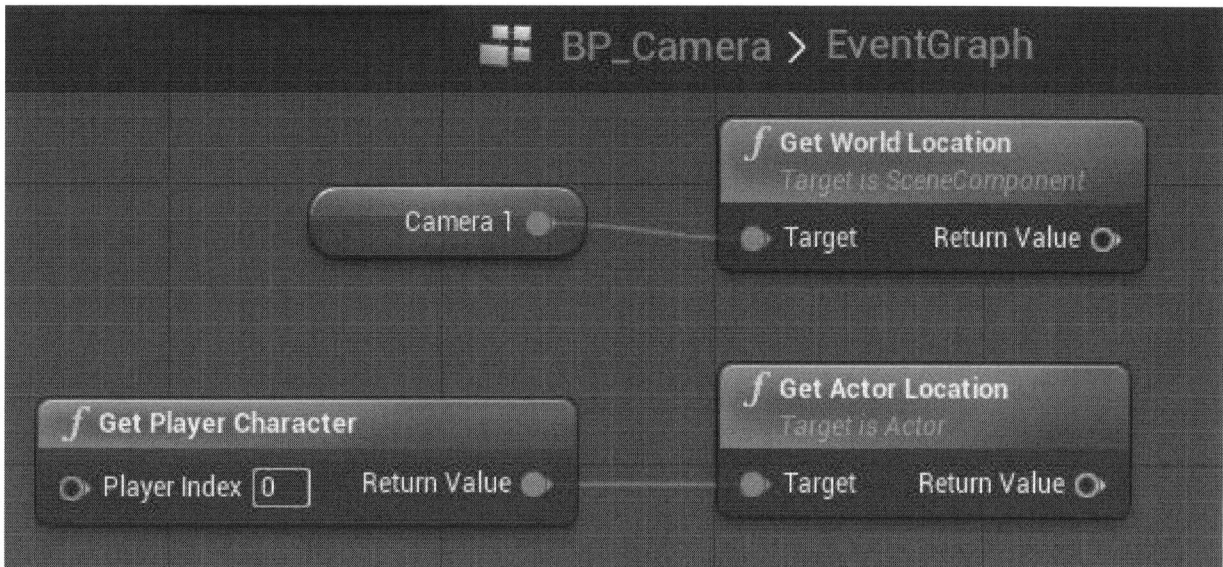

We have now got the information of where the camera is in the in-game world and where the player is in the in-game world (As we're using a tick, it will refresh this information every frame). What we now need to do is actually minus this information from each other.

Why? Because we don't want the camera looking at itself or the player themselves. What we actually want is to look at the distance in between the two. This is because the vector between the player and camera will provide the smoothest camera effect and will not follow the player if they make a sharp movement such as a high jump or a quick-turn.

What we're going to do to do this is open up the CBL and type in "Vector -" (Vector minus) and select "Vector - Vector".

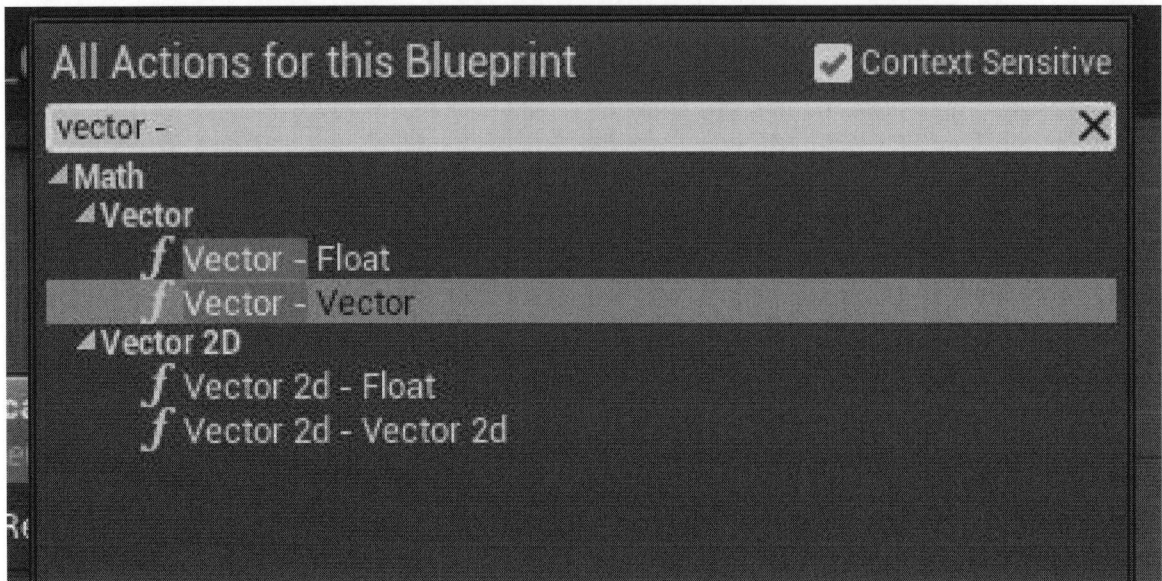

You'll now have a Vector - Vector node that needs two inputs and gives a single output. So plug in the "Get Actor Location" to one of the left-hand side inputs and "Get World Location" to the other.

Now, we need to connect the output of "Vector - Vector" and plug it into our "Target" of "VInterp To".

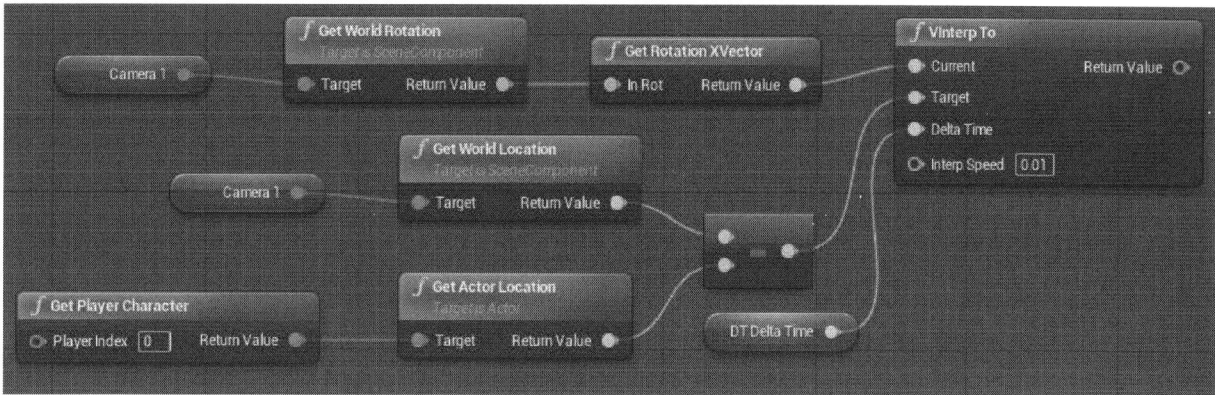

We're almost there! We are currently getting the rotation of the camera and setting it via a smooth transition to in between the player and camera.

But now we need to break the rotation of our transition as well as breaking the default rotation of the camera (When it's spawned in the world).

Once this is done, we would then get the pitch and yaw from our "Transition" rotation and use this to clamp down on the possible rotations of the camera (So it can't spin around uncontrollably).

Once we've clamped the values, we'll then re-make our rotations into a single rotation with these clamped values and this will be the magical value to plug in to our "Set World Rotation" which we set up a while ago (Feels like years. Sorry this is taking so long, I just want to make sure that you're learning everything you need to know!)

This sounds super-complicated but don't worry - Things will get a little difficult but you have me to guide you through it!

Before we continue, I've noticed a mistake I've made (Shock horror!). If we don't fix this now, the camera will do everything in it's path to NOT look at the player as opposed to looking at only the player.

I'll give you a moment or two to try and figure out what it is (Look at your code!), it took me a while but I felt extremely silly for the mistake I made.

Found it? Don't worry, we'll quickly run over the problem now and iron it out before it becomes a real problem.

Think about math for a moment, say you have two values: 100 and 51 and you want to subtract them. You can either do: *100 - 51 = 49* or *51 - 100 = -49*. Depending on what the first and second value are, it will change the answer.

Now head back to your code, in specific: Head to the part of the code where we got the "Camera" location and the "Player Controller" location and minused them before plugging them into the "TARGET" of "VInterp To".

Is your Camera's "Get World Location" plugged into the top minus input of the "Vector - Vector" node? If so, then you followed this book exactly but it's a mistake!

I'm glad I managed to pick this up before it became a problem. I could've gone back and edited the original part out but I think this is a great demonstration of how easy it is to get mixed up and get things wrong.

At the moment, we're getting the camera value: Say X=51, Y=11 and X=22 for an example and minusing that from the Player, who'll most likely always be a higher value then the camera as it's much further away (Example: X=151, Y=211 and X=512). With the current way we're minusing them both, you'll get a negative result.

What does this mean? This means that the camera will do everything in it's path to look AWAY from the player as opposed at looking AT the player.

So how do we fix this? Simple! All we have to do is plug the "Get Actor Location" of the player into the TOP input of the "Vector - Vector" node and the "Get World Location" of the camera into the BOTTOM input of the "Vector - Vector".

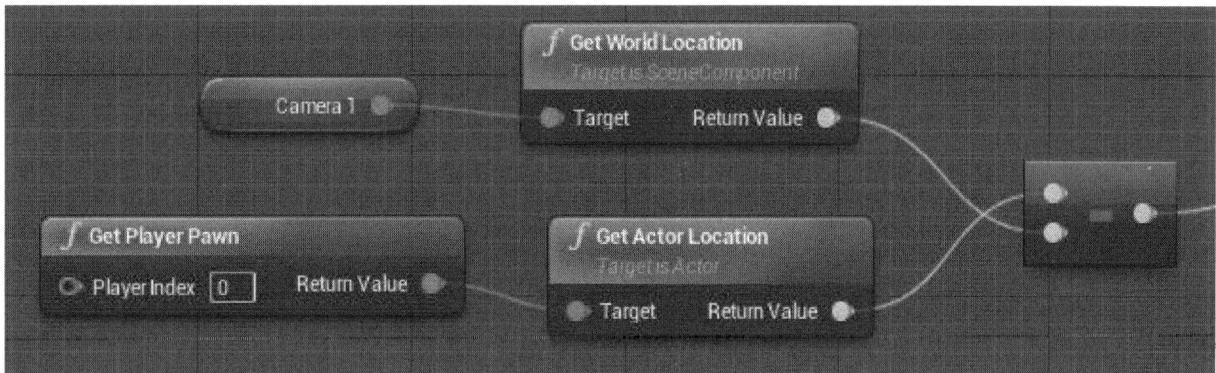

By doing this, we've just saved hours of headaches of "Why isn't this working properly?!" in which I literally just finished doing.

Anyway, once you've fixed that, we can continue back on the path we were going!

As described before, we now need to make the rotation back-up of our "VInterp To"; This is because we broke the rotation when used the "Get Rotation XVector" and now that we've added this new information to it, we need to re-make the rotation.

Open up the CBL (By either Right Clicking or using Ctrl + Click) and type in "Make Rot". When the options appear, click "Make Rot from X".

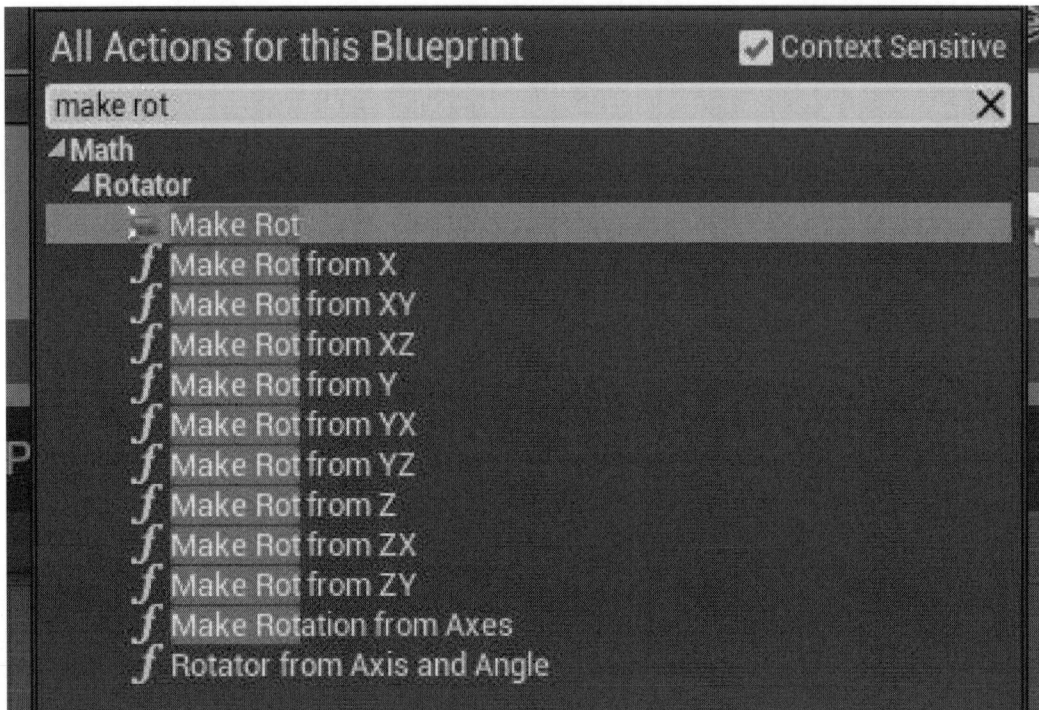

Once the "Make Rot from X" has been created, attach the "X" input pin to the output of the "VInterp" to.

We've now got our Rotation, but it's only from our the "X" input of our data. We're now going to break the rotation we've just gotten and then we're going to clamp it.

Why? We've mentioned this a few paragraphs ago, but just to confirm: We're going to be clamping our data to make sure that the camera doesn't spin out of control and is bound by certain values so it doesn't start staring at a wall away from the player.

Here is a terrible picture on Microsoft Paint to explain what we mean:

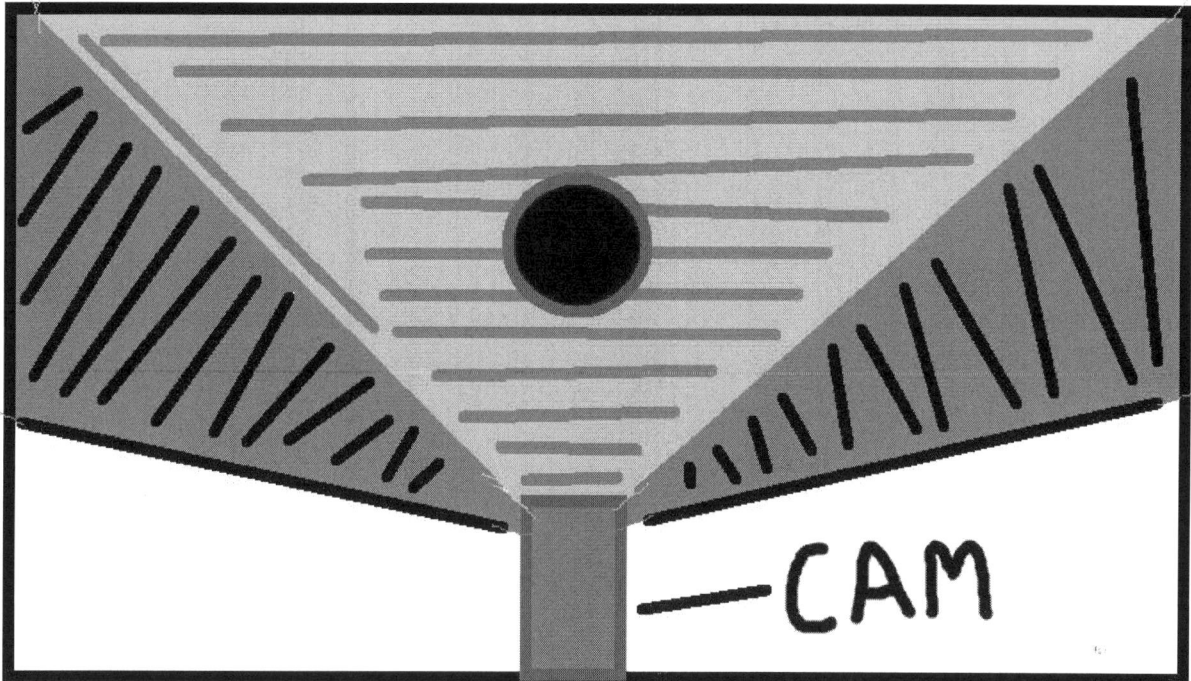

The box around the image is supposed to simulate the map area. The rectangle in the bottom middle is the camera. The black dot in the top-middle is the player and the middle cone is where we want the camera to look and the outer cone is the area we don't want the camera to look.

Don't worry, as we type the code, it should sink in. If not, when we play the project at the end, it'll definitely be apparent on what we've done.

Now that we've made the rotation from the "X" value, we now need to break this rotation.

So go ahead and use the Compact Blueprint Library to create a "Break Rot" (NOT a "Break Rot into axes!) node and hook it up to the output pin of "Make Rot from X".

We now need to create two "Clamp Angle" nodes. So go ahead and do that now (You'll have to type "Clamp Angle" into the search box as the normal Clamps (Such as Clamp [Float] won't do what we're trying to achieve):

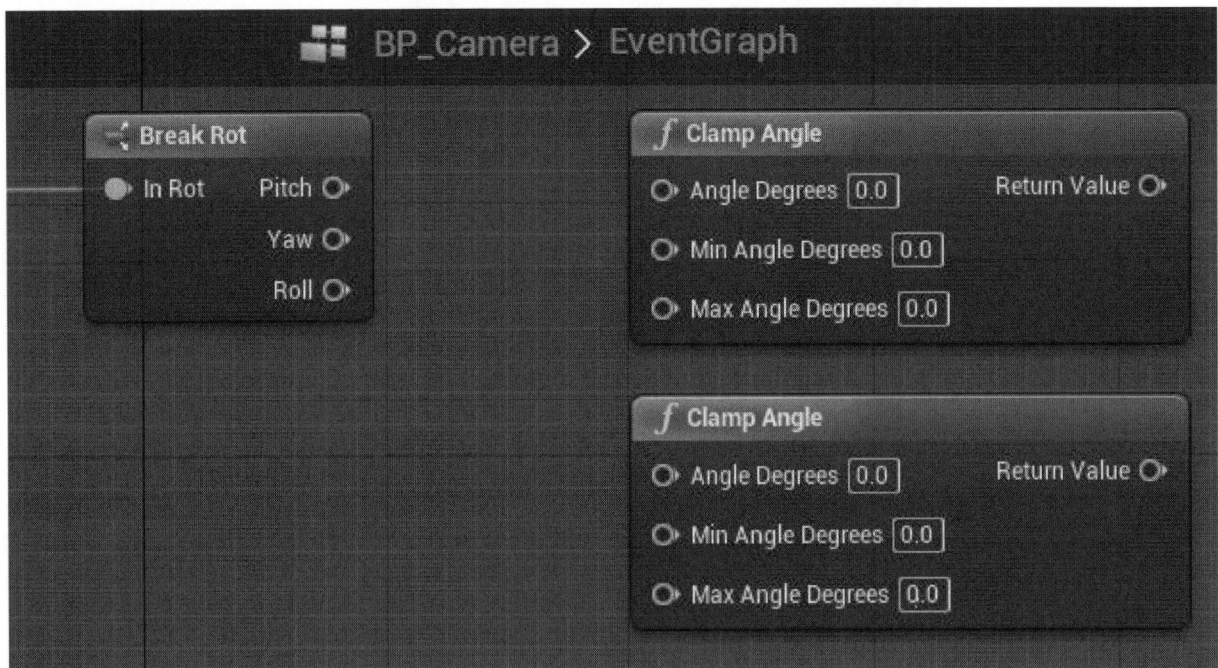

From the "Break Rot"'s outputs, connect the "Pitch" pin to the "Angle Degress" of the top "Clamp Angle" and then connect the Yaw to the bottom "Angle Degrees" (We don't need the information from the "Roll" output).

Break Rot

In Rot   Pitch

Yaw

Roll

Clamp Angle

Angle Degrees   Return Value

Min Angle Degrees   0.0

Max Angle Degrees   0.0

Clamp Angle

Angle Degrees   Return Value

Min Angle Degrees   0.0

Max Angle Degrees   0.0

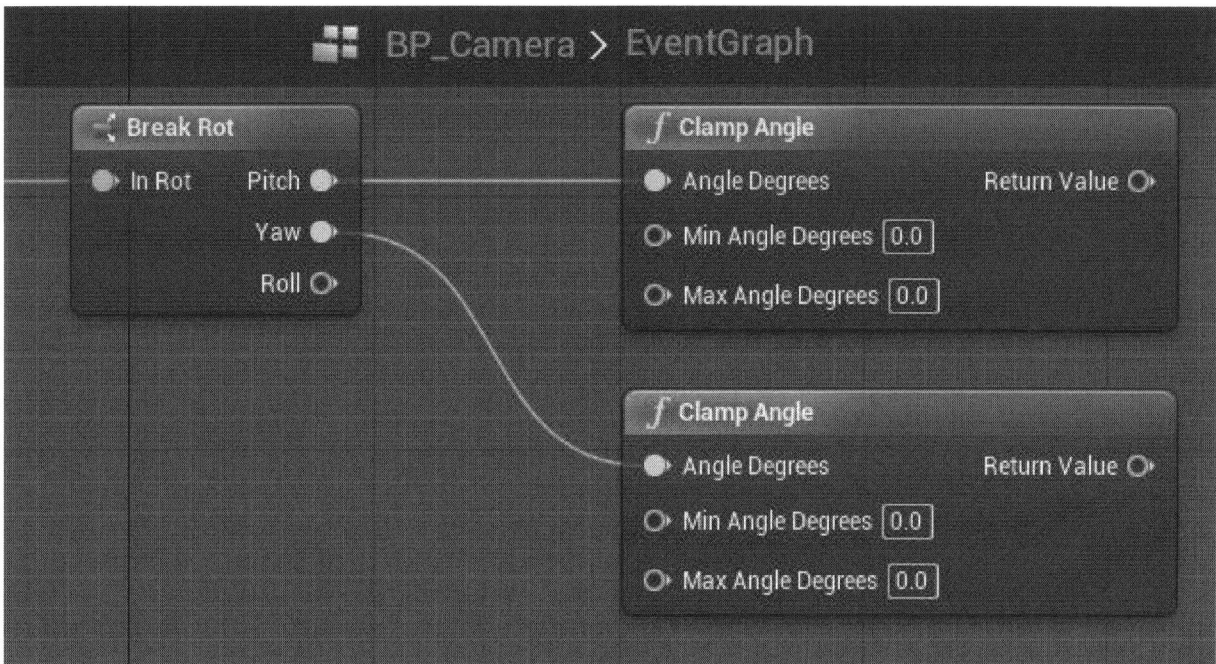

To calculate the the "Min / Max Angle Degrees" of both of these Clamp angle nodes, we need to do a little math (Don't worry, we don't have to work out the results, just the equations)

We'll be using the "Pitch" and "Yaw" for our equations, but there's one more number we'll be using: 80. What are we doing to be using 80 for? Say the camera is looking at the player, it clamps the angle to either +80 or -80, which gives 160 degrees of where we want the camera to focus on (As to not fill the screen with the player or lose the player due to sharp movement).

There's two ways we can get the number 80 into our Blueprint. We can use a "Make Literal Float" node or we can create a Variable (Type: Float) in the Variable Library and set it's default value [Once the Variable in create, Compile and Save so you can edit the default value!] to 80.

It's your choice of what route you want to take with this. I'll be using the "Make Literal Float" node and setting it to "80".

No matter which method you use, be sure to duplicate the "80" (Either Variable or "Make Literal Float" 4 times).

Do that now:

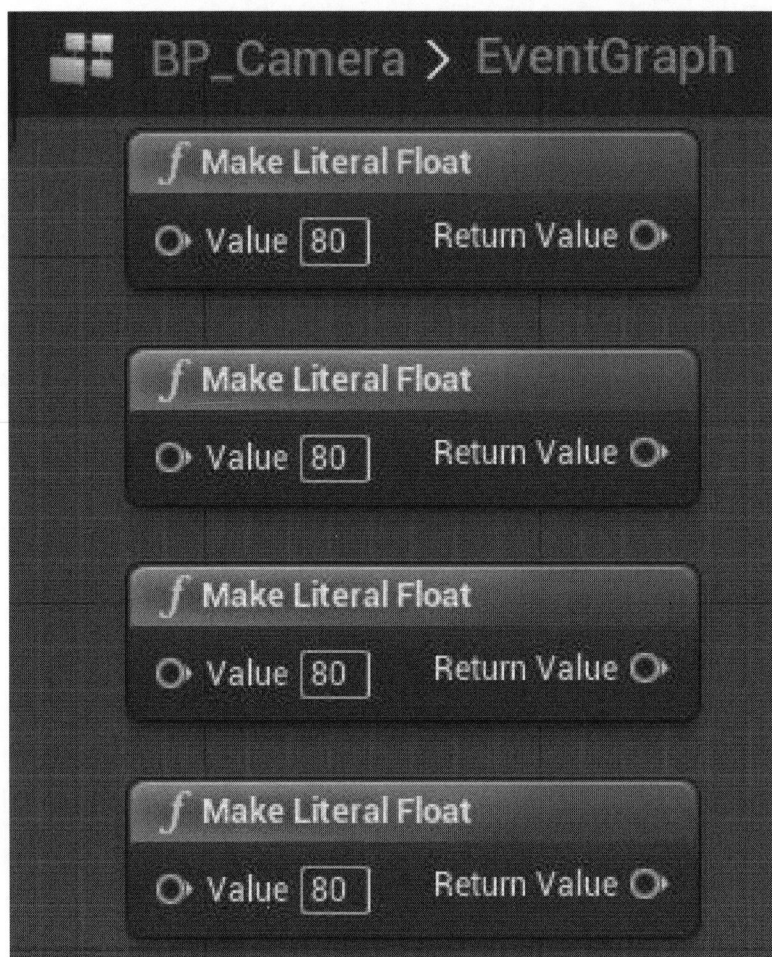

Now create two "Float - Float" nodes and two "Float + Float" nodes. When we plug these into the "Make Literal Float" (Or your Variable Nodes), make sure you plug the "Make Literal Float" / Your Variable into the SECOND input of each "Plus / Minus" node.

Connect the first and third "Make Literal Float" / Your Variable into the SECOND input of both the minus nodes:

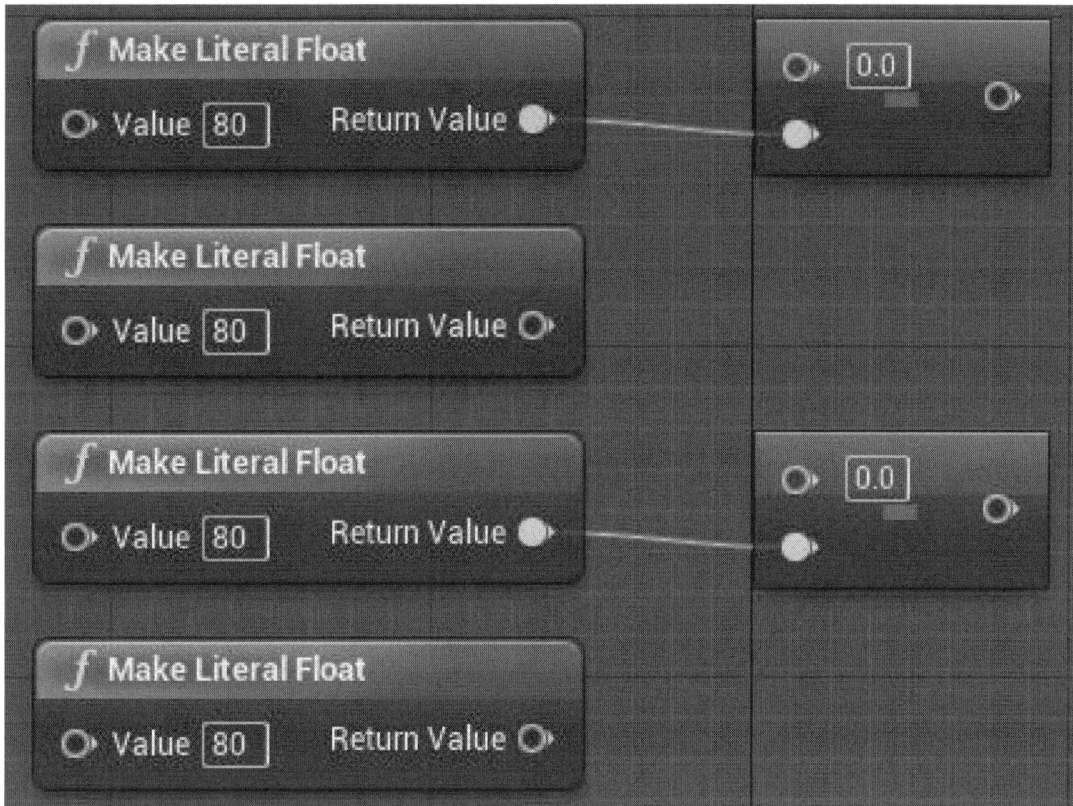

Now with the second and fourth "Make Literal Float" / Your Variable nodes, connect these to the SECOND input of the "Plus" nodes you created.

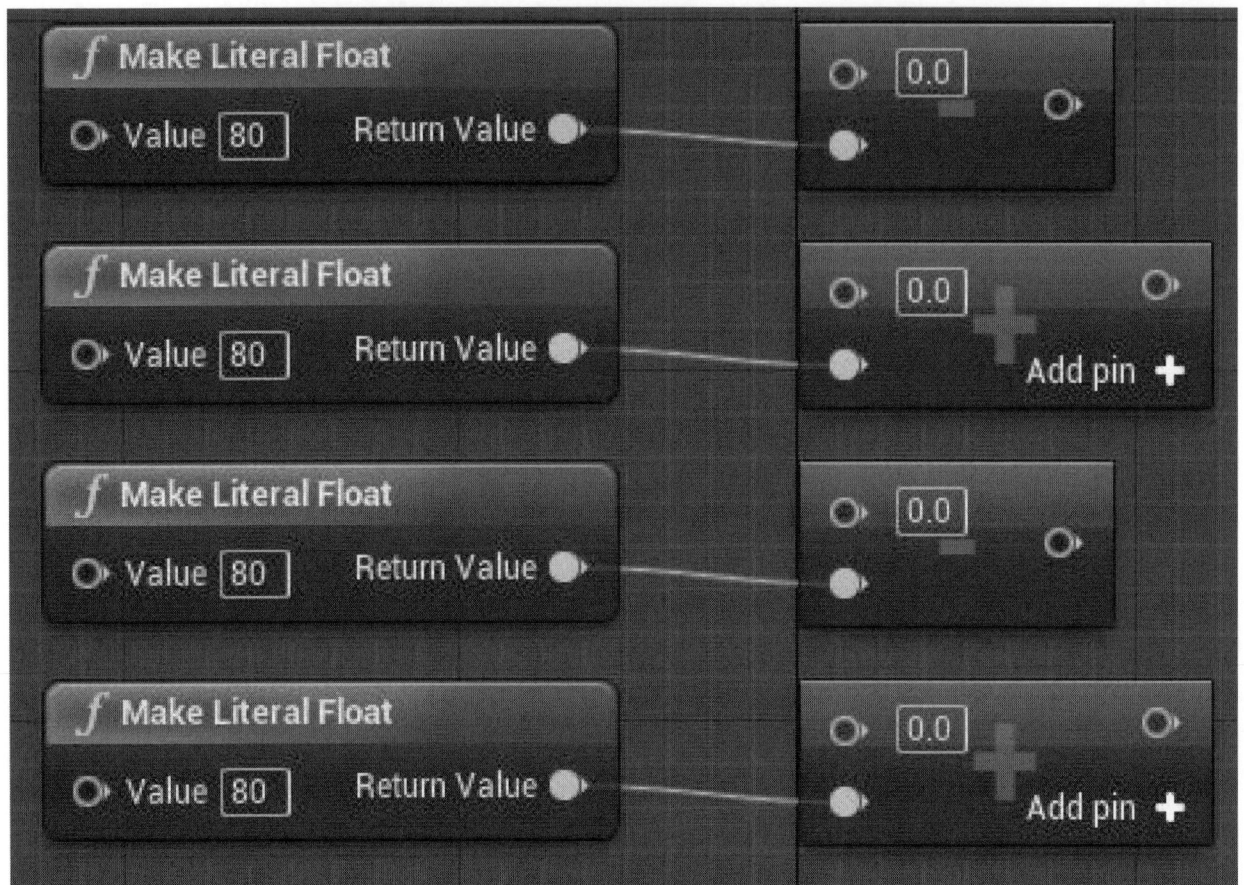

If you can't see the images (Remember, you can use http://www.kitatus.co.uk to download the high quality images version of the images in this book!), make sure you "Make Literal Float" / Your Variable nodes are connected like this:

1. Make Literal Float / Your Variable > Second Input of "Minus" node.
2. Make Literal Float / Your Variable > Second input of "Plus" node.
3. Make Literal Float / Your Variable > Second input of "Minus" node.
4. Make Literal Float / Your Variable > Second input of "Plus" node.

Now head back to the "Break Rot" which is currently connected to the two "Clamp Angle" nodes.

Even though the "Pitch" and "Yaw" outputs of the "Break Rot" are already connected to inputs, we can connect alternative inputs to these outputs and they'll stay connected (Magic!).

So connect the first "Minus" and "Plus" nodes FIRST input's to the "Pitch" of Break Rot and the second "Minus" and "Plus" nodes FIRST input's to the "Yaw" of Break Rot.

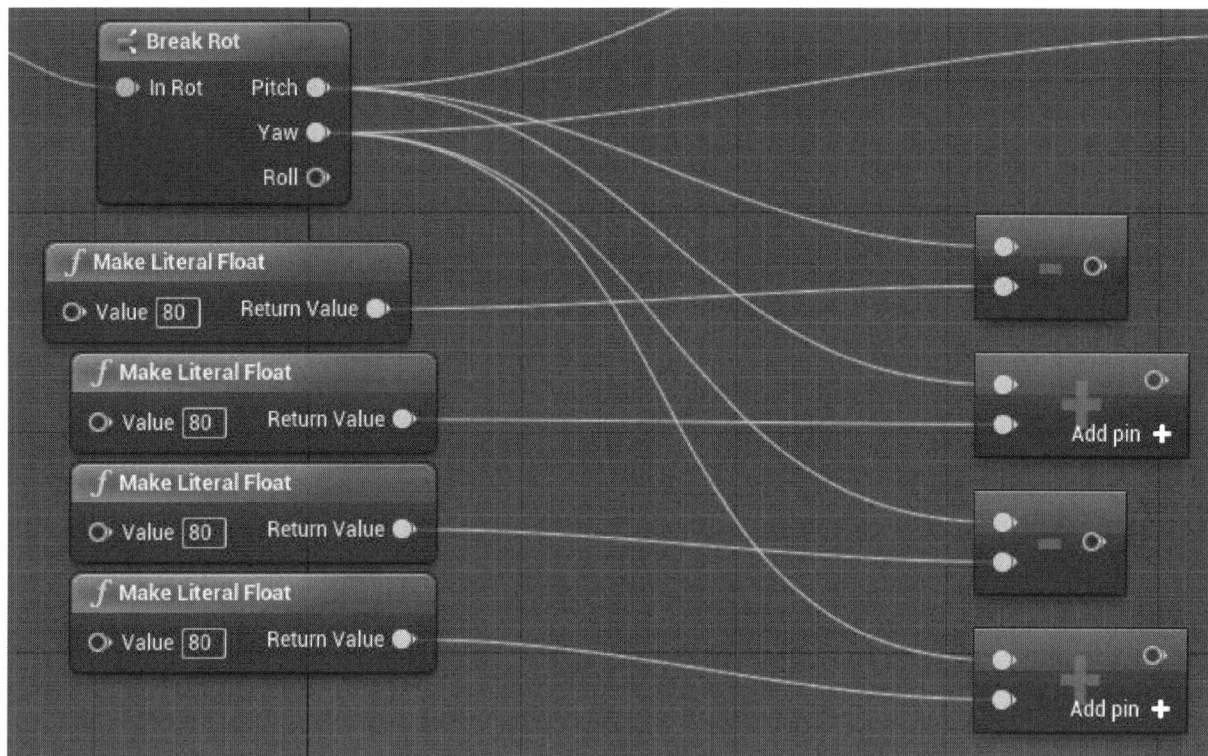

Now we're going to deal with outputs of these Plus and Minuses.

Here is a small table of where to connect them (Which will be into the "Clamp Angle" inputs of Min Angle Degress / Max Angle Degrees):

1. First "Minus" node's output - Connect this to the "Min Angle Degress" of the first "Clamp Angles" node.
2. First "Plus" node's output - Connect this to the "Max Angle Degress of the first "Clamp Angles" node.
3. Second "Minus" node's output - Connect this to the "Min Angle Degress" of the second "Clamp Angles" node.
4. Second "Plus" node's output - Connect this to the "Max Angle Degress" of the second "Clamp Angles" node.

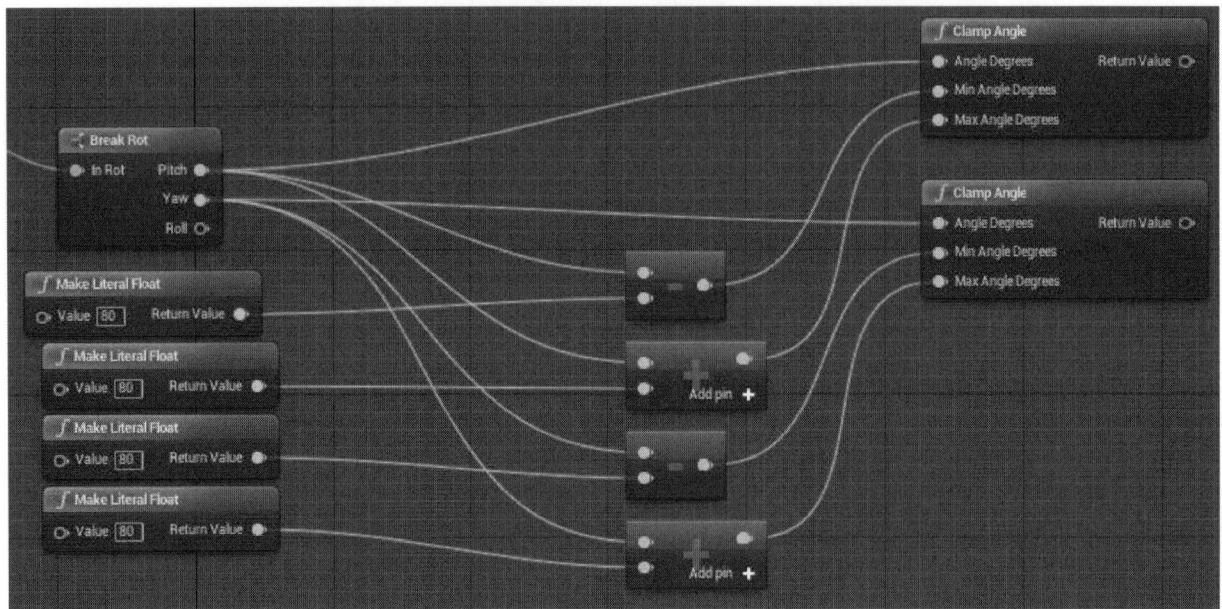

Our Blueprint is starting to look a little like a delicious spaghetti soup but don't worry - As long as you've followed my instructions, everything will work just fine.

We're almost done with this Blueprint; For real! All we need to do now is convert the current data back into a Rotation and then set this as the rotation for the camera to use!

So open up the Compact Blueprint Library by using either Right Click or Ctrl + Click and search for "Make Rot". Select "Make Rot" to create the node.

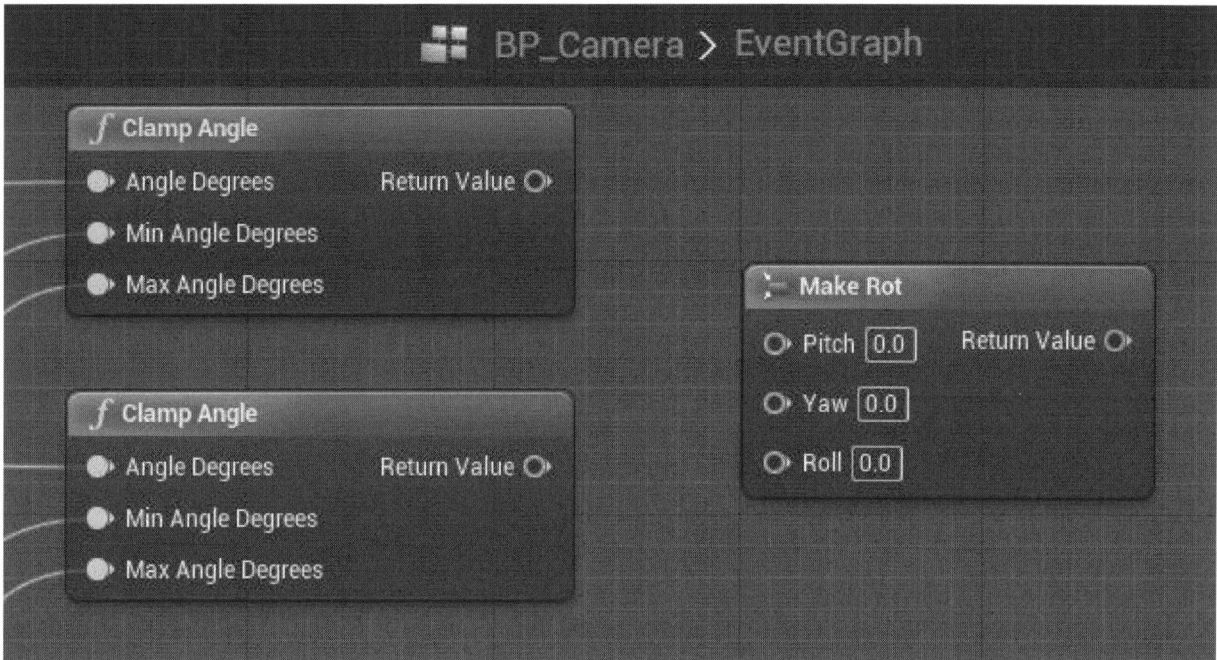

Now simply connect the output of "Clamp Angle" #1 to the input "Pitch" of the "Make Rot" node and connect the output of "Clamp Angle" #2 to the input "Yaw" of the "Make Rot" node.

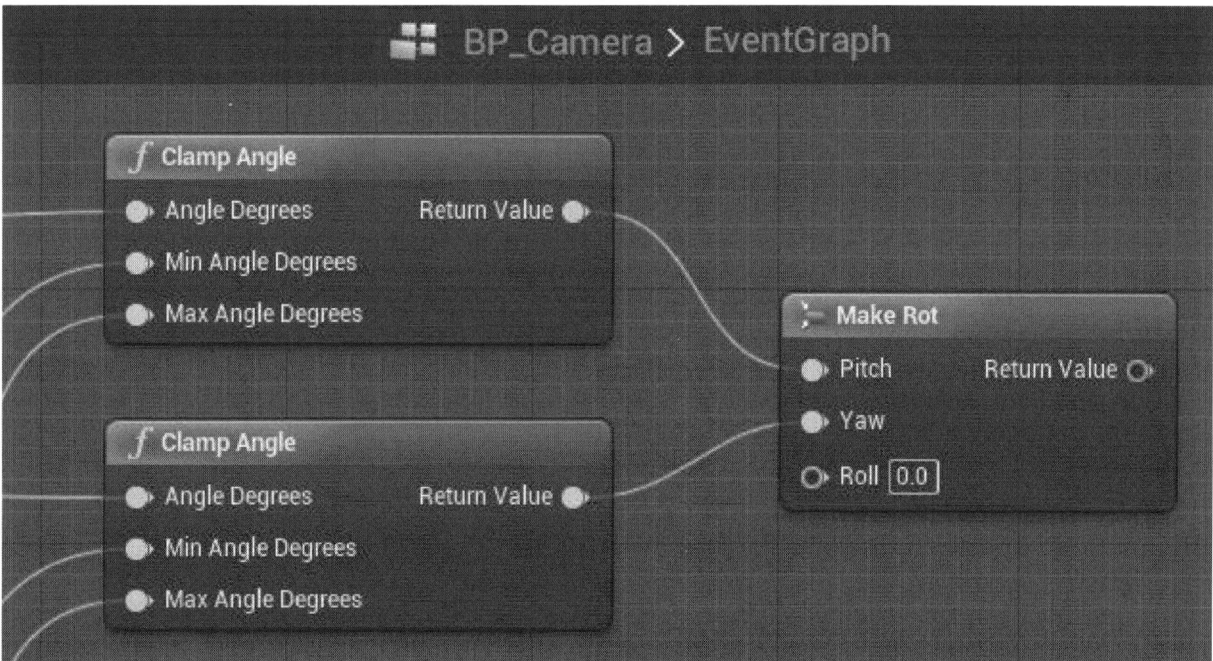

We finally have a "Rotation" output (You can tell what type of "Output" you're dealing with by the colour of the pin!).

107

Where do we plug this? We plug it into the "New Rotation" input of the "Set World Rotation" which we created quite a while ago!

So go ahead and connect the "Return Value" of "Make Rot" to the "New Rotation" input of the "Set World Rotation".

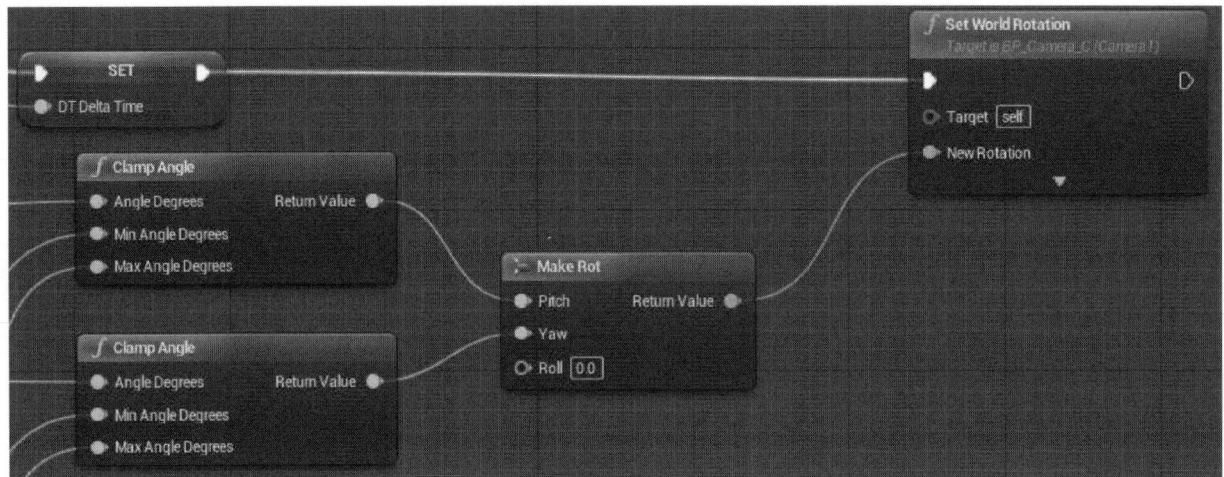

Now there's only two things we've left to do in this Blueprint before we can mark it as "Complete" !

Head over to the "Set World Location" and hit the down arrow on the bottom of the node to show the hidden options of this node:

You'll now see an option called "Sweep" which is currently "Off". We need to activate this option, so go ahead and click the empty checkbox and you'll now see a tick in the box. That's means this node will now "Sweep"! Excellent!

So what does this "Sweep" do? - This sweep makes sure that the camera doesn't continue to move if it is blocked by something such as a wall!

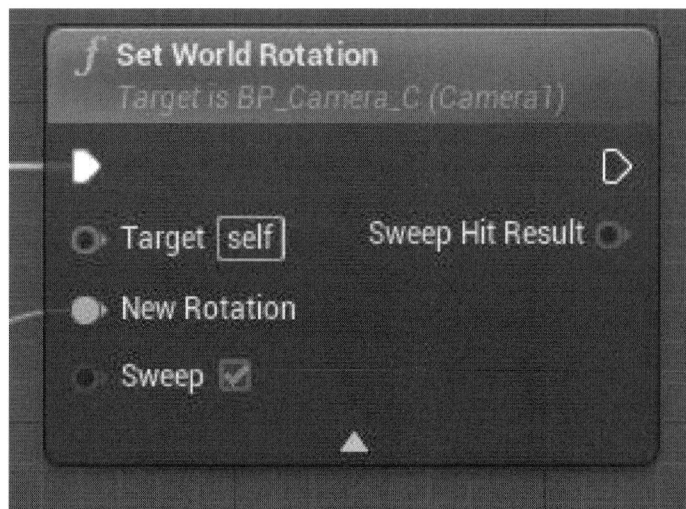

Now there's only one last thing we have to do to this Blueprint: Compile & Save!

We've covered this a few times, but just in case you missed it: On the top-left of the window you're currently in is an image of two gears with a square in front of them. If you have not compiled yet, there will be a question mark in the box. If you HAVE compiled all the recent changes to this blueprint, then there will be a tick in the box.

So go ahead and click this button now. Now, once you have compiled the Blueprint, go ahead and press the save button, which is to the right of the "Compile" button.

And we're done with this Blueprint! You can go ahead and close this Blueprint now and return to the main window of Unreal Engine 4.

At the moment, we've created the Blueprint but it's not currently in the scene and thus isn't "Active" yet. So we're just going to test it out quickly!

Go to the "Content Browser" and click and drag your "BP_Camera" into the scene.

It doesn't matter where you put it as long as you can see the player and the view isn't blocked by anything. Go ahead and use the transform gizmo to arrange the Camera into a position you're happy with.

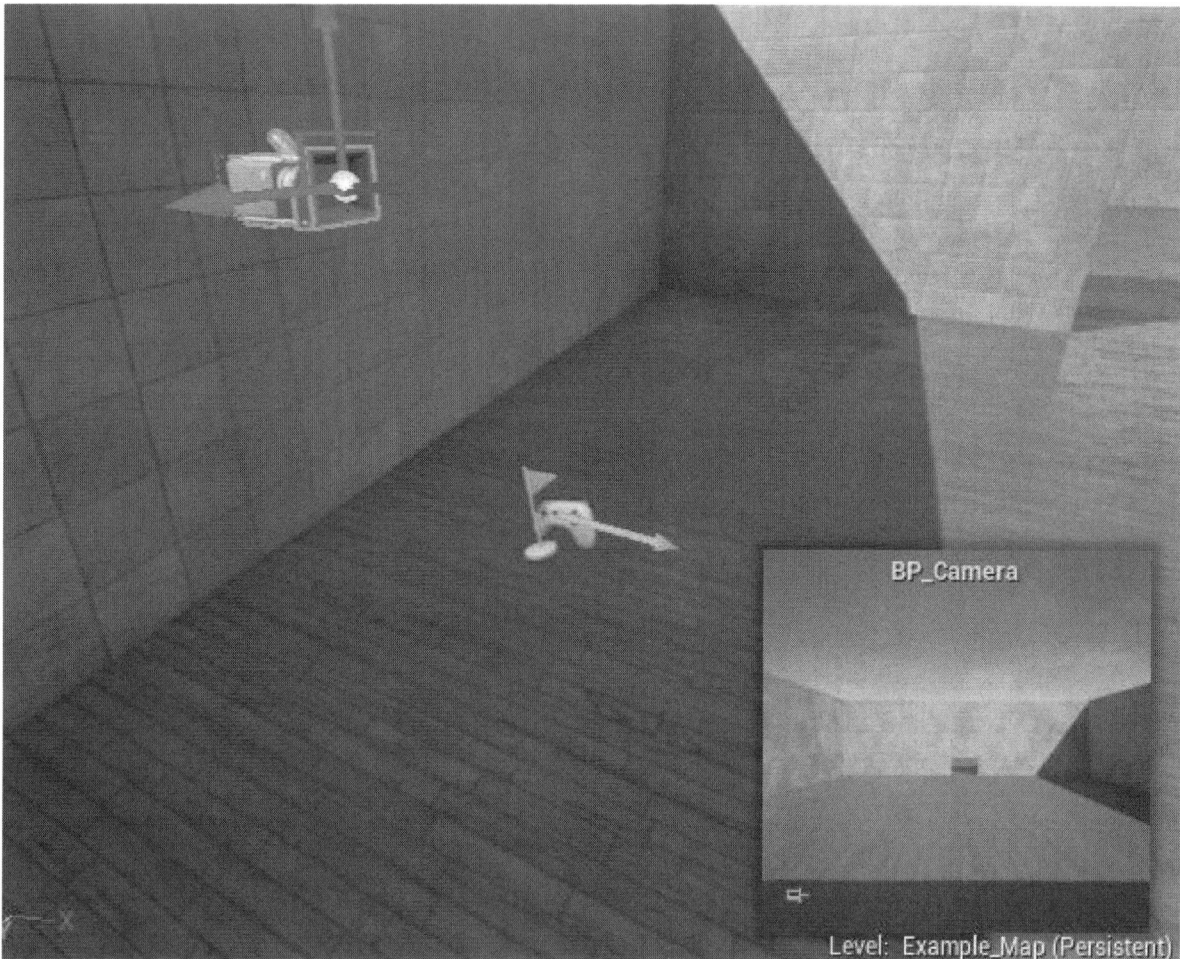

Now, we'll need to add some code to the "Level Blueprint" to make sure we set this camera as "Active".

What is a Level Blueprint? - A level blueprint is a special blueprint that applies to the current level being played (Or the map currently running). You can put code in a level blueprint for tracking score / Actor states .etc

Before we continue, make sure that you have the BP_Camera that you placed into the scene selected. You can tell if it is selected as it will have an orange outline around it and will have a transform gizmo nearby (Usually in the centre of the object).

To access the Level Blueprint, use the Navigation bar just above the scene view and select the "Blueprints" button and select "Open Level Blueprint":

Clicking "Open Level Blueprint" will do exactly that - It will open the "Level Blueprint".

Right Click (Ctrl + Click) to open up the CBL. If you had the BP_Camera that you placed in the scene selected, you'll notice that there will be an option near the top of the Compact Blueprint Library called "Create a Reference to BP_Camera". Click that to create a node that references the camera in the scene.

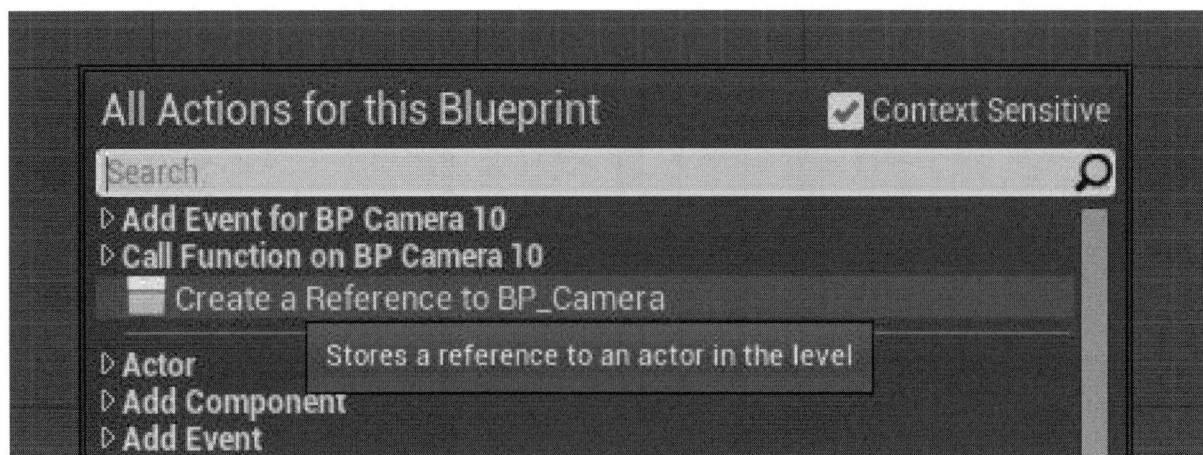

If you don't see "Create a Reference to BP_Camera", then you didn't select the object in the scene. To fix this, simply go back into the main window of Unreal Engine and select the "BP_Camera" in which you created in the scene. Then repeat the previous steps until you've added the Reference to BP_Camera into your Level Blueprint.

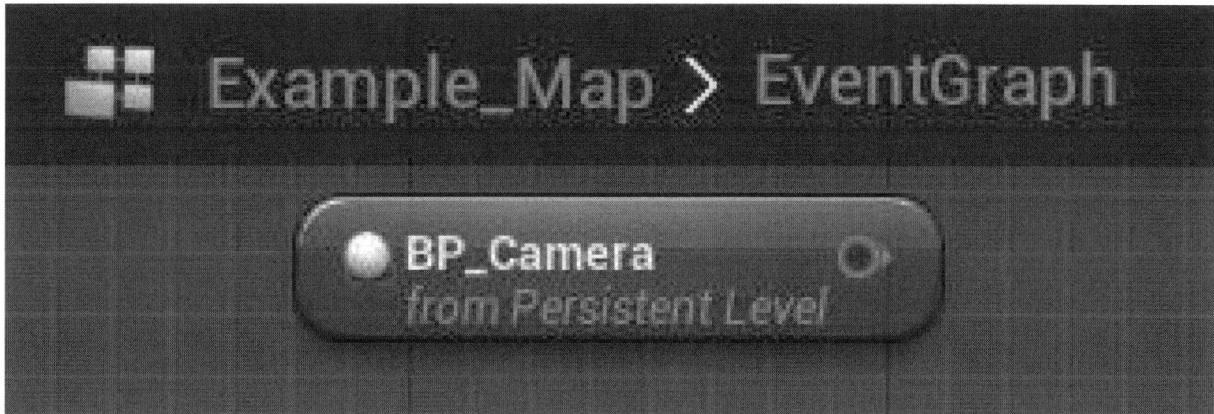

We now need to create a node to accommodate the output of the "BP_Camera" (As there are no inputs or executions in this node).

We're about to create a node which is "Hidden" to us currently. To access it, we're going to have to temporarily turn off "Context Sensitive" in our CBL. Don't worry - It's not as complicated as it sounds.

What is Context Sensitive? - Context Sensitive is a button on the Compact Blueprint Library window which shows you nodes that automatically filters the options presented in the menu based on the current context. This means it won't show you every option under the sun as you'll most likely only need specific nodes at specific times.

Turning Context Sensitive mode off means we'll see every node possible that we can place in the Blueprint. The view of the CBL can get very confusing, even for seasoned Blueprint "Experts", hence why it's suggested that you should leave Context Sensitive on where possible.

So open up the Compact Blueprint Library and turn Context Sensitive OFF by unticking the box on the top-right of the CBL.

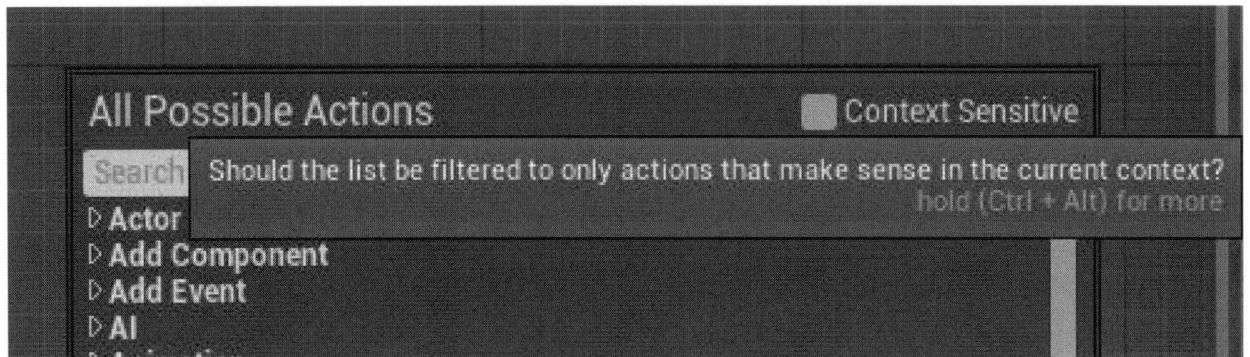

Now that "Context Sensitive" is off, type in "Set View Target" and select "Set View Target With Blend":

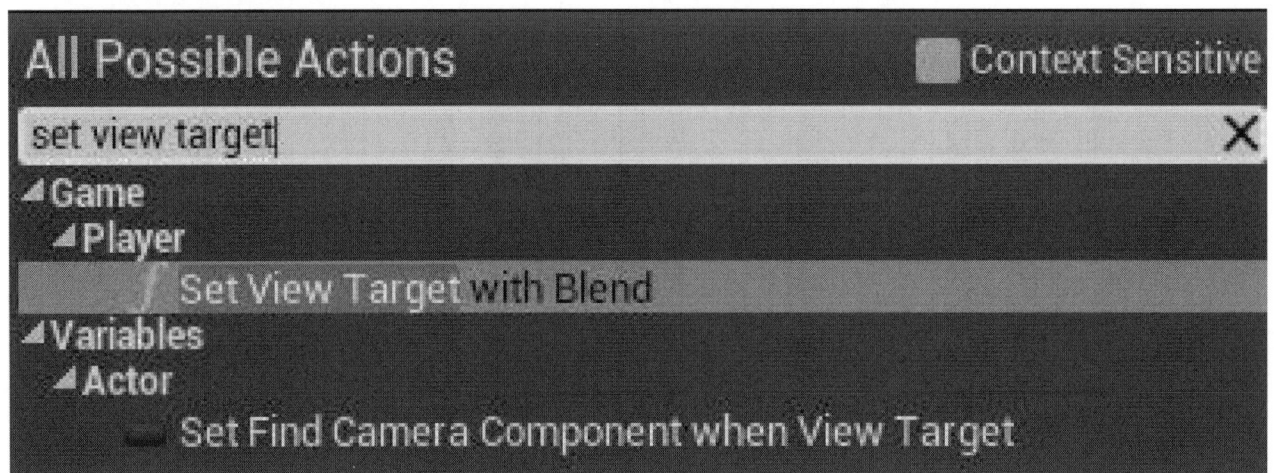

The node "Set View Target With Blend" seems very complicated but don't worry: To sum up the node in a short fashion: Set View Target (With Blend) is a node to change the current "Active" camera.

Set View Target with Blend
Target is PlayerController

Target [self]

New View Target
Select Asset

Blend Time [0.000000]

Blend Func
VTBlend Linear

Blend Exp [0.000000]

Lock Outgoing

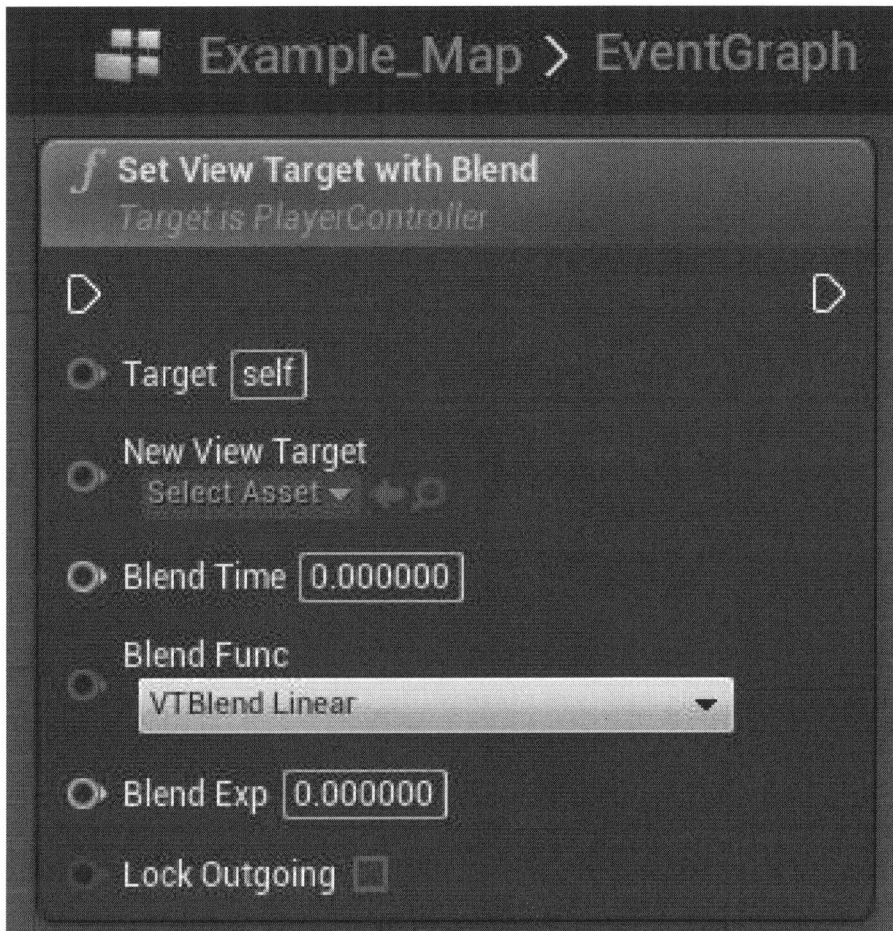

There are only three pins we need to concern ourselves with in this node: The input execution pin, the "Target" input and the "New View Target" input.

As the "New View Target" is node's answer to "New camera", go ahead and connect the output of the "BP_Camera" node to the input of "New View Target".

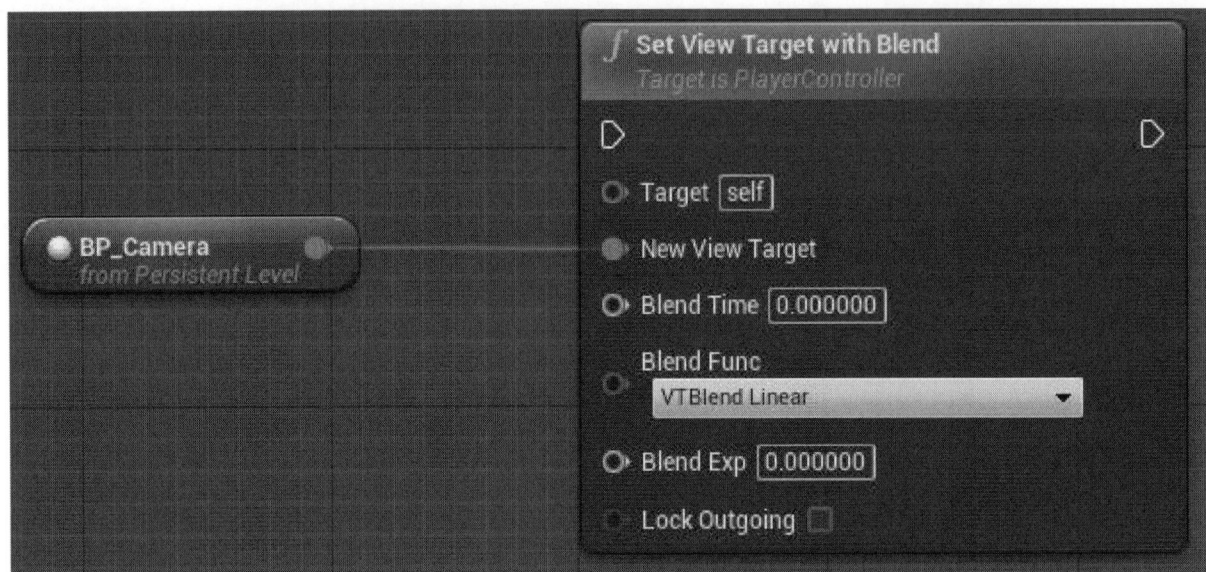

The "Target" pin is referencing the original camera in which we want "BP_Camera" to replace. So open up the Compact Blueprint Library (**IMPORTANT: Make sure you turn "Context Sensitive" back on!**) and type in "Player" and select "Get Player Controller".

Once created, connect the "Get Player Controller" output to the input of "Target" of the "Set View Target with Blend".

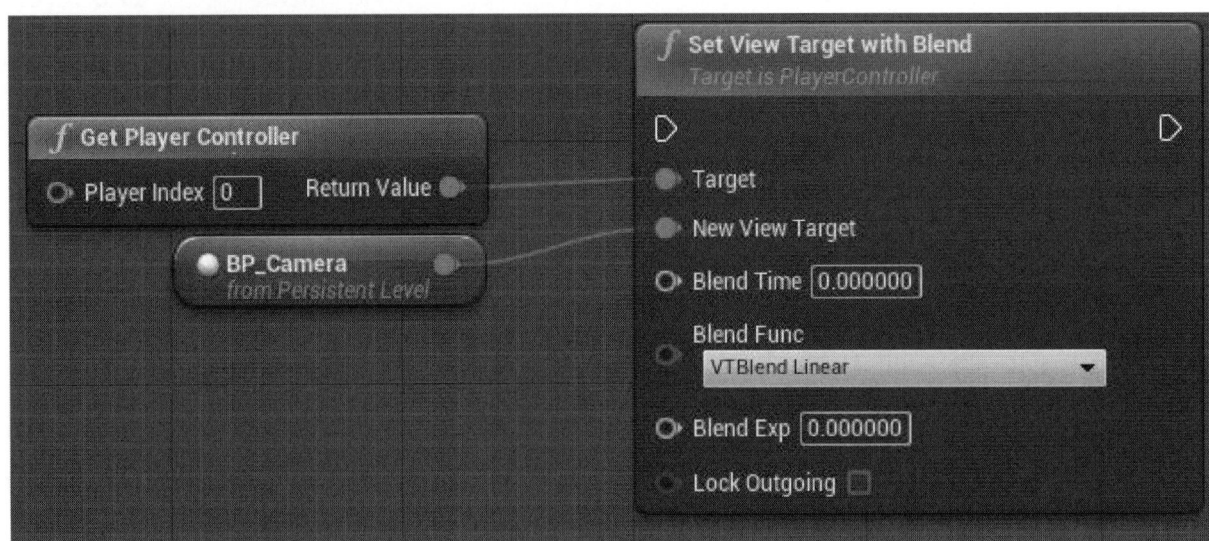

We're almost done here. But there's one thing missing. Remember what we said about Blueprints originally? Every action needs to have (Or at least stem from) an event. As there's no event that's connect to "Set View Target With Blend" in any way, it won't fire at all.

So let's open up the CBL and type in "Begin" and select "Event Begin Play". This event fires once and that's when the game begins; Which is perfect for testing if our "BP_Camera" works.

So go ahead and create the "Event Begin Play" and connect the output execution pin to the input execution pin of "Set View Target with Blend".

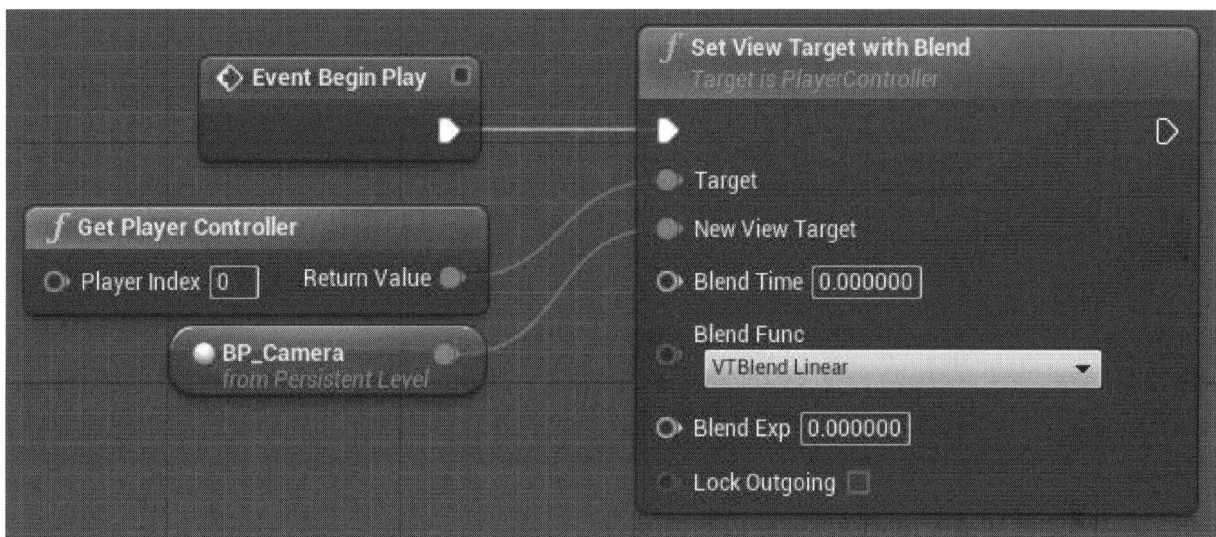

Fantastic! Just left before, hit "Compile" and "Save" and you can close this window now.

So now let's test out if our camera works! On the top navigation bar (The same place where we opened the Level Blueprint [Which is just above the "Scene View)], select the dropdown arrow next to "Play" and select "New Editor Window" to test out your project!

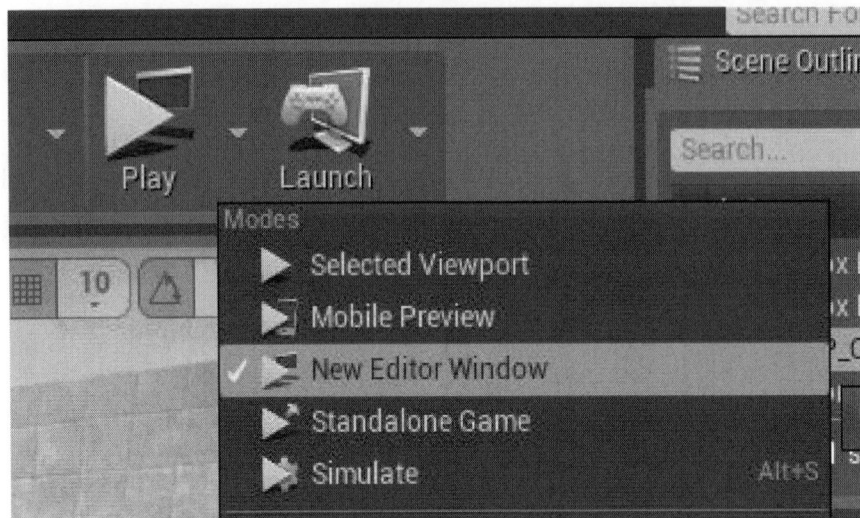

When you test your project, The "BP_Camera" you just created should work fine! If not, then skim back through the pages and make sure you've done everything correctly!

Did it work? Excellent!

If not, feel free to download the project files on http://www.kitatus.co.uk and check my work against yours, Download the file "*[LESSON1]ArtOfBP_01.zip*"!

Once everything works, Congratulate yourself! You made a brilliant first Blueprint! Now let's expand upon this a little and set a few cameras around our map to give it a true 3D point and click feel!

Don't worry, we don't need to re-create out "BP_Camera". In fact, thanks to the way we created our Camera, we can in fact just drag it into our scene multiple times and with a bit of tinkering the Level Blueprint, we can have a scene filled with "Point and Click" cameras easily!

BP_CAMERA + TRIGGER BOX = CAMERA SYSTEM

Before we continue, we need to head back into the Level Blueprint and delete all the code we put in there (The code we created which activates when the game starts! Remember…?). This is because this code will actually conflict with the code we will create in a moment.

So go ahead and head into your Level Blueprint, Click and drag over all the code we created and press either Delete on your keyboard or right click (Ctrl + Click) and select "Delete" to delete all the code we created.

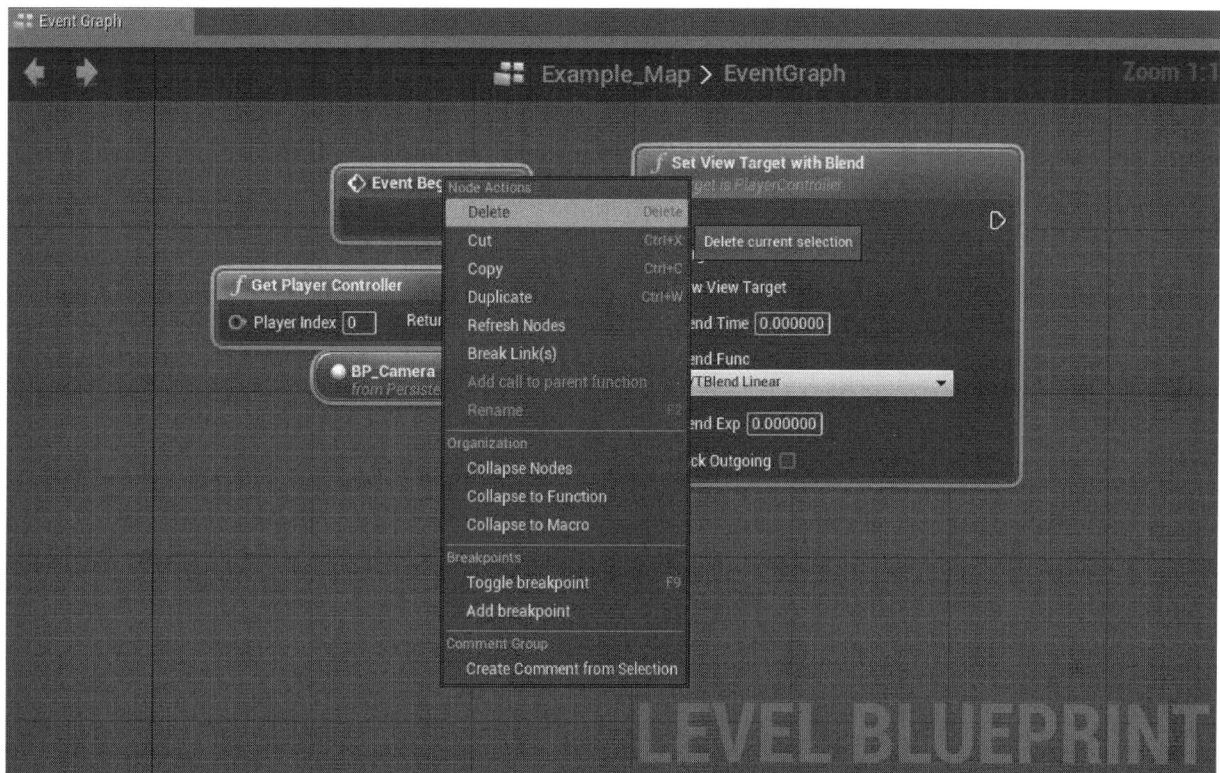

Once you've delete all of the code in the "Level Blueprint". go ahead and compile once more (Which "Refreshes" the engine's brain to realise the code is now missing). You can then close the Level Blueprint once again for now and we can begin work adding the cameras in to our scene.

As we have four "Rooms" in our project, we need to think about how many cameras we're going to need. Let's not think about cameras that zoom in on objects .etc at the moment, let's focus on cameras that are around the map.

If you are confused about what I mean think about video-games like the original Resident Evil games or the 3D point and click games which our project is based on. When you're running along, the camera will follow you no matter where you are in the World.

Now break apart our map in your mind. In fact, while typing this, I had an idea on how to better explain this part (Who needs editors, eh?):

Either open up Paint / GIMP / Photoshop or grab a good ol' pen and paper. Pretend you are a bird and look down on your map and draw what you see, like so:

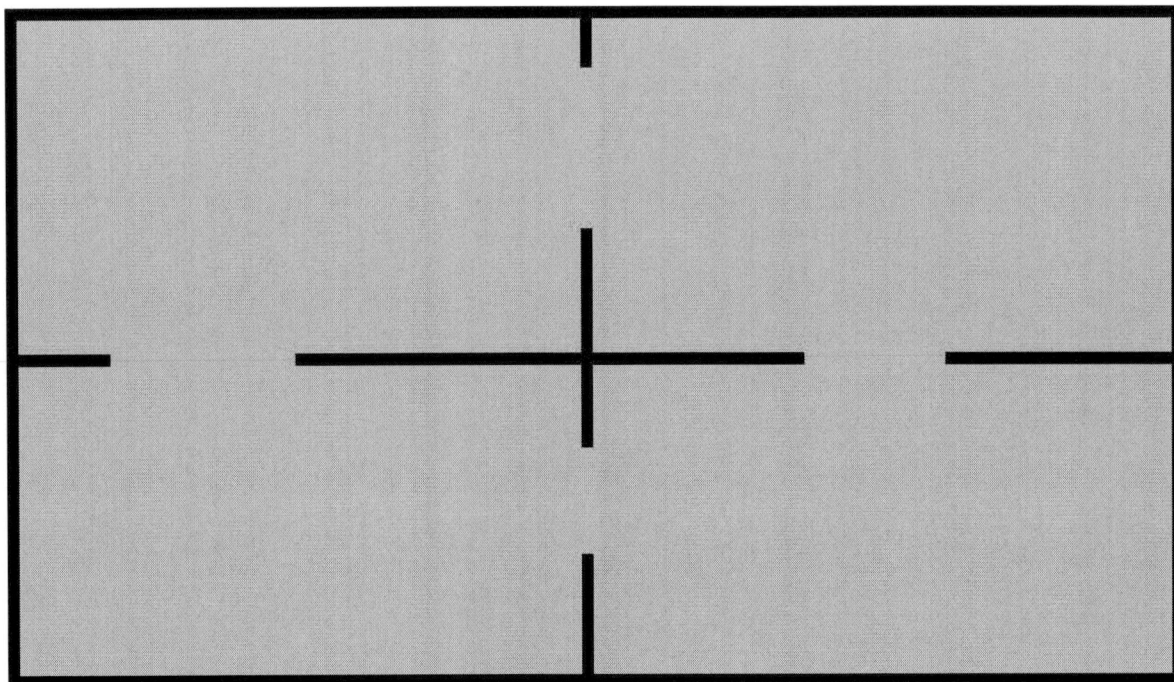

Now think about where the player can run. If you can't figure it out (It's extremely easy to overthink things sometimes!), everywhere where there is a floor in our map, the player can run to.

So how can we make sure our cameras not only look stylish but also make sure that we can ALWAYS see the player? There is no 100% correct answer for this as you'll have to sacrifice style for view coverage and vice versa but plan out where you can your cameras to go.

To help, here are three different possible routes you can take:

Route #1 - Important Corners:

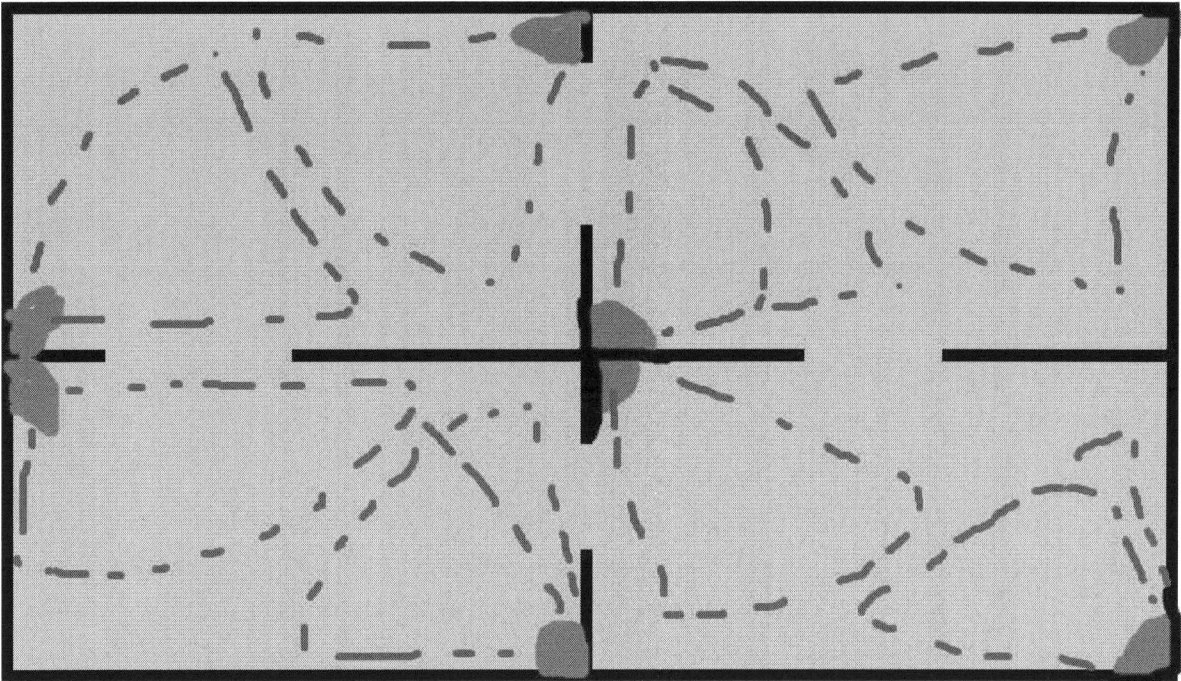

This method puts two cameras in each room in alternating corners, which covers 100% of the map but isn't very stylish at all. These days visual style is more important than ever but don't forget that the player HAS to remain visible on screen at all times.

So using this information, we now lead on to Route #2:

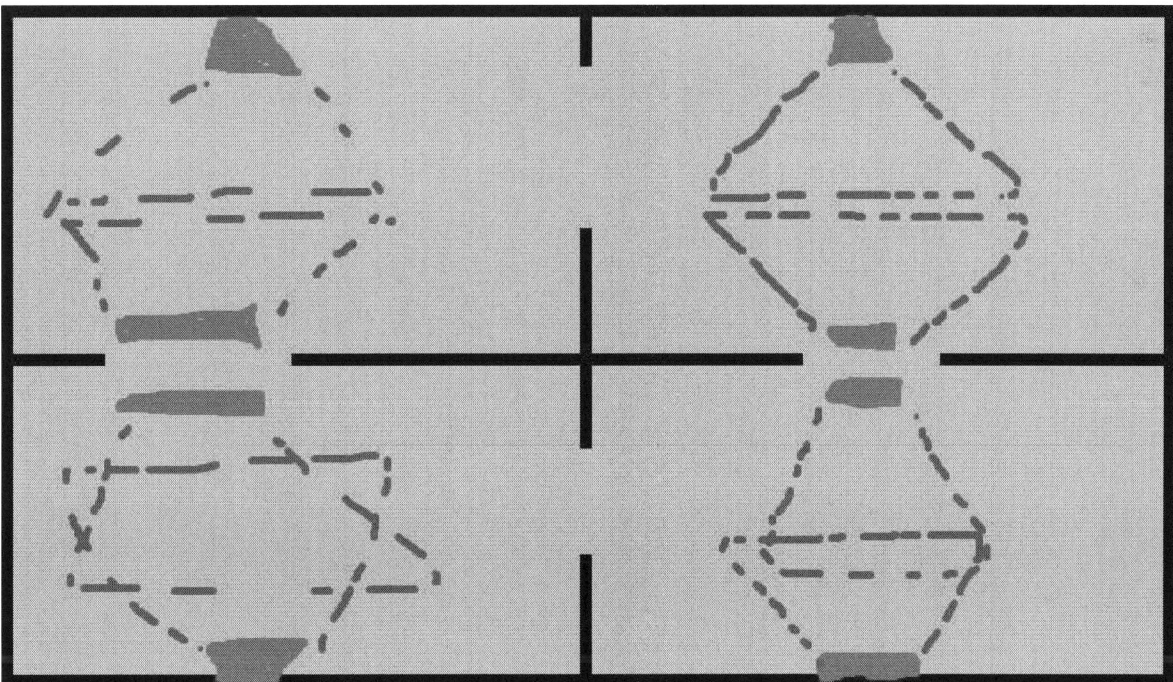

In route #2, we have four cameras on the outside walls, all facing to the centre wall. We then has four cameras on the centre walls looking away to the outside walls.

This is slightly less functional as route #1 (As the player can hide under the camera) but adds more to the style. But as we said, we need a way that we have a really good style value but at the same time make sure that our cameras are as "Functional" as possible.

So here's route #3, which I'll be personally using for the demo project (Which you can download at http://www.kitatus.co.uk):

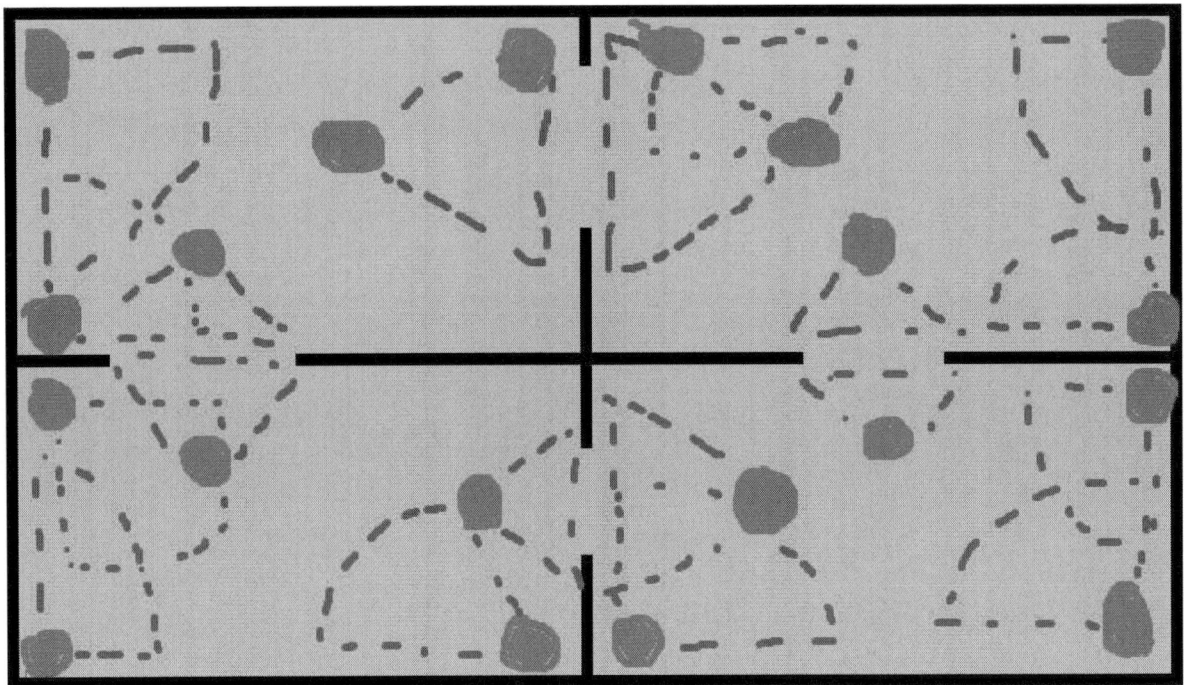

Remember: High-Quality versions of all of the images in this book can be found @ http://www.kitatus.co.uk)

If you can see the image above, you'll notice straight away that it looks like a giant mess. This is mainly because I've put in the camera's "Cone of vision".

To help simplify things, here is a description of where the cameras are and how many there are:

Camera amount: Approximately 20
Where are they: We have two cameras at every doorway on each side. This is so the player's view is always directed to the door when they are in the near vicinity. This will help to show if the door is blocked or open. We then have three other cameras in each room, covering every corner: Bar one. This is to maximise the style AND the productivity of the cameras.

Once you've figured out where you want your cameras to go, go ahead and drag them into your scene in Unreal Engine one by one (By dragging BP_Camera from the "Content Browser" into the scene) and use the transform gizmos to put the cameras into place.

If you've forgotten about BP_Camera or the transform gizmos, head back through the book, as we've covered them quite a few times now and it should be easily to pick out via skimming back through the pages.

Once you've put your cameras all in place in the scene, it's time to move on. Remember, there's no correct way of putting the cameras in the scene, as it's completely down to personal preference at the end of the day.

Once you have all the BP_Cameras in the scene, it's time to create some "Trigger Volumes" which will turn cameras on / off depending on where the player is.

What is a "Trigger Volume"? - A trigger volume is either a box or similar sized object which will trigger an event when the player or another actor (Depending on how you set them up) enters the volume.

We are going to set-up the trigger volumes in a way that covers where the camera should see the player. However, we do not and I repeat DO NOT want any of the trigger volumes to overlap at all. Not even a teeny-tiny bit. This is because it will cause a whole boatload of problems that are easily avoided and so should in fact be avoided.

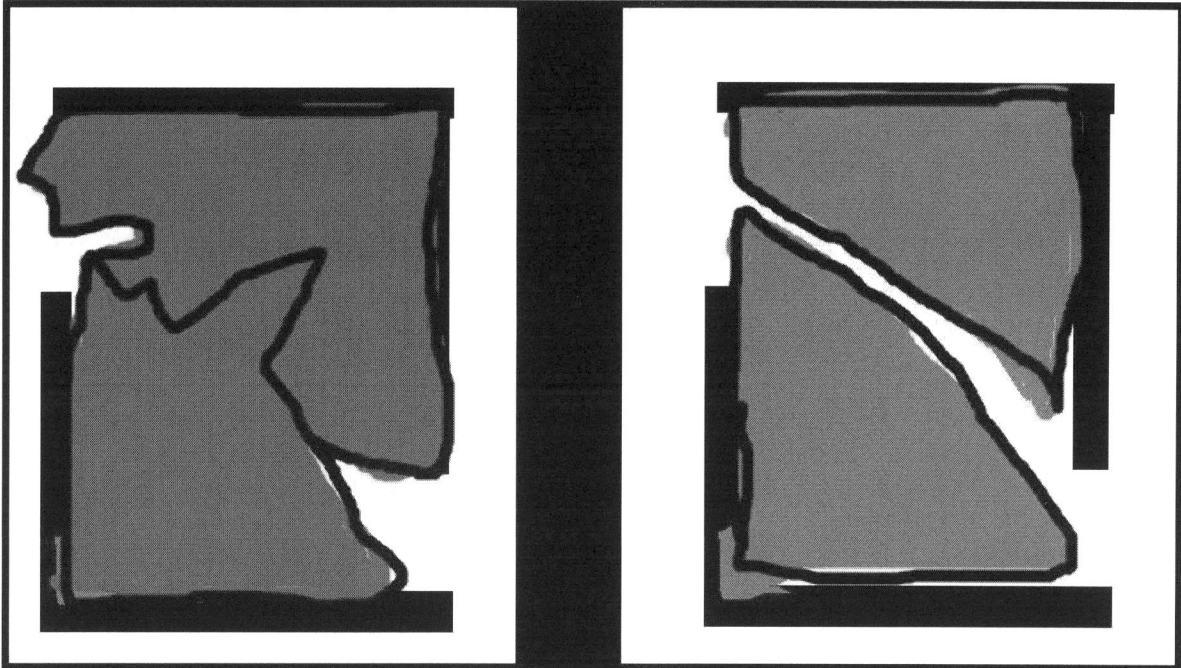

If you can see the terrible draw just above this text, you're probably thinking: "What the hell is that?". Well, it's my attempt at showing you what I mean when talking about when I say "Trigger Volumes" must not overlap each other.

On the left we see a trigger volume (Which would NEVER look like that but we'll use it for our example!) which is overlapping and on the right, we see two trigger volumes that aren't overlapping.

The trigger volumes on the left-hand side of the image will call so many problems that it's not worth doing. On the right, you should have little to no issues. So can you guess which style of trigger volumes you should use? (Insert a winky face here)!

Enough terrible Microsoft Paint images, it's time to get back to the fun!

Just before we do, grab your piece of paper or 2D art program which you drew your map on earlier (When you planned your camera placement).

Using the camera locations of this image you created, draw boxes (Or an object with four sides) around each camera where you want your player to move around the camera.

The thought process is that when the player enters one of these boxes, the camera near it will turn on and all of the others will turn off.

Remember when drawing these that they should not overlap… And not only that, it should cover 99 - 100% over the play space (The area in which the player can move).

This sounds like a difficult challenge, so I decided to overturn my Microsoft Paint image ban and draw you one last image (At least for now!) to help guide you into the right location:

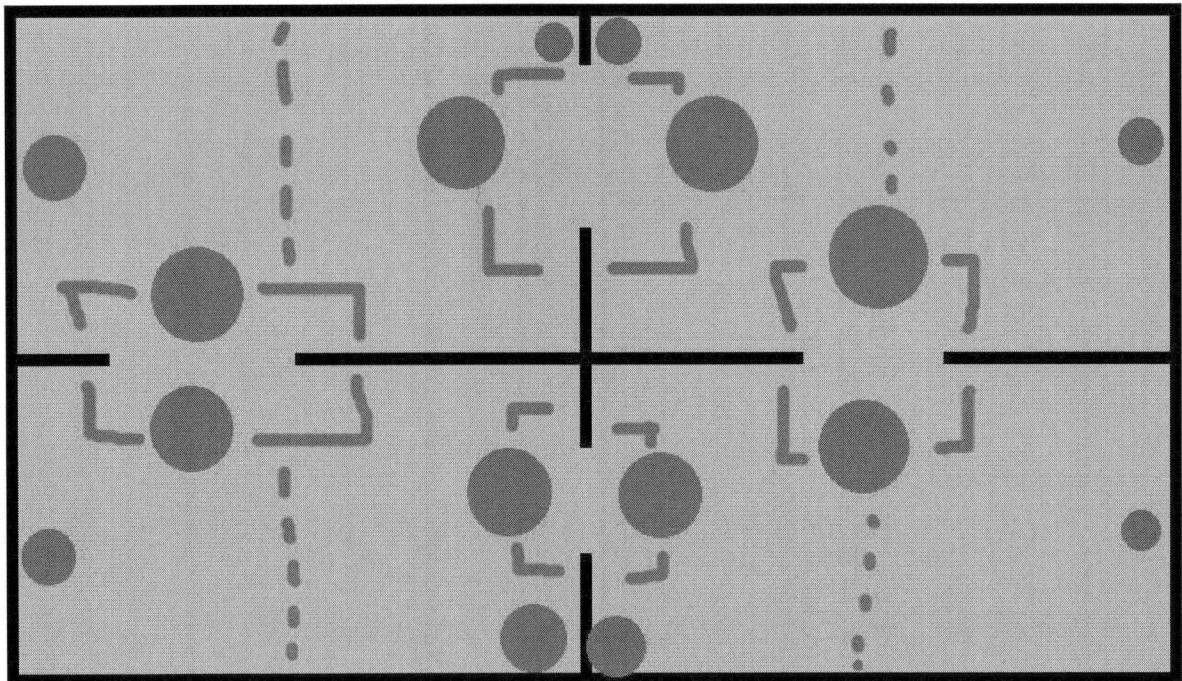

You can see in the image above that I ignored my own advice and have a LOT of overlap in my designs of the trigger volumes. This is because I have come up with an idea of using multiple trigger volumes for a singular camera.

Now I have just confused things 110% more then they were haven't I? Don't worry, let's take a breather for a moment and ease all this confusion out.

Trigger volumes can't overlap, however we can reuse code from one trigger volume onto another one. This means two trigger volumes can work as if they are the same trigger box. This helps us create some weird shapes with multiple trigger volumes that one box can't do.

Once you have your design ironed out on paper / your 2D art program, it's time to put it into our scene, So let's get to it!

Head back into your Unreal Engine project and once you're back to the normal view (With the "Content Browser" in the bottom-left, the scene view in the middle and the "Scene Outliner" in the top-right).

For those who are a little confused, I mean this view:

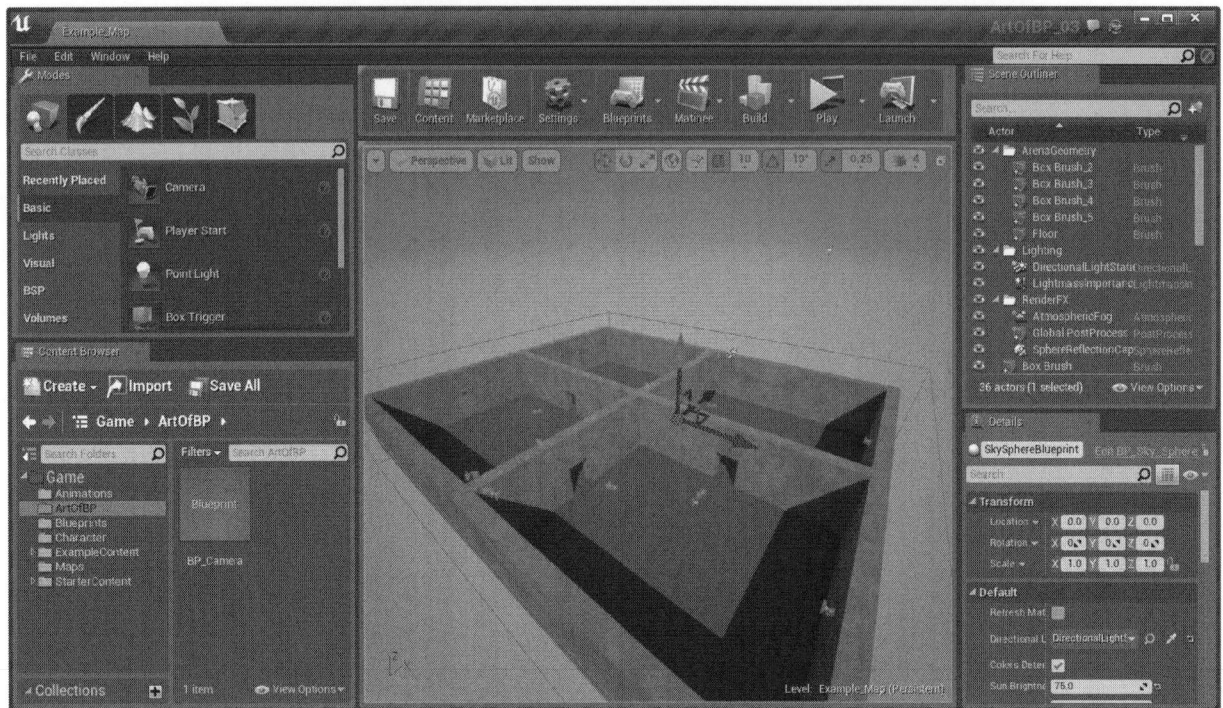

This is the main editor view and once you're here, we can continue!

Remember how we created the walls before using BSPs? We're going to use a system extremely similar to the BSP creation / placement, which uses some techniques we learnt with the wall creation (And placement!) but the process IS different. If only very slightly…

Head over to the "Modes" box in the top-left of the window (Which is where we traveled earlier to create the BSPs for our walls!). This time, we're going to use the "Search Classes" text field, which is just under the main icons but above the class options:

In the "Search Classes" text field, type in "Trigger" and select "Trigger Volume" by dragging it into the scene (Just like we did with the Box BSP).

You'll notice that this creates a box that loves incredibly similar to the BSP Box we created all that time ago. Also, you'll notice that this is a box and not the moldable shape that we've drawn on our map design.

Do you remember what we did to the BSP to mould it into the shape we needed? We used the "Geometry Edit" tool (The image on the far right of the "Modes" toolbox!). If you've forgotten about this, please skip back to the relevant section (As I don't want to spam the book with writing the same information over-and-over again).

So go ahead and use the "Modes" toolbox to drag in all your "Trigger Volumes" into your scene and use the "Geometry Edit" tool to shape them into the way you designed them when you drew the plans down on paper or your 2D art program.

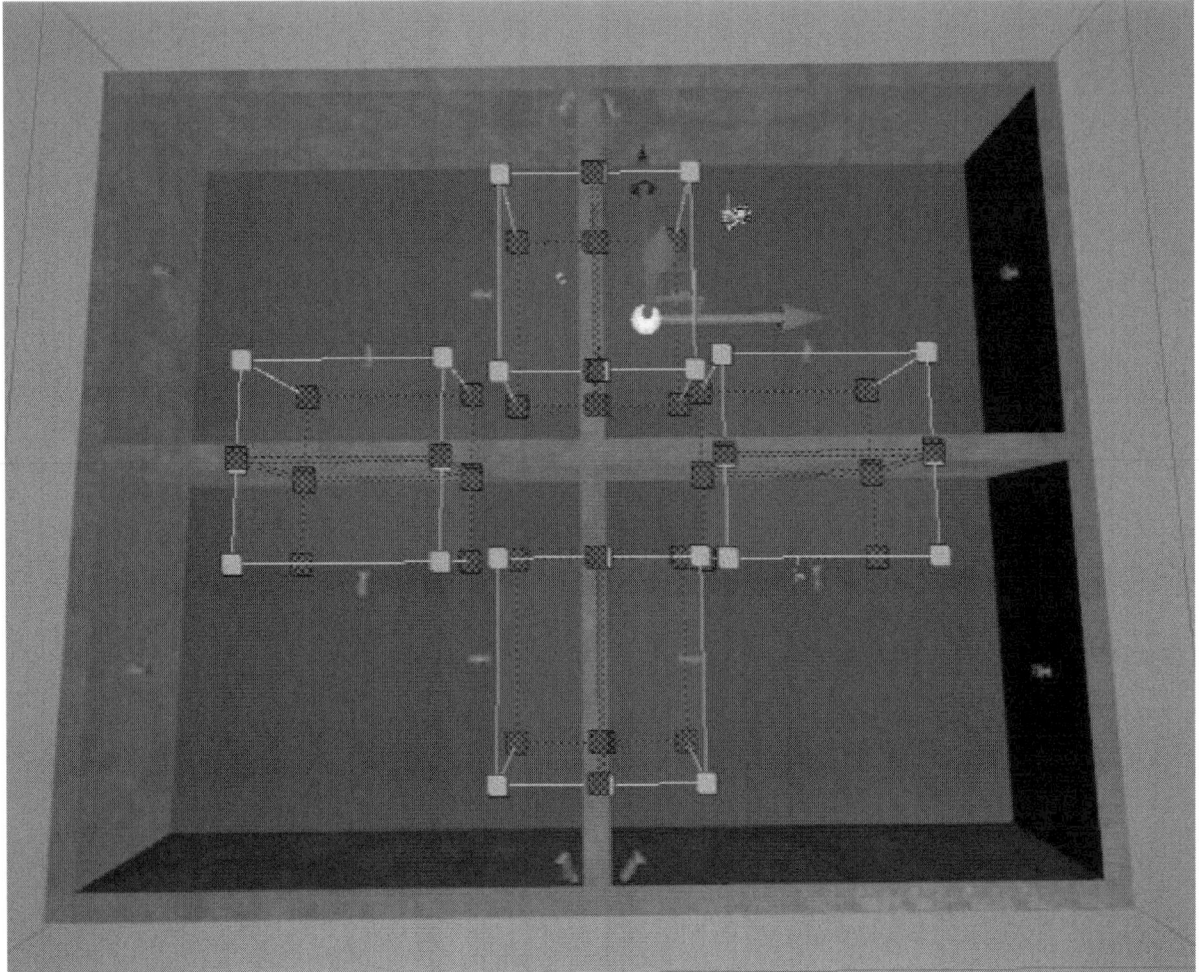

The image above is of placing the "Trigger Volumes" for the door sections. I will now add the rest of the "Trigger Volumes".

While doing this, I came up with a smart idea (This is the best thing about Game Development, You can figure things out even when you think you know things like the back of your hand!) - Instead of having Trigger Volumes for 100% of the ground coverage; We can cheat a little.

Trigger Volumes allow us to create an event if an actor overlaps the volume but they also allow us to do something (Which in all honesty I totally overlooked) that will help us create fewer Trigger Volumes. From the information I just gave you, can you guess what that trick is?

The trick is the fact we can also trigger things when an actor WAS overlapping a volume but is no longer doing so. Think of it as an "Actor is no longer overlapping" event. For those who guessed this, you get a gold star! For those who didn't don't worry, there's always next time!

What does this mean for our project? Well, if you're following my design for the trigger volumes, you can make 10% less trigger volumes. As long as you have the trigger by the door and then one for another camera in the room (But not the third camera), we can run an event like this:

Is Actor Overlapping the door trigger? No? Okay, then is overlapping the side-wall trigger? No? Then the player must be in the centre of the room.

Some of the people who are feeling more comfortable with Blueprints will be asking: "Hey, but how do we know what room are we in?". Good question! To get in a room, you'll have to go through a door. And so, we can use this information to find out what room the player is in without having to do any complicated code!

Using this ideology, we can cut out a load of unneeded "Trigger Volumes". For those who can see the images (Or you could check the site, remember!). You can see how many "Trigger Volumes" we have saved!

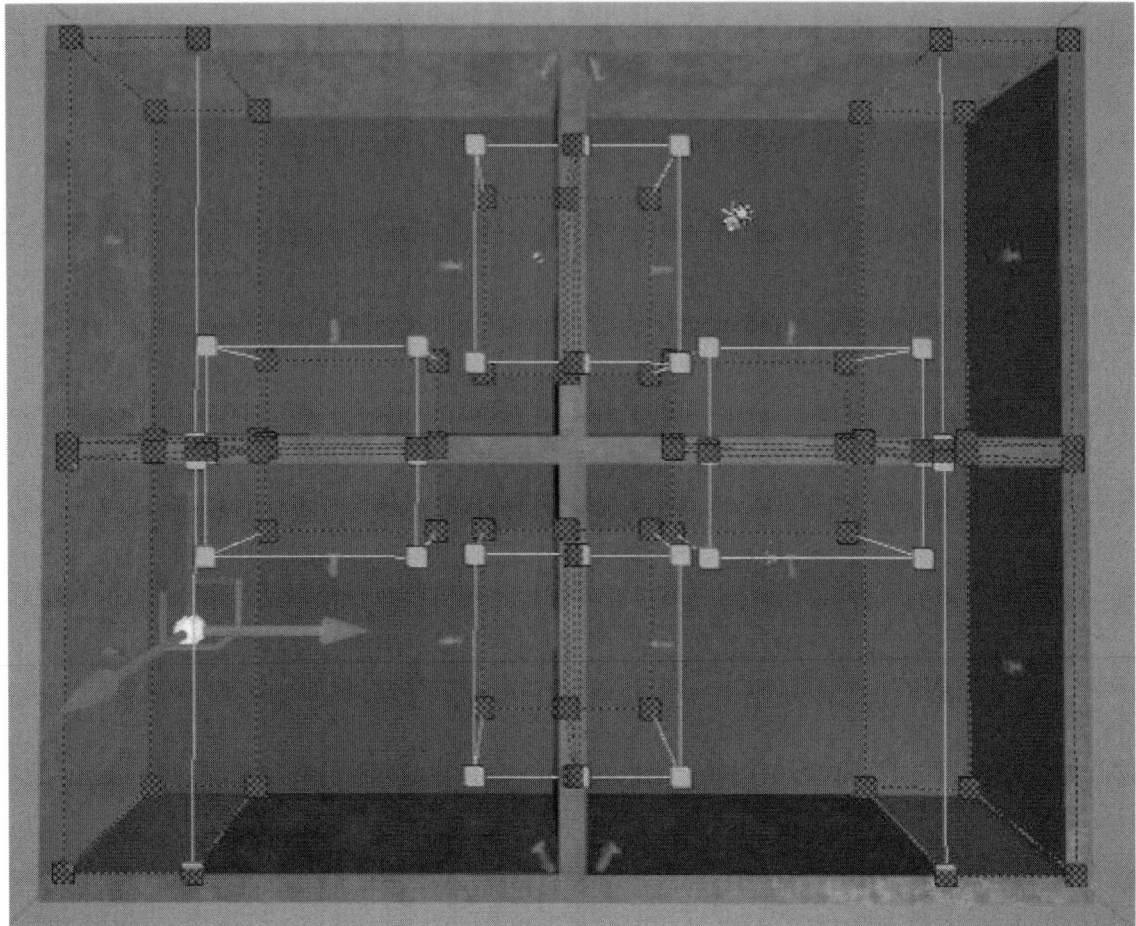

And from this, I will break my promise of no more Microsoft Paint images and show you this image as a design, so you can compare it to the older Paint image a few pages back and see just how many "Trigger Volumes" we don't have to use using this method:

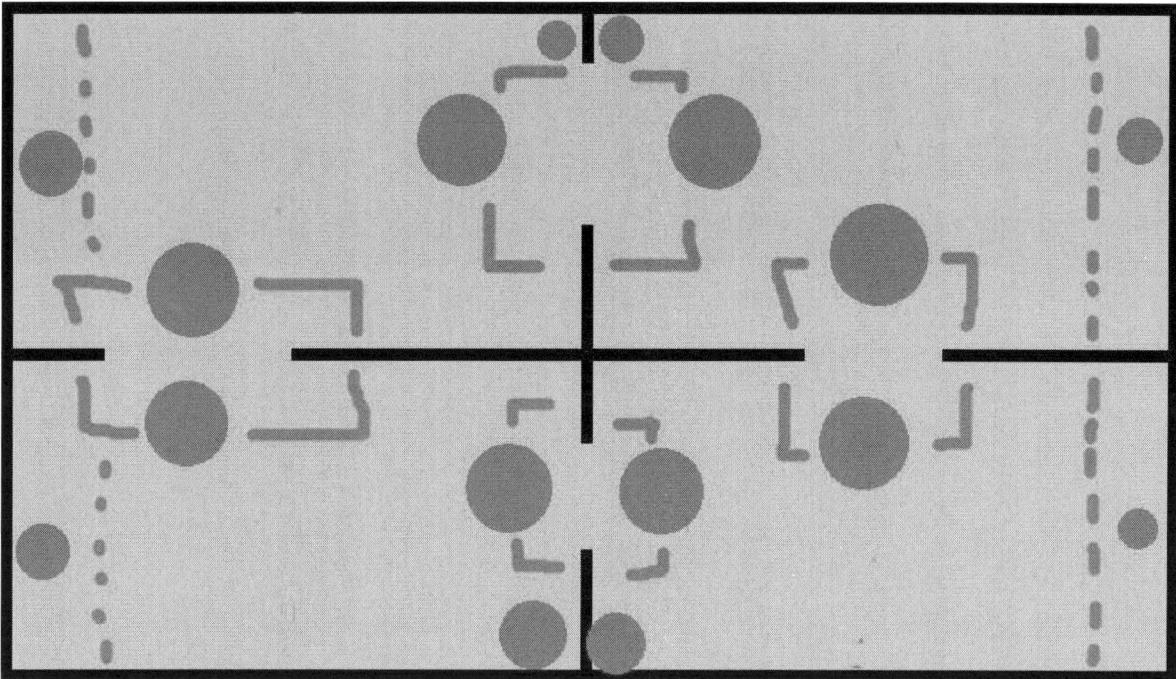

As you can see from the image above, doing it via this method saves us 16 "Trigger Volumes". This means we save time creating code as well as simplifying things. Not a bad benefit from a last minute solution, eh?

I've said this a few times, but I'll say it again: I understand that I could have edited this all out and immediately have shown you the simple method. But from doing it this way - It shows you that even seasoned Unreal Engine 4 developers can learn and figure things out.

Think of the engine as LEGO blocks. You can be given instructions on how to create specific LEGO structures but at the end of the day, that's not what you're being sold. You are being sold the LEGO blocks; The tools that your imagination will use to piece together your crazy (Yet amazing) creations!

This book works in a similar way. To some people, they'll be reading this book as an instruction manual: Do this and do that to have a 3D point and click adventure game. But that's not what this is. This book is teaching you the tools and techniques to create little parts of the 3D point and click adventure project, so that when you have finished with the book... You DO end up with a 3D point and click adventure project, but you have done it in such a way that you can expand what you've learnt and create some truly amazing projects.

Think of this book (And me!) as less as a teacher of creating the 3D point and click project and more of a tutor of the tools needed to create one! Does that make sense? I hope it does!

Getting back on topic, you should now have all of your "Trigger Volumes" that you'll need in the map and you'll now be ready to code them!

We'll create the code in the Level Blueprint, which will require us to constantly highlight objects in the scene manually for it to show up in the CBL.

So what are you waiting for? Head to the action bar above the scene and select "Blueprints" > "Open Level Blueprint" - Just like we did a few chapters ago!

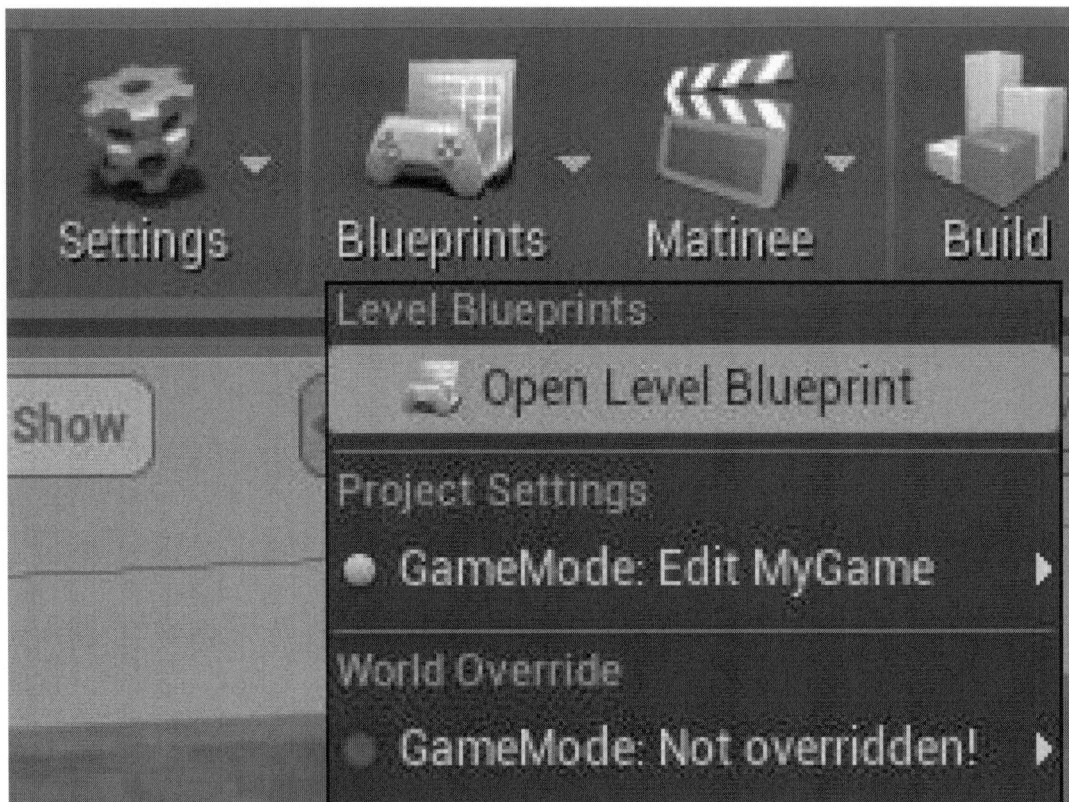

As I said before (Just to reiterate), Make sure you've deleted all the previous code we created in the Level Blueprint. This is because we were using that code to test if "BP_Camera" worked and as you'll know by now the BP_Camera is working famously.

So make sure the Level Blueprint is all "Clean" (Empty). Once it's a blank canvas once more... It's ready to help us continue our adventure to create a Point and Click Adventure game!

For the moment, we're going to focus on the "Trigger Volumes" and cameras which are facing the doorways. These next few steps will be quite difficult to describe step-by-step, so I am going to try and teach you how to do it (Instead of showing you) and let you use that knowledge to do it yourself.

So with the Level Blueprint still open as a window, head back into your main Unreal Engine 4 (Scene) view quickly and select one of the "Trigger Volumes" by the door by simply clicking it.

NOTE: It might be difficult to select it, so make sure you click near one of the green lines of the "Trigger Volume", which 9/10 will select the volume for you.

With the "Trigger Volume" selected, head back into the "Level Blueprint". Open up the Compact Blueprint Library. If you've successfully selected a "Trigger Volume" from the scene, you'll see:

- Add Event for Trigger Box <INSERT NUMBER HERE>
- Call Function for Trigger Box <INSERT NUMBER HERE>
- Create a Reference for Trigger Box <INSERT NUMBER HERE>

These options will be on the top of the Compact Blueprint Library just underneath the title of the window.

If you see those three options, then you've successfully selected a "Trigger Box" from the scene and we can add code to it here in the Level Blueprint.

If you DON'T see these options, then you haven't selected a Trigger Volume in the scene. Don't worry - By simply going back to the scene (Main Unreal Engine Window) and selecting a Trigger Volume then you should fix the issue.

Anywho, getting back onto topic: Once you're ready to continue, open up the Compact Blueprint Library in the Level Blueprint and type into the search box: "Overlap" and select "Add On Actor Overlap (Trigger Volume <INSERT NUMBER HERE>

This will create an event. As we said before, You can tell this is an event as it has no inputs (Only outputs) and has a red tint to the title.

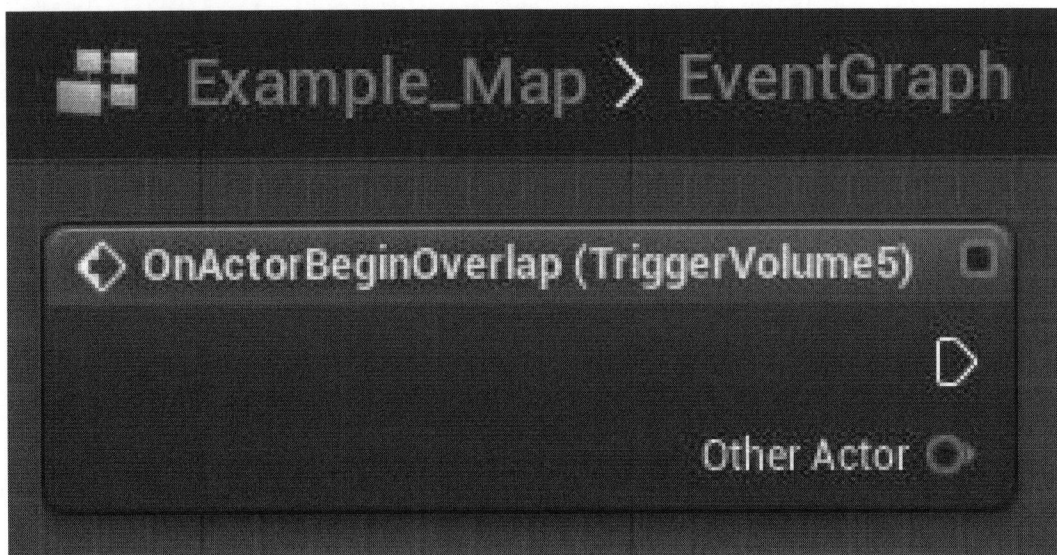

Let's take a super-quick look at the output pins: By now, you should know what the output execution pin is and what it does. If not, I seriously recommend you skim back to the previous chapter in which we talk in detail about it!

The second output pin is called "Other Actor". After the "Other Actor" text, the output pin is clearly a bright blue colour. Can you guess what this means? This means that this output will be an "Actor".

I bet some of you are confused by this. "Why the heck is the trigger event outputting an actor?!". It's doing this because it's information collected by the trigger volume which tells the Blueprint what has triggered this event.

Why is this handy? - If we know what have triggered the event, we can determine if we want to fire any code or ignore the fact that this actor is in the trigger volume.

This helps stop AI or objects in the scene messing around with our project; Making sure the camera doesn't go crazy because an AI on another side of the map has entered a trigger volume.

So how do we use this information to achieve this? Quite simply! We can achieve this "Only work if the player is in the trigger box!" with three simple nodes, which we are going to create right now:

From the "Other Actor" output pin of the event, click the pin and drag to the right, which will open up the CBL (But with nodes that specifically work the best with the "Other Actor" pin).

Type in "==" and select the "Equal (Object)" node.

For those thinking: "What the hell does this node" do: The Equal node makes sure that the input actor and another actor (Which we set) are the same. The red output pin on the right of the node is the "Answer" to this question, which we will connect to a "Branch" (True or False) node.

Seeing as we are looking for the player, the second input of this "Equal (Object) node will have to be our player. But it has to be part of the player that only exists physically in the world and not in the code.

I know this sounds darn confusing but let me break this down for you. If you open up the CBL once more and this time you type in "Get Player". There are four main options which appear and contrary to popular belief, they all serve a different purpose / function:

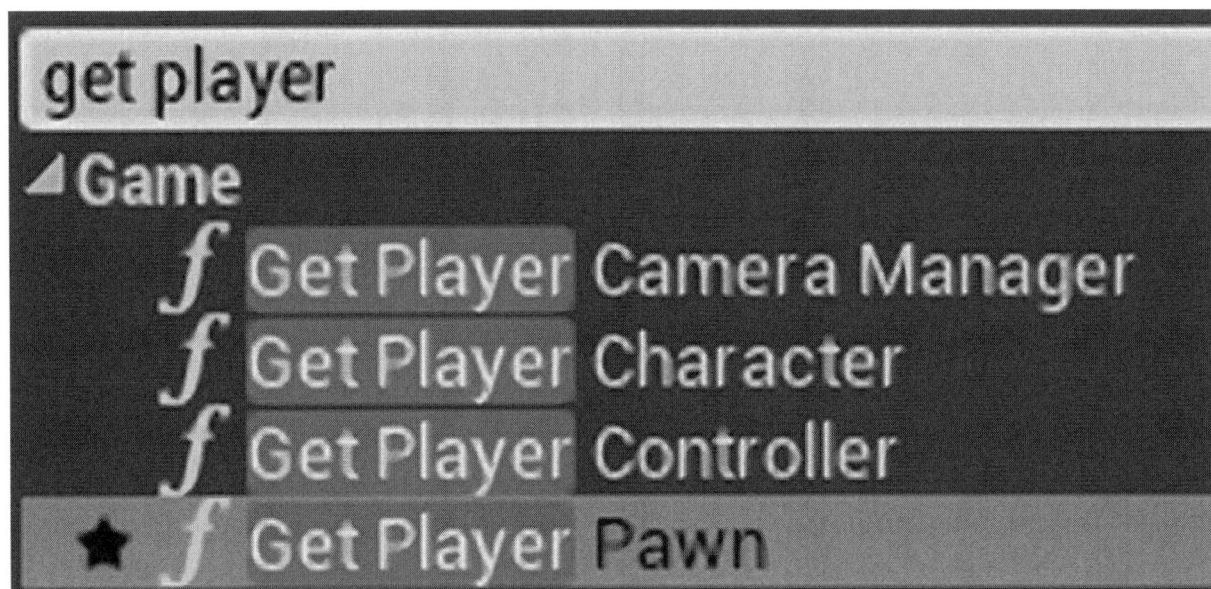

- **Get Player Camera Manager -** This node does exactly what it says: It gets the Player Camera Manager. Throughout the whole time I have used Unreal Engine 4, I have never used the node or never had the need to use the node. There's no real need for it as the other "Get Player" nodes do this job and arguably do it better.
- **Get Player Character -** This node grabs the "Character" that the user is playing. Note that this one won't work if the player pawn doesn't exist or if the player isn't playing a character that has a "Character" blueprint attached.
- **Get Player Controller -** "Get Player Controller" doesn't get the player or the pawn but gets the "PlayerController" blueprint attached to the player currently in the map (When playing).

- **Get Player Pawn** - A player "Possesses" a pawn (Moves it around). This node finds whatever the player is controller and whether or not the engine code sees this as something the player has "Possessed". This is similar to "Get Player Character" but unlike "Get Player Character", this doesn't need a "Character" blueprint attached (AKA A Blueprint with a "Character Movement Component" included)

So now we know the types of "Get Player" nodes, it's time to pick which one we want to use to represent our player when they approach the door.

Instead of making you pick though, I will give you the answer: You can either use "Get Player Pawn" or "Get Player Character" for the best results. Personally, I will be using "Get Player Pawn" as this provides the most accurate result for what we're trying to do.

So go ahead and created a "Get Player Pawn" node and hook it into the second input of the "Equal (Object)" node. Once you have done this, open up the CBL once more and type in "Branch" to create a "Branch" node (Which acts as a "Is true or Is False?" node).

139

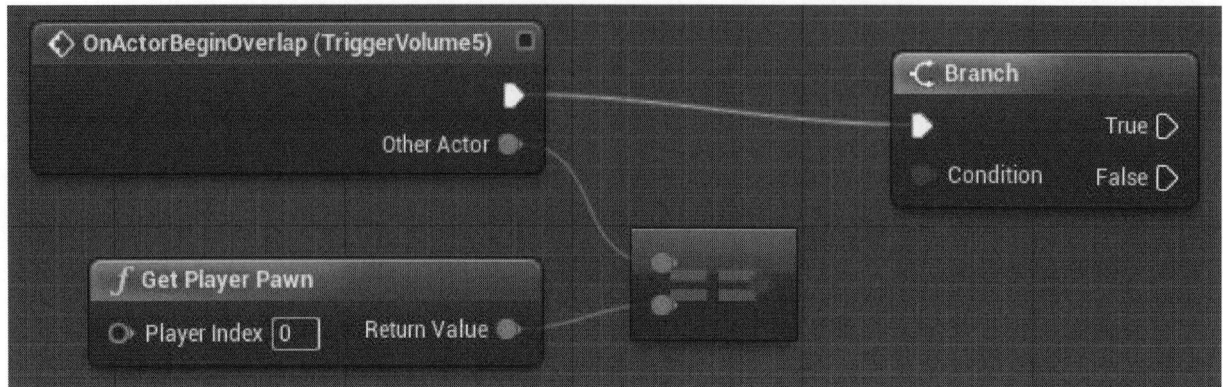

NOTE: Alternatively, you can hold B on your keyboard and left click (As this is the shortcut to create a Branch node!)

Once you've created the Branch node. Connect the output of the "Equal (Object)" node to the input "Condition" of the Branch node and connect execution input pin of the node to the output execution pin of the "OnActorBeginOverlap" node.

So how does this code work now? - At the moment, once the player enters the trigger volume, we are make sure it's the PLAYER that has entered the trigger volume (And not some AI or object!).

You'll see that the "Branch" node is outputting "True" or "False". As the "Condition" is set to "Other Actor = Player Pawn" this can be broken down into:

If the other actor IS the player pawn then… (And now it's down to us to tell the Blueprint what should happen!)

Of course we want to set the camera that's closest to our Trigger Volume to become the active camera.

To do this,o head back into your main Unreal Engine window, select the camera that is closest to the Trigger Volume (By simply clicking it!) and then back into the Level Blueprint.

With the camera selected in the scene, open up the Compact Blueprint Library (By either right clicking or using Ctrl + Click) and you'll see "Create a Reference to

BP_Camera *INSERT NUMBER HERE* near the top of the CBL. Click this to create a node that references the camera inside the Level Blueprint (Just like we've done a few times in this book now!)

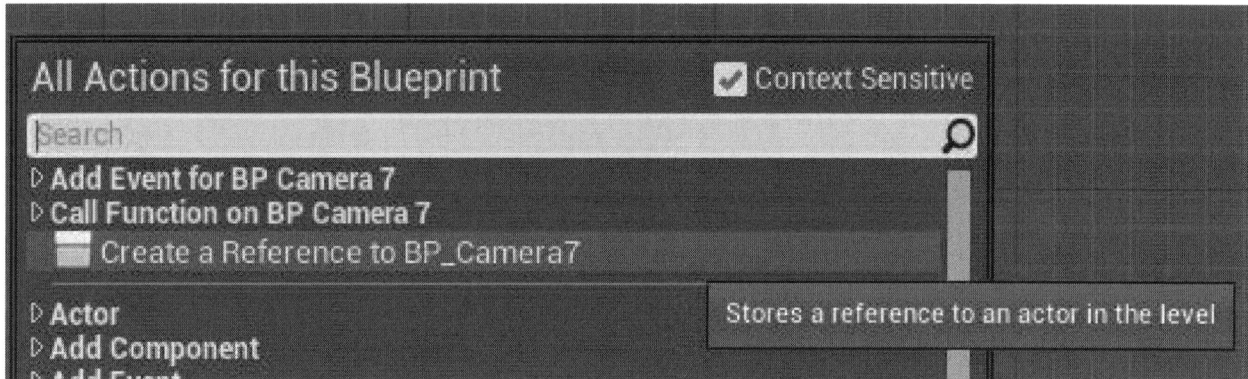

We now need to create a node we covered before (The "Set View Target With Blend"). If you remember how to do it, then perfect, but if not - Don't worry, Here's a reminder:

1) Open up the CBL by right clicking (Ctrl + Click)
2) Untick the "Context Sensitive" via the button of the top-right of the Compact Blueprint Library
3) In the search field of the CBL, type in "Set View Target"
4) Select "Set View Target With Blend" (This creates the node)
5) Open the Compact Blueprint Library once more and re-enable the "Context Sensitive" button again
6) Click away from the CBL to close it.

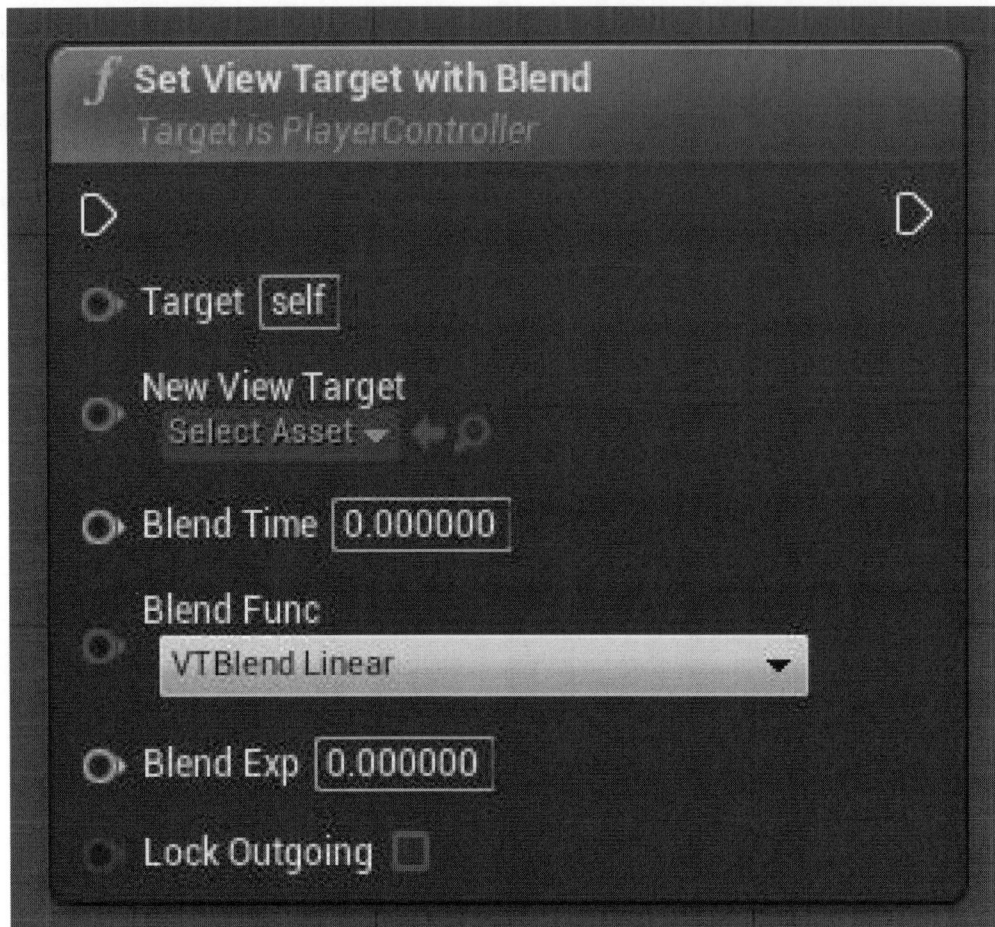

Set View Target with Blend
Target is PlayerController

Target [self]

New View Target
Select Asset ▾

Blend Time [0.000000]

Blend Func
VTBlend Linear ▾

Blend Exp [0.000000]

Lock Outgoing ☐

Just like we've previously done before, open up the Compact Blueprint Library once more and create a "Get Player Controller" node. Connect the output of this node to the "Target" input of the "Set View Target With Blend".

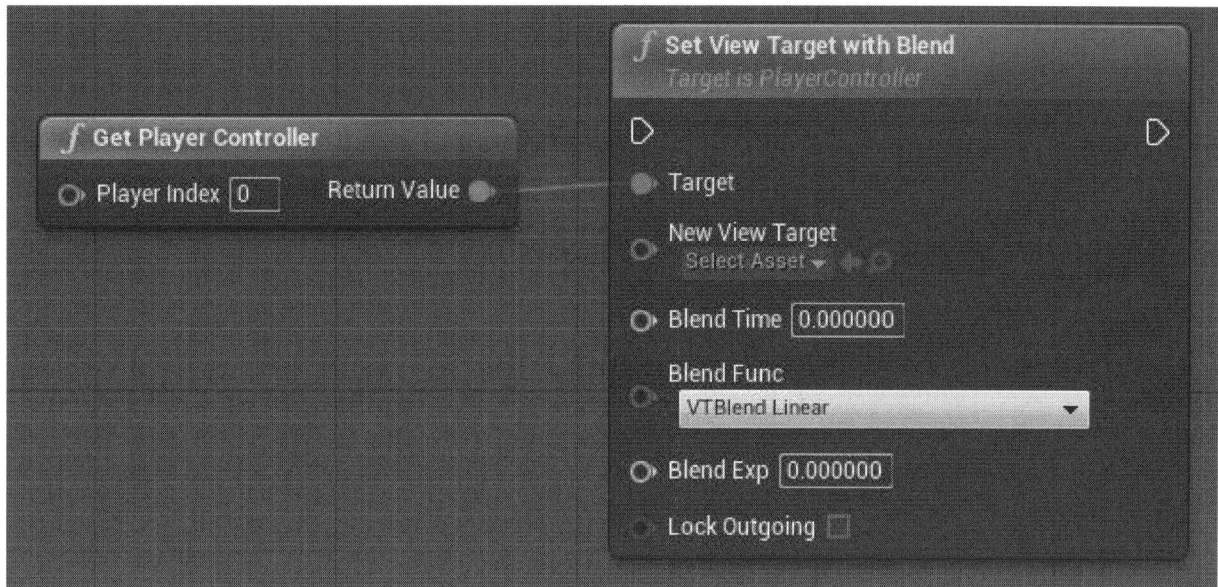

Again, just like we've previously done, connect the output of the "BP_Camera" node we created a few steps ago to the input of the "New View Target" of the "Set View Target with Blend".

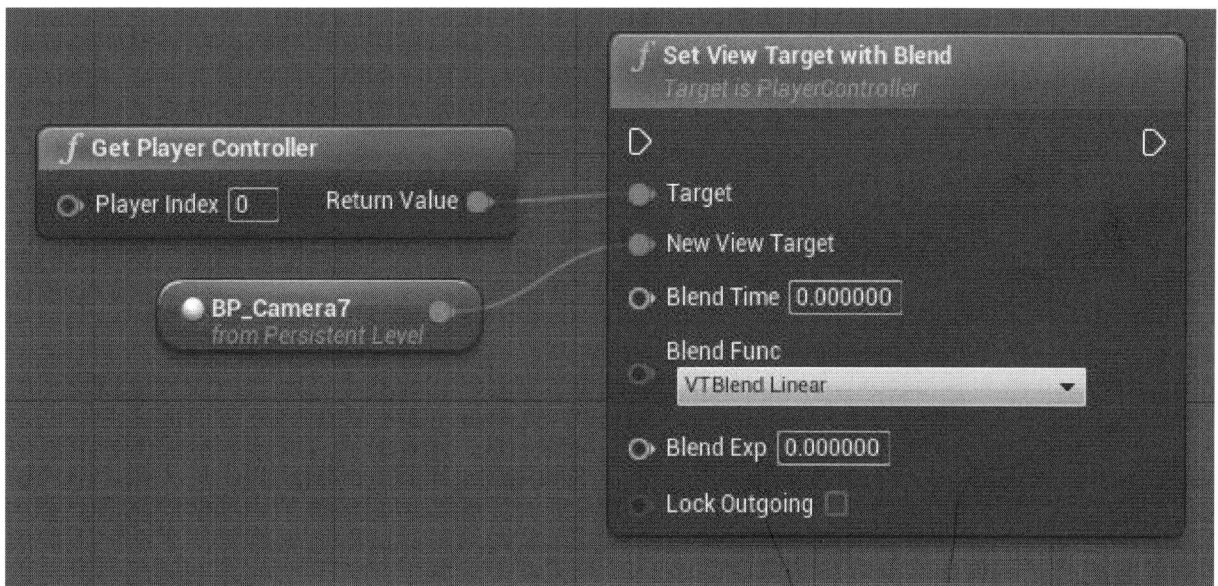

And finally, of course, connect the input execution pin of "Set View Target with Blend" to the output execution "TRUE" from the "Branch" node.

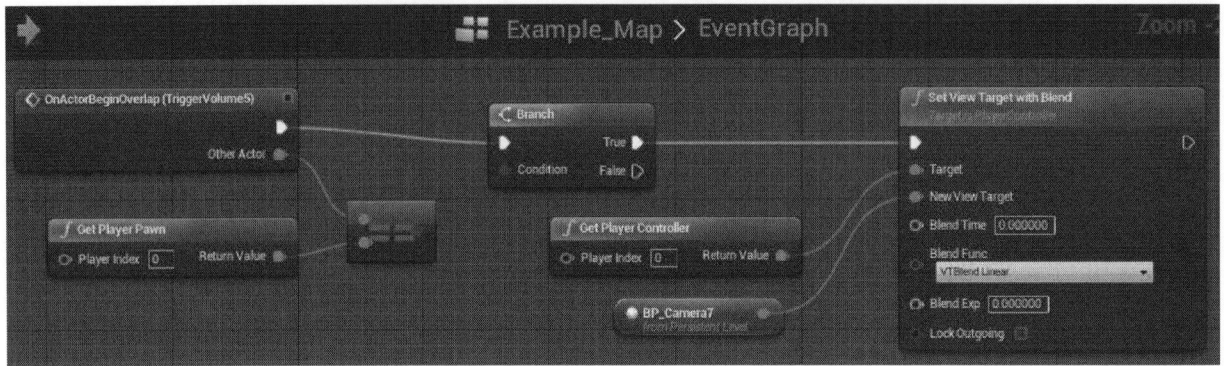

So what does is our code saying in plain english? - "If the player has entered the Trigger Volume (And we can confirm it's the player and nothing else) then change the active camera (And fire the code we created) to the BP_Camera (That we've set manually).

So compile and save your current changes to the Level Blueprint before we continue (There's nothing worse then losing work!) and once you've done so, we can add even more code to our Level Blueprint!

Remember the Trigger Box you used for the code we just created (If not, check the "OnActorBeingOverlap" event node, it will tell you which TriggerBox the event belongs to!) - Head back into the Unreal Engine main window once more and within in the scene click the same Trigger Box again.

Head back into the Level Blueprint (We'll be doing a lot of toing and throwing between them both for the foreseeable future) and open the Compact Blueprint Library.

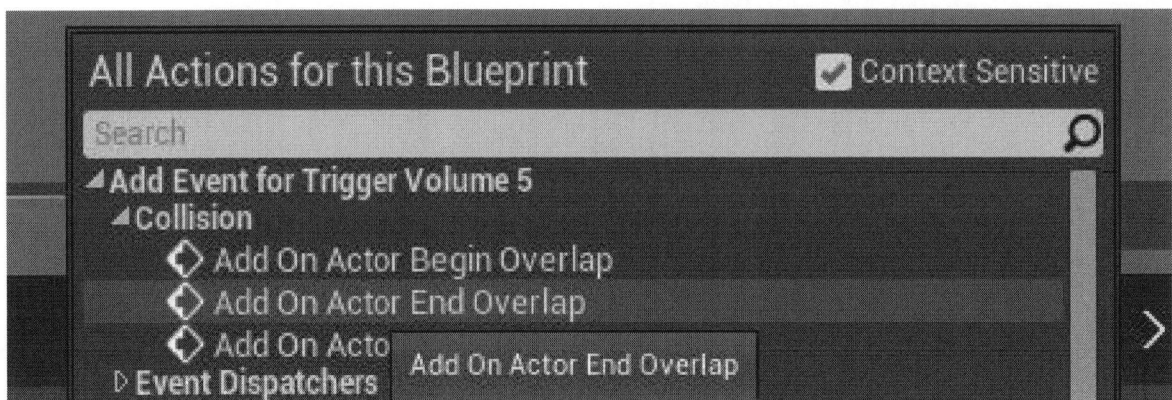

Within the CBL, if you have the Trigger Box selected in the scene, they'll be a section just under the search box titled "Add Event for Trigger Volume <INSERT NUMBER HERE>". Click this and then the "Collision" header to show our options for the events that we can use with the Trigger Box (Just like we've already done!)

This time, instead of creating an "Add on Actor Begin Overlap" node, create a "Add on Actor End Overlap".

This node will deal with what to do when the player WAS in the trigger volume but they are no longer touching any part of the volume.

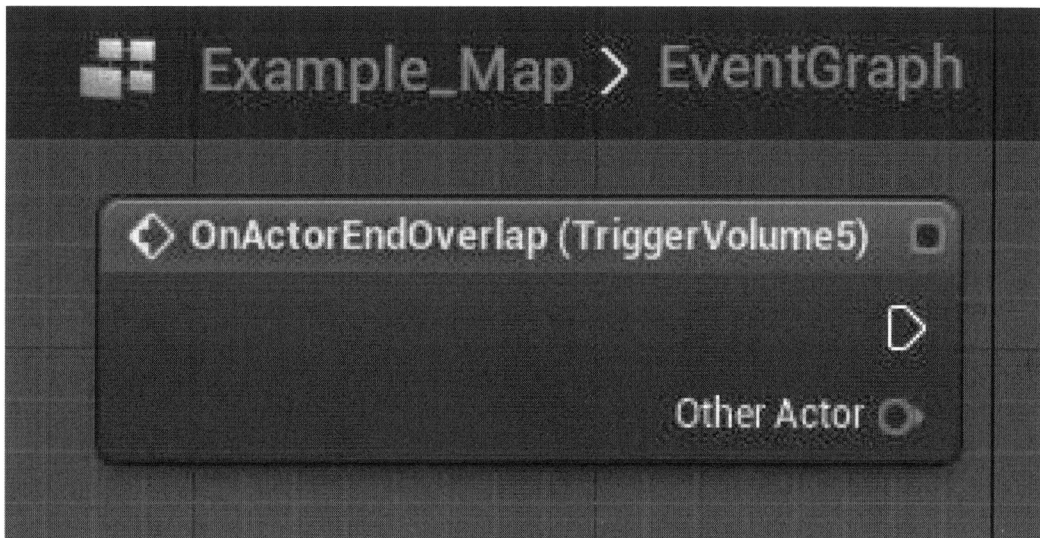

As you can see, this Event looks ever so similar to the previous event node we created:

OnActorBeginOverlap (TriggerVolume<INSERTNUMBERHERE>).

They both have output execution pins AND an "Other Actor" pin.

This is because they work in the exact same way. One ("Begin") triggers when the player ENTERS the trigger volume and the other ("End") triggers when the player LEAVES the trigger volume.

So let's set-up the "End Overlap" behaviour!

As I previously explained, when the player isn't in a trigger volume, we want the active camera in the room to be the one that doesn't have a trigger box around it: The camera that (In design) had multiple trigger boxes needed but post-design decided we could get around using multiple trigger boxes using this "End Overlap" method.

Remember the one? If not, here's ANOTHER Microsoft Paint doodle of my set-up to show which one I mean:

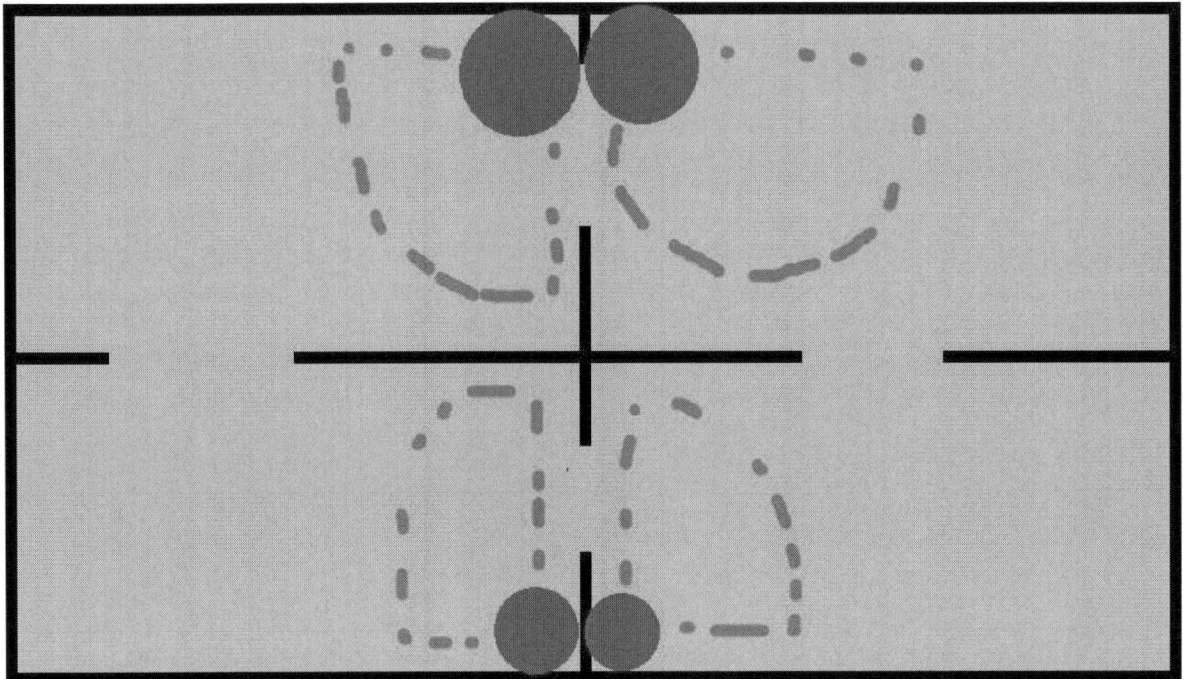

Isn't it just beautiful? In all seriousness, the image is supposed to represent where the cameras which we're currently talking about are located on my designs (Compare this recent image to the previous design images).

NOTE: As always, if you can't see the picture for some reason or it's of low-quality for you, then head over to http://www.kitatus.co.uk to view the high-quality versions of the images!

By now you should be able to tell which camera we are currently talking about. For those who have gotten a little confused: We are now talking about the camera in the room (Near the trigger box) that we didn't give a trigger box.

So let's get back to the good stuff!

Just like we've done before, head into the main Unreal Engine 4 window (Where your scene view is located) and this time select the camera we've just been talking about (It should be in the middle-corner or outer-corner of your room if you've been following my designs) but left-clicking on it.

Once selected, (Again, just like before) head back into the level blueprint and add a reference to it (By opening the CBL and near the top of the window select: "Create a reference to BP_Camera <INSERT NUMBER HERE>":

Your level blueprint should now have your "Begin Overlap" event followed by the code to set the camera there and your "End Overlap" event with no code attached but with your new camera reference.

I'm going to now get you to do something without my help. That's right, like a parent taking the training wheels off your bike, I am going to get you to walk on your own for a small time instead of crawling. But don't worry, it's not as daunting as it sounds:

As we've mentioned a few times now, the "Begin Overlap" event and "End Overlap" event work in almost identical fashion, apart from (Of course) the fact that one triggers when the player enters the trigger volume and the other triggers when the player leaves.

You can use this information to re-create the code you made for the "Begin Overlap" event but for the "End" overlap. It should all be identical code apart from the "New View Target" of "Set View Target with Blend".

This "New View Target" should be set the "BP_Camera" in which we just imported as opposed to the original camera had imported all that time ago.

So now go and attempt to re-create the code (Using "Begin Overlap" as a reference). If you get lost, you can go back a few pages in this book, where we originally created the code (But for "Begin Overlap") and use that as a template to create the "End Overlap" code.

For those who have attempted it but just need me to confirm it:

Event End Overlap > **Other Actor** (Get Player Pawn) > == > **Branch** > (True) > **Set View Target With Blend** (Get Player Controller) (BP_Camera <INSERT NUMBER HERE>)

And here is an image of both events for those who'd like to get the general gist of things:

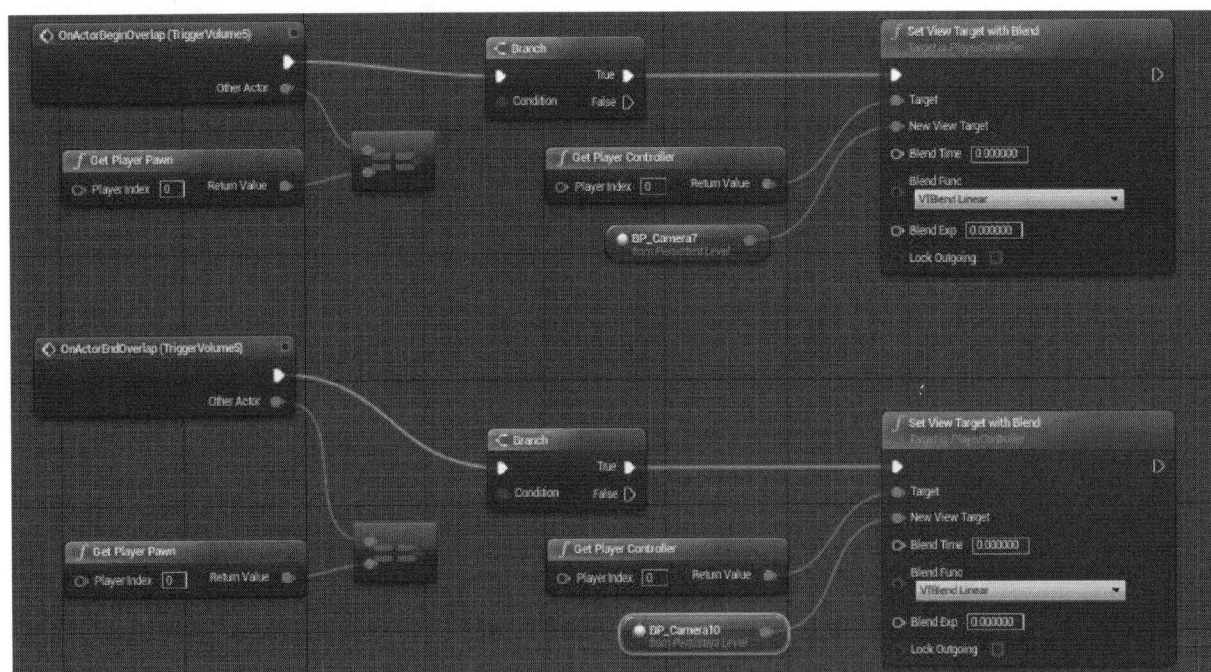

Remember, if you can't view the image, be sure to check it out on http://www.kitatus.co.uk (Where high-quality versions of the images are available).

Now, you should have been able to create the "End Overlap" node. If not, don't worry, it will be included in the project files on the website.

So once the code has been created, give you self a pat on the back and be sure to "Compile" the blueprint (And be sure to save!).

Now, I'm going to get you to do something more without my help. Something that you'll most likely not be happy with but not only does it save space in this book for important information, but it is also great practice with getting the hang of the blueprints system…

You now know how to set-up the cameras in your level blueprint. If not, then feel free to skim back through the past chapter or so. All the information and hints are there for you!

I bet you can guess where this is going… That's Right! - Use the information you've learnt about setting up the cameras and trigger volumes in Blueprint on all the cameras in your scene!

As I've stated. this is to help build your comfortable-ness (Is that even a word?) with Blueprints but it also helps save the space in this book for the super-important information!

For those who straight up can't be bothered (Shame on you!) or can't figure it out. The "Lesson #2" project download (On either http://www.kitatus.co.uk or http://content.kitatusstudios.co.uk) will have all of the work we've done so far (Including all the cameras in the scene coded into the Level Blueprint!) integrated into the project.

For those sticking with their own projects (And not using the one on the site), remember that if the player isn't in a trigger volume, then make sure that the camera in the corner of your rooms (That don't have a trigger volume attached!) are the ones that are set to active!

So go! Go now, my pretties! Go and add the code to all your cameras / trigger volumes in your scene into the level blueprint (Or cheat and download the project files from the site! Even though I am against it, I can't stop you!).

Camera Post-Mortem

You may notice that there's a few problems with our camera system: The player controls get screwed up and the weird thing that happens in doorways.

In regards to the doorway issue, as this is only a tutorial and not an end-game, it's not a burning issue. If you were using this tutorial as a final product, I would go back in and add some extra code to find out what side of the trigger volume the player is leaving and setting the camera according to that. However, to cover that in this book would take up a lot of room which is needed to cover all the other aspects of the Point and Click game.

However, if this is a burning issue for you and the camera in the doorway is bugging you to the brink of pulling your hair out, Try and come up with your own solution: You'll find that it's easier then you think! If not, shoot me an email: contact@kitatusstudios.co.uk - And I'll help you sort the issue out!

We also have the problem of the player controls. This is something that will take a LONG time to cover in the book. It's not necessarily hard to do, but it's time-consuming. We will cover this later on in the book but for now, it's not the worst problem in the world and thus we don't need to worry about it at the moment.

What we WILL be worrying about is giving the player an alternative control method. When you think of point and click, What control method do you think of? That's right: Pointing with your mouse and clicking.

Click to Move

We are now going to create a control-scheme where the player can click anywhere in the world and the player character will run to the location.

The best part about this is that it's not impossible to do: In fact, as you'll see, it's quite easy!

We'll also be learning some more important Blueprint tools, to not only add to our arsenal for when we create our own video-games, but to also help us get a better understand of Blueprints as a whole.

So, without any further delays, let's dive straight in and get started!

You should now be back into your main window of Unreal Engine (With your scene view in the centre).

To the left, as you should know quite comfortably by now, is the "Content Browser".

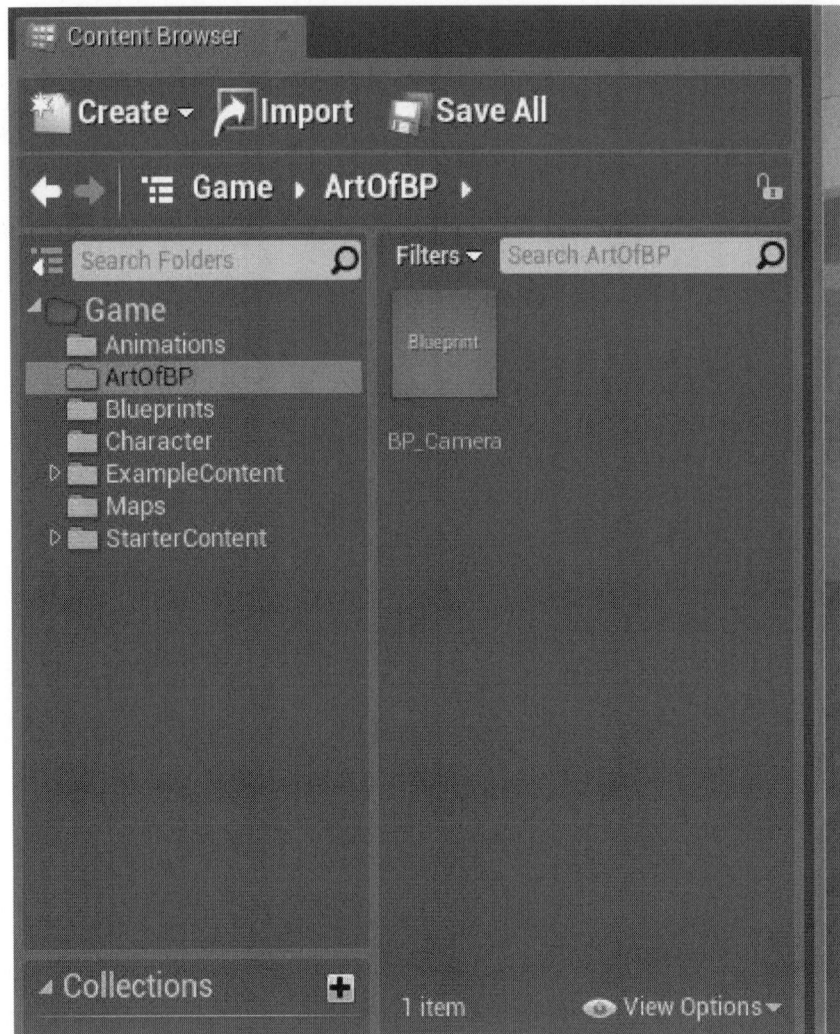

We need to create a new Blueprint. For those who have forgotten: Make sure you're in the "ArtOfBP" folder (Or a folder of your choice) within the Content Browser.

Now, when you're in the folder, go up to the top of the "Content Browser" and hit the Create Button, then press the "Blueprint" button.

The "Pick Parent Class" window will then open up.

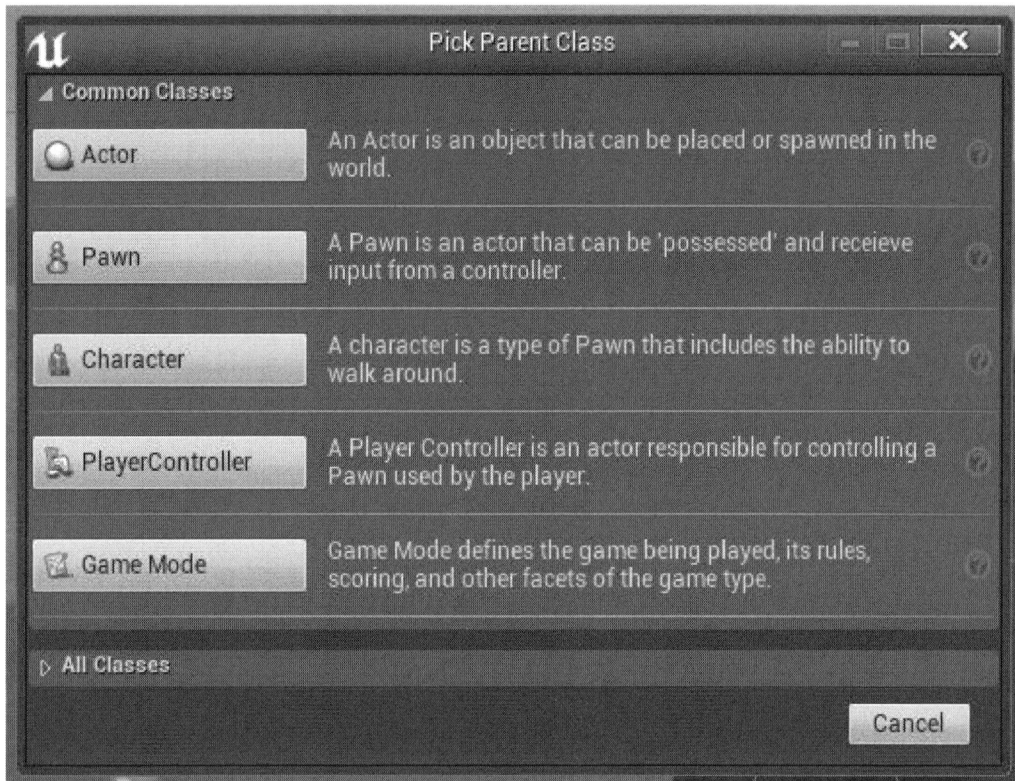

 For those who've forgotten: The Pick Parent Class window allows us to create a blueprint based on a "Template".

Here's where I explain something and totally over complicate it by accident (You've been warned!):

At the moment, the template character (Which was created when we selected "Third Person Template") has all of his controls in the "MyCharacter" Blueprint.

This is the totally wrong way to do things. Not wrong as incorrect but wrong as in "Not the right way". (See what I meant about overcomplicating things?)

Here's an example to better explain: Say you have a piece of toast and would like to put butter on it. The "Correct" way would be to use a knife. But say you did it with a fork / spoon. It's still possible, but isn't considered the "Correct" way of doing things.

That's exactly what the controls in "MyCharacter" is; The wrong way to do it. Why the template has it like this is beyond me. The correct way to actually put controls into your game is to place them in a "PlayerController" blueprint.

A PlayerController blueprint was created and designed to act as the bridge between the human player and the pawn that they should be controlling.

There are even more benefits to using a PlayerController then just being "the right method to do things". In multiplayer games, if you're putting all your movement code into the pawn - You'll run into problems. In some cases, you'll have multiple people controlling a single pawn (Which could be quite funny) and a character not responding when they die / respawn. These are just some of the problems that could occur.

While still on the topic of multiplayer games, You could do even more then put the "Controls" into the PlayerController. You could even put the player's "Score" into the PlayerController. If it was on the pawn, when the pawn dies, the score would reset. If the score was on the PlayerController, when the pawn dies and respawns, the score data doesn't reset.

These are just a few of the solutions that having a PlayerController can circumvent, but I'm pretty sure you get the idea.

So, heading back into our project, click "Player Controller" in the "Pick Parent Class" window. This will create a blueprint based on the "PlayerController" template.

It will then ask you to name the Blueprint (By highlighting the text underneath the BP icon in the Content Browser). For the sake of this tutorial, name the PlayerController Blueprint: PC_PointChar.

This stands for: PlayerController Point Character (It's super-handy to name all of your assets this way! Such as textures, calling them T_Texture or Materials, calling them M_Material. It will help when you have hundreds and hundreds of assets in your Content Browser - Trust me!)

Now, we've created a PlayerController blueprint and given the lovely name of: PC_PointChar.

The next step is to double-click the PC_PointChar blueprint to open it up.

When it first loads up, it'll open up into the "Components" tab. As we've discussed before, use the ribbon in the top-right to move into the "Graph" view.

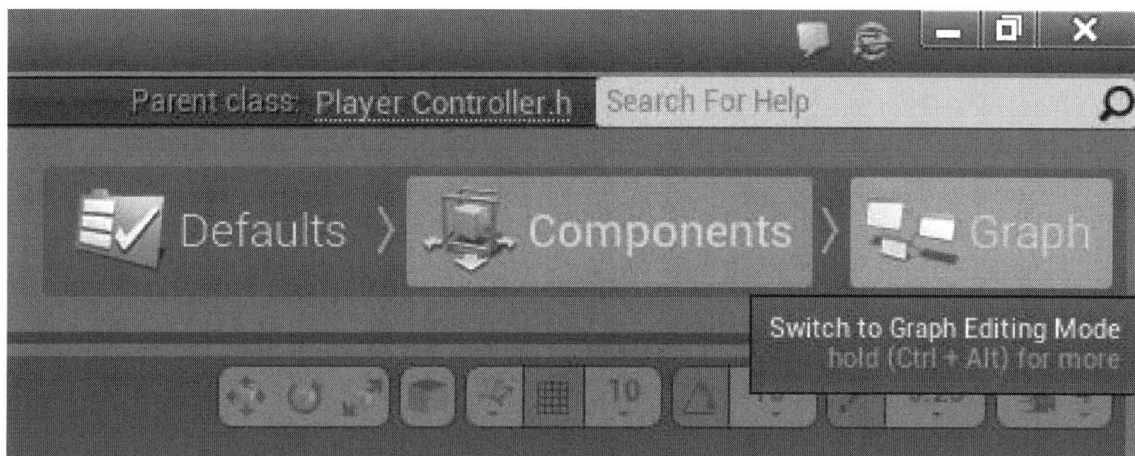

In the Graph mode now? Great! We can continue.

Functions, Functions, Functions!

We're now going to create a function. To point of this function is to use the outputs we're going to create with our own custom script, but is condensed down into a single node.

There are many benefits of using a function, but in the efforts of saving space in the book, you can find out about functions and their specific benefits by checking the Unreal Engine documentation (Which I highly suggest you do!)

However, to sum it up in a short and concise way: Think of Functions as a custom Blueprint node. We can set the inputs and the code inside and it'll not only help our Blueprints look cleaner but give us the ability to use the function in any blueprint we see fit.

While we're on the subject, Functions are extremely similar to Macros. However, there is a key difference between the two. A function will let us set the inputs and then add code whereas Macros require inputs AND outputs (And code!).

At some point during the book, we'll create a Macro as well (To show off the difference) but for now, we need to create a function. You'll see why as we're doing it.

So we need to create a function: While in the Graph view of your PC_PointChar, head over to the Variable Library. Usually, we'd use the top-ribbon of the Variable Library to create a variable (By clicking the image of the V with a little plus in front of it).

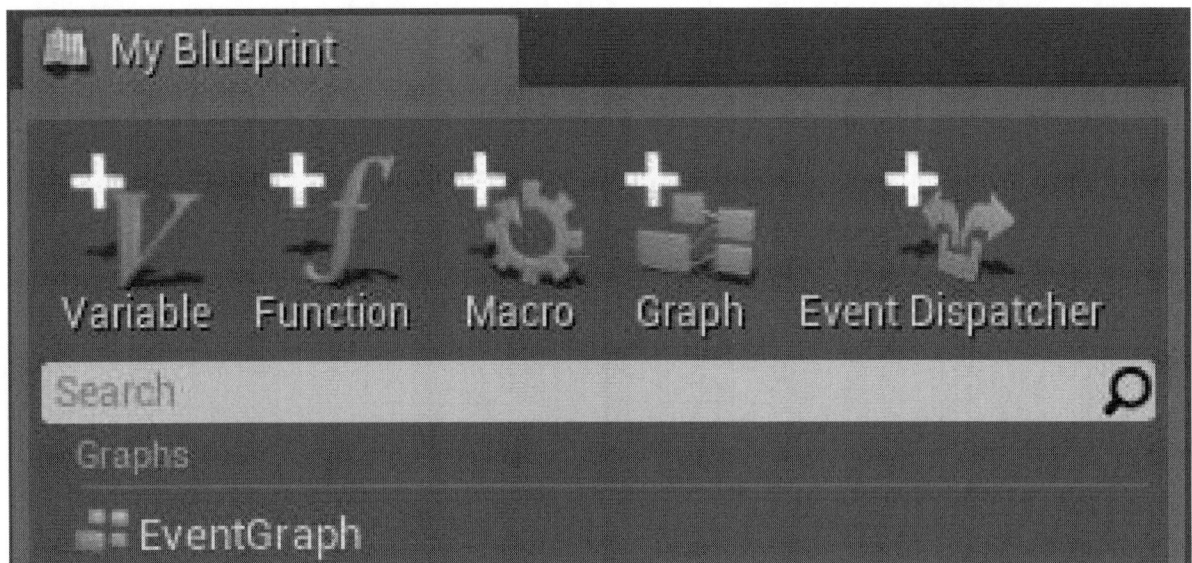

Instead of hitting the "Variable" button to create a new Variable, press the button just to the right: "Function" (With the image of an "f" with a plus next to it").

Pressing this button will create our function.

You'll see that the function has been created within the Variable Library and the name of this function is highlighted (As if it is hinting at us to change the name of it!). Go ahead and set the name as "MoveToLocation".

You'll notice straight away that there is a node pre-set in the middle of this "Function" blueprint. Don't bother trying to delete it - The blueprint won't let you. This is the "Start" of the function blueprint. Where it'll receive all the information it needs to work. It also doubles up as a handy way to see if you're in your main blueprint or a function (As the main blueprint won't have a purple node in it!).

HANDY TIP: You can also tell if you're in the Event Graph (The main blueprint) or somewhere else by checking the active tab just above the Blueprint area.

So we have our first input defined for us, the execution input. If we didn't have this input then the function would have no way to fire!

We need another input, however. This is because our function will be breaking apart a "Trace Hit" (More on what this is in a few minutes!) and then making the player move to where the hit was.

So we need to add this new input into our Function. We can do it by either clicking the purple the node or clicking the function's name in the Variable Library.

Once clicked, head over to the Variable Library and look into the details panel:

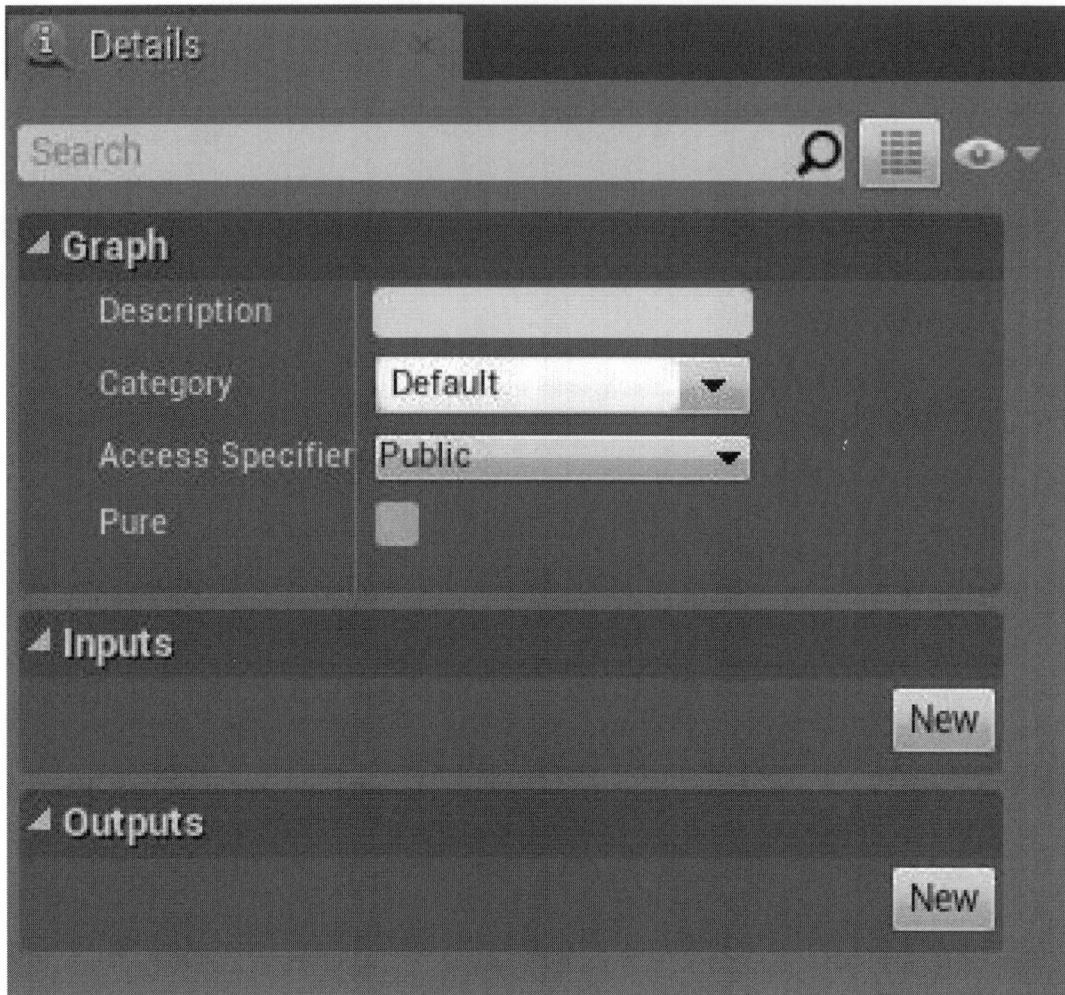

In the details panel, there's two sections marked: Inputs and Outputs.

Go ahead and head into the "Inputs" section and hit that nice, shiny "New" button.

This will create a new input, but at the moment, it's not the type we want!

As we mentioned once before in this book: A Bool is a yes / no variable. That means the value can either be: True or False. It's handy to remember that, but we don't need it at the moment, so we're going to change it into something we actually need.

We need to change the input into a "HitResult" (Which is… A result of a hit), so go ahead and click the "Boolean" button in "Inputs" and type "Hit" (Selecting "HitResult").

While we're here, Change the "NewParam" text field to: "Hit Result". This will help us when we are finished with Function as it will tell us what the blue input represents!

Excellent. So we've set up the first part of the function; It's now time to actually put some code into the function, so it… functions…

The "Hit" is where the player will click in the world. Once we've got the hit (We'll get to that part eventually), we'll have to break the result into data that we can use to actually move the player.

So use the CBL (You'll have to untick "Context Sensitive" but be sure to turn it on again once you've created the node!) to create a "Break Hit Result" node and connect the left-hand side input "Hit" to the output "Hit Result".

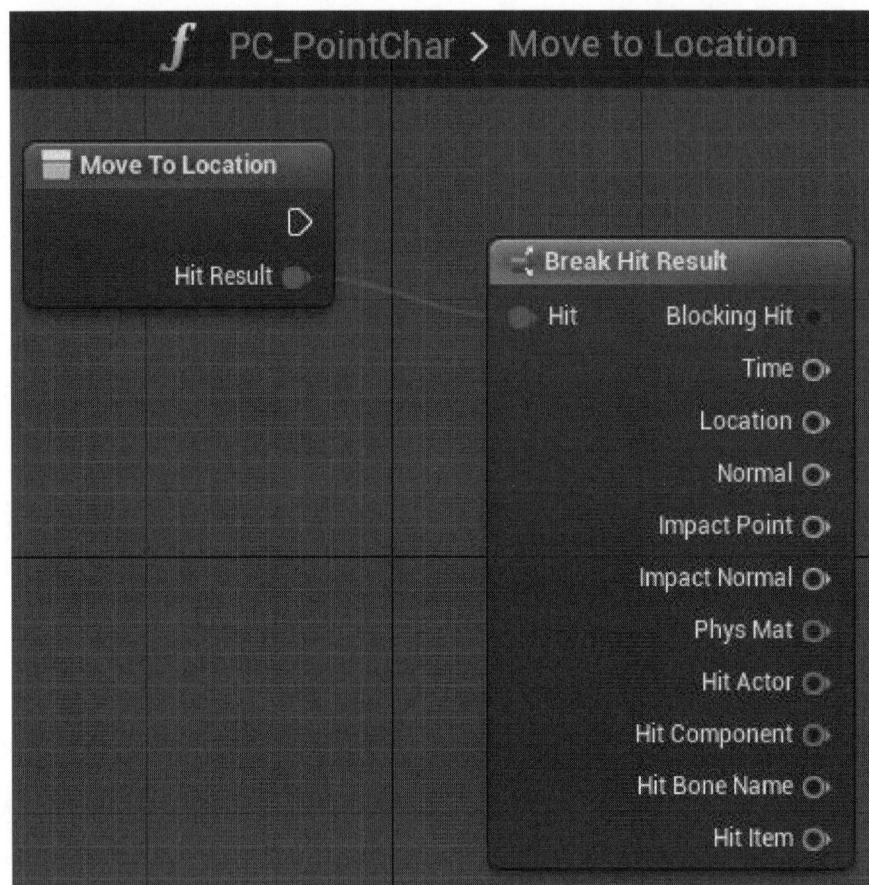

As you can see, there's a boat-load of outputs that the hit result gives us. But don't worry, they're all fairly explanatory. If there's one that confuses you, feel free to check it out on the Unreal Engine Documentation. But the chances are, if you can't figure out what a certain "Break Hit Result" output pin is used for, nine times out of ten, you won't need to use it.

Before we continue, we need to know where the player is in the virtual world which we've created. Don't worry - We don't need to use any trigger boxes or anything.

We need to get the current player that the player controller is attached to so go ahead and open up the Compact Blueprint Library and search for: "Get Controlled

Pawn" and create the node. This will get the current "pawn" (Or player character) that the player controller is currently… wait for it…. controlling. (I know, I've just gotta stop with these lame "puns")

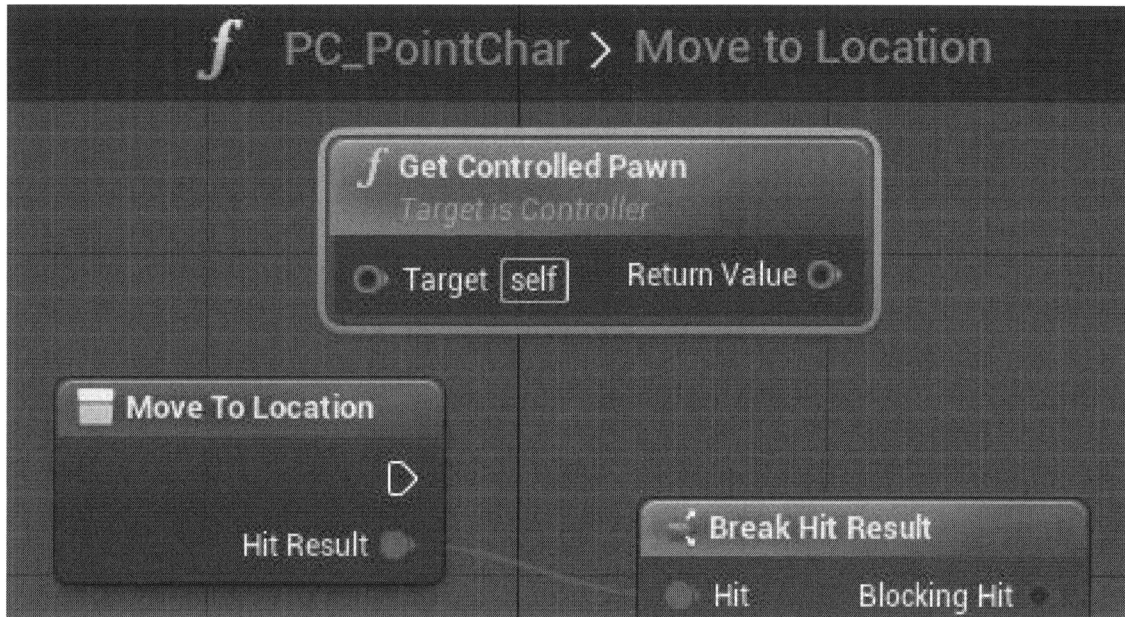

From this node, is extremely easy to get the location of the player. In fact, if you click the "Return Value" output pin and drag to the right to open up the CBL, you can type in "Get Actor Location" and the newly-created node will do just that: Get the player's location in the world!

Now, we've got the player's location in the world… What's next? Well let's think about two things for a second: We've got the player's location and from the Break Hit Result node, we will also (Eventually) have the mouse click's position in the world.

Can you guess what we do with both pieces of information? We minus them both from each other! Why? Because we need to get the distance between them both and make sure they're not clicking too close to the player (Which, trust me, isn't pretty to see when it happens!)

So open up the CBL and create a Vector - Vector node. Plug the "Get Actor Location" output into the top-left input of the "Vector - Vector" node and the "Location" output of "Break Hit Result" into the bottom-left input of the Vector - Vector node.

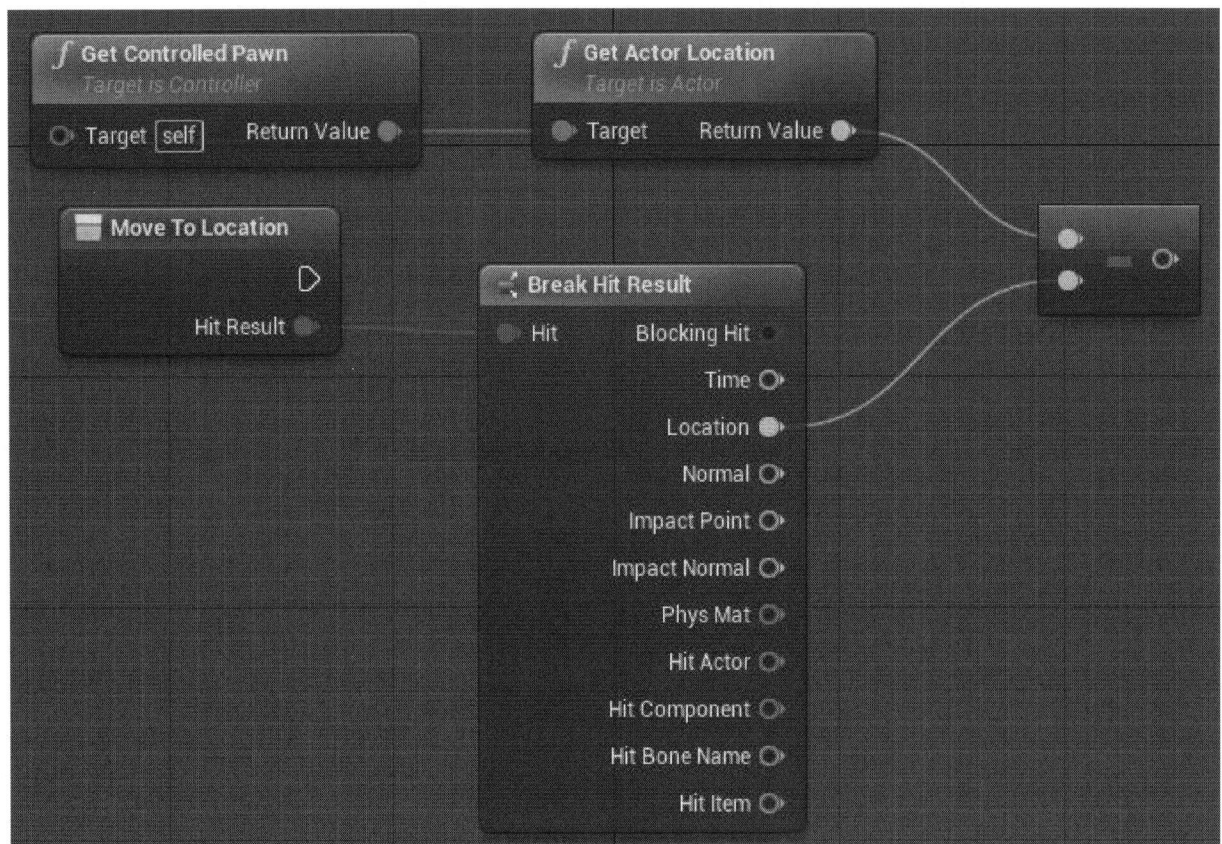

Now we're getting somewhere! Now we have the distance of the player minused from the distance of where we will click, we now have to get the length of this vector (To find out how far from the player our click really was!).

You can do this with a node called "Vector Length", so go ahead and create that now and connect it to the output of "Vector - Vector".

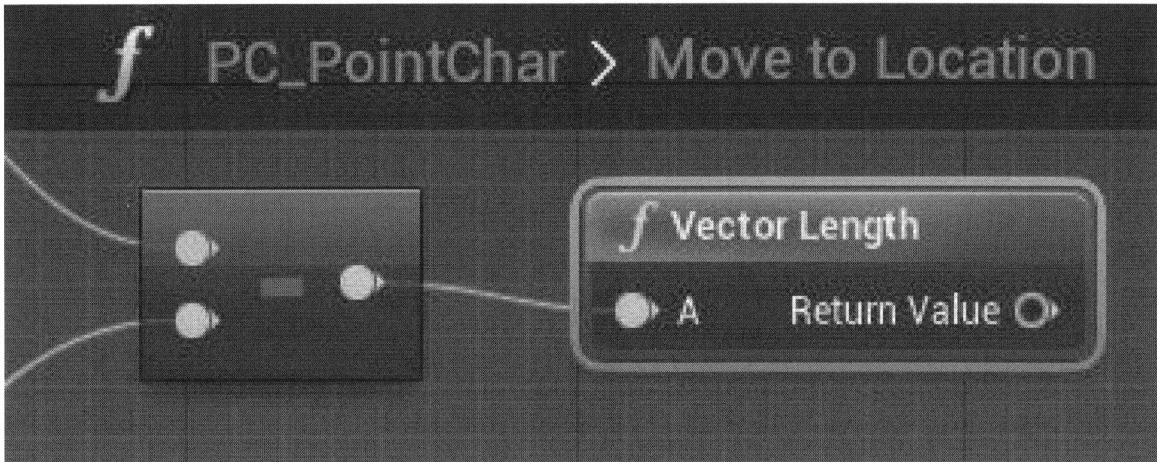

Now we're going to compare the number that his "Vector Length" gives us with the amount that it has to be MORE then. If it isn't longer then the amount we're about to create, then we don't want the code to fire as it'll cause problems (As I've mentioned before).

From the "Return Value" of Vector Length, create a "Float >=" (Float more than or equal to) node and connect the "Vector Length" output to the top input of the "Float >=" node.

For the bottom input, this will be the distance that the mouse click has to be away from the character (In order for our code to work), so let's set it at 120 for now (We can always change it later!). To set it, simply change: 0.0 to 120. Easy!

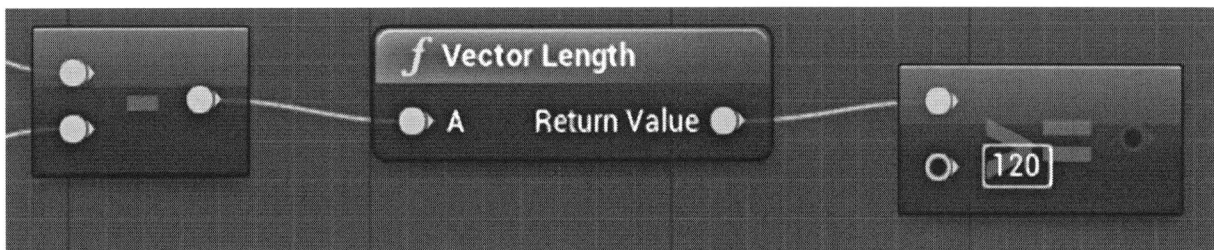

As you might have guessed by now, the colours of the output MEAN something: They're not just there to look pretty. You should've been able to guess by now that:

- Yellow = Vector

- Green = Float

But what you've already done (But might not remember) is that you've already figured out what the red output stands for. If you want to guess, you've got three seconds to guess what is means… Ready? 3… 2… 1… The red output stands for a Bool (True / False).

No doubt by now, you're getting a little confused about all this talk about "Vector, Float, Bool"and whatnot. For those who are new to coding, they'll think that they are words created just to confuse, but in reality, they are terms (Or rather Variables) to help your game making adventures.

Here's a super-quick, super-simple breakdown on what the most common Variables are and what they mean (I will also include a helpful table at the end of the book AND as a download on http://www.kitatus.co.uk)

- Vector: X Y Z value of an object in the world (An object's location)
- Float: A number between 0 - infinity (That includes decimal places)
- Integer: A number between 0 - infinity (That DOES NOT include decimals)
- Bool: True (Yes) / False (No) values.

These four are the most common variables that you'll use in your adventures, so here is a breakdown on where you'll most likely find us for these variables:

- Vector: Getting an actor's location in the world (Such as a player) OR getting the distance between two objects (Like we're doing right now!)
- Float: Recording the time or a specific value (Such as speed: 1510)
- Integer: Good for a menu selection (0 for option A, 1 for option B .etc)
- Bool: This one is pretty self explanatory. You could use this anywhere where you need a "Is true / Is false" answer, such as "Is it raining" or "Is the Character doing this?"

As you can see, these variables are much less scary when you know what they mean!

As I said before, I'll provide a table for you (Not a real table. If only I could afford it!) at the back of the book and as a free download on the Kitatus website, so you can always refer back to it when you get stuck!

Anyway, we're getting a bit side-tracked, Let's get back to the project!

Remember where we left off? (Sorry about taking off on that tangent there, but it was super-super important information!) We have a "Bool" output (Which is giving us a True / False value). Where do we plug this in? Into a "Branch" (True / False" node of course!

Use the CBL to create a Branch (Or hold "B" on your keyboard and left click!) and connect the "Condition" to the output of the "Float >=" node.

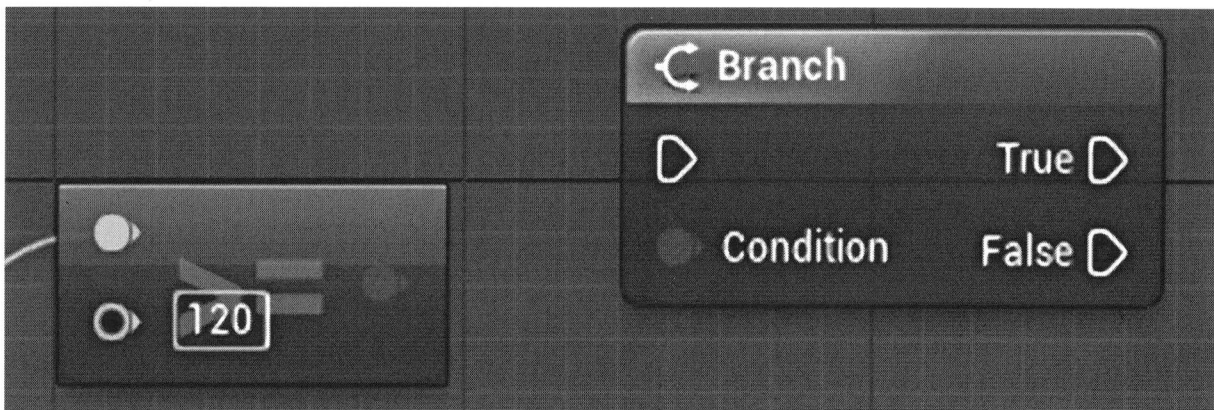

Notice how, unlike the other nodes we've created thus far in the Function that our "Branch" has an input execution. Go ahead and connect the "Execution Output" of our purple "Move to Location" node to the "Execution Input" of the "Branch".

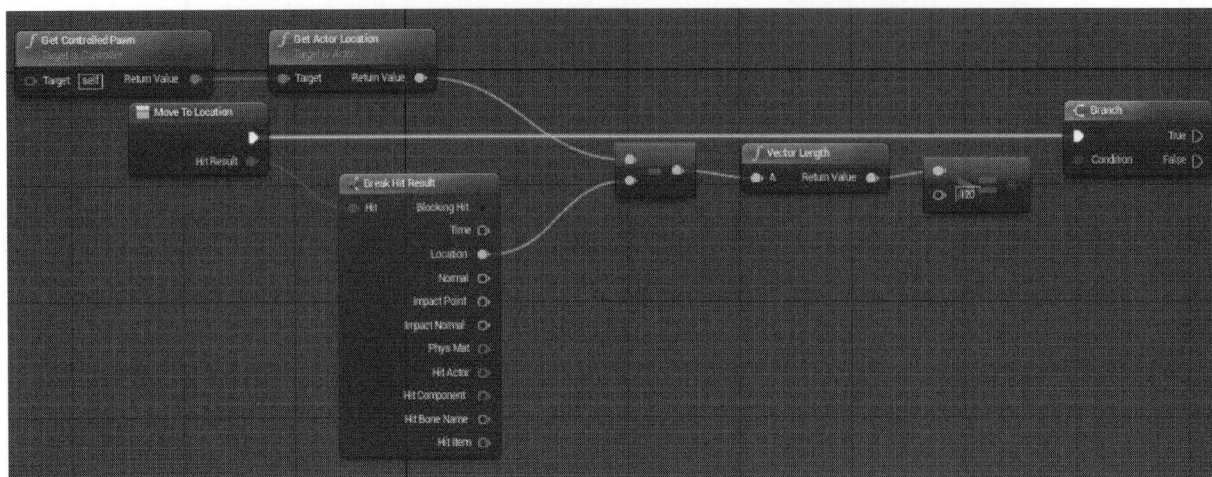

Now we're getting somewhere!

To complete this Function, we only need to few extra things! So use the Compact Blueprint Library to create a "Simple Move to Location" node.

Attach this newly created node to the "True" output of "Branch".

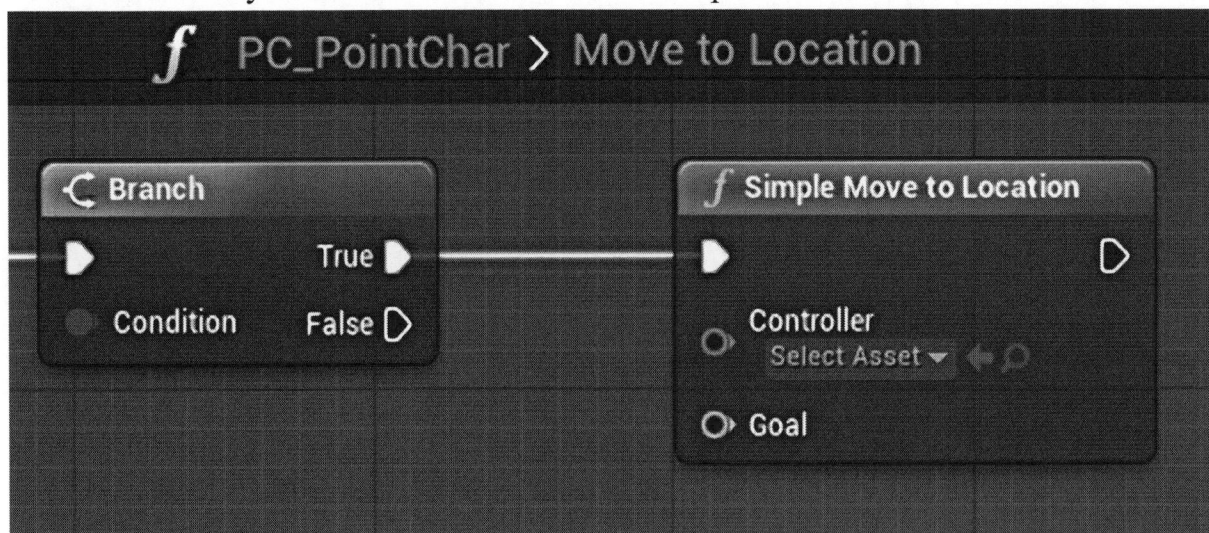

It's pretty obvious what this node does... Right?

For the "Controller" input in "Simple Move To Location", click the pin and drag to the left. When the Compact Blueprint Library opens, type in "Self" and select "Get Reference to Self".

This basically tells whatever the player controller is controlling to move to the location specified.

But we haven't specified the location yet…

Remember the "Location" from the "Break Hit Result?" (Which we plugged into the "Vector - Vector" node?

Let's just simplify our code for a second (See if you can figure out the input for "Simple Move to Location" as we quickly break down the code):

The code reads like this: When this function is fired, check where the player is and where the mouse click was. If the distance is greater then 120, then move the actor to where the mouse click was.

Did you guess it yet? If you did, you're amazing! If not, don't worry, I know things get a little daunting with Blueprints, but you'll get the hang of it - You're still amazing!

For those who didn't get it: Grab the "Location" pin of the "Break Hit Result" (Yes, I know it's already plugged into "Vector - Vector" but that's the wonders of Blueprints: You can plug most things into more then one input!) and plug it into the "Goal" of "Simple Move To Location".

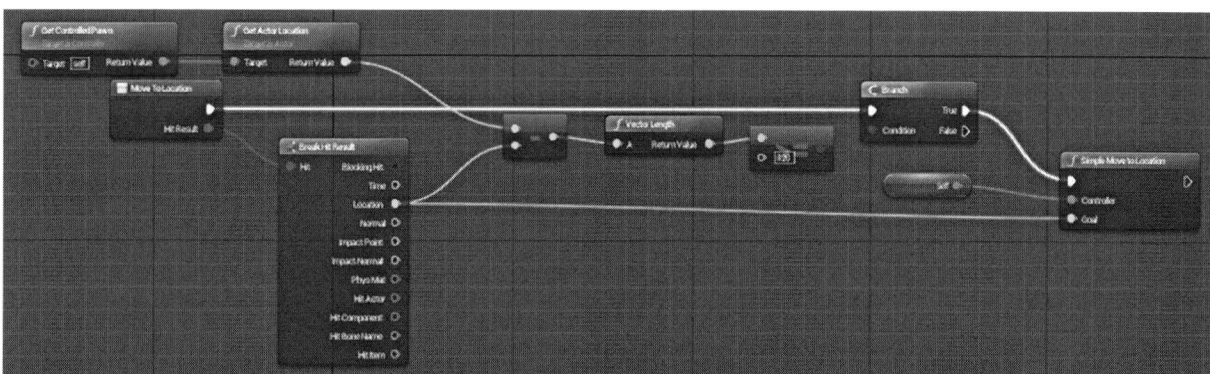

NOTE: This image will be hard to make out (Both in-print and on the e-book. The best way to view this image is to check it out on the website, In all it's high quality glory: http://www.kitatus.co.uk)

And that's all the code we need for this function. You made your first function: Great job!

Now it's been created, it's time to head into the Event Graph and make our function "LIVE" so to speak!

Player Controller Event Graph… Bring our Function to life!

Once the function has been created, it's time to head back into the Event Graph (The main code of our Blueprint). You may or may not have noticed that Events can't be fired with functions, which makes Event Graphs the key part of all Blueprint adventures!

To head back into the Event Graph, we can do it in one or two ways: By either using the tabs just above the blueprint area or use the "Variable Library" (By double clicking "Event Graph!")

So do whatever method you're more comfortable with and head back into the "Event Graph" now.

Before we continue, we need to learn about something in Unreal Engine 4 which we haven't touched yet: The "Project Settings". The reason we need to know about the project settings is because we're going to set-up a custom "Input Action", which will allow us to use the mouse button in-game.

So compile and save your blueprint and temporarily close it, heading back into your main Unreal Engine 4 view. Once you're back into the view of Unreal Engine where you see your scene in the centre, go up to the top navigation bar, which has "File, Edit, Window and Help".

Click Edit and go to "Project Settings".

This loads up the "Project Settings" windows. There's a whole load of information here, a lot of it we'll get to later. For now, use the left navigation pane to go to "Engine > Input".

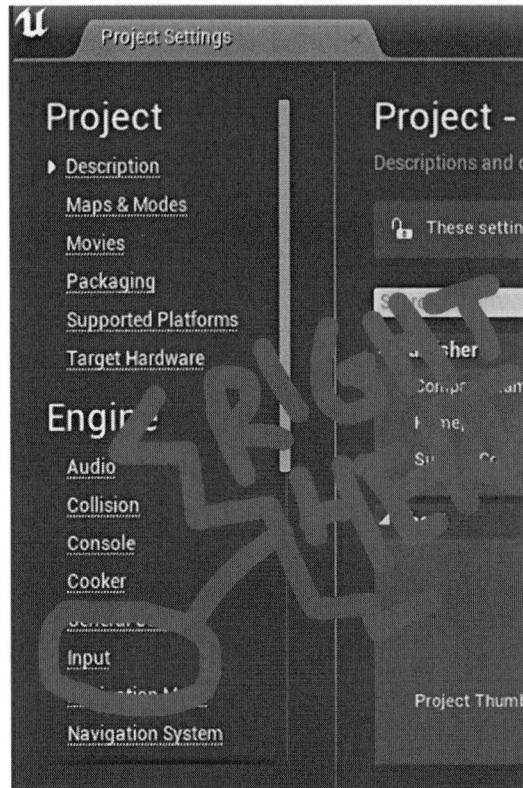

Click the "Input" button to head into the "Input" tab.

While in the "Input" tab, head to the "Bindings" section and select the "+" sign next to "Action Mappings" to create a new "Action".

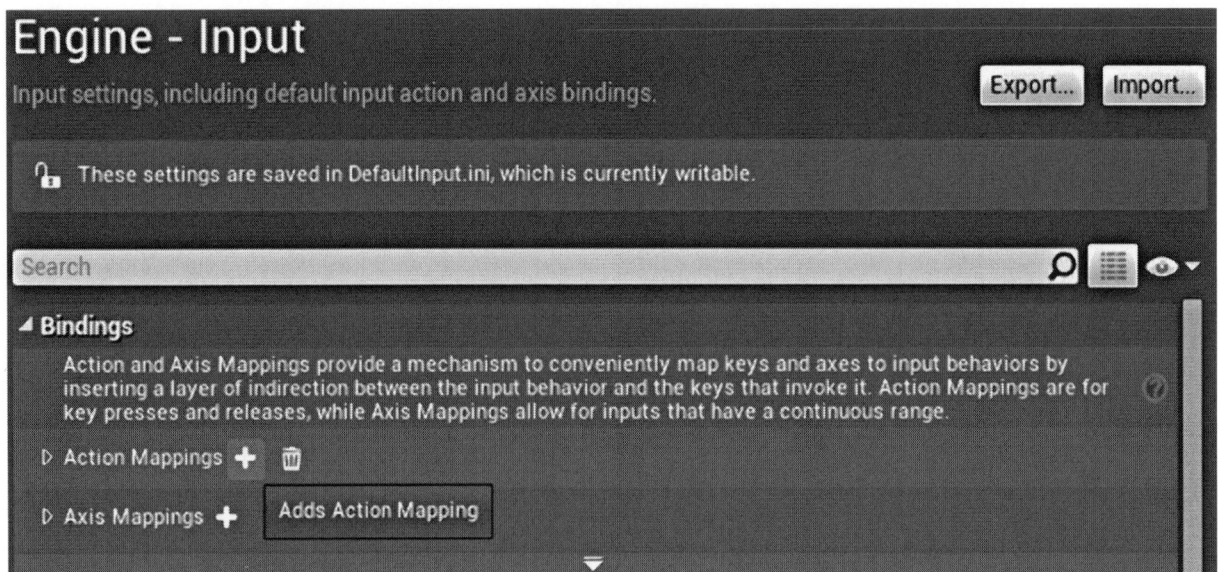

Once you've pressed it, head a little to the left, where you see the empty right-hand arrow just before "Action Mappings". Press this arrow to reveal the current Action mappings: Jump & "NewActionMapping_0".

Rename "NewActionMapping_0" to "LeftMouseClick".

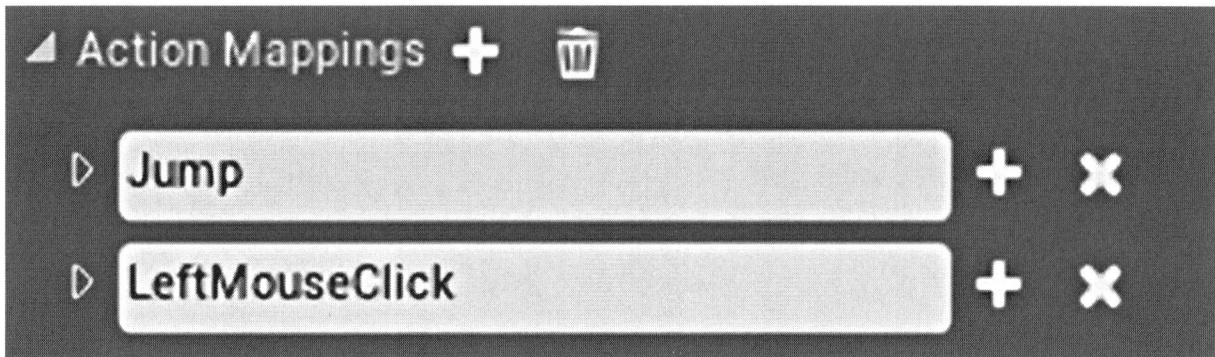

Just like we did before, see where there's a hollow arrow to the left of "LeftMouseClick"? Click that and you'll be presented with a button to set the button of this InputAction. If you need more buttons, just hit the "+" next to "LeftMouseClick".

For now, set "None" to Left Mouse Button. This sets "LeftMouseClick" to Left Mouse Button which is exactly what we want and exactly what we need.

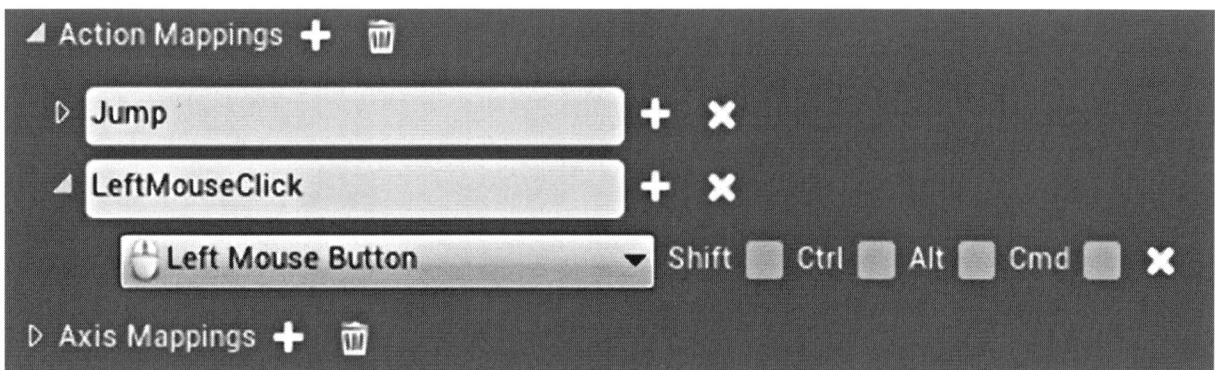

You are now free to close "Project Settings" for now. Be sure to go to "File > Save".

Once you've saved, head back into PC_PointChar (By double clicking the blueprint in the Content Browser).

When in the Event Graph, use the CBL to create "LeftMouseClick" (Or whatever you named the input action, and as if by magic, the input you just created with be created as an event. How nifty!

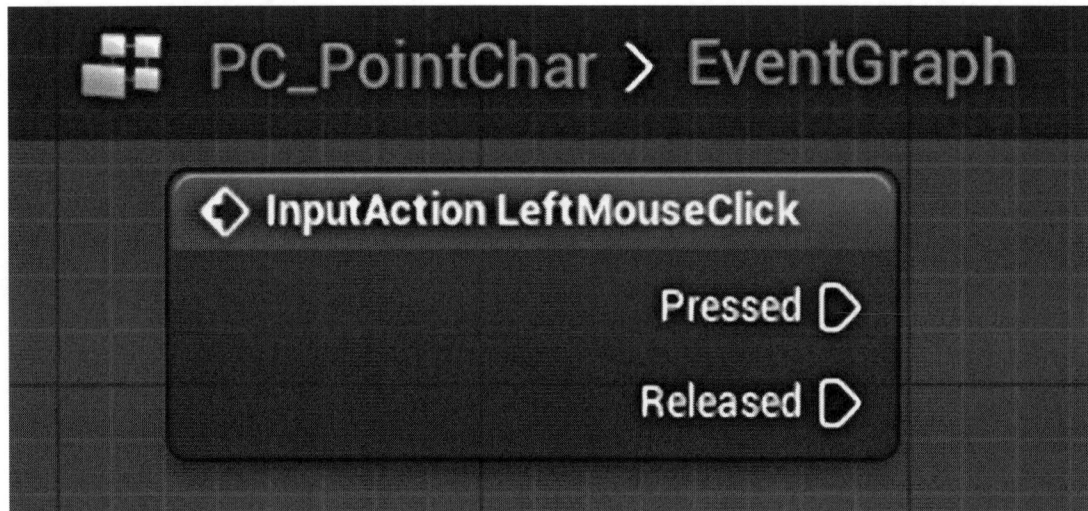

We're now going to create a "Gate" node, so go ahead and use the Compact Blueprint Library to create one.

A "Gate" node is pretty hard to explain, but I'm going to try my best to break it down into a simple form:

A gate is like a traffic light. You use execution pins to "Enter" the gate. This is like pulling up to the traffic light. You then use execution pins to determine if the gate is "Open" or "Closed", so image that Open means green light and Closed means red light.

Any code that is on the "Exit" of the gate will continue to fire until given the "Red light".

Hopefully this gives you an insight to what a gate is and does. If not, just hit me an email at: contact@kitatusstudios.co.uk and I'll try my best to explain in detail.

Alternatively, you can always check the Unreal Engine Documentation on their website.

You'll notice that I keep mentioning the documentation, this is simply because it's a gold-mine of information, just waiting for you to devour.

I'm sure some of you read the title and think "Man, that sounds lame!" but I honestly recommend you check it out - You'll learn lots of little (And big!) things that you'll wonder how you lived without. I mean, how do you think I learnt the knowledge to be able to write these books?

Back to our project. Our "Red light" and "Green Light" will be our mouse click. When the mouse button is pressed down, this will be our "Green" light and when the mouse is no longer pressed down, the theoretical traffic light will go "Red".

So connect the "Pressed" execution of "InputAction LeftMouseClick" to the "Open" of Gate and the "Released" execution pin to "Close".

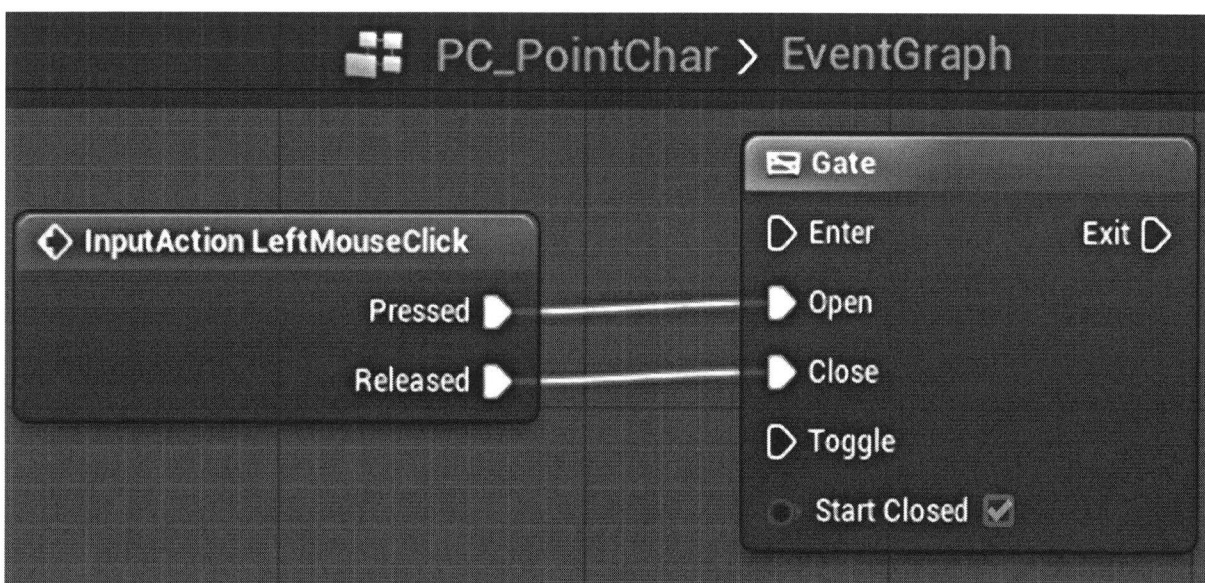

Now it's time to bring our function in!

You can either click and drag your function in from the "Variable Library" or use the Compact Blueprint Library and type in "MoveToLocation" (The choice is yours!), so go ahead and bring the Function into your Event Graph... Now!

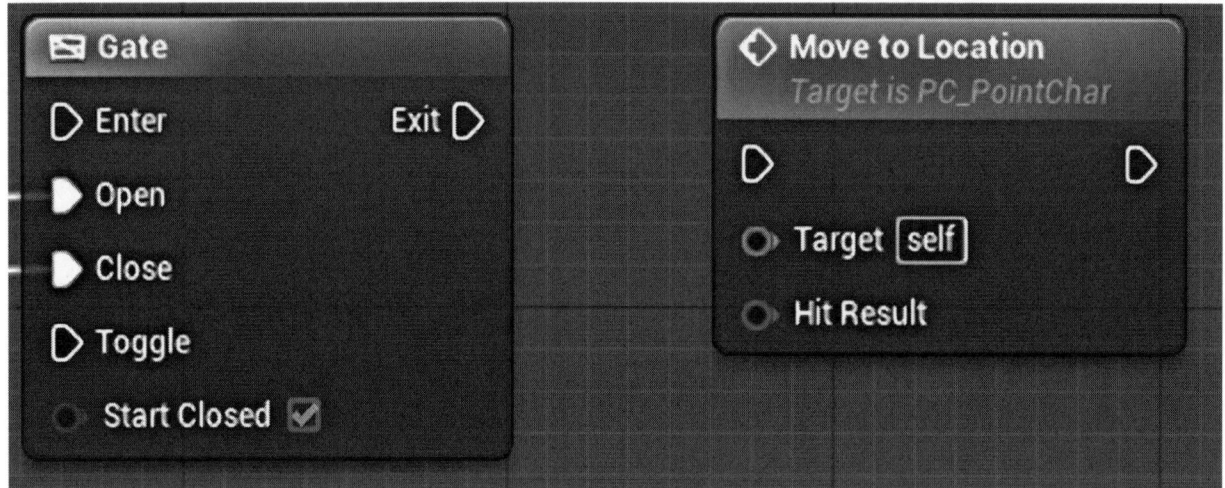

Connect the "Exit" of "Gate" to the Input node of "Move to Location".

Remember how we have the "Hit Result" as an input to our function? Now we have to create a node to connect to that input!

As it's the mouse cursor we have to trace the hit from, go ahead and open up the CBL, typing in "Get Hit" and selecting "Get Hit Result Under Cursor by Channel".

Go ahead and connect that straight into the "Hit Result" input of the "Move to Location" node.

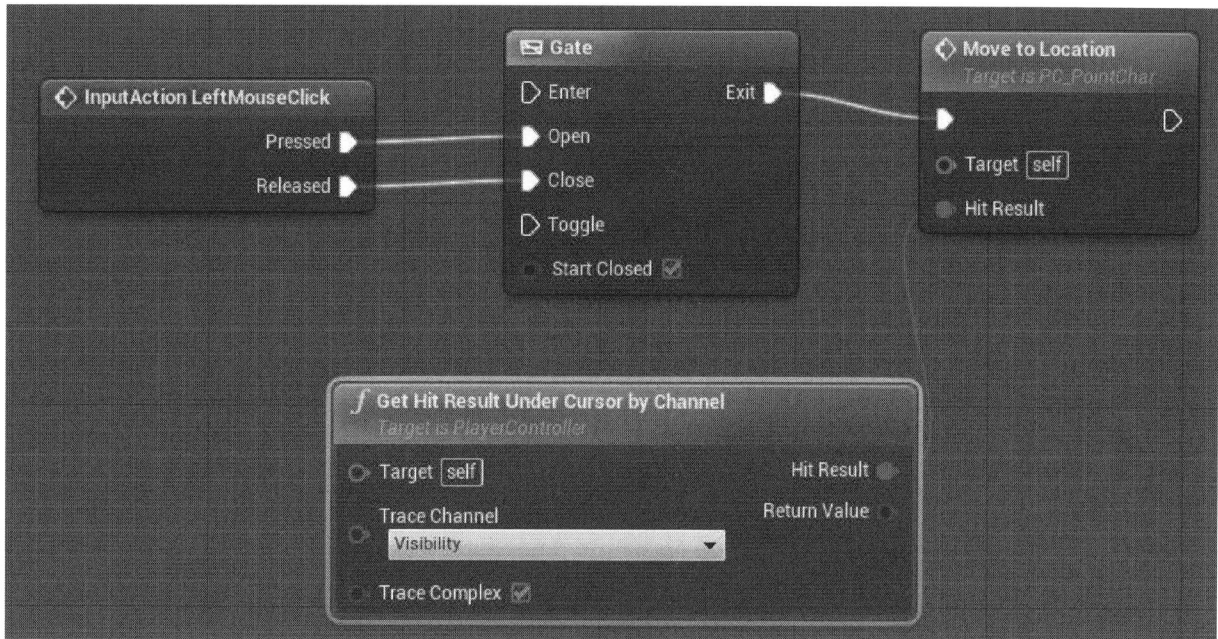

We're almost done with this Blueprint. We have most of the ingredients, but we're missing one key ingredient:

When I originally mentioned the "Gate", I used a traffic system with a car as an example. When you look at the script we currently have, doesn't it feel like there's something... Missing? That's right! Our theoretical car is missing to "Enter" the gate.

So what is going to be our car? Every single frame. Every frame we want to check if we can execute our function or if it's locked away behind a gate... literally.

Do you remember what we can use to get every frame? That's right - A Tick Event!

Go ahead and use the Compact Blueprint Library to create an "Event Tick" and connect it to the "Enter" of the gate.

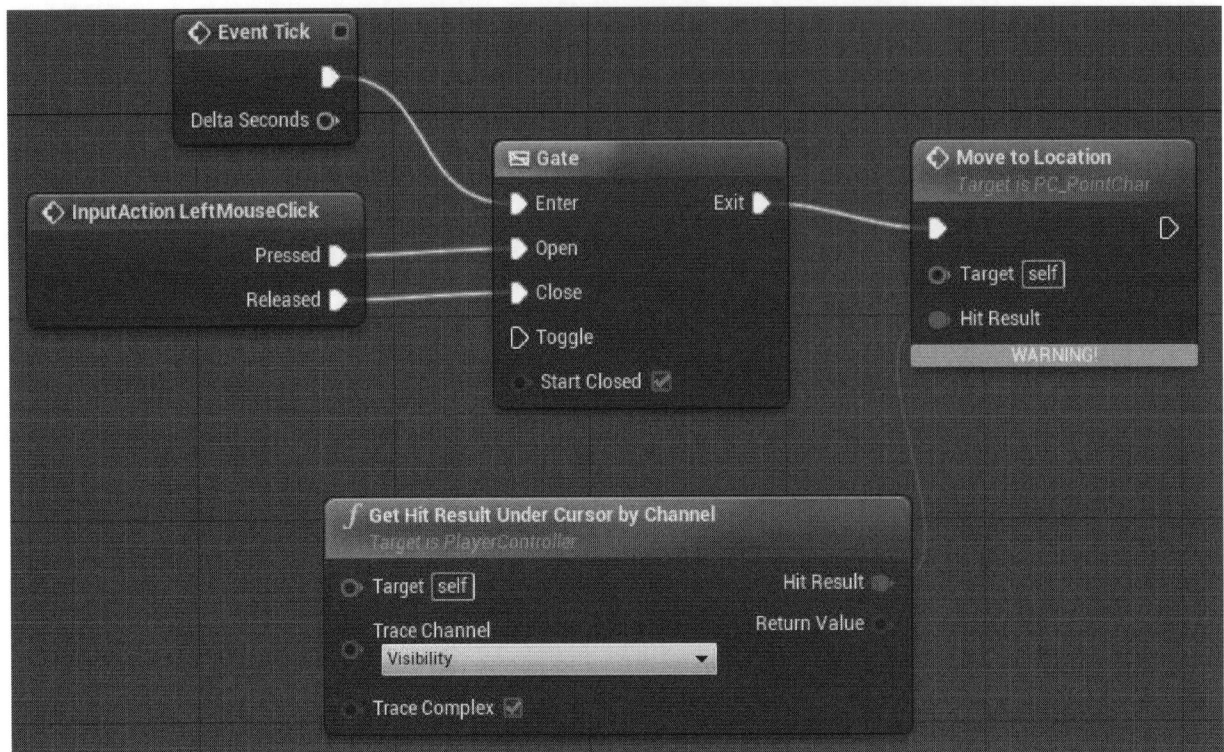

So let's break the code down real quick: Every frame (If we've got 60 frames per second, then this will be 60 times a second!), we're checking if the mouse button has been pressed down. If it has then we'll send the player on a path to where the mouse click was. If it hasn't then we won't tell the player to move where the mouse is anymore.

Nice work! Now compile and save and you're free to close the blueprint and head back into the main Unreal Engine window.

My mouse…. Doesn't move the Player?!

If you have already gone ahead and previewed the game, you'll notice that the mouse isn't working. Don't get annoyed - Yes, we have put the code in but we're missing some key settings in order for our code to work:

1. We need to set our "PlayerController" that we just created and refined as the "Active" playercontroller

2. We need to set up a Navmesh (More on this in a minute!)

First, we're going to go ahead and set-up the PlayerController to become the "Active" PlayerController.

Don't worry, it's not as hard as it sounds!

Go ahead and head into the "Content Browser" once again (Into the folder where your PC_PointChar" is located!) and create a new Blueprint.

This time, when "Pick Parent Class" opens up, select "Game Mode" to create a blueprint based on the "Game Mode" template.

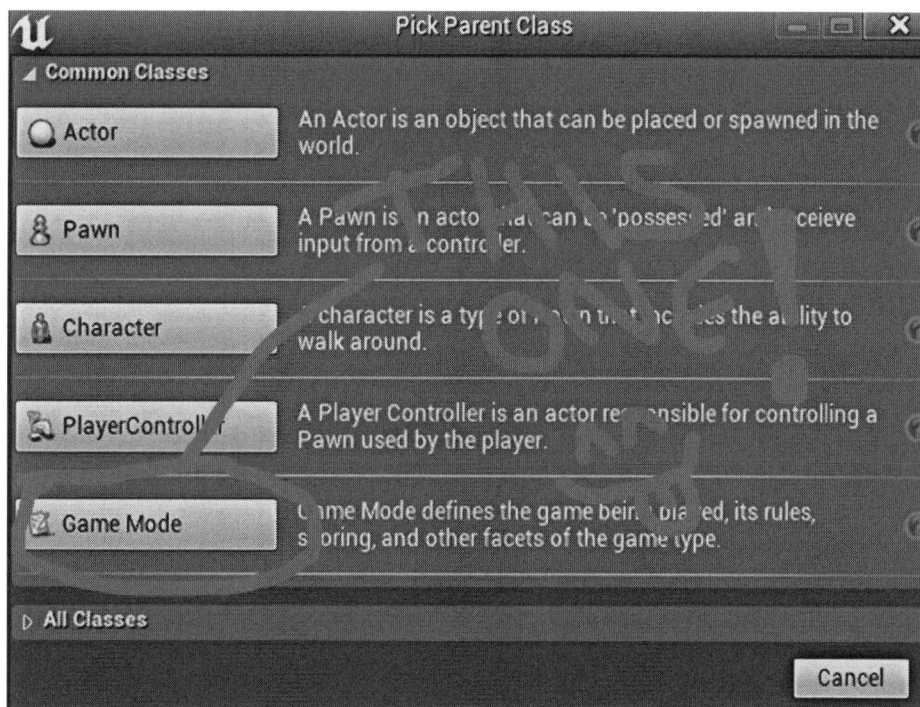

Don't worry though; This Blueprint doesn't actually require any code. It simply requires us to change one or two settings inside!

So name the Game Mode blueprint: GM_ArtOfBP (Or something along those lines!). Once you've named the Game Mode blueprint, double-click it to open it up.

You'll load up into the components tab, but as this is a Game Mode blueprint (And not an actor .etc), this Blueprint doesn't need any component editing.

A few of you will immediately go to head into the "Graph" tab (By using the navigation ribbon on the top-right) but this isn't what we need to do. We DO need to use the navigation ribbon but it's not the "Graph" tab we'll be using today. Instead, use the navigation ribbon on the top-right and head to the "Defaults" tab.

At first glance, this tab looks very confusing but don't worry, it's super-simple to use.

Take a look at the section near the top called "Classes". You'll see that it has five sections labelled:

- Default Pawn Class
  - HUD Class
- Player Controller Class
  - Spectator Class
  - Game State Class

Each of these sections have a dropdown button with a value already filled in. Remember how I told you that using this Blueprint was simple?

All we have to do is set the Player Controller class to "PC_PointChar" (By clicking the grey box with "PlayerController" in it!) and set the Default Pawn Class to "MyCharacter" (Instead of "DefaultPawn").

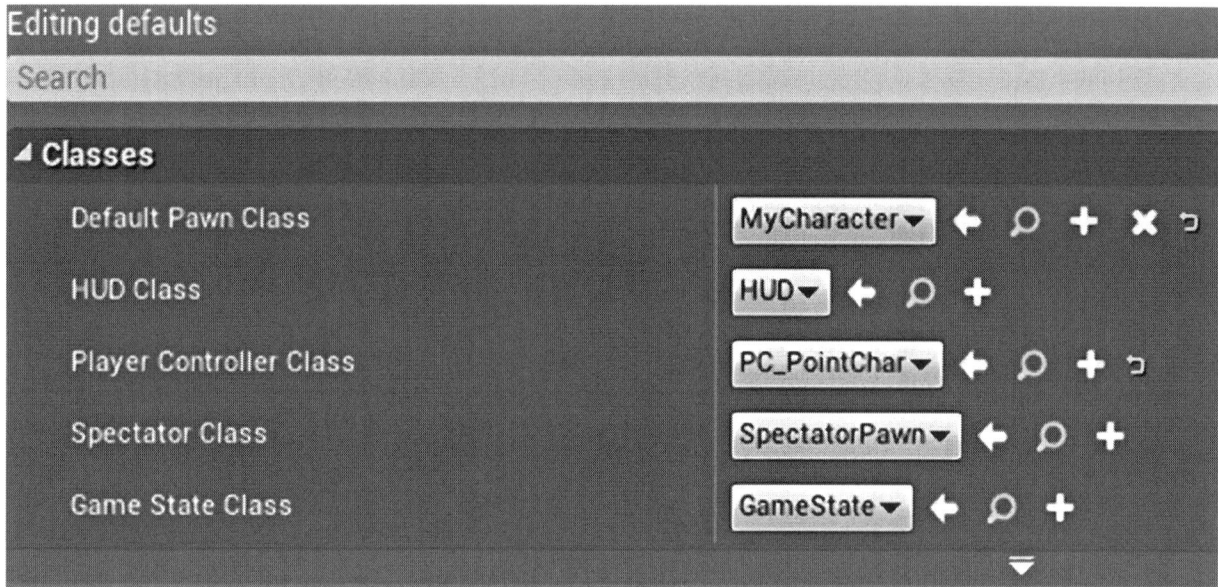

… And that's literally all we have to do to this Blueprint. Be sure to compile and save it. Once you've done that, it's now time to "Set" it as the "Active" GameMode, so close this Blueprint and head back into the main Unreal Engine 4 window.

GameMode… Activate!

Remember how we opened up the Level Blueprint? That's right, we used that nice Blueprint button just above the scene view. I bet you're wondering: Why the heck is he bringing this up now?!

Well… That's because we need to head to that Blueprint menu! Go ahead and press the Blueprints button. If you've forgotten where it is, it's just above your Scene view in the main Unreal Engine window and is in between: Settings and Matinee.

So click the Blueprint button now (If you have already) and select "GameMode: Edit MyGame" (Under the "Project Settings" category).

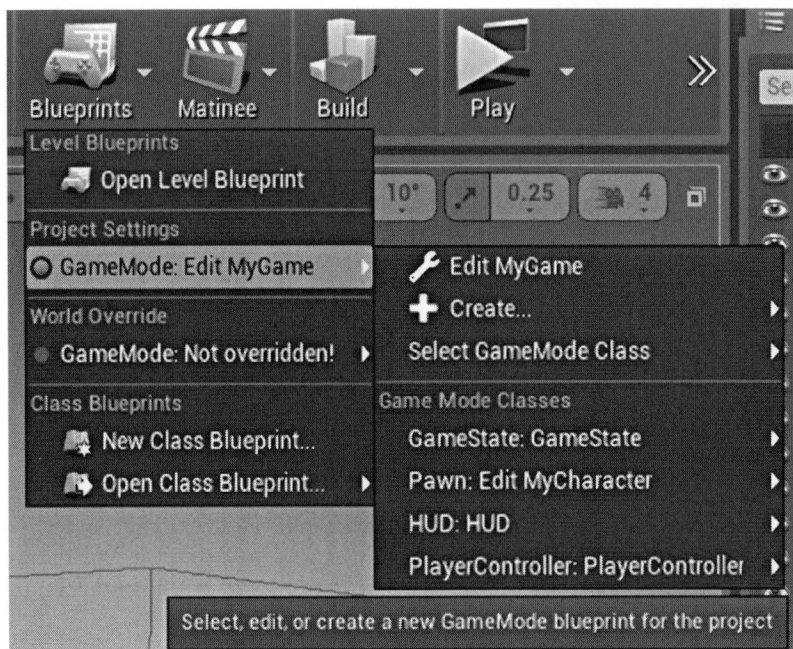

Within this menu, select "Select GameMode Class" and then select your "GM_ArtOfBP" (Or whatever you call yours!)

We've now set the GameMode that we created as the GameMode to use in-game. If you test your project now, you'll notice... Nothing has changed.

This is because of a certain node we've used in our Player Controller: The Simple Move to Location node. This node is pretty important to what we wanted our code to do (Move the player to where the arrow is clicked!), so deleting it is out of the question. Instead, there's one thing we have to notice about the node before we can move on.

Nav... Mesh?!

Some of the more keen-eyed readers here may have noticed when creating the node with the CBL that it was housed in a category called "AI". This is because the node was originally created to move AI (Which stands for artificial intelligence, often more commonly referred to as computer-controlled characters AKA the enemy!) to locations specified.

Using the node in the way we have is using the code in a different way that it was originally intended to be used - But don't worry, we can add something to our project to make the node work!

We're now going to create a NavMesh. This is something that we'll cover in more detail in a future book (An A.I focused book!), but for now, here's what you NEED to know:

NavMesh stands for Navigation Mesh and it tells the computer controlled characters where they can and can't go in your in-game world.

In order to create a NavMesh, you need to create a NavMesh bounds volume, which can be created from the "Modes" toolbox.

To use this tool, drag the "NavMesh Bounds" into the editor, just like you did with your box BSPs (To create the walls) and your Trigger Volumes. Once in your scene, re-size / re-scale the NavMesh Bounds using the "geometry edit" tools (Again, just like you did with the BSPs and Trigger Volumes) so it fills all the walkable floor in your scene (And any other walkable surfaces!)

So go ahead and do this now. Head into your "Modes" toolbox in the top-left of your editor and use the "Search Classes" function to find: Nav Mesh Bounds Volume.

Bring into your scene and in re-size it (Using them geometry edit tool!) so it covers all of your floor of your map.

Once you've created your NavMesh, you're almost ready to rock and roll! We now need to "Build" it!

Remember how I said a while back (Around page 60!) that pressing the "Build" button builds lighting and other settings?

(The exact quote was: Clicking the building image will "Auto-Build", which means the project will build the current lighting, as well as other settings in which we'll cover in the future.)

Well the Nav Mesh is an example of one of these settings! With NavMesh, you only need to build once for it to become "Active" and in the world. Once you've built it into your map, it'll create a "Recast NavMesh" object in your scene, which you can use to update the NavMesh at anytime!

So go ahead and click that shiny "Build" button now! If you've forgotten where it is, feel free to skip back to around page 60 or alternatively, just look above your scene view (To the right of the "Blueprints" button).

Your map will take a moment or two to build.

When the build has completed, you'll see… nothing different. Don't worry, the NavMesh is now working (Well, it should be!) but we need to find out if it's working and where in the map we've missed out / we don't the player to go to!

So how do we see it? Simple! Click inside your scene view and press "P" on your keyboard. Once you've done that, you should see a green layer of… green all over your floor! (Or maybe red if you didn't set the NavMesh up correctly!)

If you see all green? Excellent! If it's red? You need to use the geometry edit tool on the NavMesh Bounds to make sure all the floor is covered with the NavMesh Bounds volume!

So the Nav Mesh has been built, the PlayerController we have created (And the custom GameMode too!) are all set and active. So what's left to do? Nothing!

Go ahead and try your project out! You'll notice that it's super hard to find your mouse cursor but clicking somewhere in the world (As long as it's far enough from the player!) will get the player to move to that location!

Great work, you're doing excellent!

We've just now got to fix that problem where the mouse is invisible. We could do this in one of two ways: Either by showing the mouse itself or creating something in the in-game world that will show the player where the character will move to!

As the second option sounds way cooler (And cooler = better here at Kitatus HQ!), we're going to sort that out now!

So THAT'S where I was going!

First things first, click IN your scene and press "P" again to get rid of the green all over your floor. It's handy but extremely distracting!

Gone? Awesome!

Now head into your "Content Browser". Remember when we first originally created the project all that time ago now? When we first created the project, we selected "With Starter Content". This means we have some handy meshes / objects we can use for prototyping!

Head into your Content Browser and navigate to: "GAME > Starter Content > Architecture".

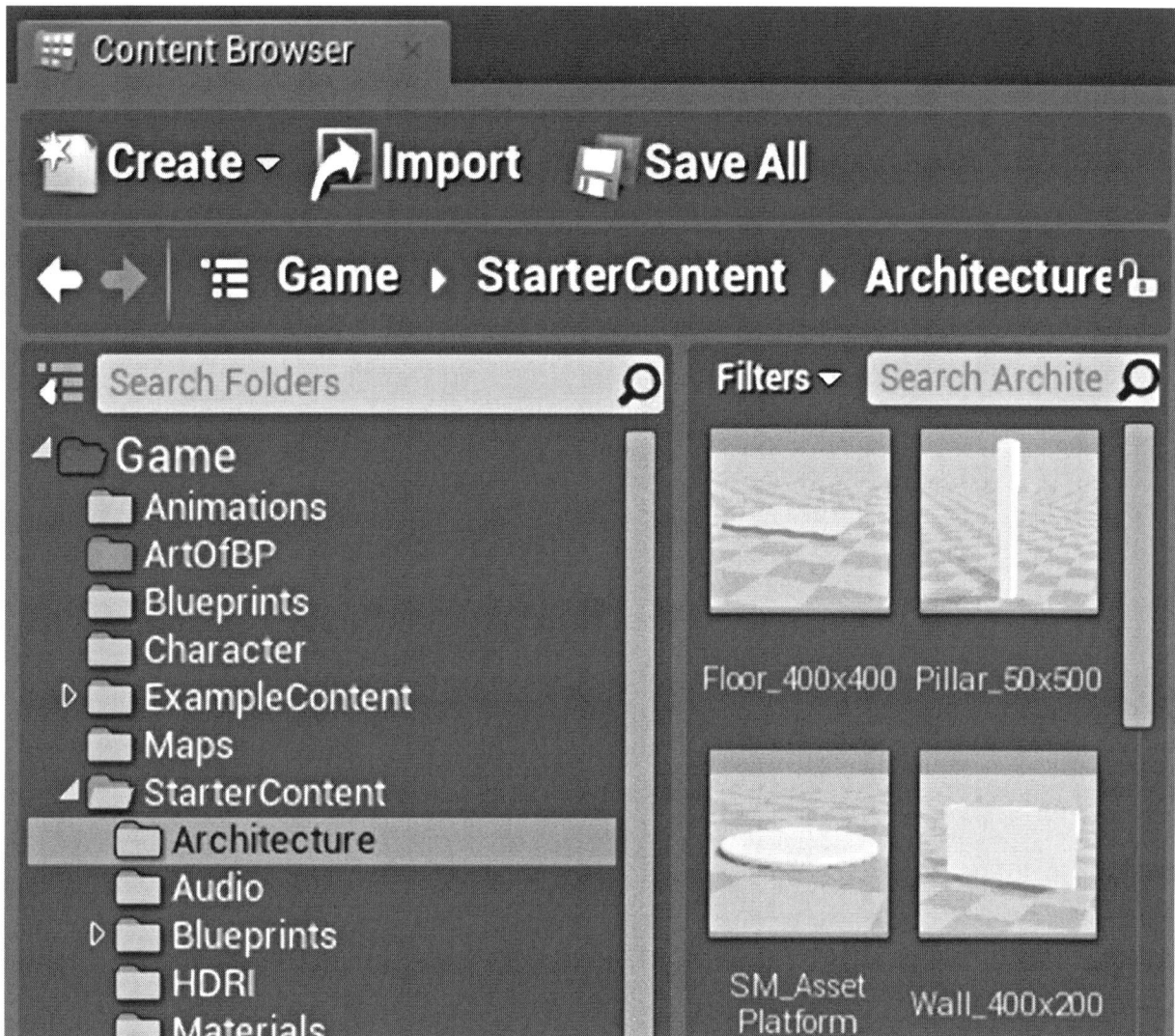

Now you're here, do you see the UFO-looking disc (Called SM_AssetPlatform)? Click it and drag it into the scene! This is going to be our mouse locator!

Before we can get to work adding some magic to this UFO-looking thing, we need to set a few of its properties! So: Click the newly created SM_AssetPlatform from the scene and you'll see it's details on the bottom-right hand side of your screen:

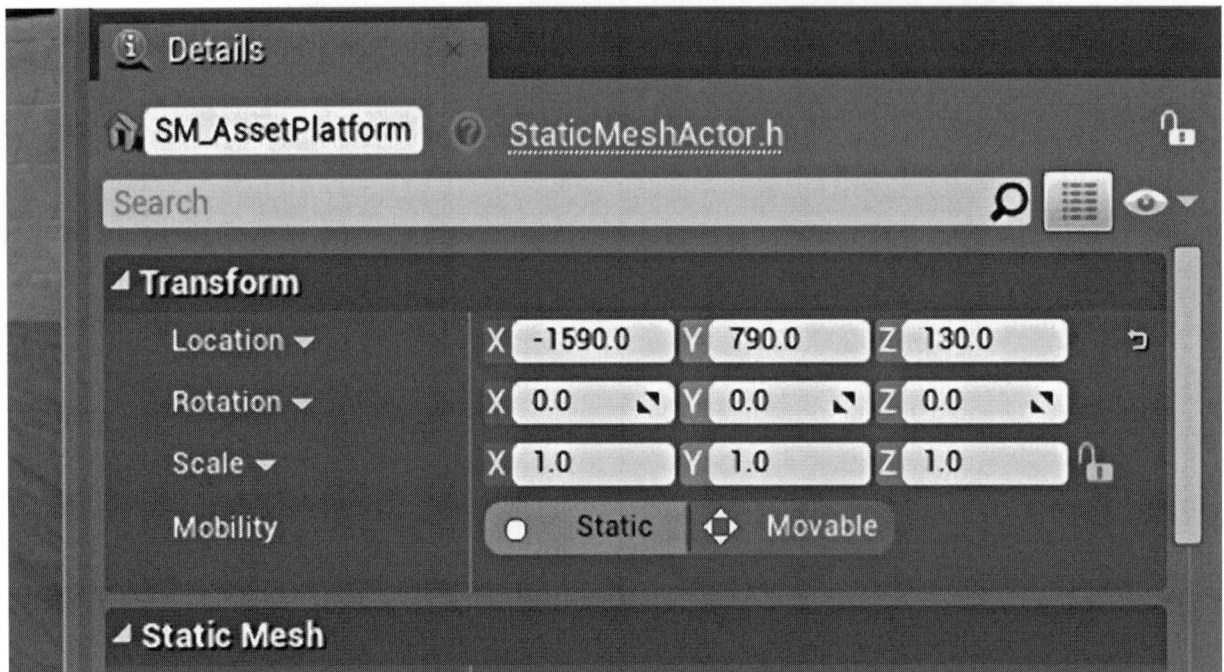

The first thing you're going to want to do is set "Mobility" from "Static" to "Movable".

What does this mean? Exactly what it says on the tin: Static means "This object doesn't move, so don't let it!" whereas "Movable" means: "This object might move, so let it move!"

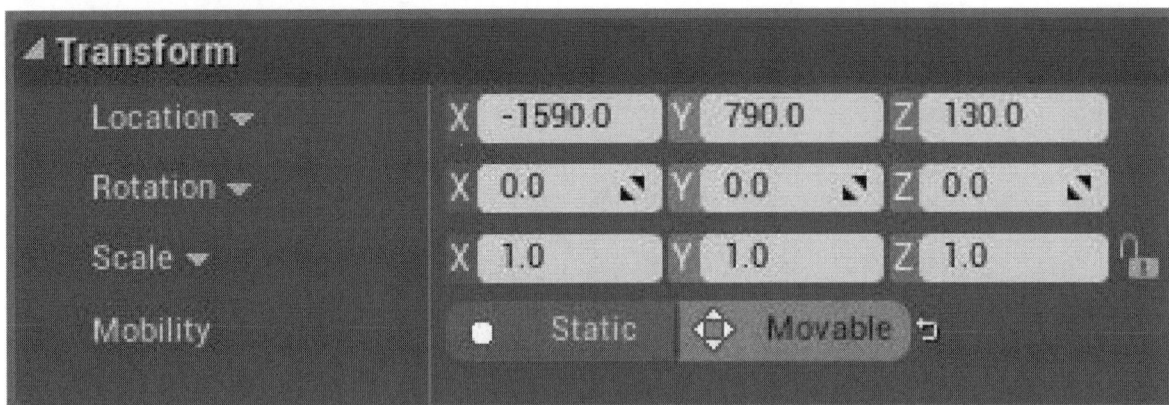

Scroll down the details panel some more until you get to the section called: "Lighting".

In this section, set "Cast Shadow" to false by clicking the tick-box (Make sure it's empty!)

Once you've unset "Cast Shadow", scroll down the details panel a little more until you get to the category named: "Collison".

You'll notice at the moment, it's set to "BlockAll". We're going to have to change that!

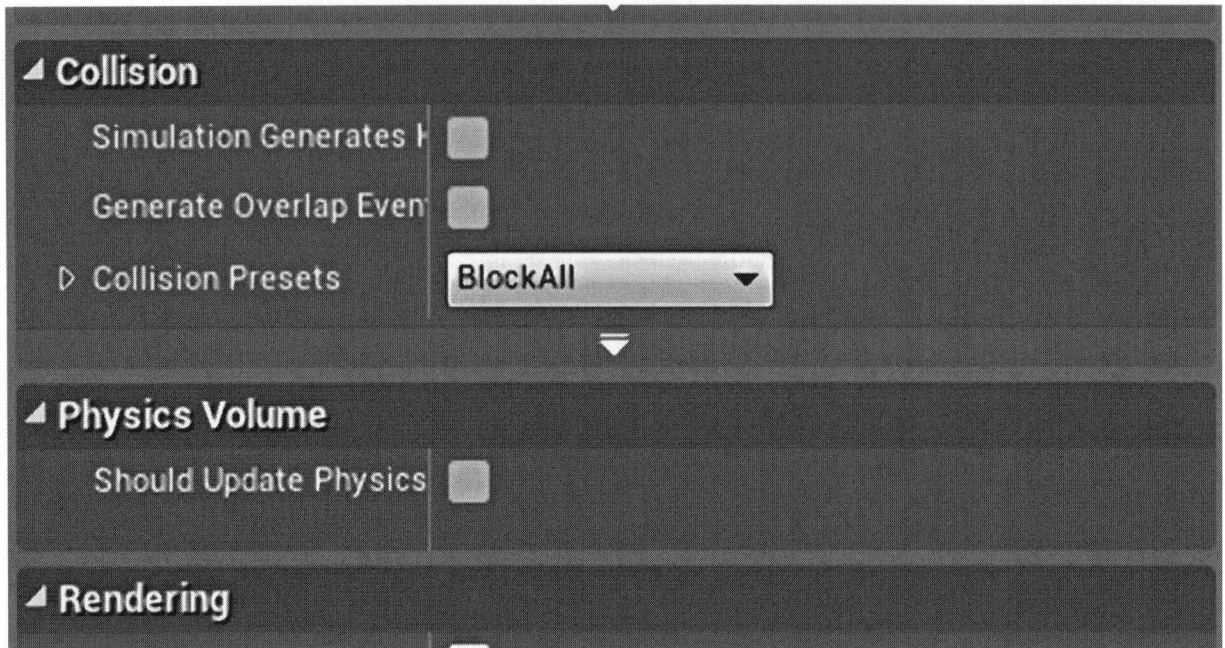

As we don't want this little UFO-thing to have No Collision whatsoever, click the dropdown button that currently says "BlockAll" and change it to "NoCollision"!

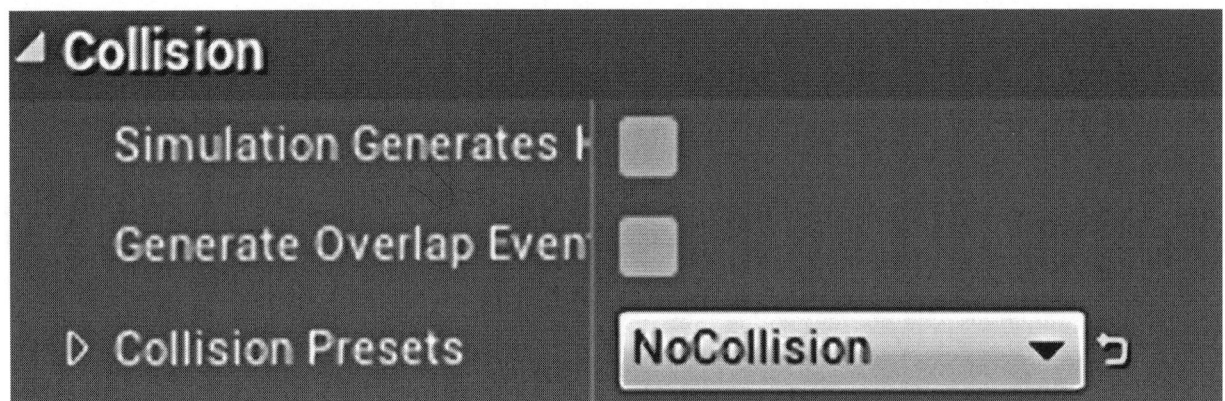

Now would be a great time to save your project via File > Save All!

Once you've saved, click the UFO ("SM_AssetPlatform") in your scene once again and head into the Level Blueprint (With "SM_AssetPlatform" selected in the scene!)

Now, we've covered what all of the nodes we are about to create do, so we're going to pick up the pace here for the rest of the chapter. If you have any questions, flip back a few chapters and you'll find the answers to your questions already answered!

Within the Level Blueprint, create two nodes: "Get Player Character" and "Get Player Controller".

From the "Get Player Character" node's "Return Value Pin", create a "Get Actor Location" and connect it to the "Get Player Character Node" and create a "Vector - Vector" node and connect the output of "Get Actor Location" to the top-left input of "Vector - Vector".

Now, from "Get Player Controller", Click the "Return Value" pin and drag to the right (Which will open the Compact Blueprint Library). When it opens, type in "Get Hit Result" and select "Get Hit Result Under Cursor By Channel".

Next… Open up the CBL and untick "Context Sensitive". Now type in "Break Hit Result" to create the node with the same name. Once the node has been created open up the CBL again and re-tick "Context Sensitive"!

Connect the "Hit Result" from "Get Hit Result Under Cursor By Channel" to the "Hit" of "Break Hit Result".

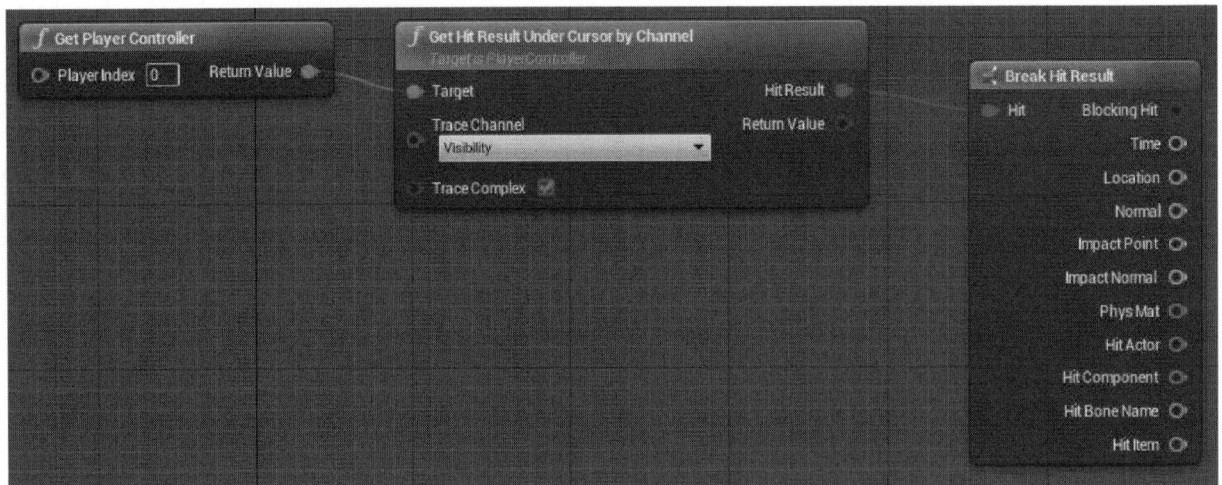

Remember the "Vector - Vector" node we created? Connect the "Location" output of the "Break Hit Result" to the bottom-left input of the "Vector - Vector" node.

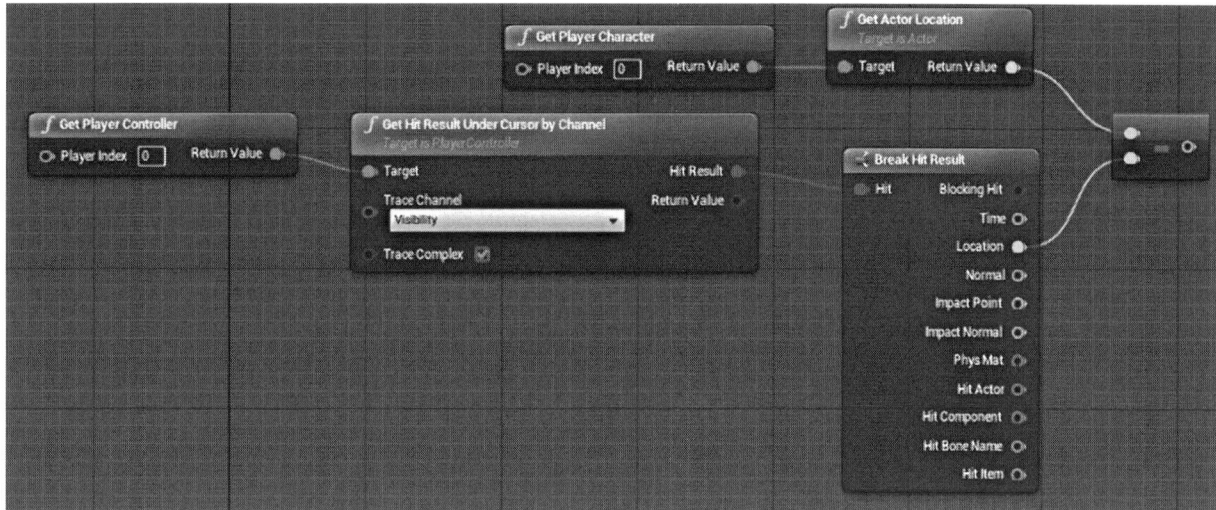

Is this looking a tad familiar? From the output of "Vector - Vector", create a "Vector Length" node and connect it to the output of "Vector - Vector".

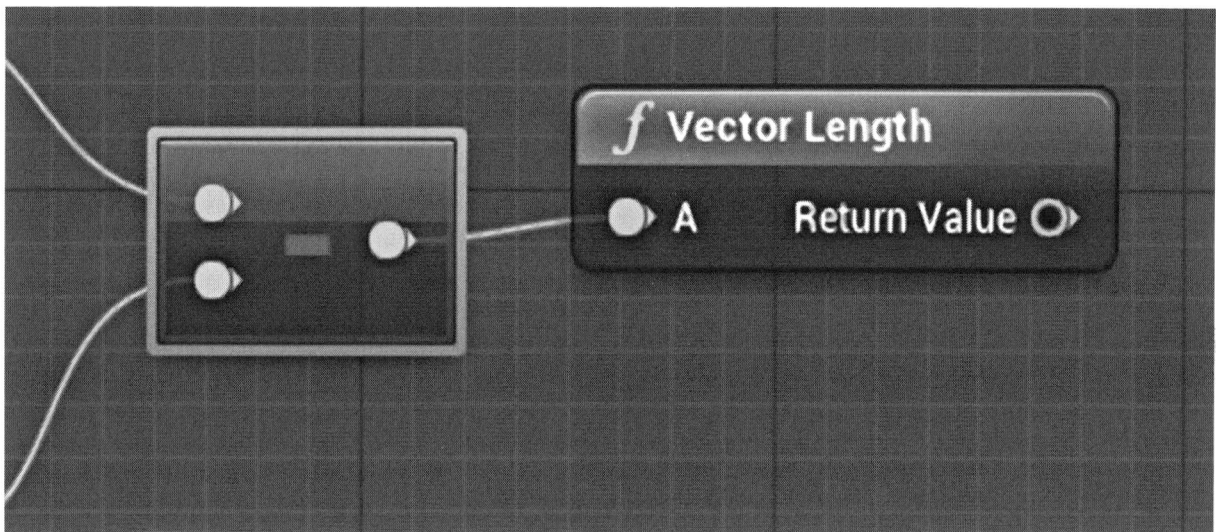

Now, Just like we did for the Function we created ages ago (See! Didn't you get the feeling of Deja vous?!), create a "Float >=" (Float more than or equal to) node and connect the output of "Vector Length" into the top-left input of the "Float >=" node.

Just like before, type in 120 manually into the bottom-left of the "Float >=" node (Or whichever number you assigned to the Function in the PlayerController!)

193

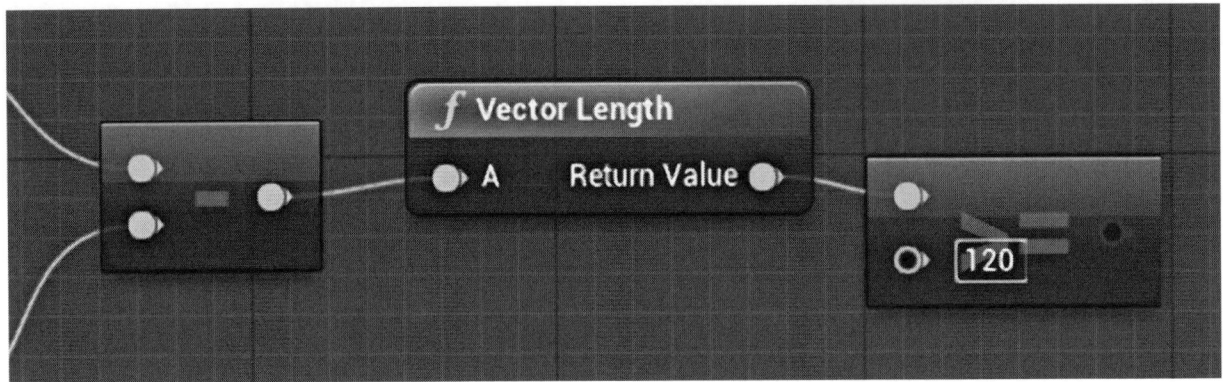

Now either hold B and click with your left mouse button or use the compact blueprint library to create a "Branch" node. Connect the output of "Float >=" to the "Condition" of the "Branch" node.

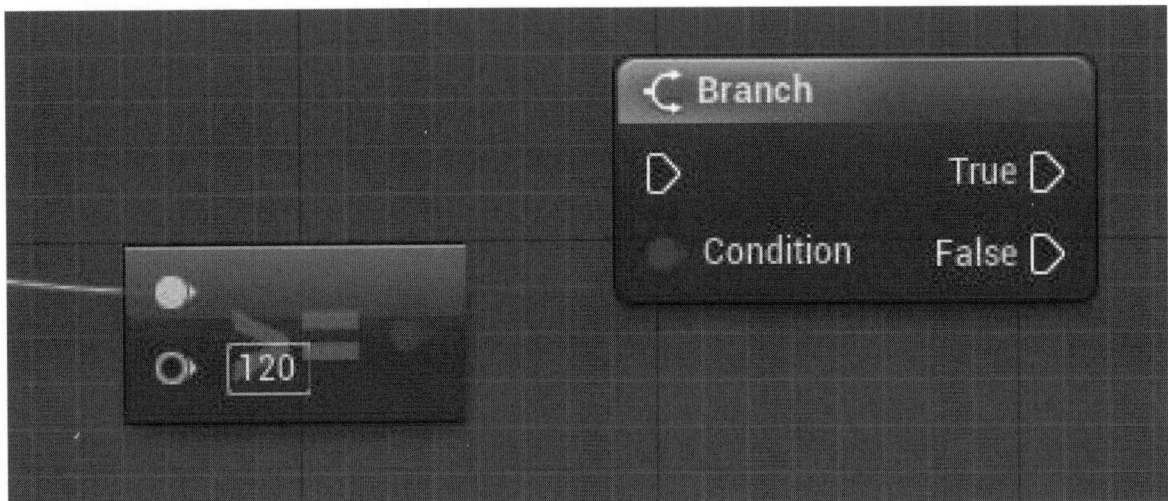

(Don't worry, we'll sort the input for "Branch" in a little while!)

This is the part where things differ to the function that we created in the PlayerController.

We could have copy and pasted the code from the function into this Level Blueprint but there's a specific reason why we didn't: To help you learn. Repeating things over and over helps set it in your mind!

Anywho, going back to our code, We're now going to create the last bit of code to make our UFO move to the mouse location!

Create a "Set Actor Hidden in Game" node via the Compact Blueprint Library. Depending on how you do it, the "SM_AssetPlatform" may be connect to the "Target" input of the node.

If it hasn't, don't worry, just open the CBL again and type in "Add Reference" and select "Add Reference to SM_AssetPlatform". If it's not there, they quickly head back into your main Unreal Engine window and select it in the scene!

If you've had to create it manually, connect it to the "Target" input of "Set Actor Hidden In Game"!

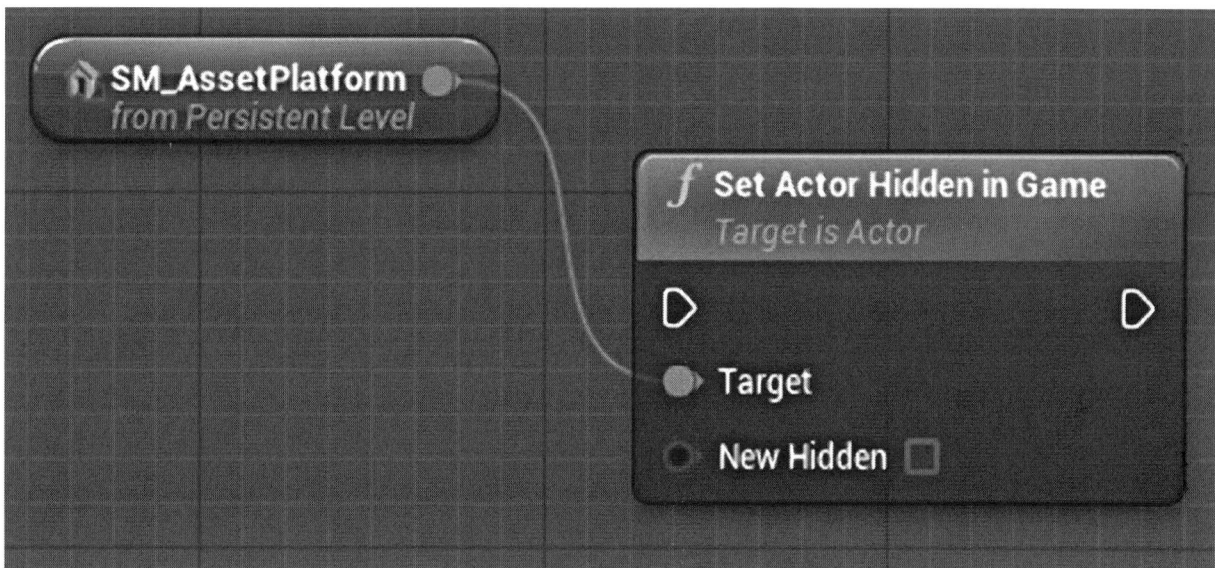

Do this twice so you have two "Set Actor Hidden in Game" nodes with "SM_AssetPlatform" connected to the input of both!

On the top "Set Actor Hidden in Game", see the empty tick box next to "New Hidden"? This translates to "Shall we hide this in-game?".

Set the top "Set Actor Hidden in Game" to true (By clicking the tick box) but leave the second "Set Actor Hidden in Game"'s "New Hidden" empty!

Connect the input of the top "Set Actor Hidden in Game" (The one with "New Hidden" marked as "True"!) to the "False" of the "Branch" node.

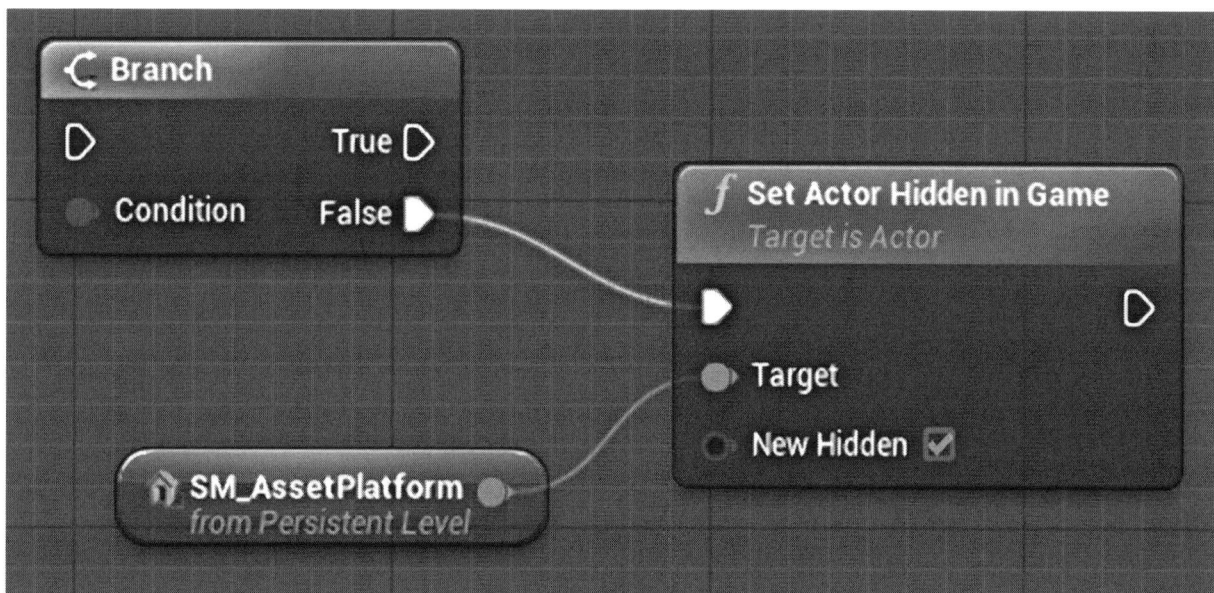

I'm sure you can guess where the other "Set Actor Hidden in Game" (The one with "Hidden" not ticked!) goes? That's right - Into the "True" of the "Branch" node!

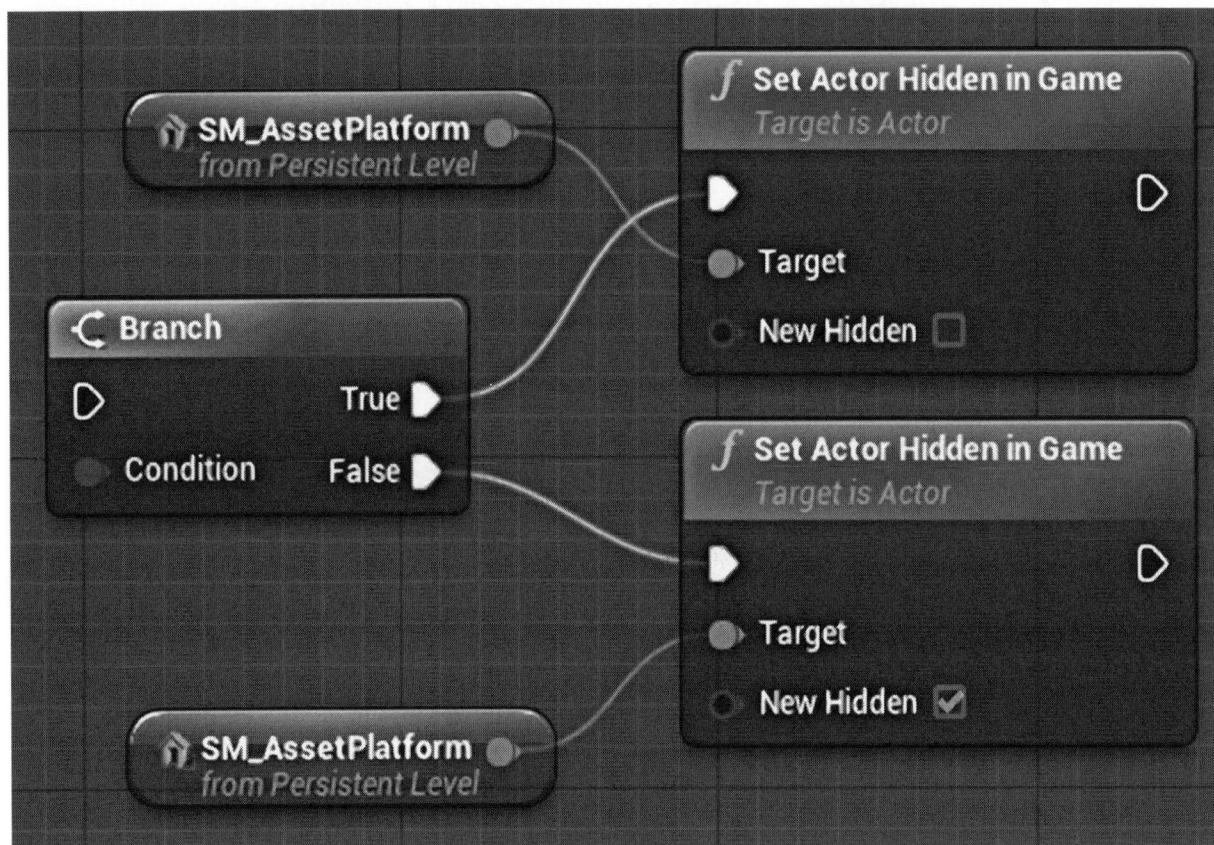

From the output execution pin of "Set Actor Hidden in Game" (The one that's connected to the "True" of the "Branch"!), create a "Set Actor Location" node.

Just like before, "SM_AssetPlatform" should be automatically connected to "Target". If it isn't, just add it in manually.

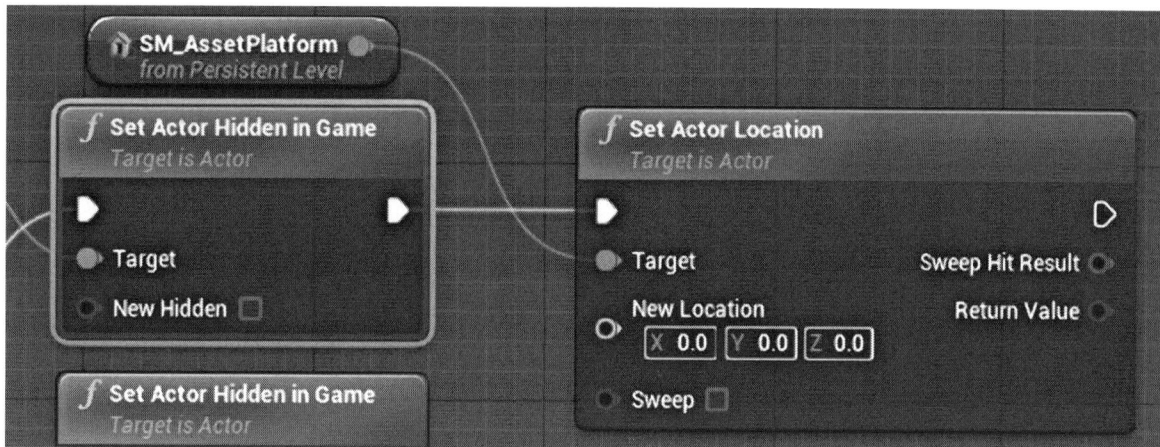

Remember the "Break Hit Result" node? Grab the "Location" output pin and drag it to the "New Location" of this "Set Actor Location" node (This will connect the two!).

Our code is almost finished! Let's take a really quick breakdown of the code to figure out what is missing:

"Where is the mouse at the moment? Where is the player? How far is the distance between them both? Is it more then 120 units? Yes? Then set the "SM_AssetPlatform" to where the mouse is. No? Then hide "SM_AssetPlatform" from view and don't do anything!"

Notice anything missing from that? Give the code a little glance over and see if you can figure it out!

That's right, no event is triggering this code at the moment so the code simply isn't firing!

So what event do we need? Well, we need this code to constantly fire… So we need an Event Tick! Go ahead and create it now.

Connect it to the input execution pin of the "Branch"!

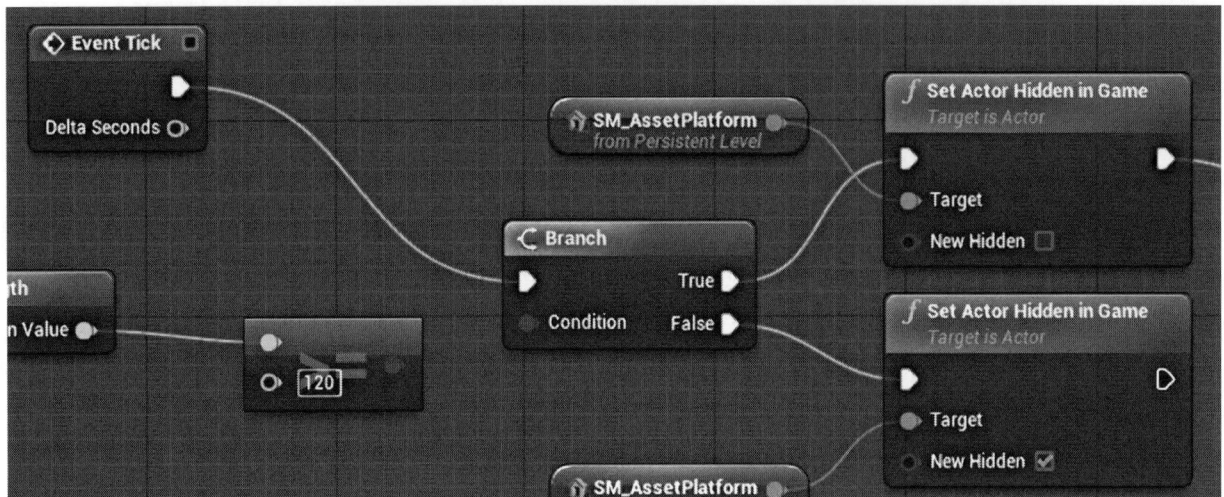

… And we're finished with this Blueprint!

Be sure to Compile it and then give the project a test, you'll see that it's now working as intended: The player can see where he (Or she!) will move when they click, and when they do eventually click…? Bam! They'll move to that location!

Great job. We're just over 200 pages in and you've already created something awesome! But even though it resembles something similar to a Point and Click game, we're not quite there yet.

The next step is to create doors to lock the player out of all the rooms. Once that's done, we can add goodies, puzzles and more to give them a goal and a mission! Everything we have done up until this point will be available with the rest of the project files over at http://content.kitatusstudios.co.uk or http://www.kitatus.co.uk so be sure to compare your current BPs to mine if yours isn't working correctly!

It's time for Lockdown!

Things are falling to place quite nicely!

We're now going to create doors that will lock / unlock when we want to! Sounds cool right?

For the sake of this book, we'll also be covering something extra: Converting BSP to real meshes!

If those terms are confusing, don't you worry:

BSP: Temporary geometry that sucks for performance but is great for quickly blocking out your level / worlds!

Mesh: A static mesh is a piece of geometry in the world (That consists of polygons). Think of them like lego pieces and that'll give you a great insight into what a mesh is: Something you can make that you can bring into Unreal Engine and use to build levels (Such as a wall, door or in some cases, a whole level!)

Earlier in the book we used BSPs to create our walls and we'll be using the same system to create our door. We'll then turn it into a "Static Mesh" and then turn it into a Blueprint, In which we'll add code to make it work however we like it to!

So let's not wait around, let's keep this train rolling!

We've talked about creating BSPs before, but here is a super quick run-down:

In your main Unreal Engine view, go to the "Modes" toolbox (Which is situated) in the top-left. While in this section (You might need to drag it down to make it bigger and show all the options!) , select the "BSP" menu option and click on the "Box" button and literally drag it into your scene.

Then use the "Geometry Edit" tool to change the shape of the box and mould it into whatever shape that you need.

I seriously recommend skimming back to where we talked in depth about all of this as we covered some crucial information (Such as don't EVER move your BSPs while in Geometry Edit mode as you'll accidently edit the shape of the object!)

For this tutorial, we are making a door. So move your BSP box to the doorway and use the "Geometry Edit" tool to literally fill the doorframe (Make sure it fills the doorway but doesn't spill OUT of the doorway!).

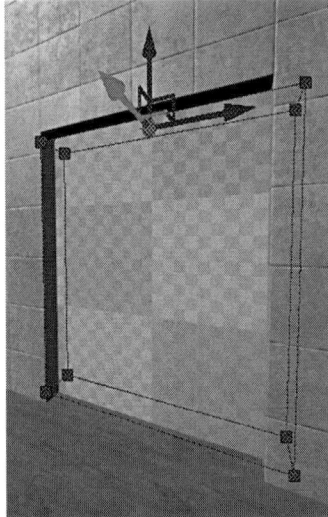

By the way, if you're wondering: Chill, we only have to create this once (When we convert it to a Blueprint, we can simply copy / paste the BP with the code already created to the other door frames)!

Once you're happy with the look of the BSP, come out of "Geometry Edit" mode and click on the BSP again (Make sure you're out of "Geometry Edit" first!).

Time for the magic: Convert the BSP into a Static Mesh!

Remember the details panel (In the right of the Unreal Engine window!). If you've selected the BSP correctly, You'll see categories such as "Brush Settings" .etc

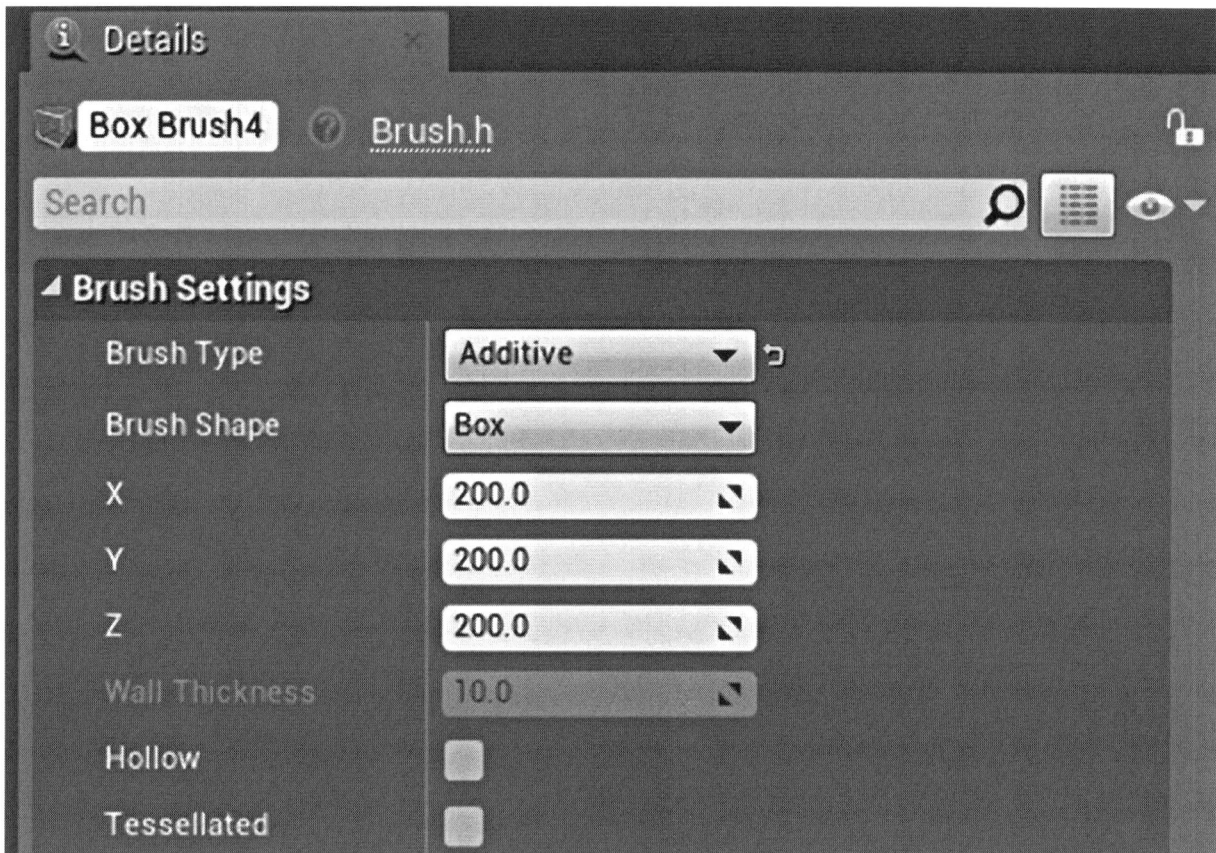

We're now going to convert this BSP into a Static Mesh. When you eventually work on your own projects, this will be a really handy feature. Here are a few reasons WHY:

1. Once you have converted a BSP to a Static Mesh (Or multiple BSPs to one Static Mesh!), you can export it into your favourite 3D program and create your final 3D art using the Static Mesh as a guide!
2. You can improve the performance of your test scenes by convert all those performance sucking BSPs into much "Performance-lighter" Static Meshes!
3. You can export the Static Mesh into a program like Substance Painter (Or 3DO / DDO) and create some amazing looking 2D art on-top of your 3D work!

These are just a fraction of things you can do JUST by doing the next few steps, so pay attention!

To turn this BSP into a Static Mesh, you'll have to find the "Hidden" options in the details pane. Take a look at the brush settings again:

Did you see it?

Look just underneath the "Hollow" and "Tessellated" options. See it now? That tiny, tiny arrow pointing down?

Click it and the "Hidden" options will reveal themselves like the thieves hideout in Aladdin.

Once you see the hidden options, you'll see the button we've been after: "Create Static Mesh"!

What are you waiting for? Click it!

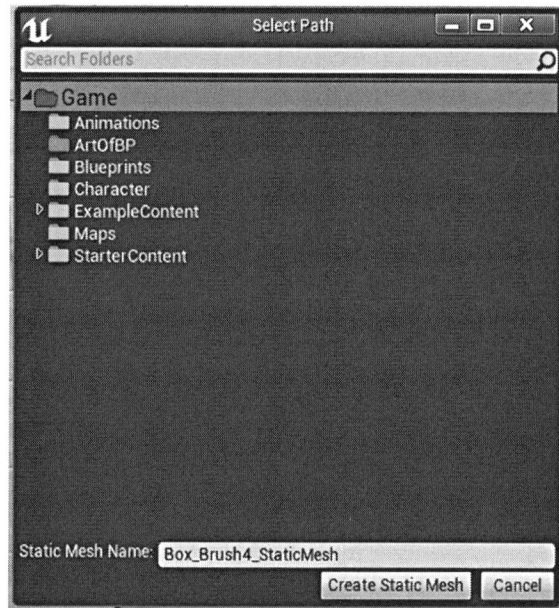

It will ask you where you want to put the Static Mesh (In the "Content Browser") and what you want to name it.

So we don't lose it, go ahead and select your "ArtofBP" folder and set the "Static Mesh Name" to: SM_Door.

Once you've got it ready, go ahead and click "Create Static Mesh" and you'll notice something odd about the door...

Invalid Lightmap?!

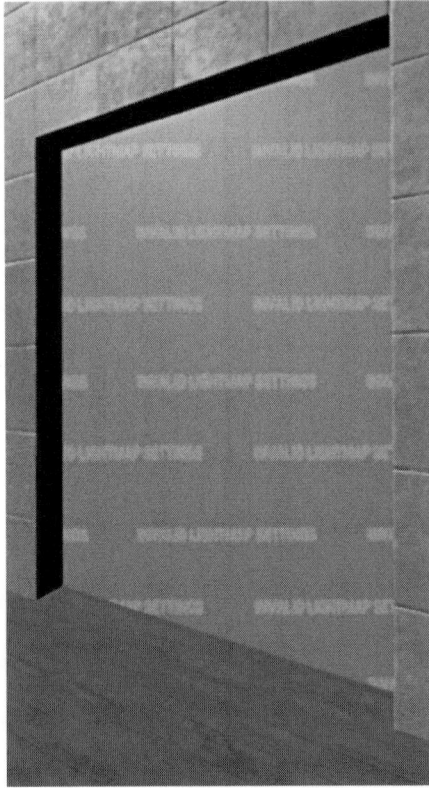

It's gone all grey. Not only that but it says "Invalid Lightmap Settings" all over it. Don't panic - This is normal. This always happens when you convert a BSP to a Static Mesh.

Why? - It happens because when the engine converts a BSP to a static mesh, it sets the "Lightmap Resolution" to 0.

What is a lightmap? A lightmap holds all the data to with… You guessed it, lighting. All of the how shadows work on the object as well as diffuse interreflection are all data that the lightmap contains.

Unreal Engine 4 - Being the sexy powerhouse that it is, calculates all of the lightmaps and such for us, saving us time and companies money.

However when bringing a BSP into the world of a Static Mesh, it doesn't know how detailed you want this lightmap. We don't need that much detail (Less is more performance!) but we still need some.

So we're going to set our Lightmass setting for the Static Mesh now.

Head over to your "Content Browser" and into your "ArtOfBP" folder (Or whatever folder you put your Static Mesh in!) and double-click your SM_Door to open up the Static Mesh editor.

You'll immediately notice that the Static Mesh editor looks both familiar but non-familiar at the same time. It has parts resembling what we've covered before, but with the way it combines this part it makes for a scary-looking window.

Don't worry though, as we've learnt a few times, Everything in Unreal Engine 4 looks more complicated then it actually is.

While in your Static Mesh editor, do you see the details panel on the right? Head over there now and scroll down to the section called: "Static Mesh Settings".

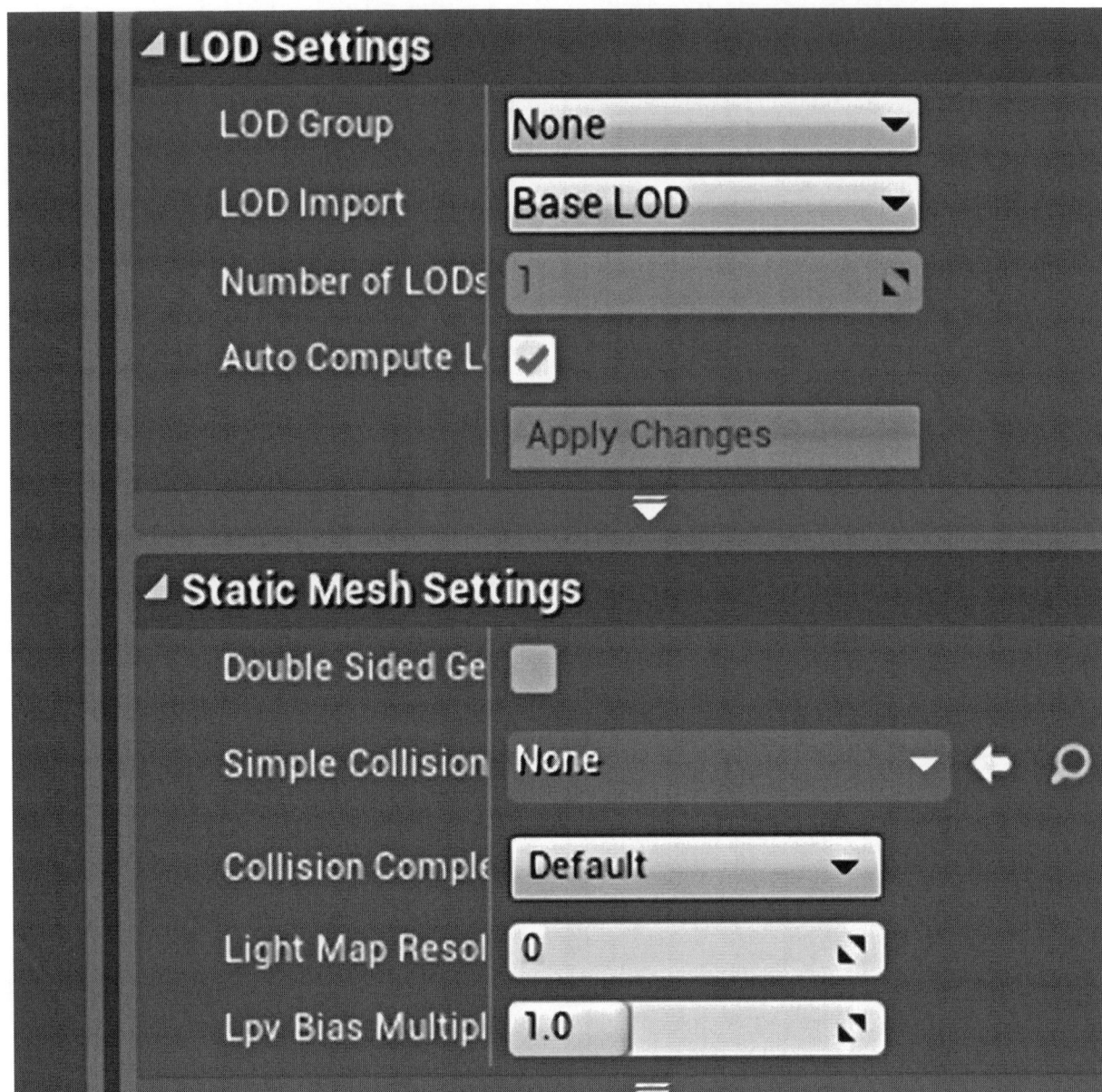

LOD Settings

LOD Group   None

LOD Import   Base LOD

Number of LODs   1

Auto Compute L   ✓

                          Apply Changes

Static Mesh Settings

Double Sided Ge   ☐

Simple Collision   None

Collision Comple   Default

Light Map Resol   0

Lpv Bias Multipl   1.0

While looking at the "Static Mesh Settings" (In the "Details" panel INSIDE the "Static Mesh Editor") Do you see the option called "Light Map Resolution" with a "0" value next to it? That's the number we have to change!

For the sake of the tutorial, put 512 in there. Normally, we'd mess around and try and get the best lowest number (To save on performance), but as we're learning what everything does, 512 will do fine for our adventure.

Go ahead and replace the "0" with "512" now.

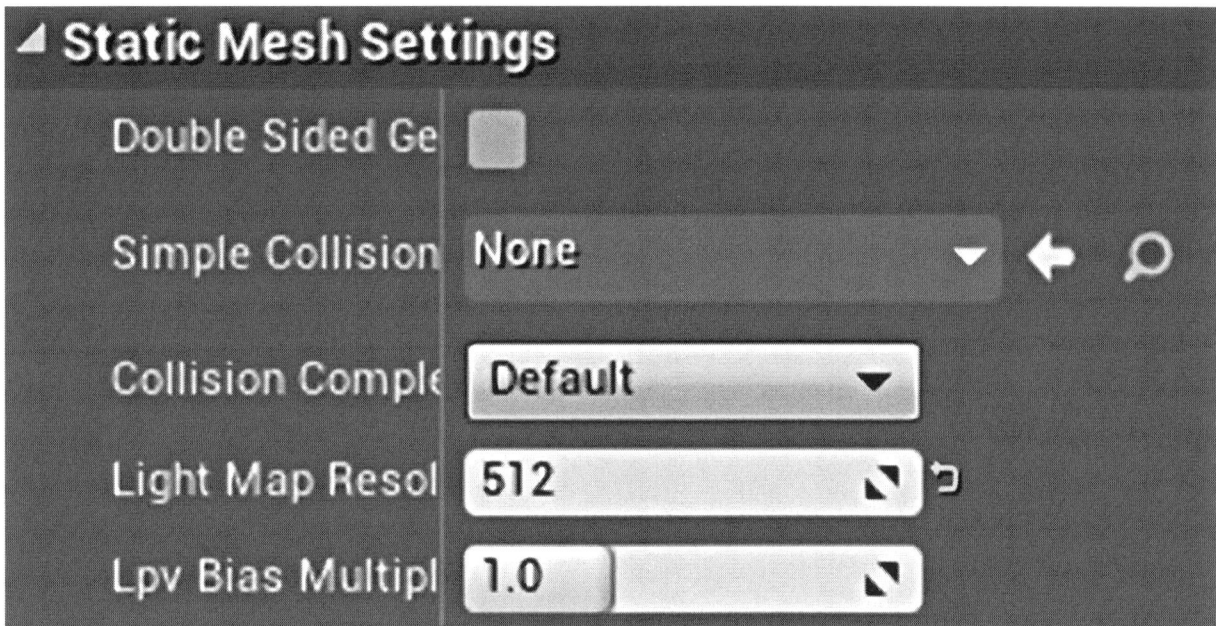

Static Mesh Settings

- Double Sided Ge ☐
- Simple Collision **None** ▼ ← 🔍
- Collision Comple **Default** ▼
- Light Map Resol **512**
- Lpv Bias Multipl **1.0**

Once you've changed the value, be sure to "Save" (Using the floppy disc button on the top-left of the "Static Mesh Editor"). Once saved, you can close down the "Static Mesh Editor" and you'll see we are no longer plagued with "Invalid Lightmap Settings" all over our Static Mesh!

So what's next? Turning this Static Mesh into a Blueprint!

Time for the magic: Static Mesh > Blueprint

To convert this Static Mesh into a Blueprint, there's two main things we have to do: Actually convert it and replace the Static Mesh in the scene to the converted Blueprint!

Head back into the "Content Browser" and find your "SM_Door" (But don't open it!)

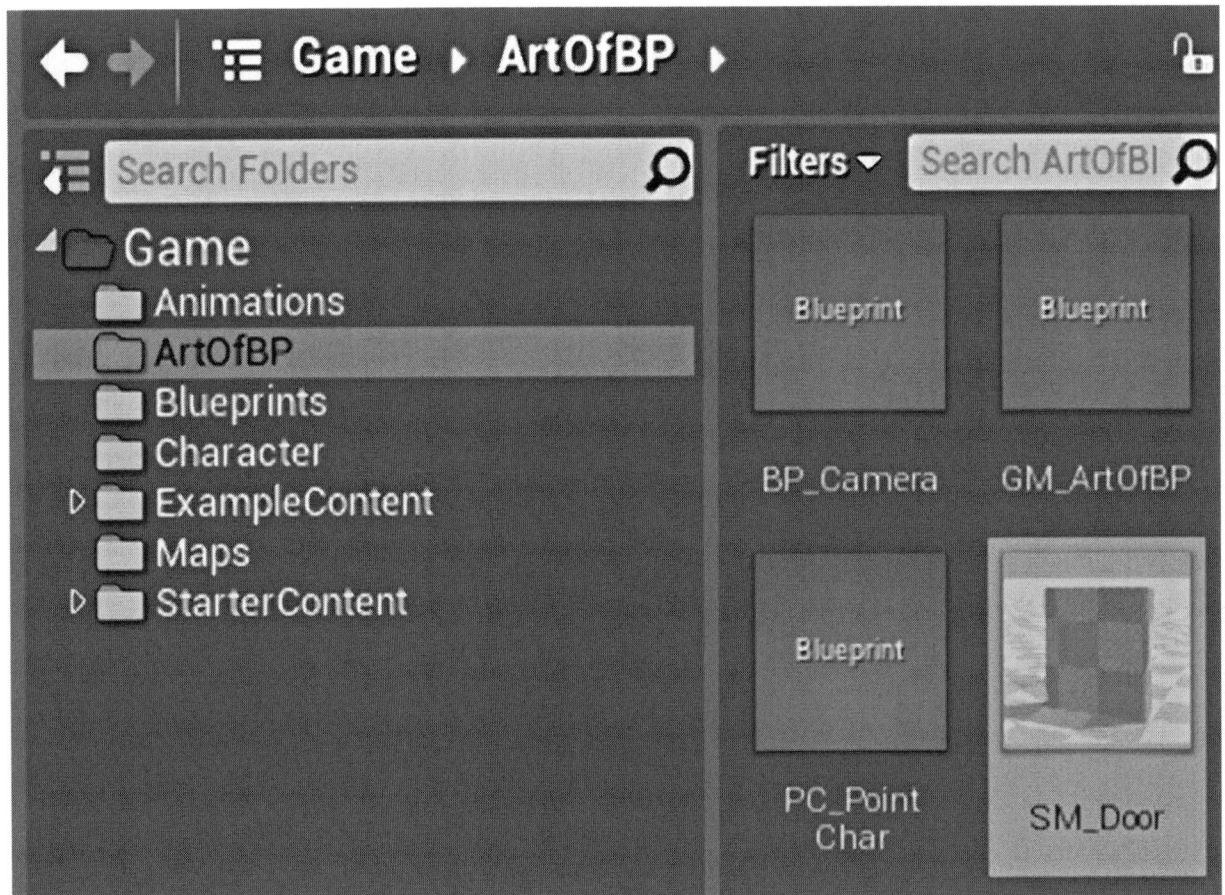

This time, instead of double-clicking "SM_Door", right click (Ctrl + Click) it to bring up the options menu:

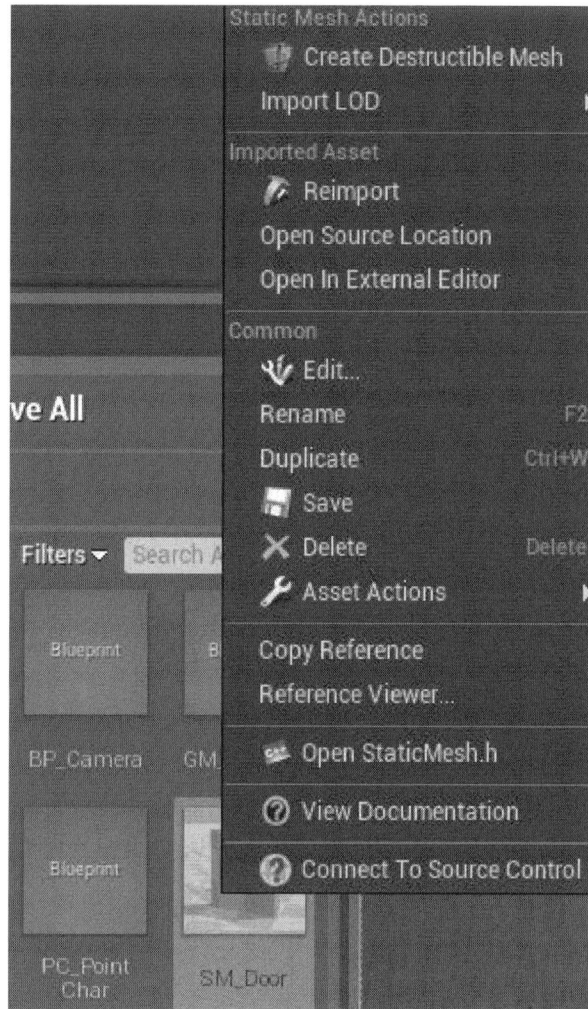

Within this options menu, go to "Asset Actions" (It has a spanner image next to it!). Hovering over it will show you a second options menu.

At the top of this second options menu is a button that says: "Create Blueprint Using This..." - As this is exactly what we need, go ahead and click it.

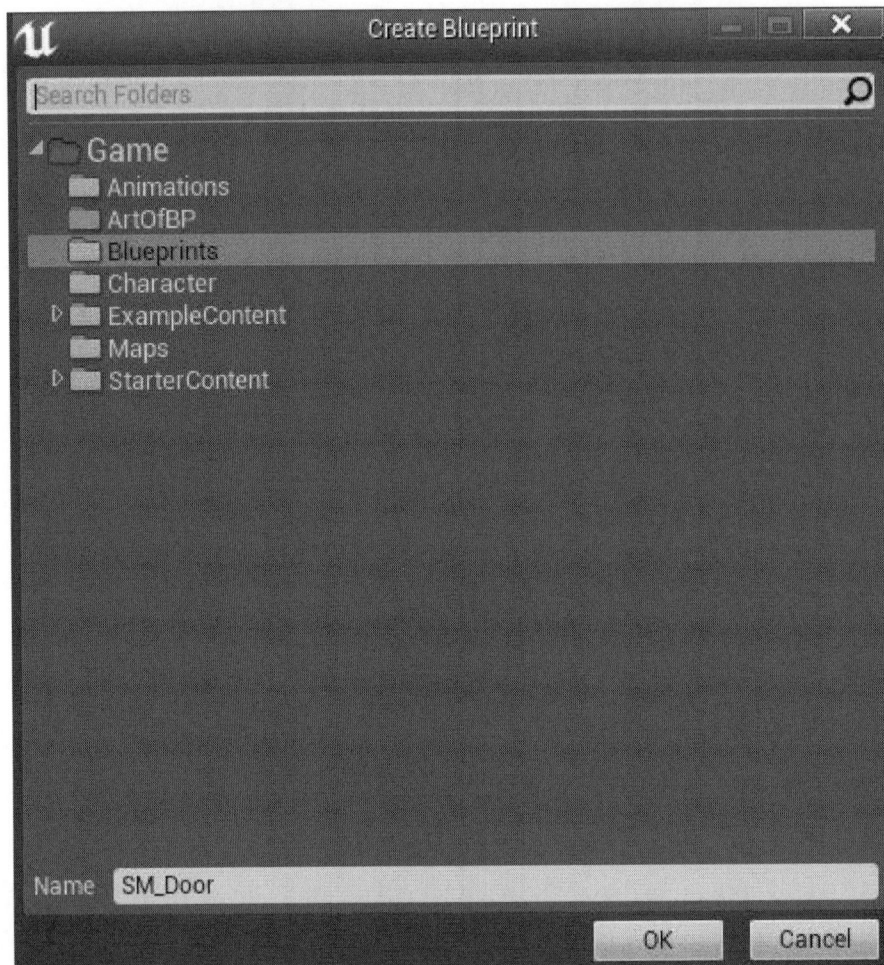

Just like before, it asks you to pick a folder and a name for this new Blueprint. So pick your "ArtOfBP" folder (Or your named equivalent) and set the name to BP_Door.

Once you've done this, hit "OK". Unlike before, it throws us straight into the Blueprint (Which is super-helpful!).

Having learnt everything up until this point, you'll no doubt first head to the "Navigation Ribbon" in the top-right to navigate to one of the other tabs but don't!

If you have, slap your wrist and stop getting ahead of yourself! The tab you need to be in at the moment is "Components", so double-check that's where you are!

Root? Root-a-toot-toot!

You'll see that the door is now in the Blueprint, which is perfect. The engine automatically created an Actor Blueprint for us and put the door in. But there's one change we have to make to the components!

Before we actually change anything, let's figure out WHY we have to change something: When you convert a static mesh into a Blueprint, Unreal Engine 4 assumes that your Static Mesh won't need to move (It assumes it'd be… Static. Get it?).

Of course, that's not the case in this scenario: We're going to need the door to move (Open) once certain conditions are met.

Some of you may be thing that we need to change something from: Static to Movable but this isn't what I'm getting at.

If we were to move the door in it's current state, it would be 10x harder to remember where it's origin location is if we didn't do what I'm about to tell you to do: Make the SM_Door a "Child" of a "RootSceneComponent".

I bet you must be thinking: What the heck is that?!

Very simply: A root scene component is an empty object. It's invisible and holds no data. Absolutely none. To the end-player of our project, they won't even know it's there. The only person who's going to know it's there is me and you.

So what's the point in it if nobody will see it and it does nothing? Think of it like this: Say you're waiting in line at a fast-food restaurant but you really need the toilet. What the "RootSceneComponent" would do is remember where you were in

213

the queue - leaving you the ability to go to the toilet and do whatever you want to do before returning and finding exactly where you were before.

And that's the whole point of the "RootSceneComponent". It sits at 0 X, 0 Y and 0 z (Aka Wherever you place your Blueprint in the world) and remembers that this 0, 0, 0 is home. If you were then to move the door down 10 or 20 units, the Root is still 0, 0, 0. This means we can then just go up by 10 units on the door and be right back to where we were.

So think of the "RootSceneComponent" as a location rememberer. This will become more handy when you have things like two meshes in a Blueprint and you need them to return home at some point (Like a double-door that opens / closes).

In that case, you'd put the "RootSceneComponent" in and then make the door meshes a "Child" of the "RootSceneComponent". This way we can return them to 0, 0, 0 whenever we want (Which would be our closed door position in that scenario).

So in your "Component" view, you'll see a toolbox on the left-hand side called "Components". This is where you add the components to your blueprints, it could anything from cables, audio emitters, particle emitters, mesh .etc

We're going to add a "RootSceneComponent" now, so go ahead and click "Add Component".

If you search for "Root", you're not going to find anything. I'll explain why in two seconds but for now, search for "Scene" and select it to create it into the Blueprint.

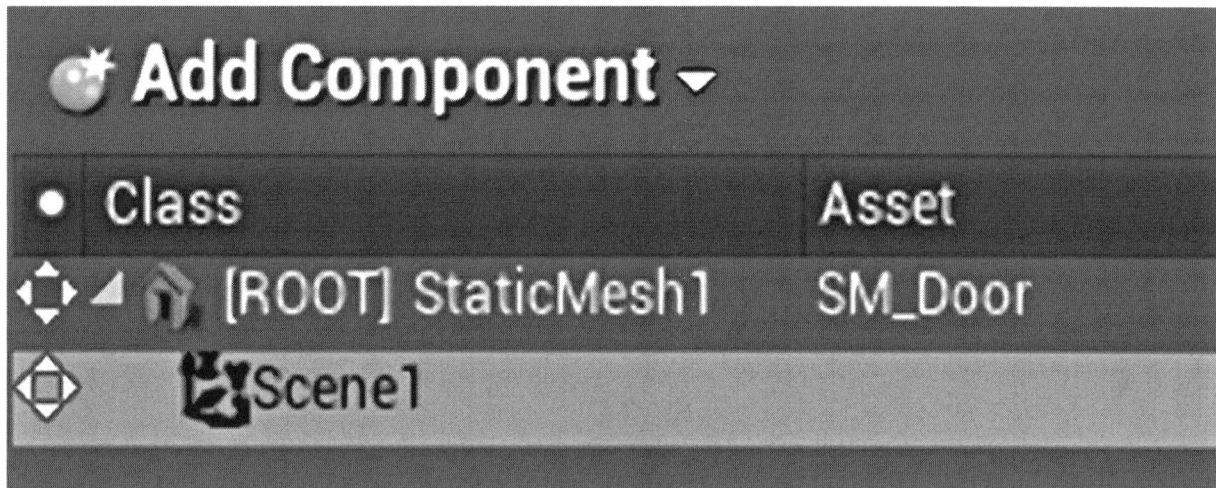

You'll notice that the "Scene" isn't called a "RootSceneComponent". When we talked about the "RootSceneComponent", it should be noted that we're not talking about an object called "RootSceneComponent", we're talking about a Component called "Scene" which is the root component.

So how do we turn our Scene into a "RootSceneComponent"? Simply by clicking and dragging it where the "[Root]SM_Door" is! This will stop the "Door" being the "Root" component and will get our empty object (The "Scene" component) to become the new "Root".

I know this is all sounding a little confusing, but don't worry. "Root" is basically the "Home" component. The home component is 0, 0, 0 and it's good practice to make the "Scene" component the "Home" component.

This is because everything in the blueprint (Component-wise) is a child of the "Root" component. Think of a paper-clip chain, it all begins with the first paperclip and everything after could be considered "Children" paperclips, as they all need the original paperclip to be where they are.

I'm probably confusing things more so let's just get to the practical; If you still don't understand, you'll pick it up on the way.

If you haven't already, drag your "Scene1" onto the "ROOT[SM_Door]". When it does, you'll see that the "Scene1" will change it's name to "Root[Scene1]".

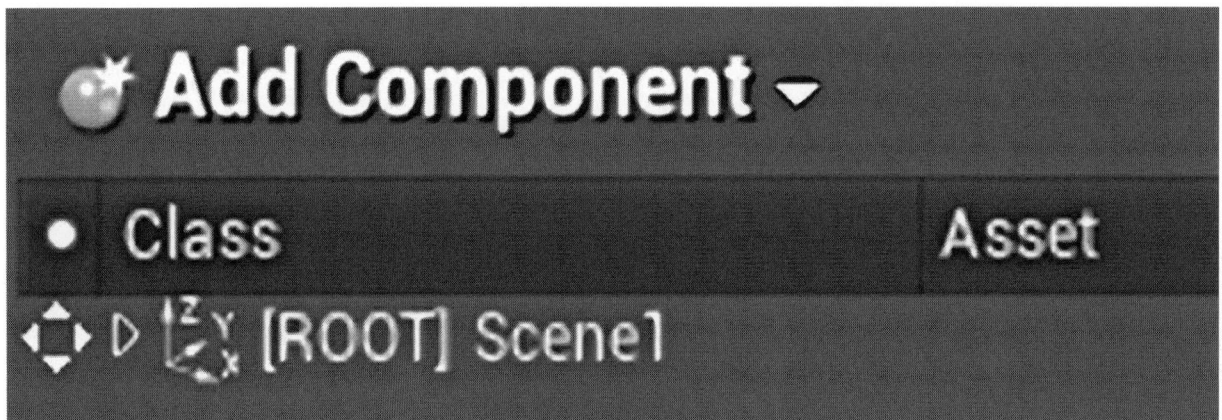

You'll notice that the "SM_Door" has disappeared from the "Component" toolbox but don't worry, by simply clicking the arrow that's pointing to the right right before the XYZ image (That's next to "[ROOT] Scene1"] it will appear once more.

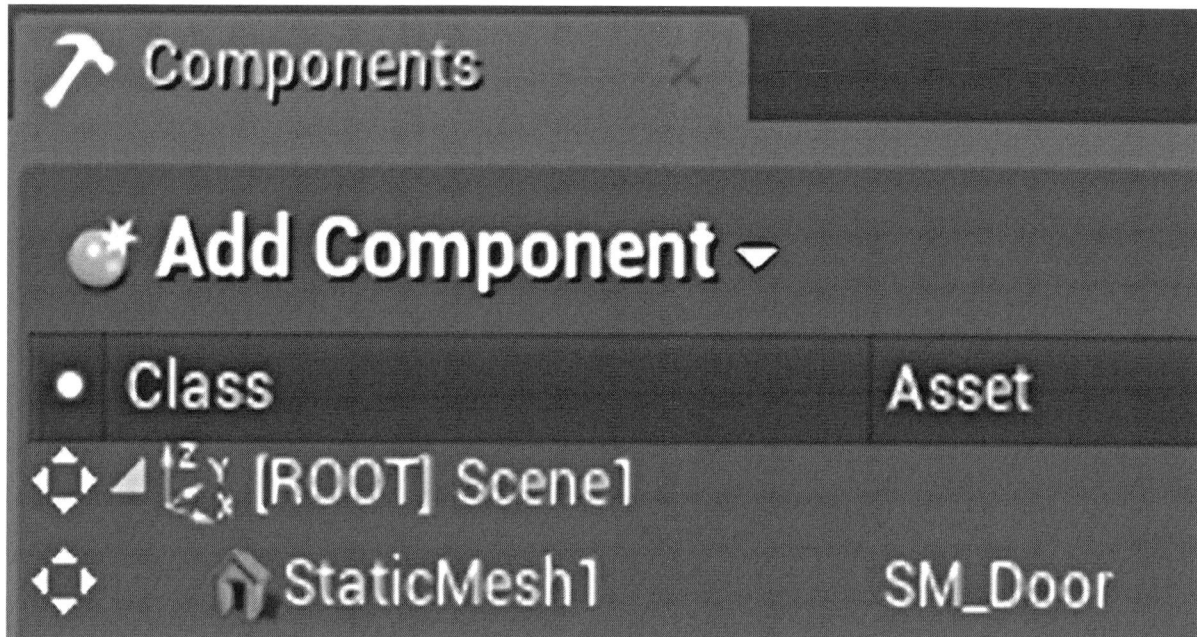

That's all we need to add into our Blueprints components at the moment. What you could do (After you've finished all the steps of this book!) is go back into the "Components" of this Blueprint and add a particle emitter, so when the door opens, it smokes, sparks or whatever you'd like!

But we're not going to cover that in this book (Not for now anyway), I was just giving you some inspiration on how to build on everything you learn from this book!

Custom Event Time!

It's now time to head into the Graph view of our blueprint. By now, you should be quite comfortable with navigating between the "Defaults, Components and Graph" tabs using the navigation ribbon on the top-right.

Once you're in the graph view, it's time to create our first Custom Event! You should be able to guess what this is, but in case you can't figure it out:

Remember how we've been using an Event Tick a lot? How about the Begin / End Overlap events? These events fire under their own certain circumstances but as we've described before, an Event gives the node connected to it the "Power" to fire. What triggers these events is what sets them apart from each other.

A custom event is an event created by us, in which we decide when it fires (And when it doesn't!). This is another thing that's easier to understand in a practical environment, so we're going to create a Custom Event now!

Before we continue, make sure you're in the graph view of your "BP_Door". Once you're there, open up the Compact Blueprint Library and search for "Custom Event", selecting "Create a Custom Event".

It will then ask you to name the "Custom Event". For the sake of this book, we're going to call it "OpenDoor" (Nice and simple!), so go ahead and do that now.

Later on, we'll get to firing the Custom Event, but for now, we'll focus on this blueprint.

When creating the rest of the code, be in the mind-set that all the conditions have been met for this door to be open. Be it a key has been collected, a puzzle has been solved or a riddle has been answered; It doesn't matter. Just think that whatever has triggered it has the permission to fire this code.

What you'll need to do next is head into the Variable Library and create a new variable: Call it "IsOpen" and set the type to bool (Which is yes / no data!).

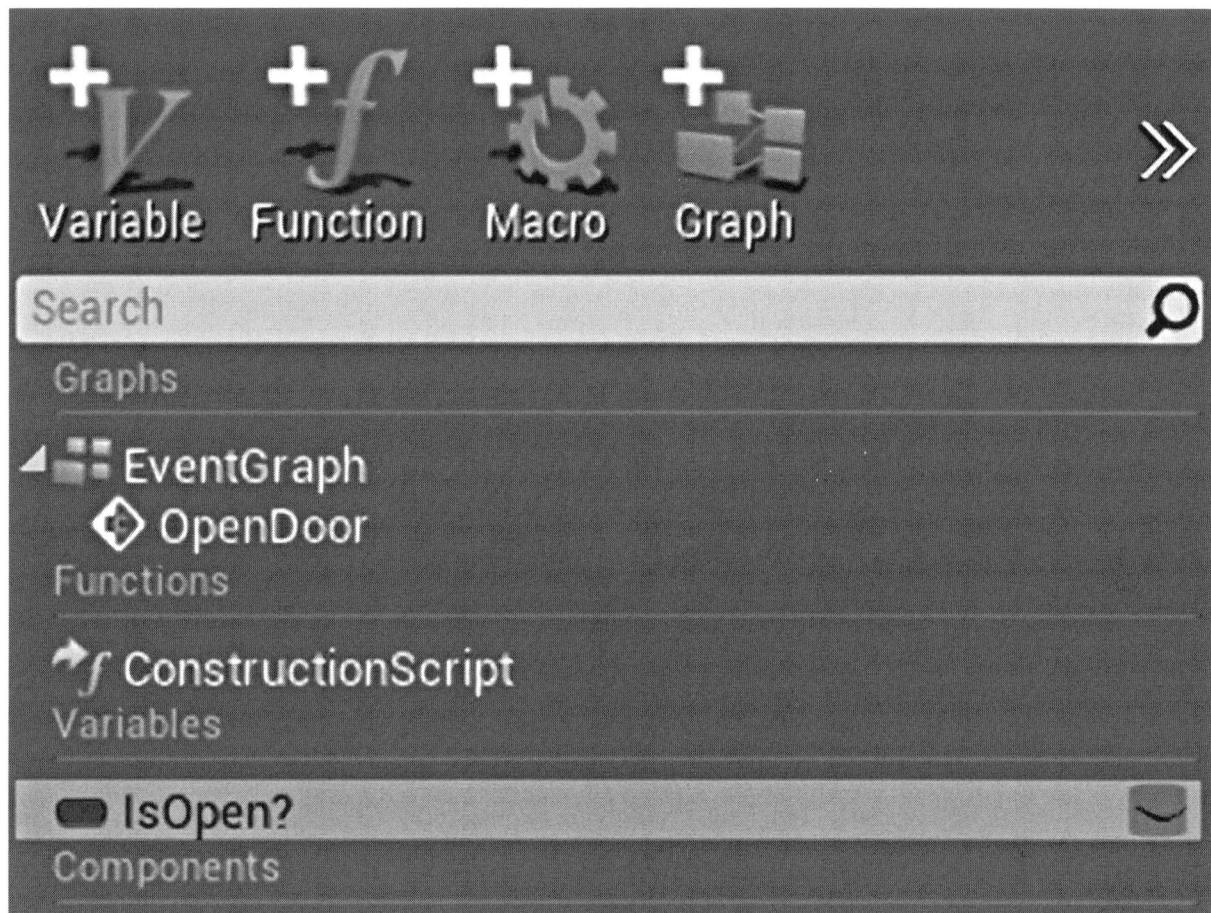

Once you've created it, drag it into your Blueprint and when the options come up, select "Get".

The reason we've created it this is because we want to know if the door has already been opened. If it has, we don't want the code to fire again: Once the door is open, it should stay open!

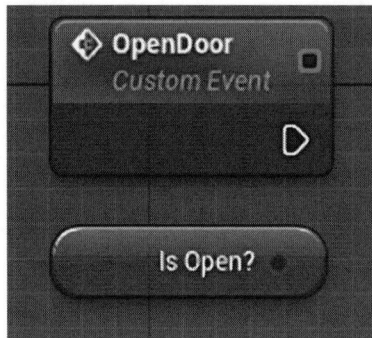

As you might have guessed by now, as we've brought the bool in: We need a "Branch" node. So go ahead and create it now (Either via the CBL or by holding B and left clicking with your mouse!) and connect the "Is Open?" node to the "Condition" input pin.

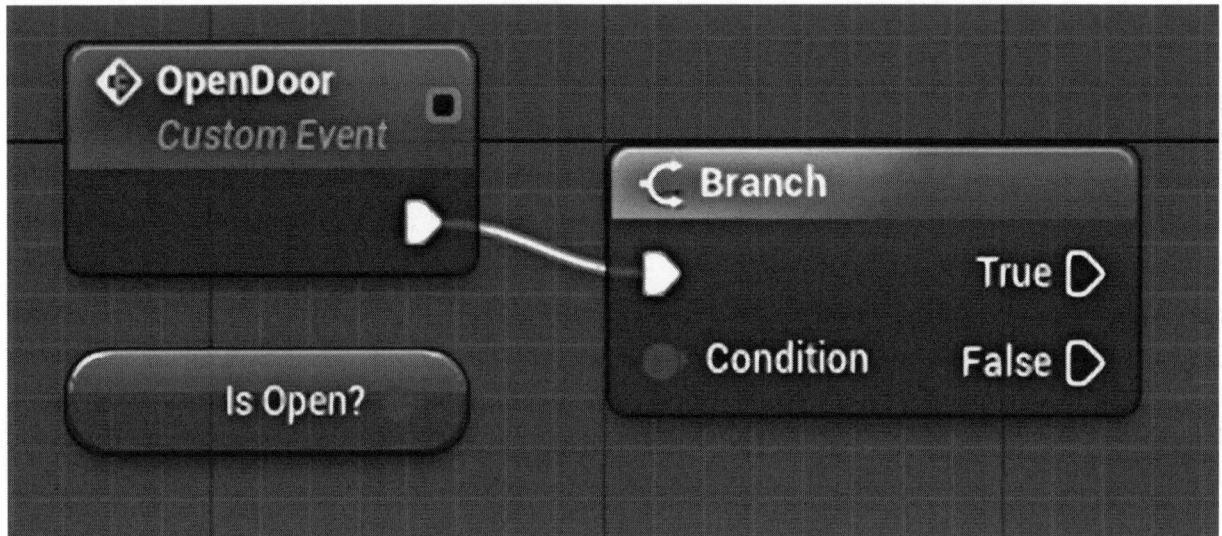

We don't want the BP_Door to do anything if it's anything, so we'll leave the "True" output of the "Branch" node well alone.

It's Time to Write (Right) the Timeline!

We're going to create a node now and connect it to the "False" output pin of the "Branch".

So open up the Compact Blueprint Library and search for "Timeline", selecting "Add Timeline…"

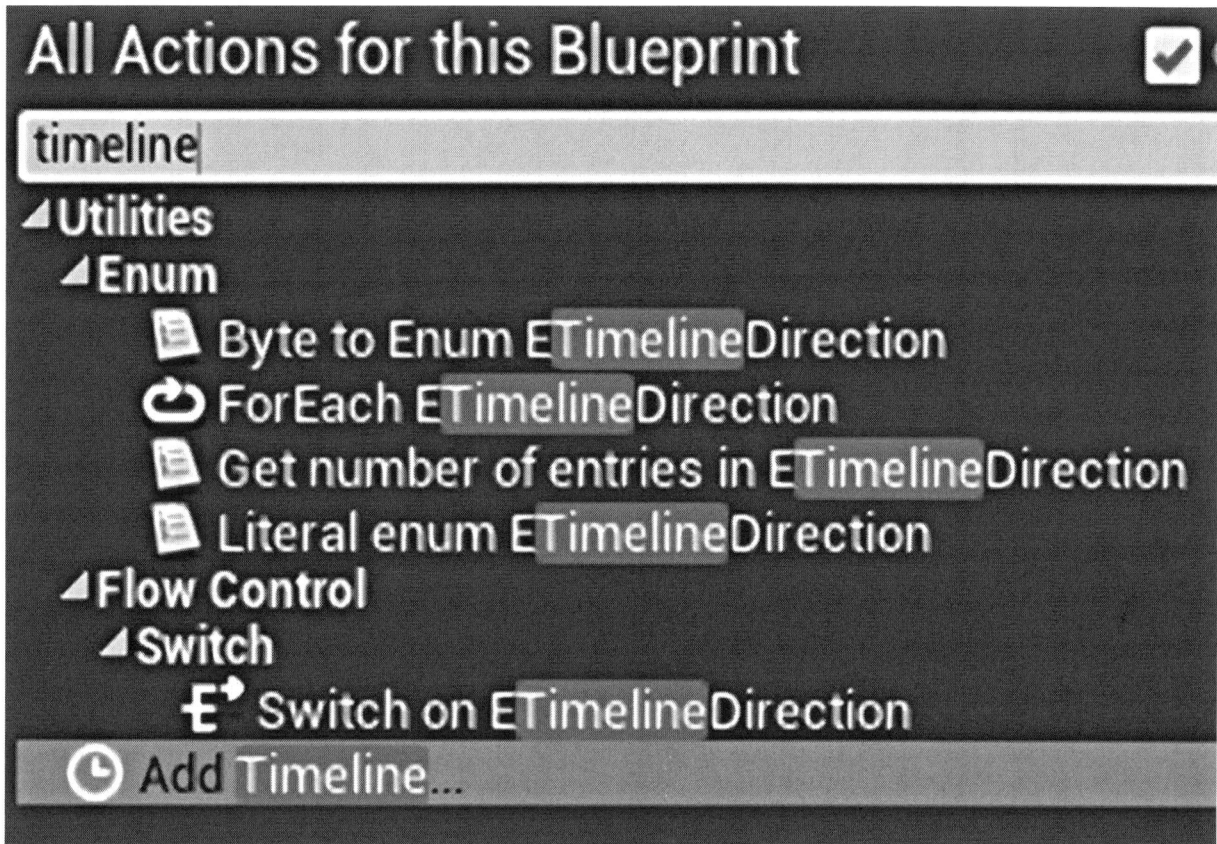

All Actions for this Blueprint

timeline

▲Utilities
  ▲Enum
    📄 Byte to Enum ETimelineDirection
    ↻ ForEach ETimelineDirection
    📄 Get number of entries in ETimelineDirection
    📄 Literal enum ETimelineDirection
  ▲Flow Control
    ▲Switch
      E⁺ Switch on ETimelineDirection
  🕐 Add Timeline...

It asks you to name the Timeline but it doesn't really matter what you name it. Once it's created, plug the output "False" from the Branch into either "Play" or "Play from Start" of the "Timeline" node.

Now here's a super-quick description of the Timeline node and what it'll do for us!

A timeline node allows us to set a value over time. Be it a door opening or something like a timer counting down. It's all possible with Timeline. The node was originally created with animation in mind, but due to the fact that you can set values over time, It makes a good alternative for a whole bunch of code on a Tick.

Inside the Timeline node looks a little worrying, but don't worry, You've got little old me to guide you through the adventure!

You'll notice that I said "Inside" the Timeline node. To get "Inside" the node, simply double click the node and you'll go from the blueprint view to inside the Timeline node!

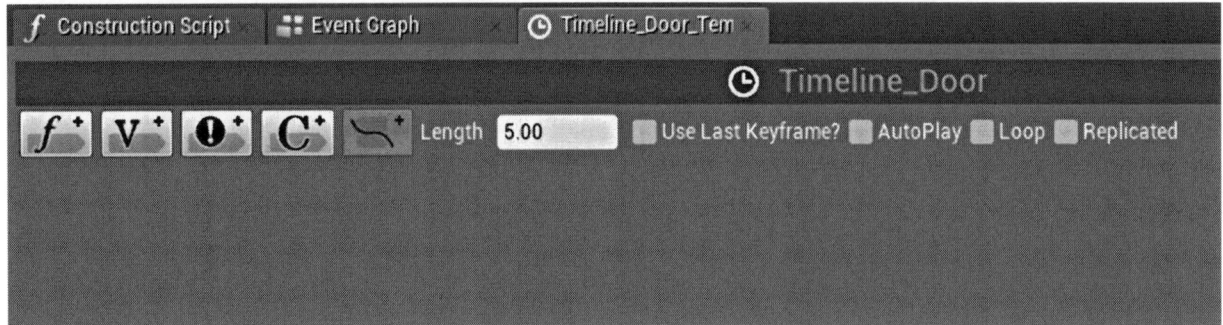

You'll notice that things look a little bare at the moment. Things will get pretty interesting soon: I promise!

Just underneath the title (Which will be whatever you called the timeline), there's a number of buttons. Ranging from "F+", V+" all the way to radio buttons "Loop" and "Replicated" .etc

These buttons have specific purposes, here's a quick rundown for reference:

- "F+" - New "Float" track
- "V+" - New "Vector" track
- "Exclamation Mark in a bubble" - New "Event" track
- "C+" - New Color Track

The other buttons along the chain are self-explanatory.

What we first need to do is set the length of this timeline. As we want the door to open quickly, we'll only need to set the timeline to last for 1 second.

To change the length, simply go to the "Length" label on this button bar. At the moment, it's set a 5 (This is the default value), which stands for 5 seconds. Change the 5.00 value to 1.00.

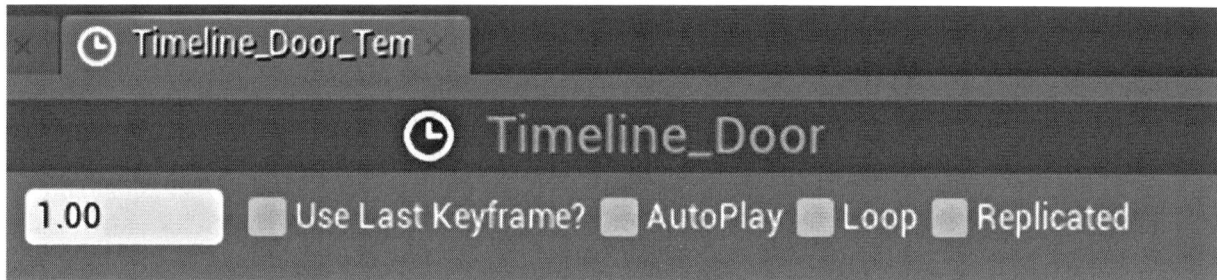

We now need to create a "Float" track. We'll then use the output of this with some code to set the location of our door!

The reason we're doing it as a "Float" track instead of a "Vector" is because with the "Float" track, when we add the code, we can set the "Relative" location of the door (And not the world location).

If you're wondering "What the heck does that mean?", let's break it down super-quick:

- Relative Location = Local location (Within the Blueprint (As if the RootSceneComponent is at coordinates 0, 0, 0).
- World Location = The location within the in-game world (As if the RootSceneCompoent is at coordinates that are not specifically 0, 0, 0)

As you can tell, Relative location is perfect in our scenario, As we'll have multiple doors that run off this Blueprint!

So getting back to the Timeline, go ahead and create the float track now, using the "F+" button.

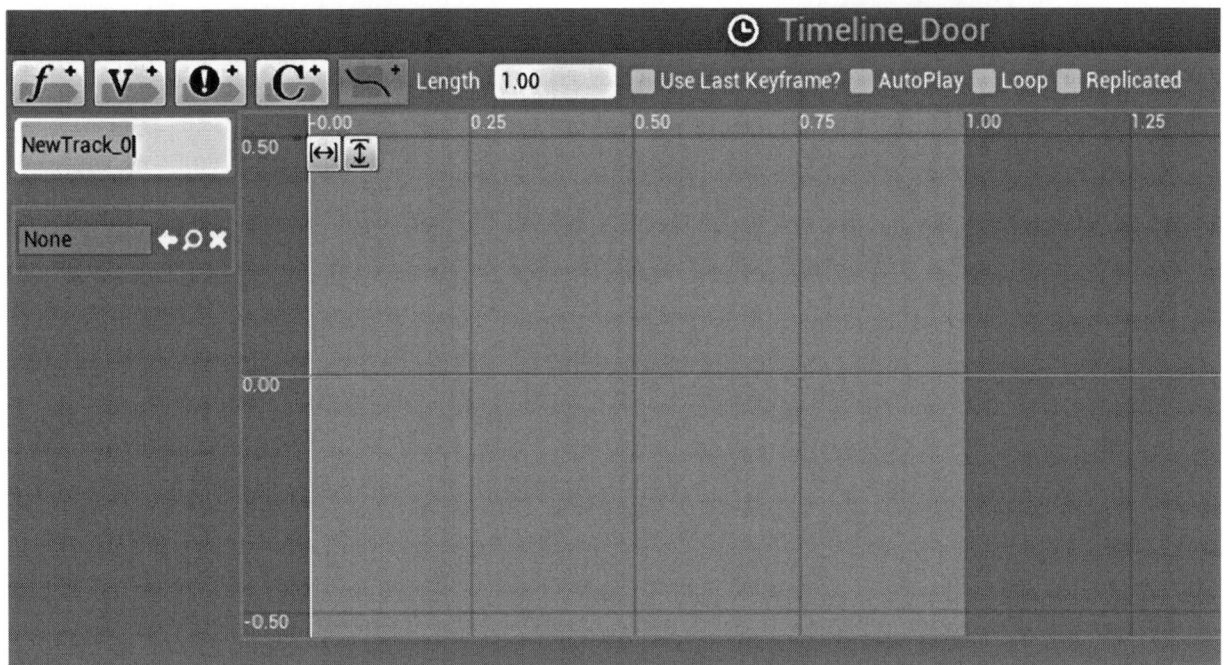

I warned you things will look scary! Don't worry, it's dead simple to use this interface!

First things first, rename the track to "FloatData". You can do this by right-clicking (Ctrl + Click) "NewTrack_0" (If the text field isn't editable already!)

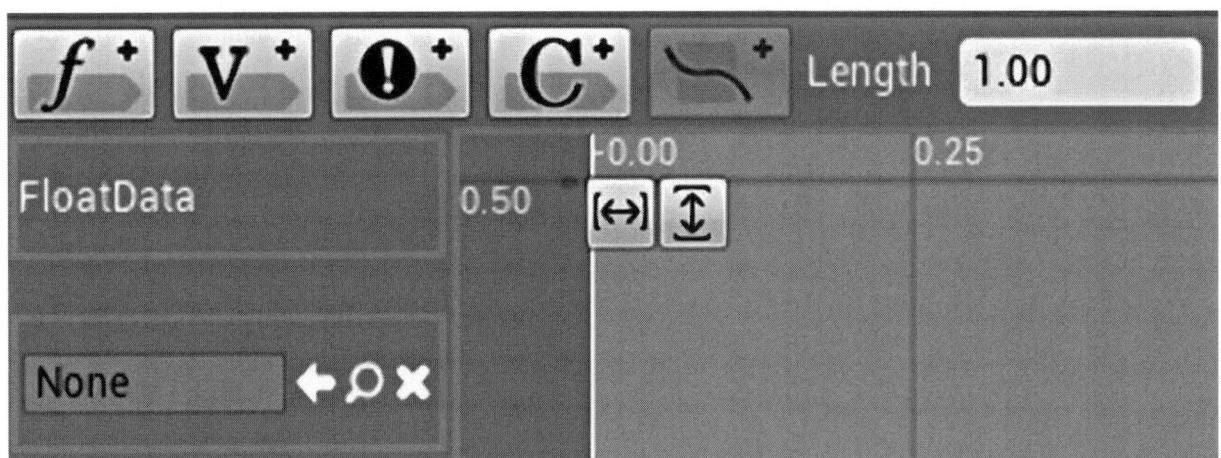

We're now going to create two keyframes! This will alter the outputted "Float" depending on the time!

Around the 0.00 mark of the grid (With the red line through the middle), Shift + Click the red line around the 0.00 mark and again at around the 1.00 mark (Don't worry, you don't have to be precise!)

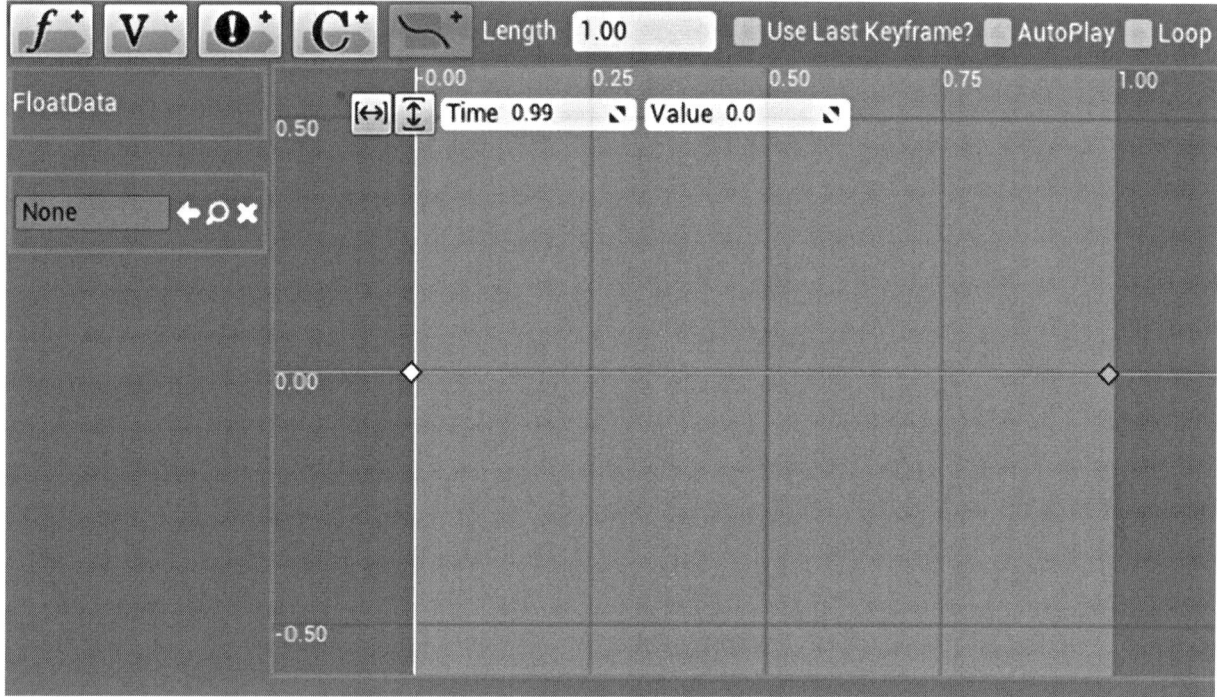

You'll notice the keys now in your Timeline (Albeit very tiny!)

Click on the keyframe that was created at around the 0.00 mark, you'll notice that just underneath the buttons which we used to create this track, they'll be two fields that have appeared: "Time" and "Value".

At the moment, my time is set at "-0.07" and the value is set at 0.0. The value is correct but the time is a little off. If either of your values aren't 0, you can use the fields to change it so it's correct. Do that now!

Now click the second keyframe (That's around the "1.00" mark). Make sure the "Time" is set to 1.0 and the value to 1.0.

NOTE: You might have to press "Enter" on your keyboard after entering the value!

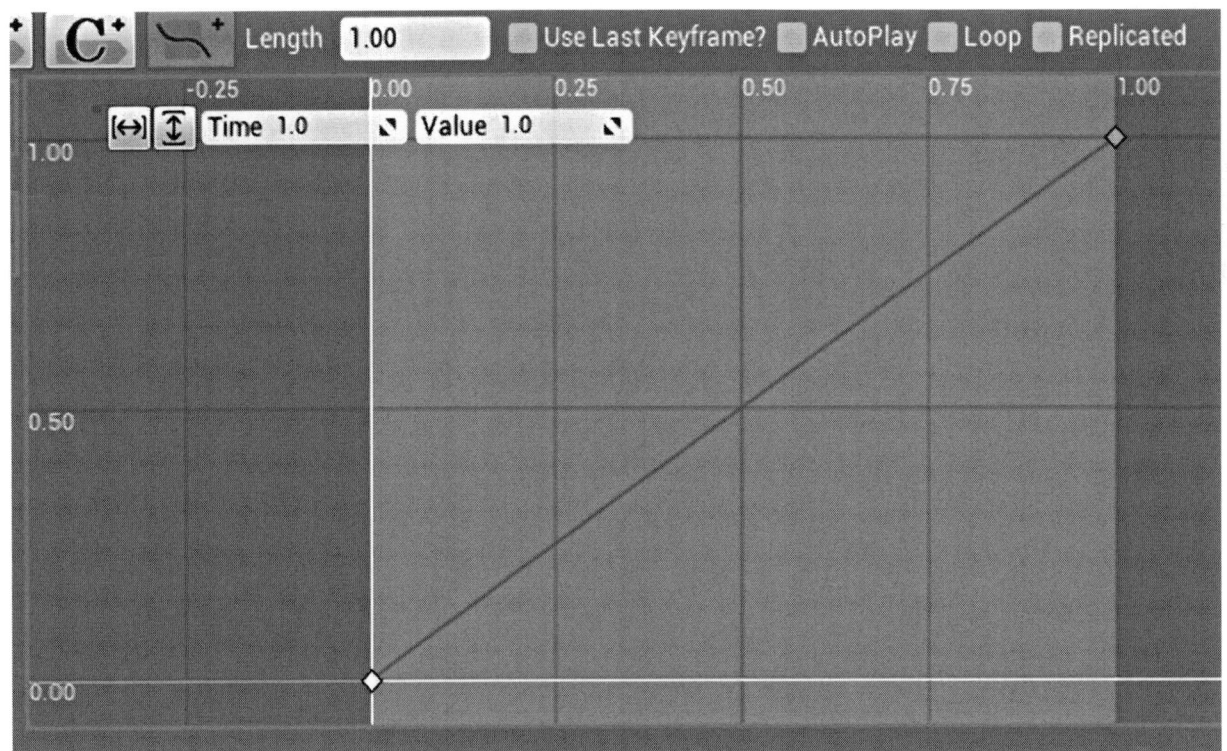

You'll notice that the red line will now go up on a tangent. Notice the grey lines going down? This means at the time of the grey bar (0.00, 0.25, 0.50, 0.75 and

1.00), where the grey line and the red line meet is what the "Float" output will be at that time.

So at 0.5, at the moment, our door will be halfway to its destination.

But we want to smooth our Float track. it's not necessary but helps give the door opening animation a bit of an artistic edge!

To smooth our values out, head to the first keyframe and right click (Ctrl + Click) it. A small menu will now appear.

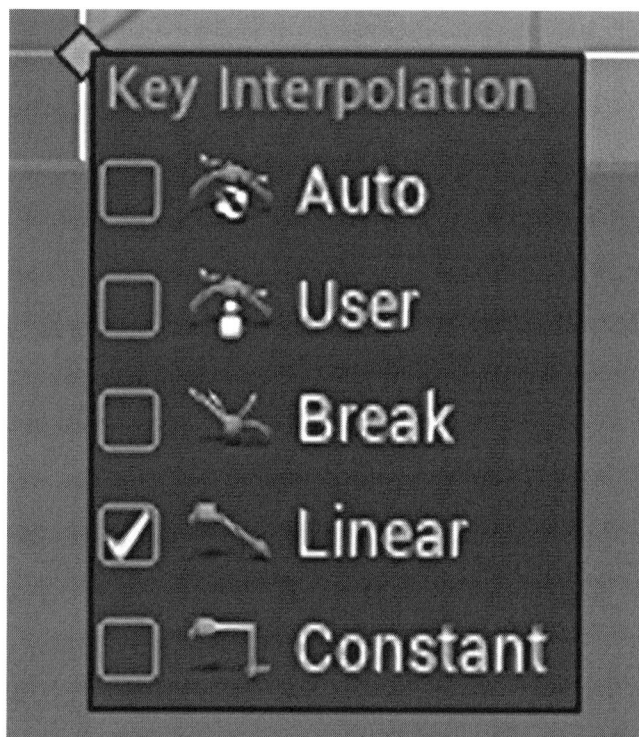

You now have a choice. You can experiment with whichever one you like or simply select "Auto" (Which is what I'll be doing). Whatever your choice, go ahead and make a selection.

Once you've made your choice, go ahead and do the same for the other keyframe. You'll end up with a graph that's no longer a linear tangent, but you'll (Hopefully) have a nicer looking shape that either feels smoother or feels like it has more weight behind it.

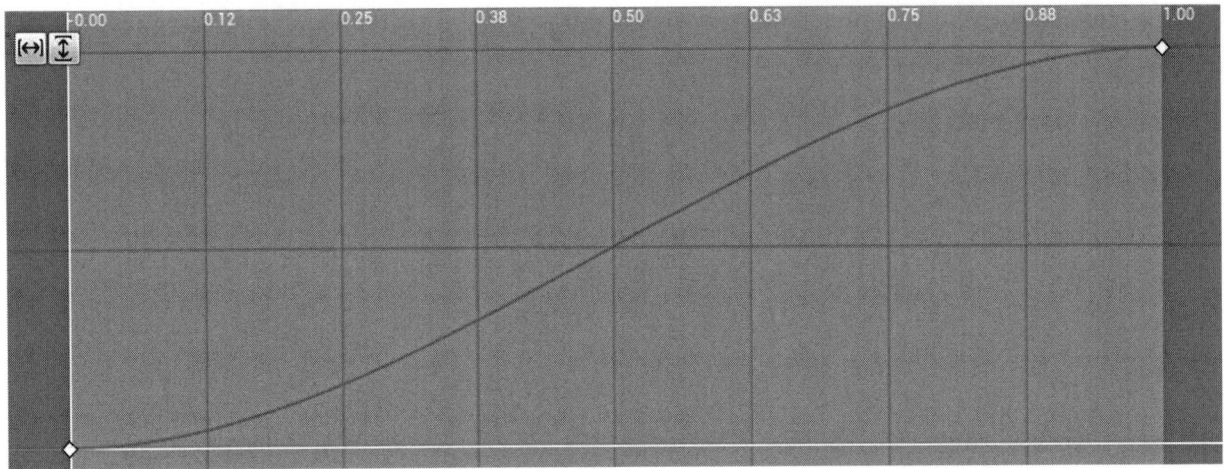

But what does the change in this graph mean? As you can see in the image above, my line has gone from a straight angle into more of a curved line.

This means my door won't go straight done but will slowly open at the start, then it will speed up as it's going down and finally it will smooth off once it's come to the end of its movement animation.

Pretty nifty for a simple line, eh?

We've done all we can inside this Timeline. Use the tabs just above the buttons we used to create this "FloatData" track to close it down and head back into the main "EventGraph" again.

You'll now notice that our "FloatData" has appeared as on an output on our Timeline node!

Groovy! If you haven't already, go ahead and connect either the "Play from Start" or the "Play" input execution pins to the output of "False" from the "Branch" of the previously created node!

Lerp...Lerp!

Now we're going to get to the actual door movement! We've sorted everything else out but now is the time to actually move the door!

For this, we're going to have to create a "Lerp (Vector)" node. A Lerp stands for linear interpolation. Linear interpolation is essentially changing one value to another, which is what we're going to use get the door from local 0, 0, 0 to underneath the map (Which will give the effect of the door opening!)

Go ahead and create the "Lerp (Vector)" node now.

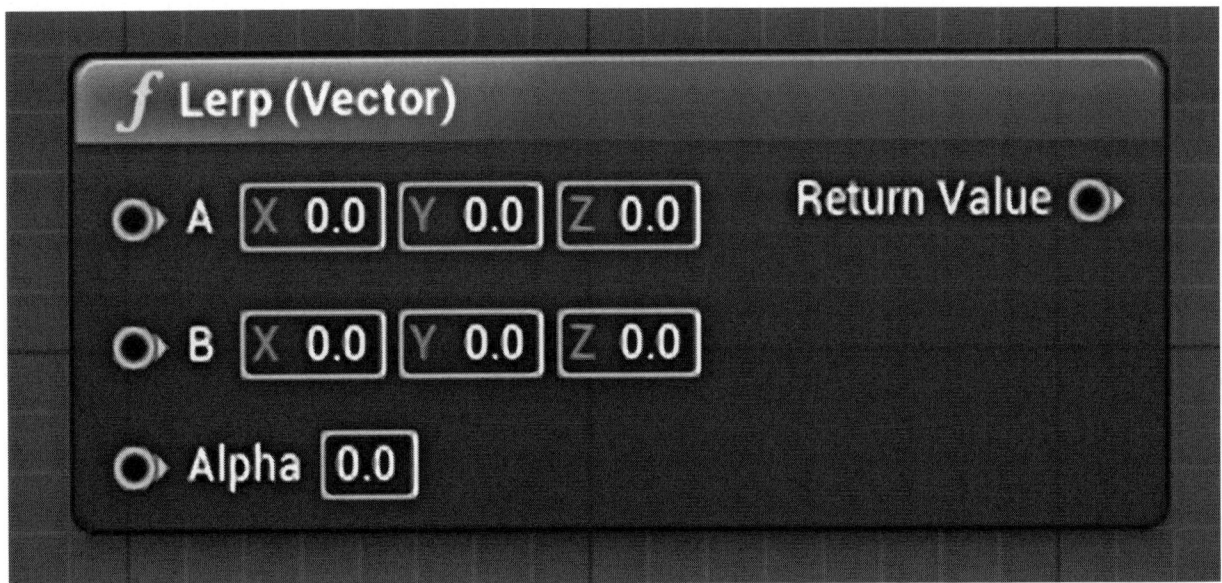

The first thing you'll notice is that in this "Lerp (Vector)" node, the "Alpha" input pin is a "Float" variable; Which is exactly what we just made in the timeline node!

As we have already created the data that needs to fit in this alpha, simply connect the output "FloatData" from the Timeline node to the input "Alpha" of the "Lerp (Vector)" node.
This alpha basically acts as the "Speed" of this "Lerp" node. So within a second we go into a fast start, slow middle part and fast end, this will reflect when the code switches the door from location A ("A" of the Lerp node) to location B ("B" of the Lerp node!)

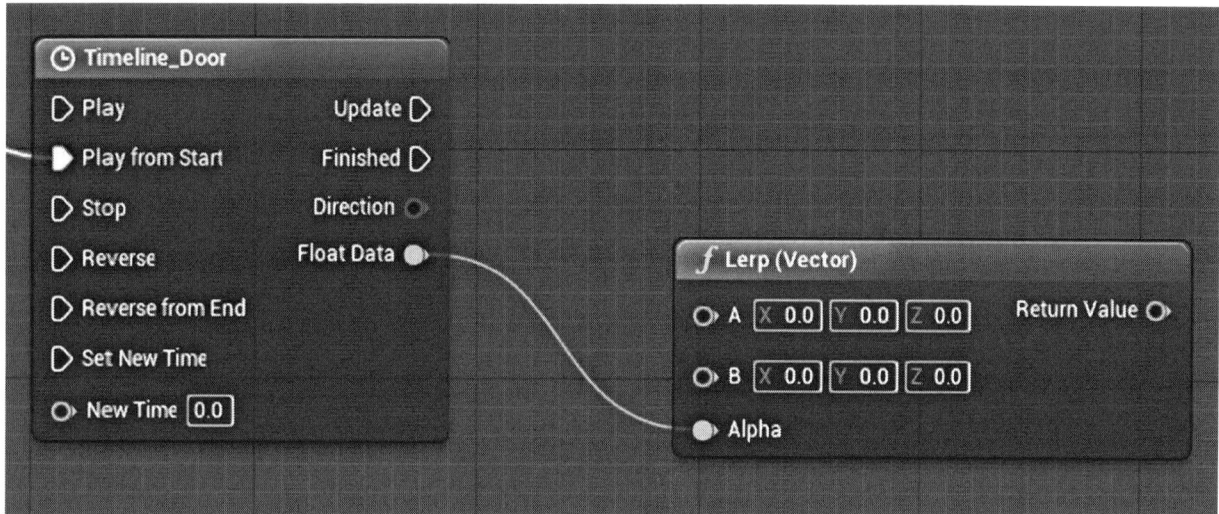

Now let's deal with the "A" and "B" inputs of the node! As you can guess, A is fine and can be left alone as the door starts it's life at 0, 0, 0. As we want the door to do downwards (Which is the "Z" of the world!), set the Z of "B" to -450.

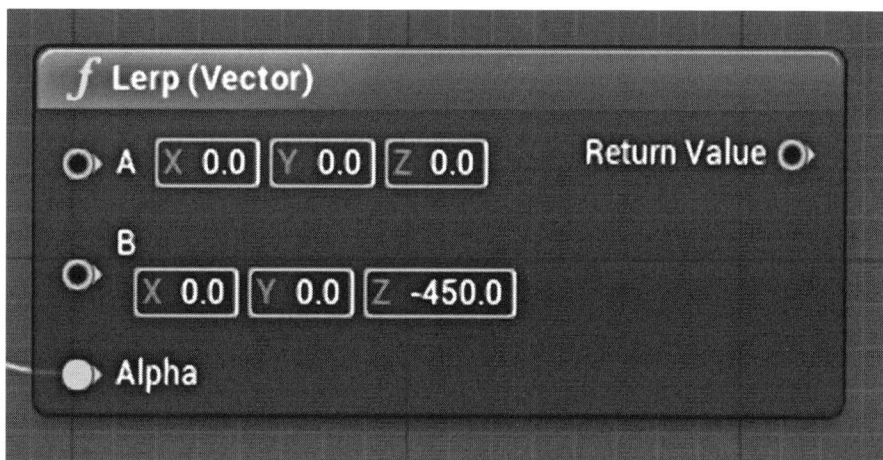

Now we have to actually tell our door to be affected by this change of data!

This next step will depend on your engine version: Pre 4.6 will have to drag their Static Mesh in manually into the blueprint via the Variable Library and then click the output pin and drag to to get the option, whereas 4.6 and above users will simply have to open up the Compact Blueprint Library and search for it.

So go ahead and do that now. When the CBL opens up, search for "Set Relative Location" (If you're using 4.6 it will be called: Set Relative Location (StaticMesh1) <Or the name of your door static mesh!>

This is how the node will look in 4.6:

The node will look awfully similar pre-4.6, but you'll have the Static Mesh connected to the "Target" pin.

Go ahead and connect the "Lerp"'s "Vector" output (Plug it into the "Set Relative Location"'s "New Location" input.

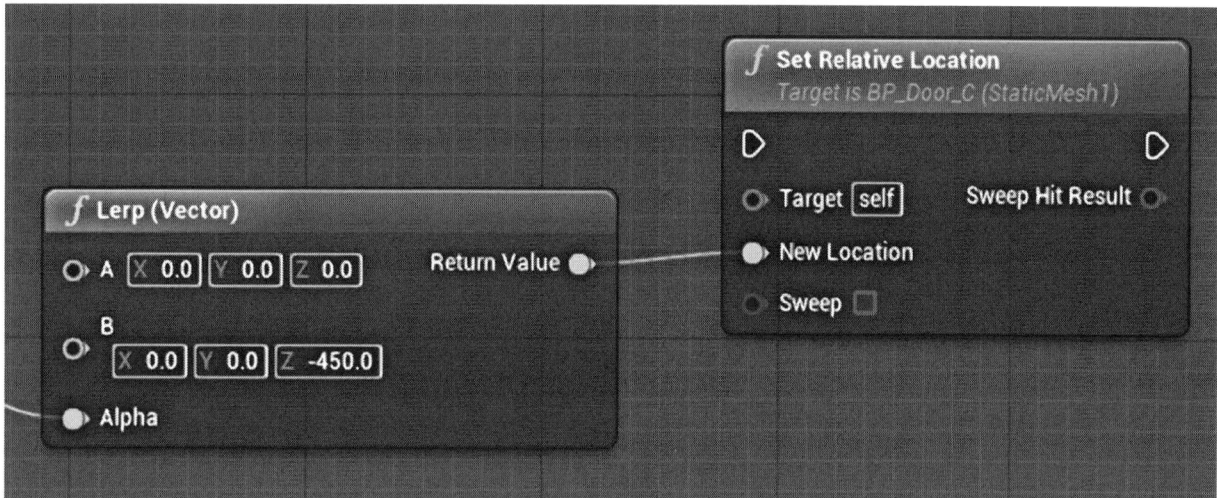

Now, connect the input execution pin of the "Set Relative Location" to the output "Update" of the timeline.

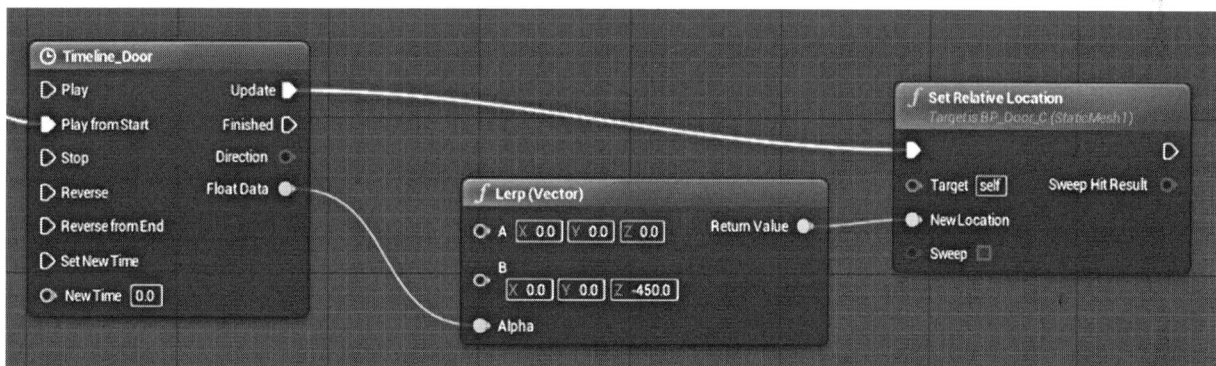

We're almost finished in this blueprint, there's just one last thing that we have to do. Before we do, let's take a quick review of the code:

"Once we send the message for this code to fire, check if the door is already open. If it's not, then "Open the door" by moving the door under the map."

Notice anything missing? That's right! We never actually tell the door that it's open now.

To fix this, head into your Variable Library and drag your "IsOpen?" variable into the scene. When it asks, select "Set" and plug the input execution of this node into the "Finished" node of the timeline.

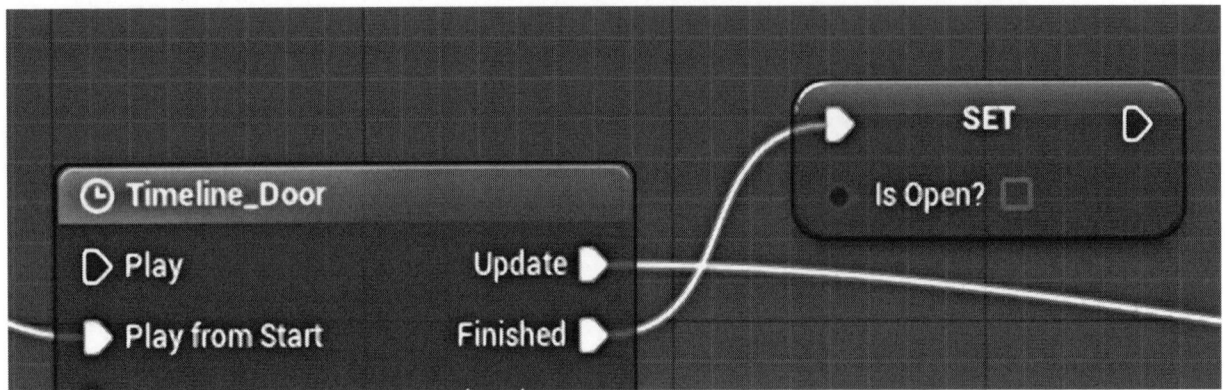

Then click the box inside the "Set IsOpen?" node to set it to "True".

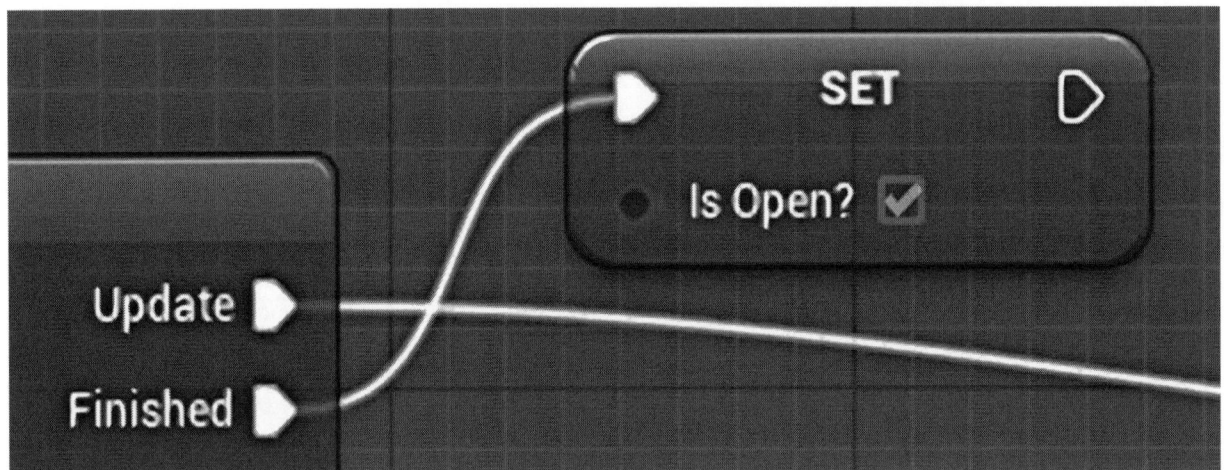

This means that once the one second is up, the door is now known as "Open" and because we ask the code "IsOpen?" at the start (And connect all the code to "False), the code won't be fired again.

Brilliant! That's another Blueprint completed! As you'll remember though, we set a custom event to fire this code. We don't currently have anything setting off this code, so it won't fire.

But we're getting ahead of ourselves, there's still two things we have to do before we can call this Blueprint 100% completed.

So save and compile the blueprint. Once done, you are free to close the Blueprint down. Once you're back in the main Unreal Engine window, head to wear the door originally sat.

Static Mesh? Go Home! BP_Door? It's your time to shine!

If you click the door in the scene, you'll notice that it's not the Blueprint yet: It's still the static mesh!

Deleting it and putting the BP_Door in it's place is extra effort, especially when there's an easy way around it!

To do the easy way, head into your Content Browser and make sure your "BP_Door" is selected.

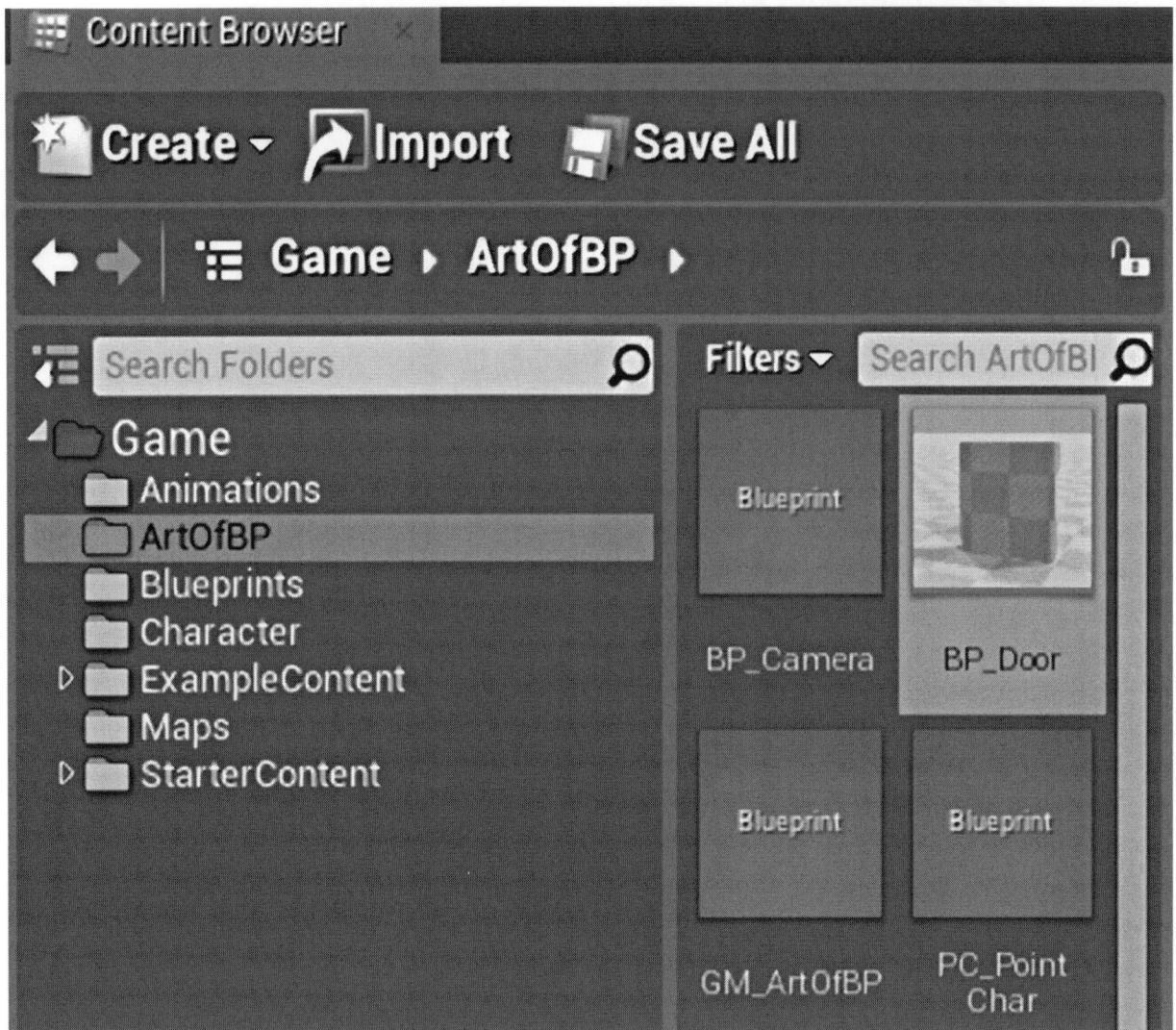

Now, take a look in your scene and select the door. Right click (Ctrl + Click) to see some options that you can play with.

Near the bottom of this list, you'll see an image with the text "Replace selected actor with "BP_Door". Perfect! Simply click this button and your Blueprint will replace the Static Mesh!

Give the game a go! I know the custom event hasn't been connected up yet, but give it a test anyway. Try and walk through the door.

You'll quickly see why I asked you to test it out...

Where's the collision?!

You'll notice if you tested your scene that you walk right through the door as if it's not there. This is because when we converted the BSP into a Static Mesh, it lost all of it's collision data.

Don't worry though, it's a cinch to get back!

Simply head into your "Content Browser" and find your Static Mesh of the door (Not the blueprint!) and double click on it to open up the editor.

On the top, there's a number of buttons which all have their own special functions.

Due to the fact I don't want to overwhelm the book with TOO much information, run your mouse over each button and you'll get a small description of what each button does and what they were created to do.

Once you're familiar with all of the buttons, it's time to get to work! Normally, you'd use the "Collision" menu (Which is ABOVE the this menu of buttons) and select the collision type that's best for you.

But we're not going to do that today. Instead, I'm going to show you a trick that you can use in the future if your mesh needs better collision then simple shapes!

Head over to the details panel on the right hand side and find the section marked "Static Mesh Settings". You might remember that we've been here before (To set the lightmap resolution!)

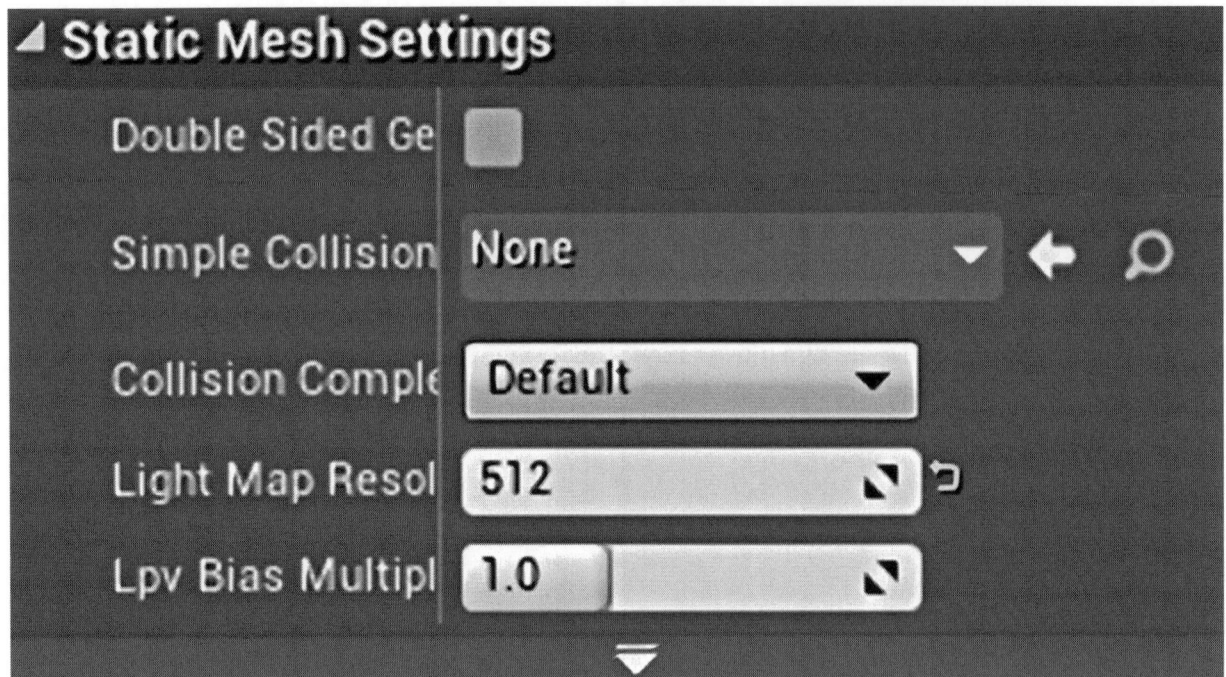

◢ Static Mesh Settings

Double Sided Ge ▢

Simple Collision **None** ▼ ← 🔍

Collision Comple **Default** ▼

Light Map Resol **512** ◣ ↺

Lpv Bias Multipl **1.0** ◣

See the option marked "Simple Collision" (Full label: Simple Collision Physical Material)? At the moment it is set it to default. If you set it it to "Use Complex Collision as Simple", you'll automatically have collision on your box.

This would work for any static mesh (Such as a tree or something that you needed the collision to be the exact same shape as the mesh itself and not a generic box / sphere).

To be completely honest with you, In all the times I've used this method as opposed to using generic collision (Box, Sphere .etc) , I have not noticed any performance differences. You might discover some, I don't know. But I'm using this method in my commercial product and haven't come across any problems doing it this was at all, but I could be wrong on this (Shock horror!). So just be cautious!

Once you've changed it to "Use Complex Collision as Simple", Save it and close the window (Heading back into the main Unreal Engine window).

Test out your project. If you did it correct, then you won't be able to walk through the door anymore! If you do end up still walking through the door; Then you've done something wrong (Skim back the past chapter or two and retrace your steps!).

Our First Puzzle!

So now that the door works, there's one thing we've got to do before we continue. I think you can guess what it is; Copy the door to all the doorways in the scene!

At the moment we have the door covering one doorway and there's three more that need doors. You can simply copy & paste your BP_Door (Or drag it in from the "Content Browser", it's completely up to you!), just make sure that before you continue; Each doorway has a door in it, so a player can't run from one room to the next without a door being in the way!

If you can't be bothered or would like to "Back-up" your work, I have included all the work up until this point on the website (http://www.kitatus.co.uk or http://content.kitatusstudios.co.uk) under the title [LESSON4] (Make sure you're download the file for THIS book and not another book!)

You should now be able to continue; Each room should be locked off with doors and you should be ready to create our first puzzle! (We'll get back to the "Custom Event" for the door later!)

We're going to do a very simple puzzle for this first room: Combining two items together to unlock the door.

This means we'll have to create a simple inventory system!

Before we begin, there's many different methods that you can use to create an inventory; Every one will change depending on your need for that inventory.

As we only need a simple inventory, we'll be using a structure (A collection of Variables) as well as a Blueprint interface to store what is in our inventory, and using UMG to show the player what is in the inventory.

Creating our Inventory!

Before we continue, we're going to need two images to act as our icons in the UMG so the player knows what he / she has picked up.

For those who don't know UMG stands for Unreal Motion Graphics and it's a tool in Unreal Engine 4 that allows you to create menus, pause screens, health bars .etc. Basically, anything that you want to appear on the screen (That's not in the in-game world) as a 2D object, you'll be using UMG to bring them to life.

Now that we've got that little description out of the way, As I said just before the UMG description: We need two images to that we'll put on the UMG to show what the player has picked up.

You can do this in two different ways. You can create the images yourself or download my pre-created ones from the project files on the KITATUS website (http://www.kitatus.co.uk).

If you're creating the two images of your own, make sure image #1 is of a can and image #2 is of a small button. Please make sure that the images you created has an empty background and that you can see the object from a distance (As our UMG won't be that big!).

For reference, here are the two images available to you on the KITATUS website:

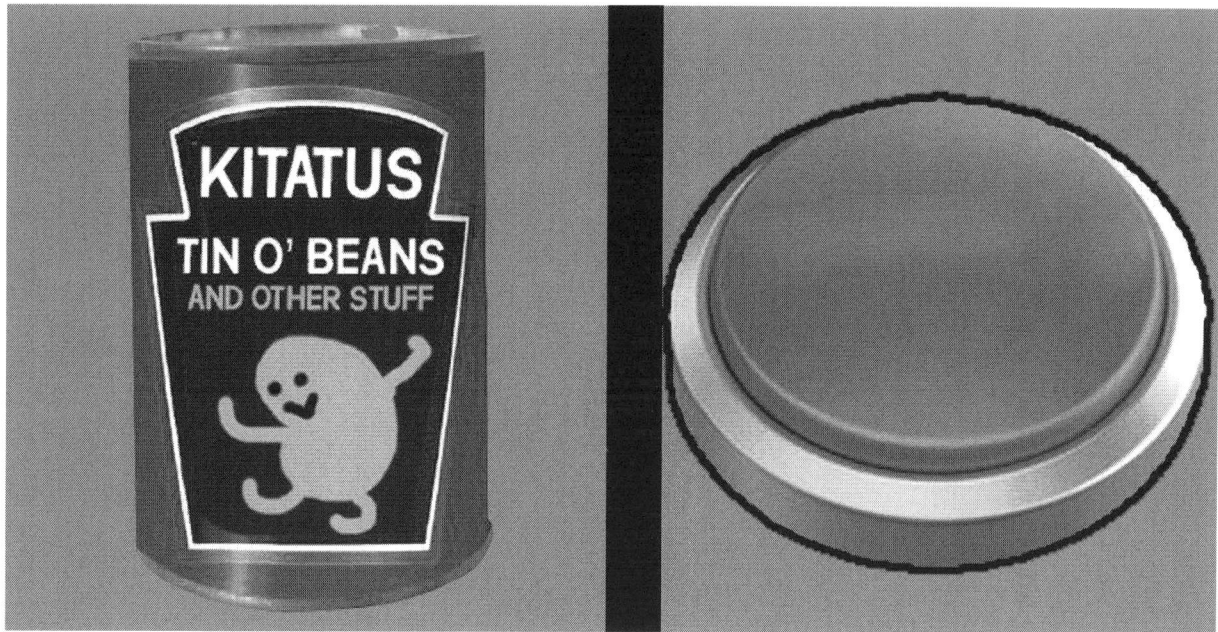

I created each image at a 500 x 500 resolution with a clear background and a simple image in the middle. This means that if I scale it down, you'll still be able to make out what the image represents.

Once you've either created your two images or downloaded mine, import them into your project by going into your Content Browser (Make sure you're in your "ArtOfBP" folder <Or whatever you called that folder!>) and selecting "Import".

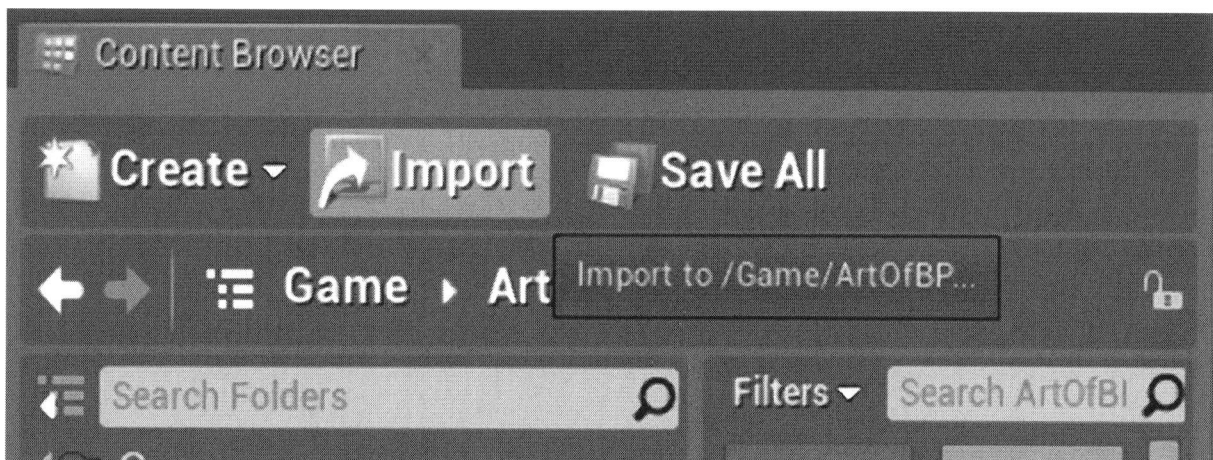

When the window opens up, navigate to wherever your images are and highlight them both to import them into your project!

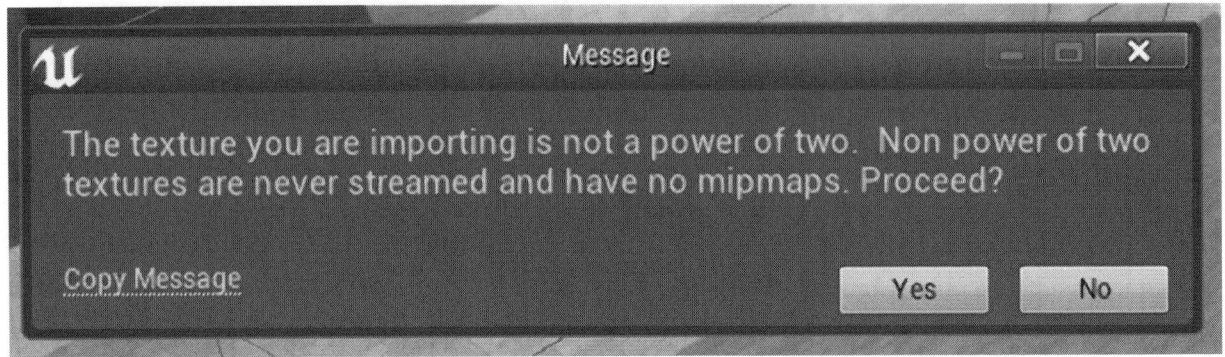

Message

The texture you are importing is not a power of two. Non power of two textures are never streamed and have no mipmaps. Proceed?

Copy Message   Yes   No

It then might tell you: "The texture you are importing is not a power of two". Don't panic, this is something we don't have to worry about in this instance (I'll bring it up in the future if it ever gets in our way), so just hit "Yes" and it will import the two images as textures!

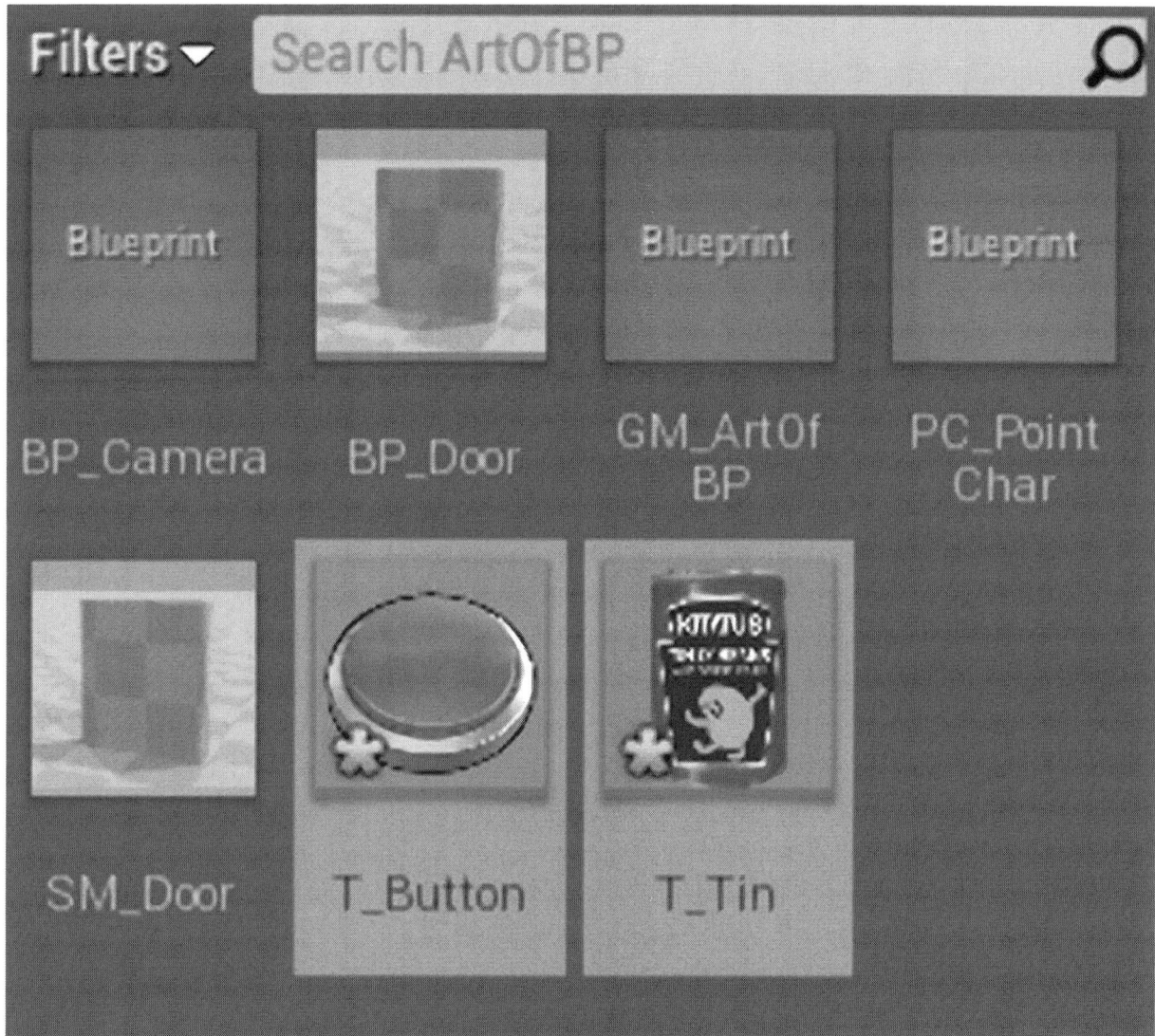

Excellent! Now would be a great time to save your project up until this point.

Blueprint Interface? Huh?

The next thing to do before we have a working inventory is to create a Blueprint Interface Blueprint (Man, that sounds confusing!)

A Blueprint Interface acts as a "Middle man" if you will for our data. Imagine sending money abroad to a friend or a distant relative. You don't normally send the money directly but instead you would send it via a third-party (Such as Western

Union or a similar international money transferring service), which would then send the money to the person in question.

Imagine the Blueprint interface as that international money transferring service. It will take data from one blueprint and give it to another, a lot like casting (More on that later!) but with less of an overhead.

So go ahead and into your Content Browser again. This time go to "Create" > "Blueprints" (NOT "Blueprint" but the menu button that says "Blueprints") > "Blueprint Interface".

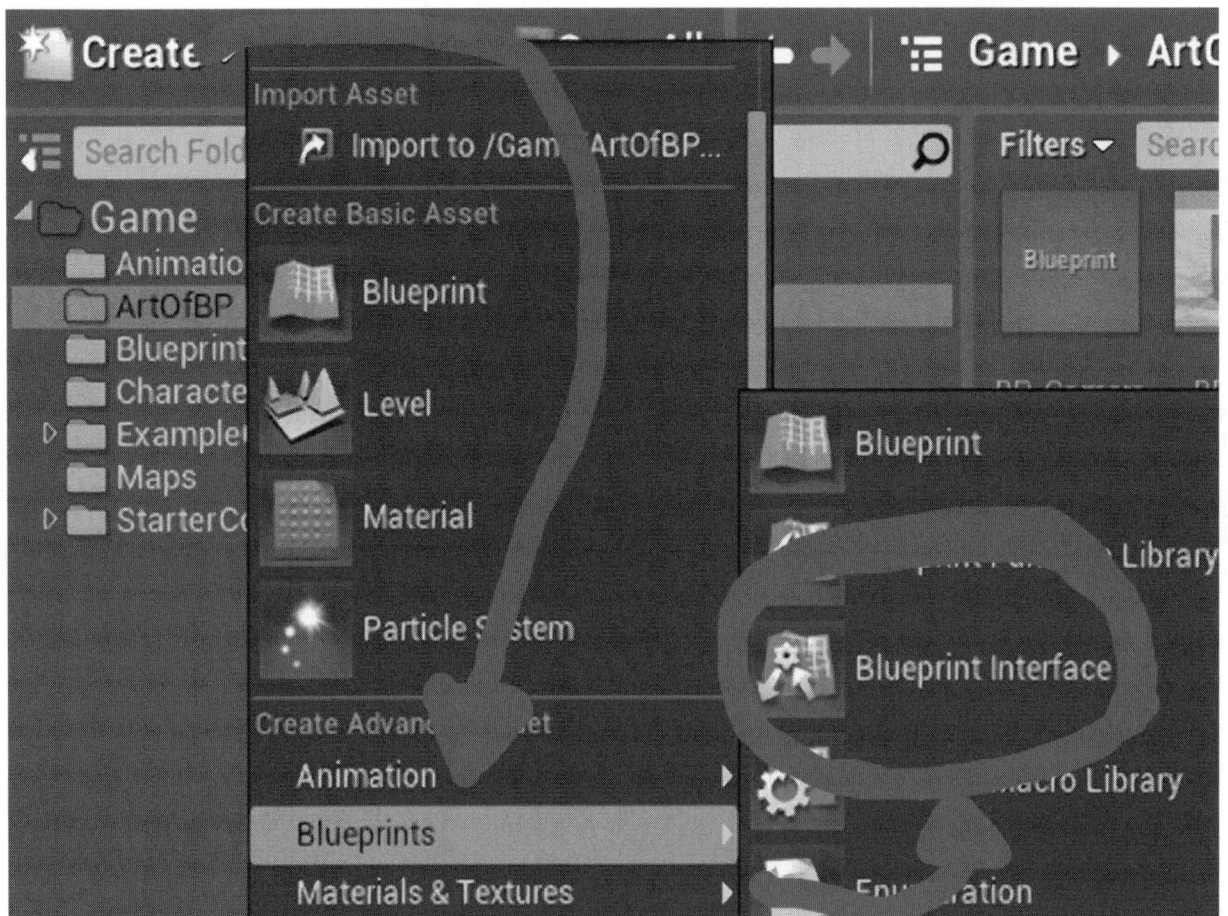

Name the newly created Blueprint interface: "BI_Inv" which stands for "Blueprint Interface: Inventory".

Once you've named the Blueprint Interface, double click it to open the Blueprint Interface editor.

You'll notice immediately that it doesn't look like a normal blueprint at all! (That's because it isn't!)

For one, there isn't a way to navigate to any "Defaults, Components or Graph", as there is no navigation ribbon!

Instead, we are given one option in those regards (At first anyway!) and that's the "Defaults" view. This is where we will store the information to send between Blueprints.

To send the information between the two blueprints, we need to create a function. We've done this before, but it works a little differently inside a Blueprint Interface.

Go ahead and click the "New Function" button (Which has an image of the F with a +, just like before!).

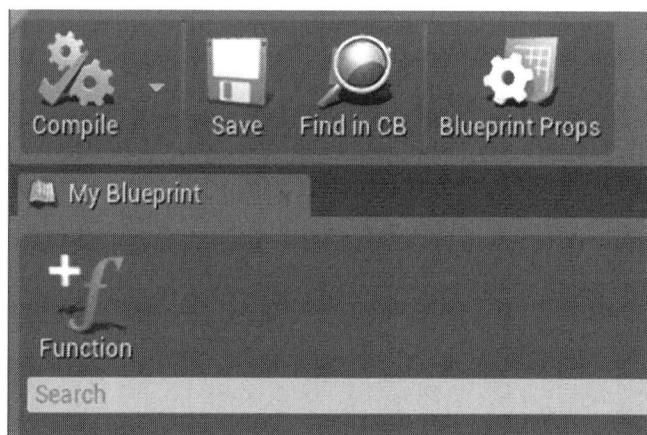

After you've clicked it, we're now looking at a scene that looks strikingly similar to a Blueprint…

Use the Variable Library on the left to name the function "Action_Use". We are then going to create yet another function, but this time call the function "Action_Drop".

This is just as a little extra so that the player may drop whatever is in their inventory. It's not needed for our example but it will help you get a better gist of things in terms of learning about Blueprint Interfaces / getting a deeper understanding of functions .etc

You'll see why now:

Double click on the "Action_Use" in your Blueprint Interface. All you have to do here is click "Compile" and then "Save" (On the top bar).

Now head into your "Action_Drop". We need to add an input which let's us "Get" the actor, so we know which Actor needs dropping. So go ahead and scroll down in the "Variable Library" until you get to the section marked "Inputs".

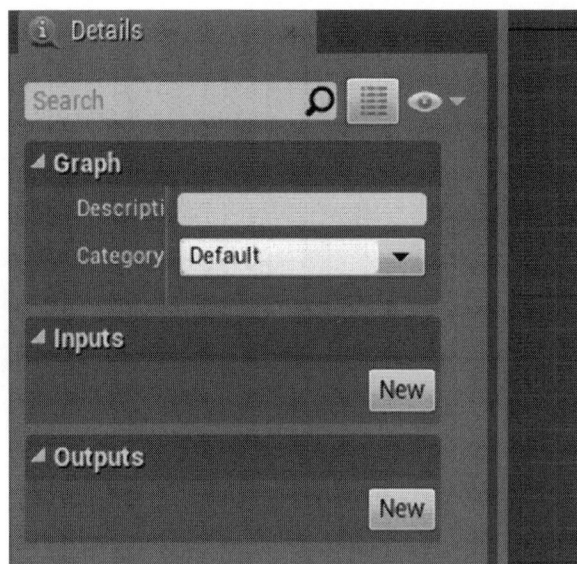

Hit "New" and set the "Variable Type" to "Actor" (You can do this by typing "Actor" into the search box when you click the Variable Type!). Once set as "Actor", go ahead and name the Variable "Actor" and then compile and save.

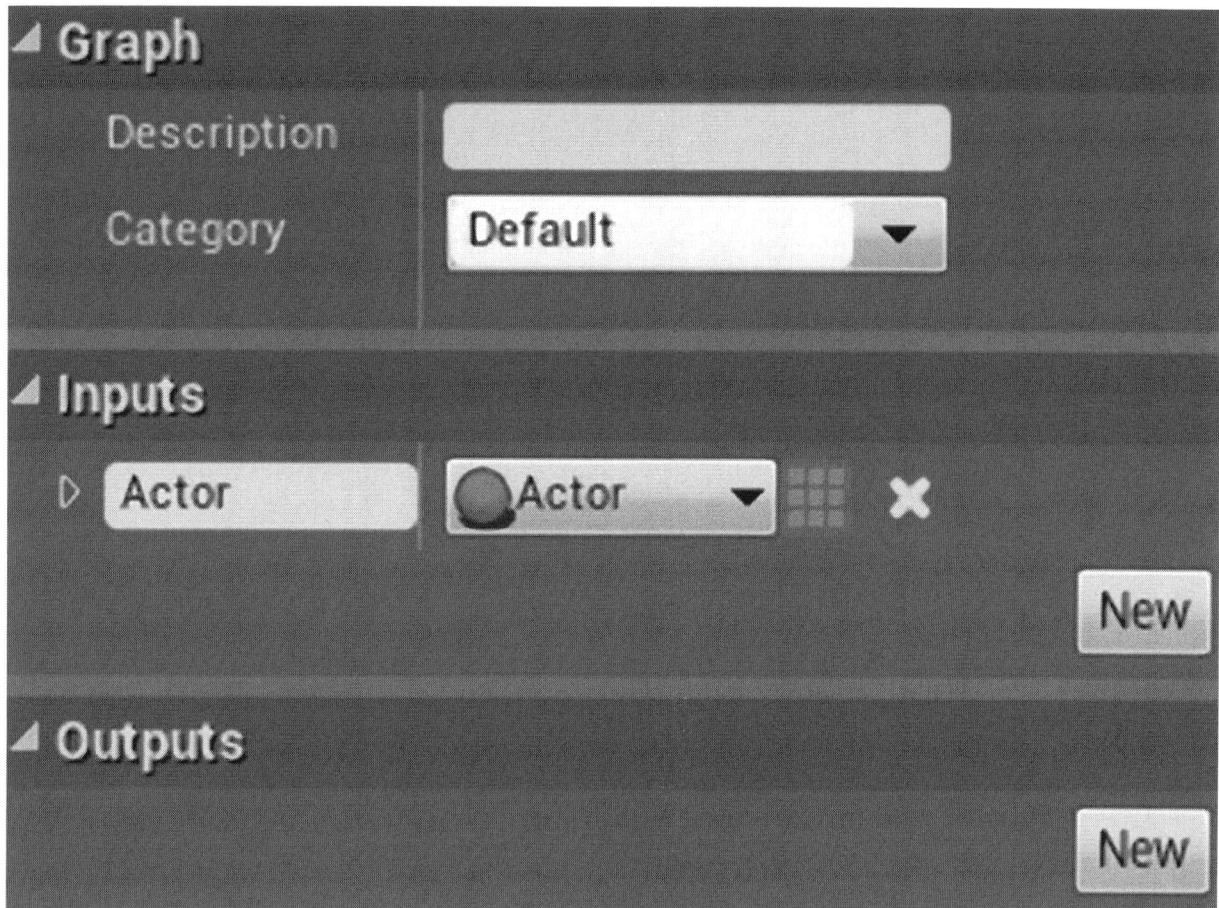

Once compiled and save, you can now close down the Blueprint Interface and head back into your main scene view.

Structure? What is this?!

Just like we created the Blueprint Interface, we need to create a Structure blueprint.

A structure blueprint is a lot like an array (A collection of variables), however they differ in the fact that a structure can contain different types of variables whereas an array can only have one type of array.

A good way to explain this without getting too confusing would be: Imagine you're in a shop that sells fish and chips. You have two shopping baskets, one is the Structure and one is the array.

You are told that you need to make a delicious meal of fish and chips for 500 people, so you walk along and add a fish and one lot of chips to your array basket. That's when you discover that the array basket can only have one type of food in there and you have to decide: Either get yet another basket (And carry three baskets!) to carry fish in one and chips in the other, or use a structure, which would allow you to carry all 500 fish AND chips in the one basket.

That was a bit of a silly analogy but I hope you get the picture!

Go ahead and head into your "Content Browser" and go to "Create" > "Blueprints" (NOT "Blueprint"!) > "Structure".

Name this Structure Blueprint "Struct_Inv", which of course stands for: Structure: Inventory. Once named, double click it to open up the Structure editor!

You'll notice that the Structure editor seems a lot simpler then some of the other editors we've had to deal with on our journey, so let's dive right in.

We need three variables:

- Name: "Object" - Type: "Actor"
- Name: "ObjectTexture" - Type: "Texture2D"
- Name: "ActionText" - Type: "Text"

Go ahead and create these now in your Structure Blueprint.

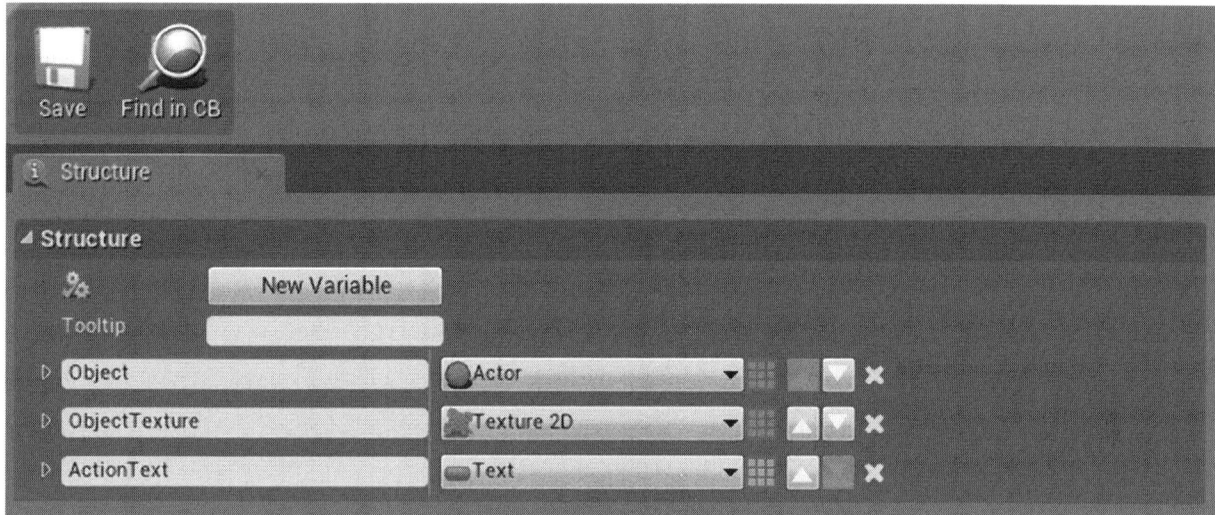

Once you've created them all, you can go ahead and click "Save" and close down this Structure Blueprint for now.

Creating our Tin and Button!

Now we're going to use a lot of knowledge we already picked up to create out Tin and Button blueprints!

First things first, make sure you in the main Unreal Engine window (With your scene view in the centre).

We're going to start off by creating our can. Just like we did with the BP_Door, we're going to use a BSP to create the can then we're going to convert it to a static mesh. From there, we'll convert it to a blueprint and then add our code to turn it into an inventory item!

In an effort to save space in the book, I'll task you with either creating the can and tin via BSPs or you are free download the Static Meshes from the website (In the project files).

So go ahead and create the two BSPs now [And convert them to Static Meshes!] (Or download them from the project files!).

Once you've got the two Static Meshes (One for the Tin and one for the Button!) it's time to create our next Blueprint!

As you well know by now, there's a number of ways that you can create your blueprint with the static meshes in question. One way would be to right click (Ctrl + Click) the static mesh in the content browser and select: "Asset Actions > Create a Blueprint Based on this", but we're going to do things a little differently…

We are going to create a Blueprint in which we can set the pick-up whenever we like; Which means we only need to create the one Blueprint for both of our Static Meshes!

The reason we're doing it this way is because this allows you to expand on the blueprint in the future in case you want to make a bigger inventory for your future point and click projects!

One Blueprint Fits All

So we're now going to create a blueprint for our inventory items that adapts to our needs.

It sounds complicated but to be honest, it's not much different at all to how we've been doing our Blueprints up until this point… So let's jump right in!

As we've done a number of times, head into your Content Browser (Into your "ArtOfBP" folder!) and create a new Blueprint. The parent class of this Blueprint should be "Actor" and go ahead and call it "BP_Pickup".

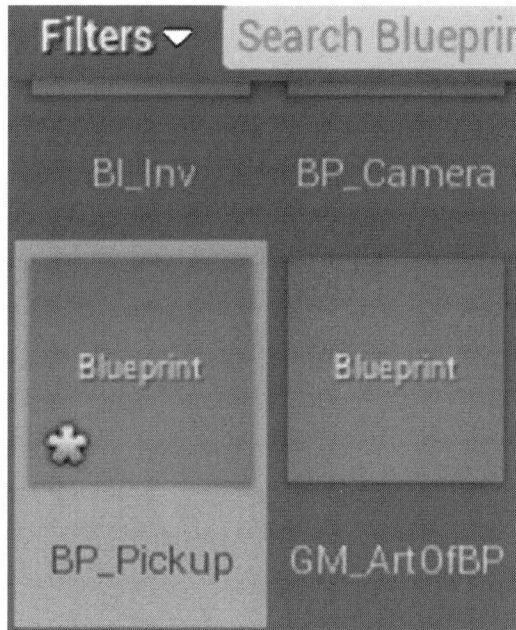

Once you've created the blueprint, go ahead and double-click it so we can get to fun stuff!

Just like we did for the BP_Door, head into the "Components" view and make sure you create a "Scene" and make it the "Root" component.

If you don't remember how to or why we need to do this, go ahead and skim back to the section of this book where we talked in detail about the benefits of doing so (When we created the Door Blueprint)!

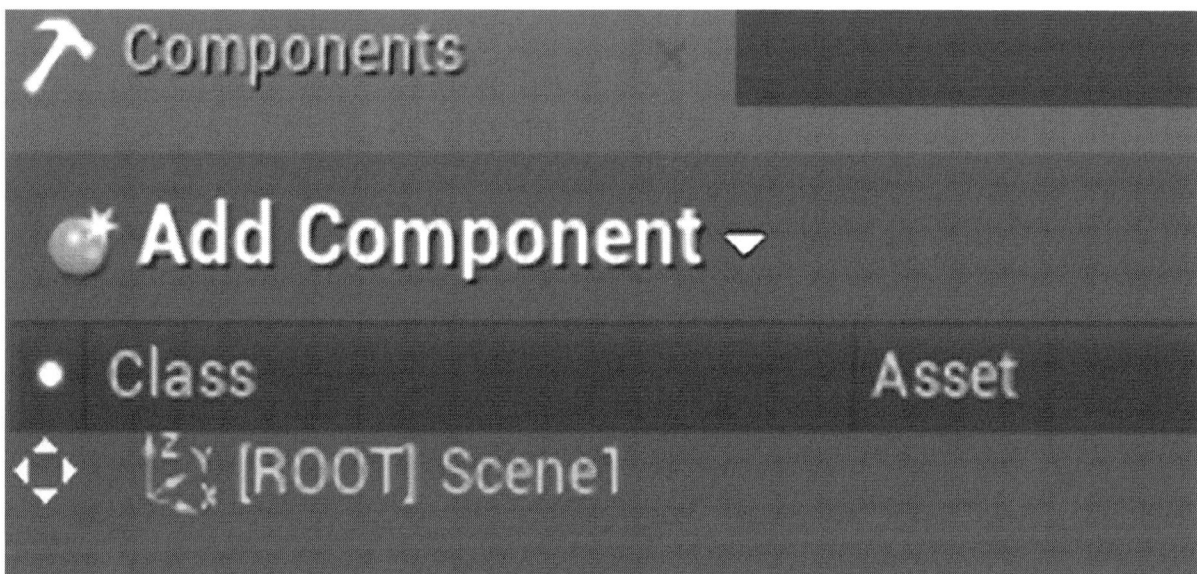

Once you've created the "Scene" component and made it the "Root" component, go ahead and create a "Static Mesh" component, just like we did for the "BP_Door".

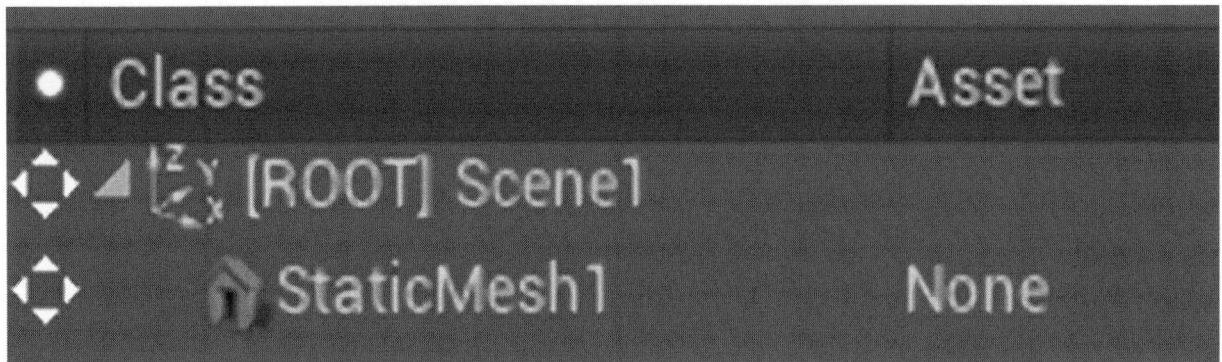

Go ahead and name the "StaticMesh component" from "StaticMesh1" to "PickUpMesh".

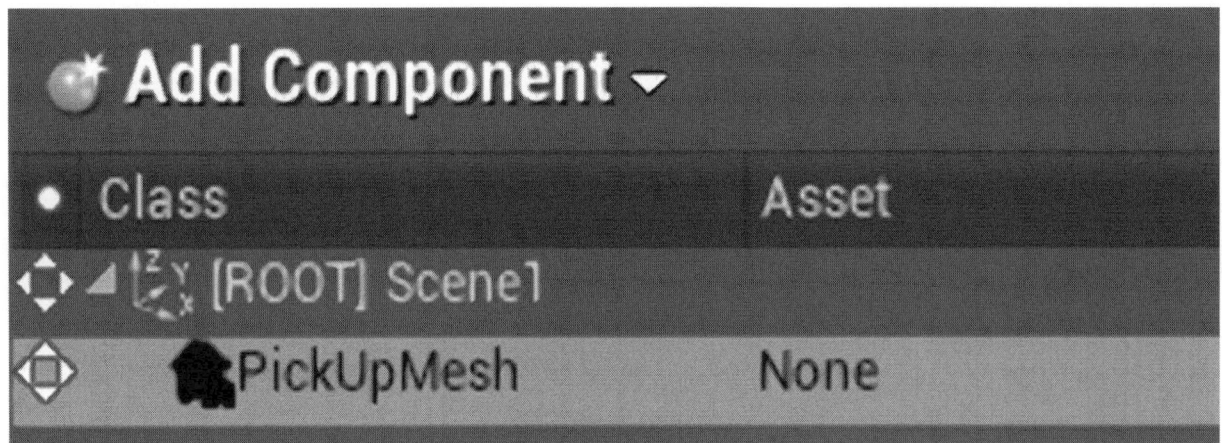

Unlike the "BP_Door", we are not actually going to set a Static Mesh for this "Static Mesh component".

I bet you're thinking "What, Why?!". This is because we'll actually be setting the mesh in our code (As we'll be unsure if this Blueprint will be representing the Tin can or the button until the code has been finished!).

We'll be adding one more component: A "Box" component. We'll be using this to see if the player has walked up to our object and from there we'll be able to see if they can pick it up or not!

So go ahead and add this "Box" to your Blueprint now!

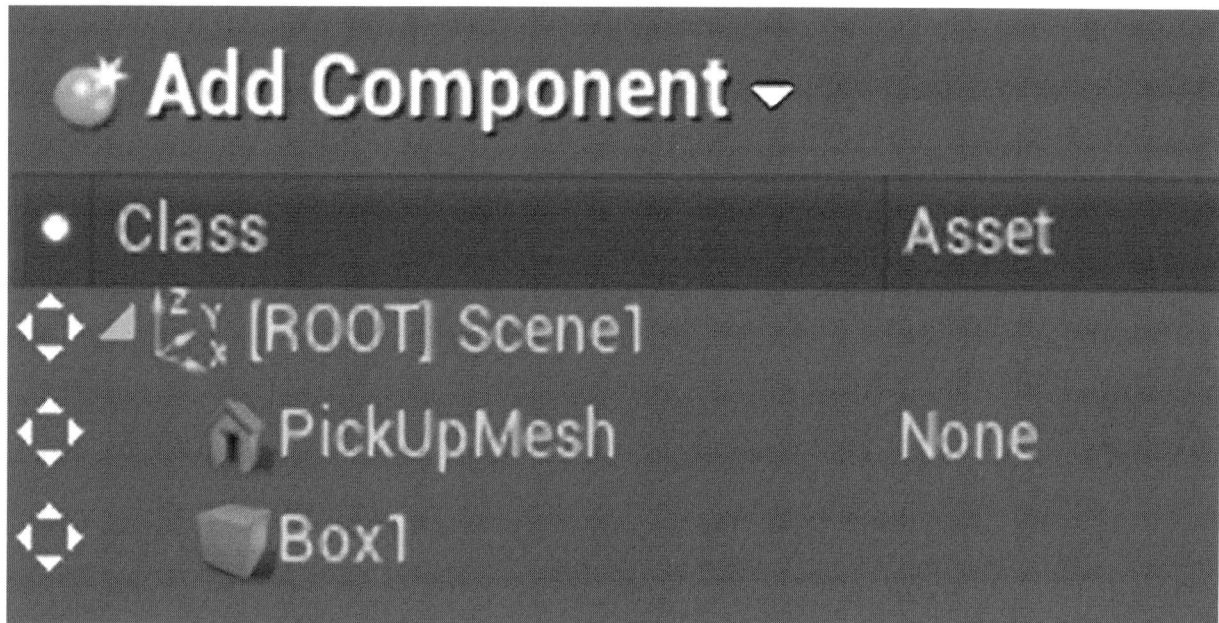

You'll notice by looking at the scene view of your "Components" view that the box is a bit too small. This isn't a problem as we can quite easily resize the box!

If you click the "Box1" component, you'll notice it's properties show up just underneath the "Component Class" list.

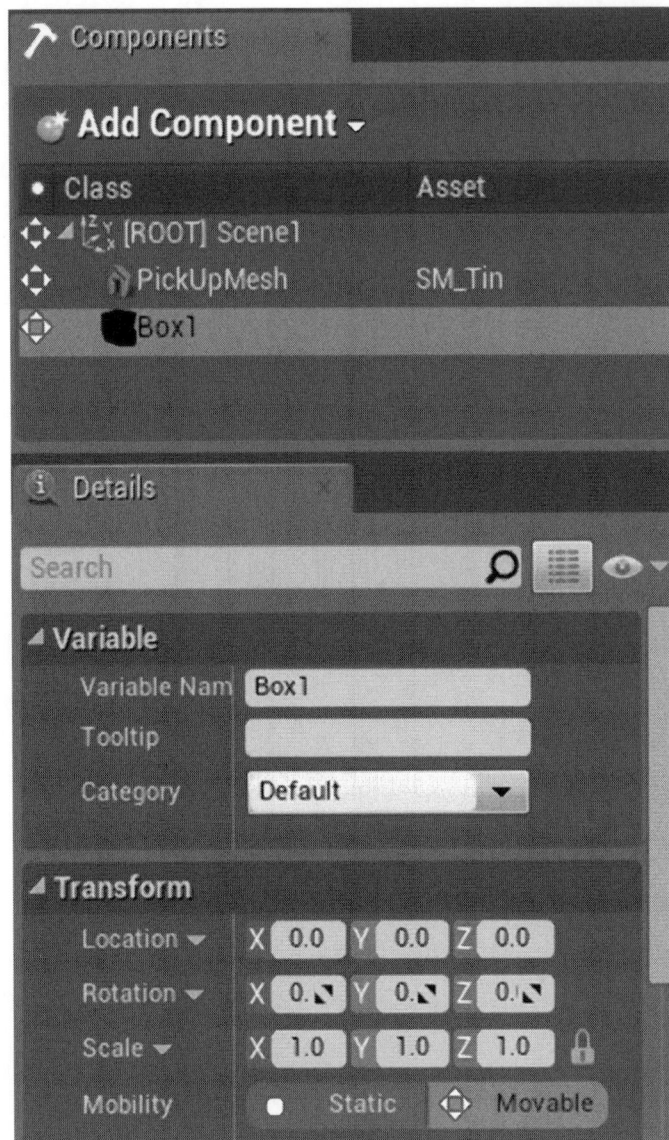

Within these settings, you'll see a section marked "Transform", with settings such as "Location", "Rotation", "Scale" and "Mobility". We've covered these all throughout the book and for those who have forgotten, it's all rather self-explanatory.

Location changes the location of the box, Rotation… You guessed it! Scale makes the box either bigger / smaller and mobility says if the box will move or not (Just leave it a "Movable" for now!)

I've messed around with these settings and found that setting the scale to "3" on X, Y AND Z gives an optimal result. So go ahead and change it now, change the X, Y and Z from "1" to "3"!

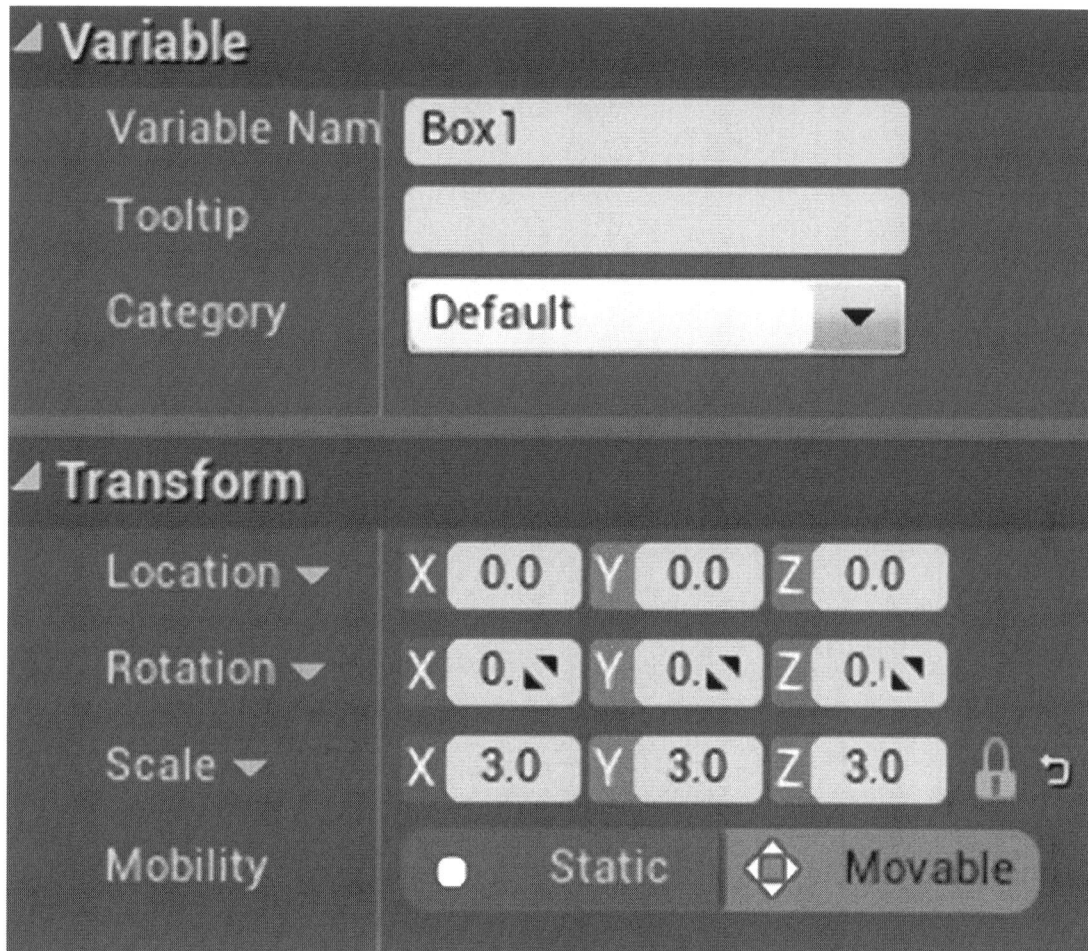

We've now got all the components we need, it's time to create the code to bring our Blueprint to life!

Use the navigation ribbon on the top-right to go from the "Components" tab into your "Graph" tab.

Before we can code all of the usual business (Overlaps and whatnot), we first need to code the part which will tell us what Pickup we want this to be. As we want to set this in the editor (Without constantly mucking about with code)!, we'll have to add some code to the construction script!

I briefly explained around page 80 about what the construction script is / does:

"The construction script is where you create code to set-up the blueprint - For example, setting the mesh of the blueprint, telling the BP to do a certain thing when we're messing around in the editor .etc"

I know that sounds a little weird at first, but don't worry, once we get into adding some code to it, it will all make sense!

Do you remember how to get to the Construction Script? I mentioned it around page 80, but for those who can't remember: Click the tab just above the Blueprint area!

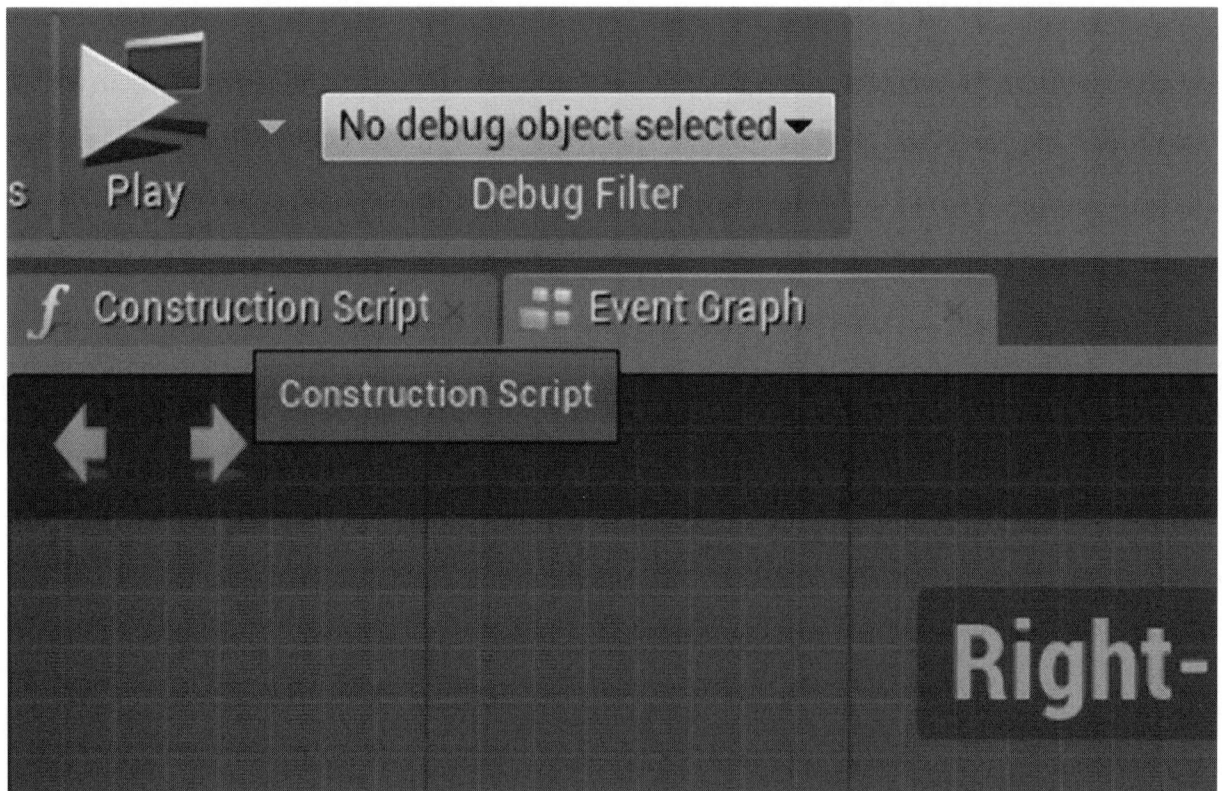

So go ahead and dive straight into the "Construction Script" tab now! To double check that you're in the construction script, you'll see this pre-created node in the centre of your Blueprint area:

Drag Off Pins to Create/Connect New Nodes.

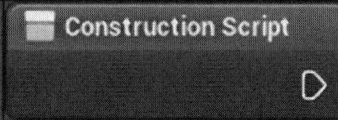

Construction Script

You'll notice that the node is called "Construction Script" and has a single output execution pin. Knowing your inquisitive brain, you'll be asking: Well, when does the code attached to this fire?!

The code created in the construction script will fire as soon as the actors exists. This could be when the level starts (And the Blueprint is present!) or even when you create the Blueprint within the editor.

It will even fire when you change a property or move it around in the editor! Groovy!

So to recap, As soon as the actor exists within the world, all of the code attached the "Construction Script" node will fire. Which, might I add, is JUST what we need for picking out static mesh and setting our properties!

So let's get coding!

First things first, we're going to need to do is set the mesh in the "Mesh component" slot (As it's empty at the moment!

The way we're going to do this is by using an integer. Remember when I first told you about integers? I explained to you that they can be any number (As long as it's a whole number AND not a minus number!) for example: 0, 1, 2 .etc.

We're going to use this functionality to tell our blueprint when it should be the tin and when it's supposed to be the button!

How does this work? Well, we'll assume that if the Integer we're about to create is 0, then the BP should be a tin and if it's 1, then assume the Blueprint is supposed to be the button!

You can use what you learn next in many different circumstances. I use this method A LOT for when I'm creating a menu: If the Int is 0 then the player can select "New Game" but it's it's 1 then the player is hovering over the "Options menu", if the Int is 2 then they're looking at "Quit Game" .etc.

I could preach about this method all day long but it'll fall upon deaf ears unless you can see the magic for yourself, so let's sort it out for our project now!

Go ahead and head over to your Variable library and create a new Variable, Setting it's "Variable Type" to Integer (Int) and it's name to "PickupType".

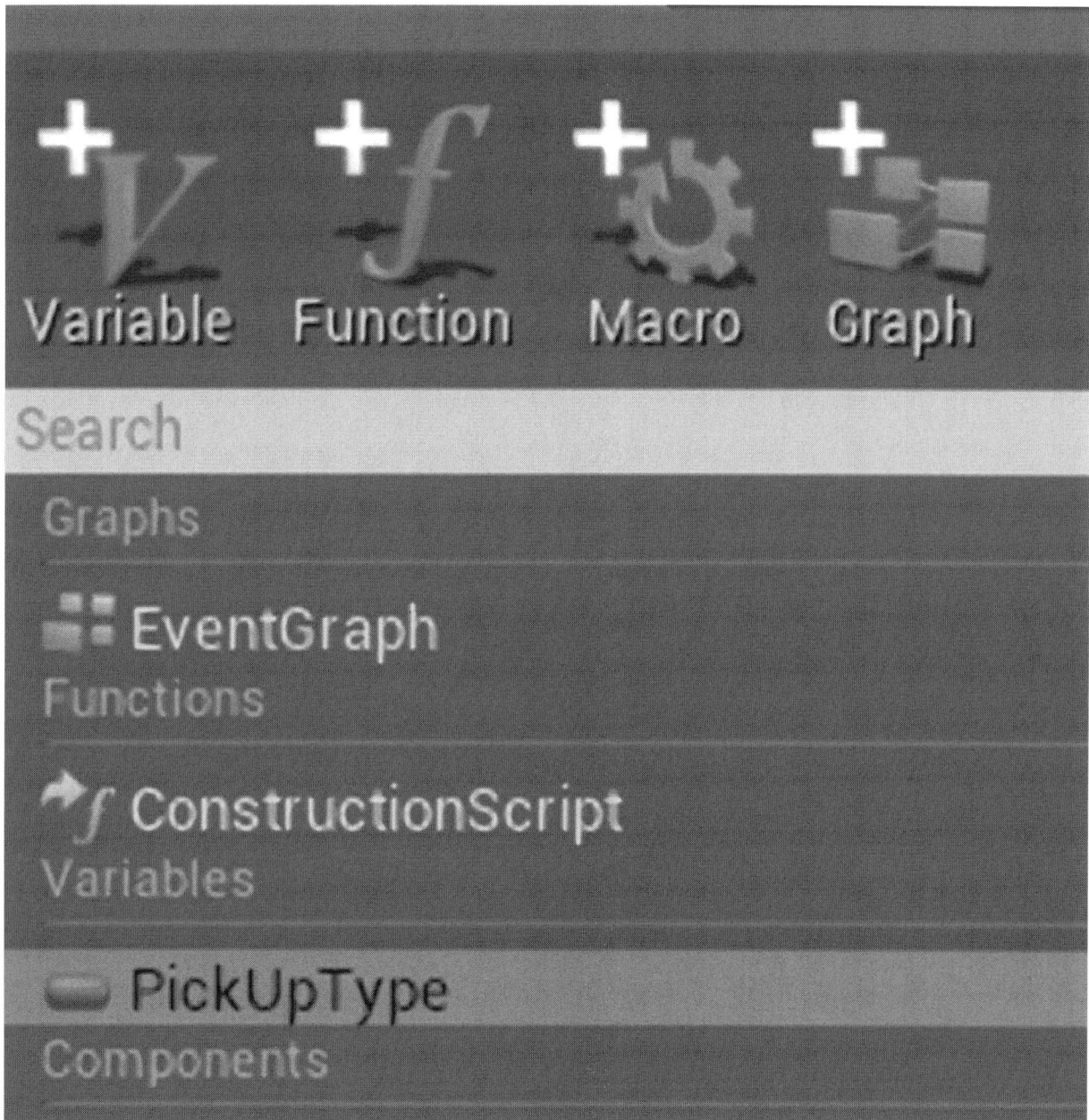

Excellent. We now need to set this variable as "Public" (So we can see it and change it while in the Editor!). You can do this by clicking the closed eye to the right of your variable. Clicking it will "Open" the eye, which means the Variable is now editable.

 Be sure to Save + Compile right now by the way. For some reason, the whole "Variable being Editable" doesn't work until you compile your Blueprint - So go ahead and do that now!

Once you've saved and compiled, we can continue!

We've created our Variable but at the moment, it's "Empty". So let's add some code to put some information into it.

In your Blueprint area, open up the Compact Blueprint Library and create a "SwitchOnInt" node.

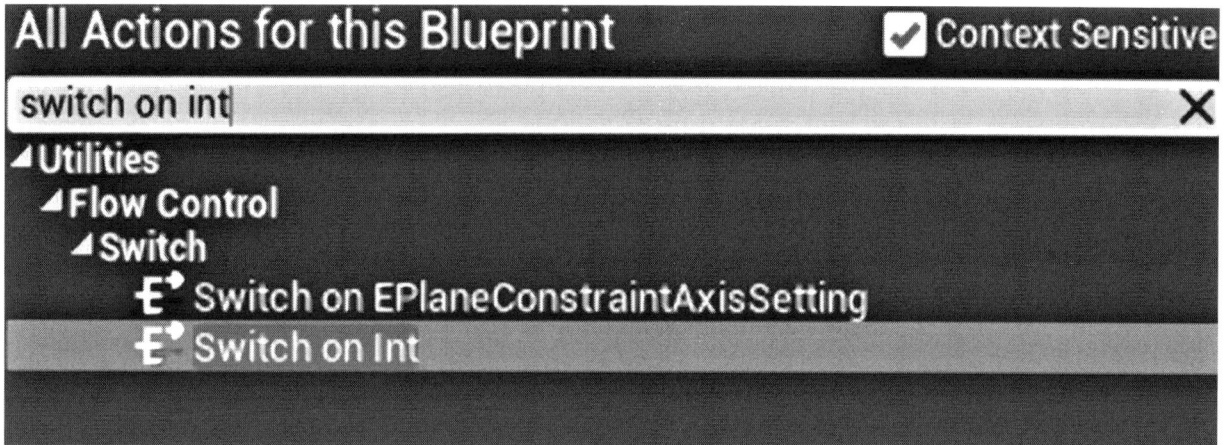

This node will take an Integer variable and depending on it's current value, fire different code.

As I just described, we need to have separate code depending on our "PickUpType" int. If the Int is 0 = Fire the code that sets this Blueprint up as a Tin and if it's 1 = Fire the code that sets this Blueprint up as a button.

At first glance of the node, It looks almost impossible to have create that functionality:

So how do we set the node up? Quite easily! First things first, click the node and check the area just underneath the "Variable Library".

See the selection that says "Has Default Pin?" - Untick that box.

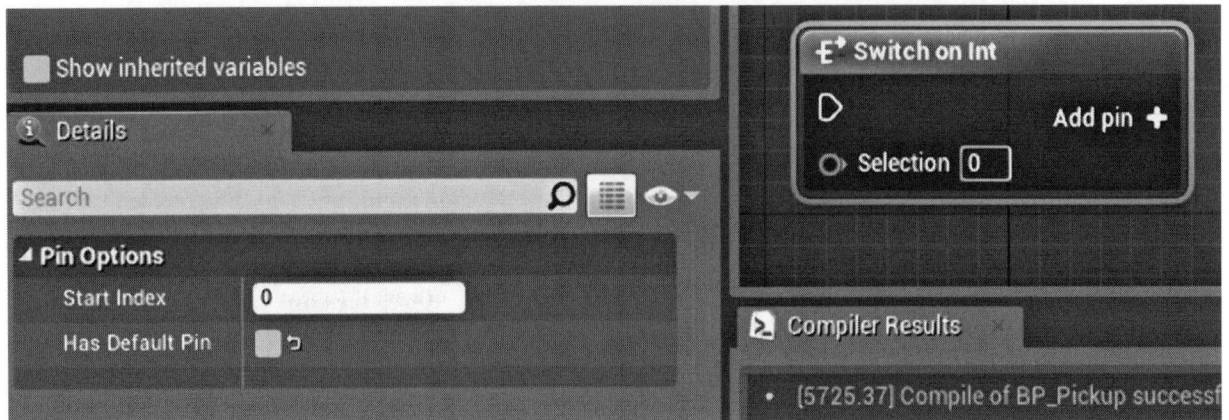

There's no real need for it and by not having it keeps our node clean, tidy and easy to read!

Now head back to the node itself. See the part that says "Add pin +"? Go ahead and click the plus twice and you'll end up with two output execution pins: "0" and "1".

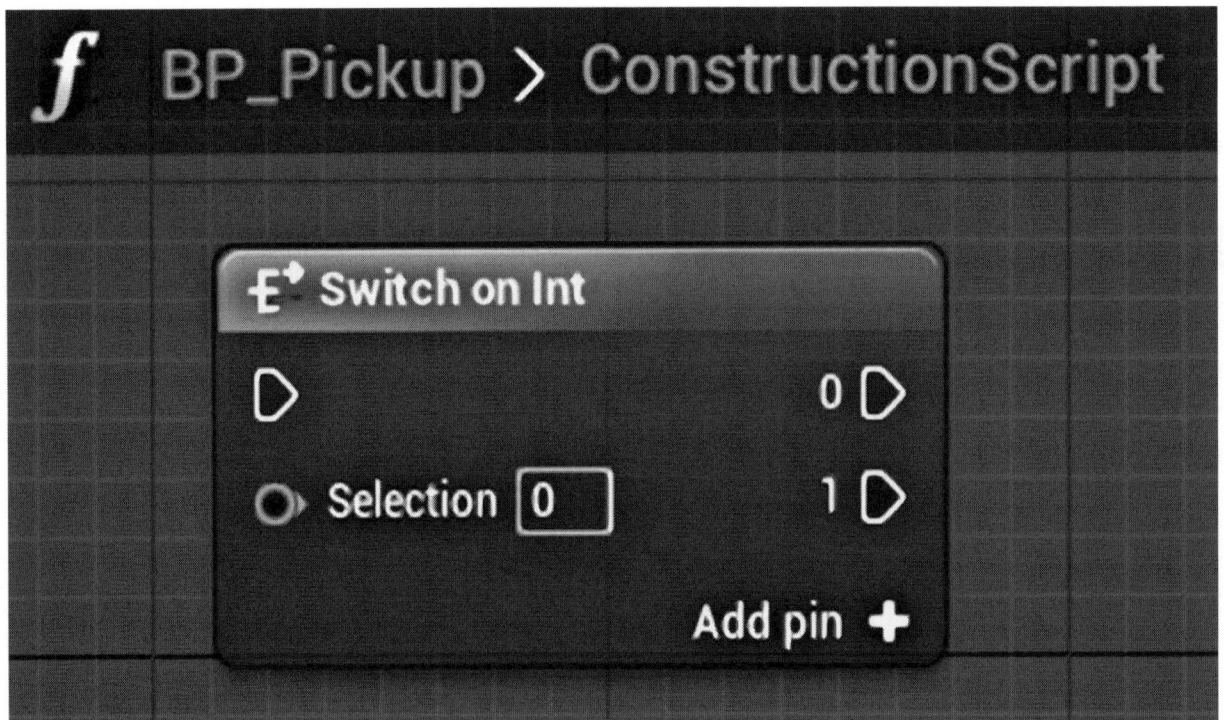

I bet you're wondering what this means? These are the choices from the Int! If the Int is 0 then do the code connected to "0" whereas if the Int is "1" then… You know the rest.

If you're wondering why the default number is 0 then you're not alone. A lot of people (And I mean A LOT) make the mistake of setting the first number of the Ints to 1 when in fact Ints start at 0.

As a way of remembering this, think of Metal Gear Solid 4 (If you've played it).

SPOILERS FOR MGS4 IN THE NEXT PARAGRAPH!!!

At the end of Metal Gear Solid 4, there is a monologue from a character in which states that the world doesn't start a "1" like most people believe, but it in fact starts at "0". You can't have any less then "0" but "0" can grow and grow and grow. No matter how much "0" grows, you can't go below "0". This is EXACTLY how Integers work!

END OF SPOILERS.

Enough spoilers, Let's get back onto topic!

So at the moment, you'll notice something missing. Take a look at "Selection" of the "Switch on Int" node. Do you notice something… missing? No? Think about it. We created an Int… Doesn't it feel like it should be somewhere?.... !

You guessed it! You've got to bring your "PickUpType" Variable from the Variable Library (Select "Get" when asked!) and plug it into the "Selection" input of the Switch on Int node.

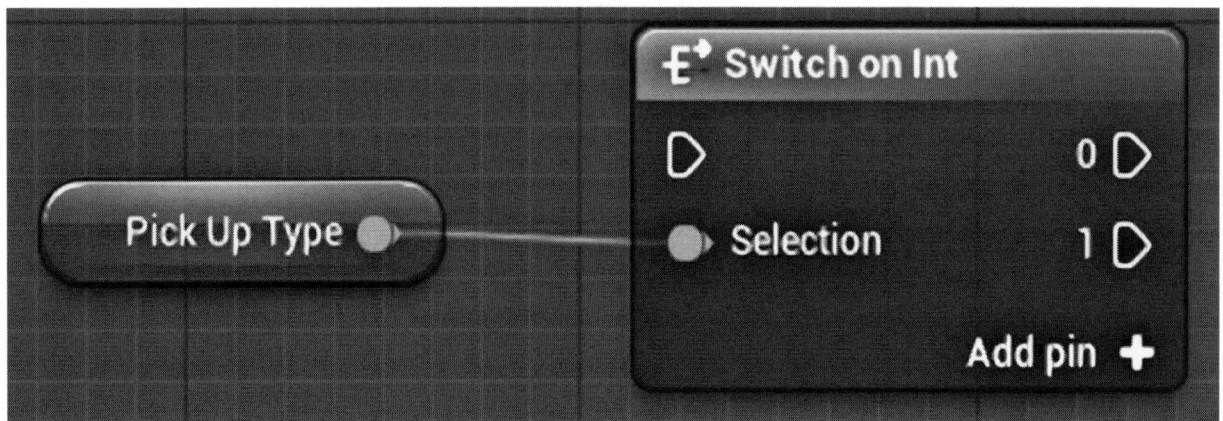

There's almost one thing left to do before we can add the rest of our code! We've got to connect the "Switch on Int" input execution pin to the output of the "Construction Script"'s output execution pin!

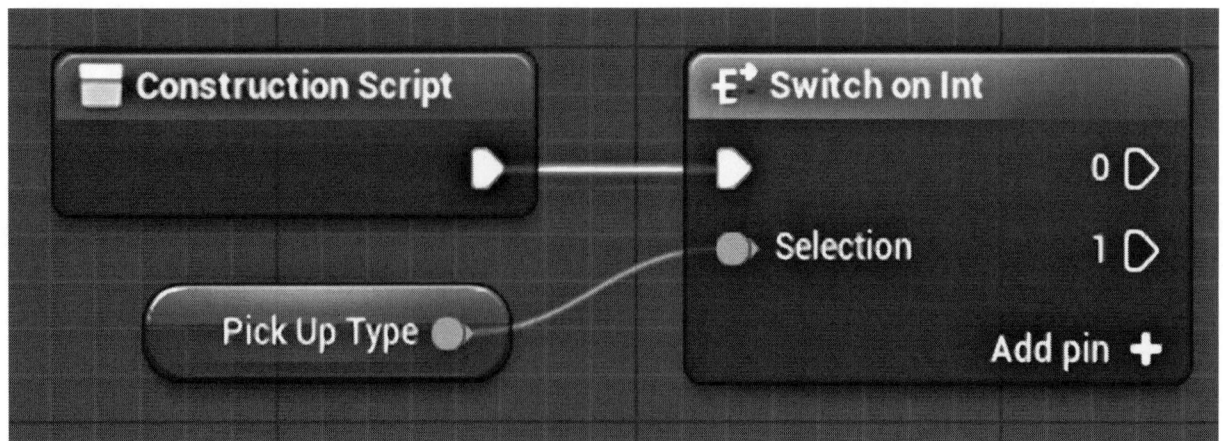

Awesome! Now we have code that is saying:

"When this code fires, check what value "PickUpType" is and set what code to fire accordingly".

A few of you keen-eyed people might be asking: "Well, when / where is PickUpType actually set?" - Remember how we set the variable to: "Editable"? This means we'll be able to set the value of the variable ourselves in the editor!

Which basically means when we're ready, we'll tell the Blueprint what type of object it should be! How awesome / simple is that?

So the foundations of our code is nearly complete, We simply now need to set the mesh to show and we can then begin to add code to the main area of the blueprint!

This is another one of those things which will vary between engine versions:

1) If you're using Unreal Engine 4 (4.6 or above) then all you'll have to do is open up the CBL and select: "Set Static Mesh <Insert Component Name Here!>" to select the connect node.

2) If you're using any version of Unreal Engine 4 that predates 4.6, you'll have to manually drag in your static mesh component from the Variable Library and from the output pin, creating a "Set Static Mesh" node.

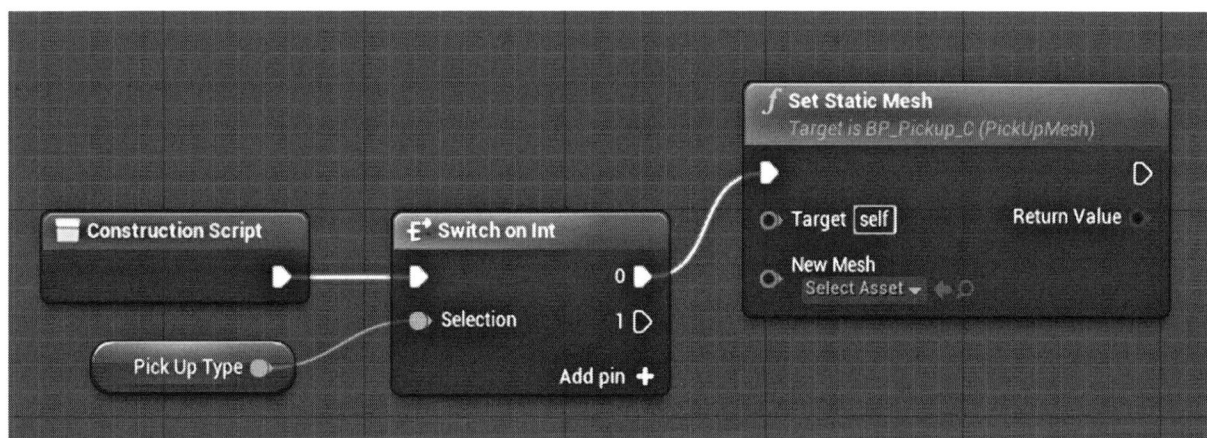

Repeat the previous step so you have two "Set Static Mesh" nodes, one connected to the "0" output and one connected to the "1" output of the Switch on Int node.

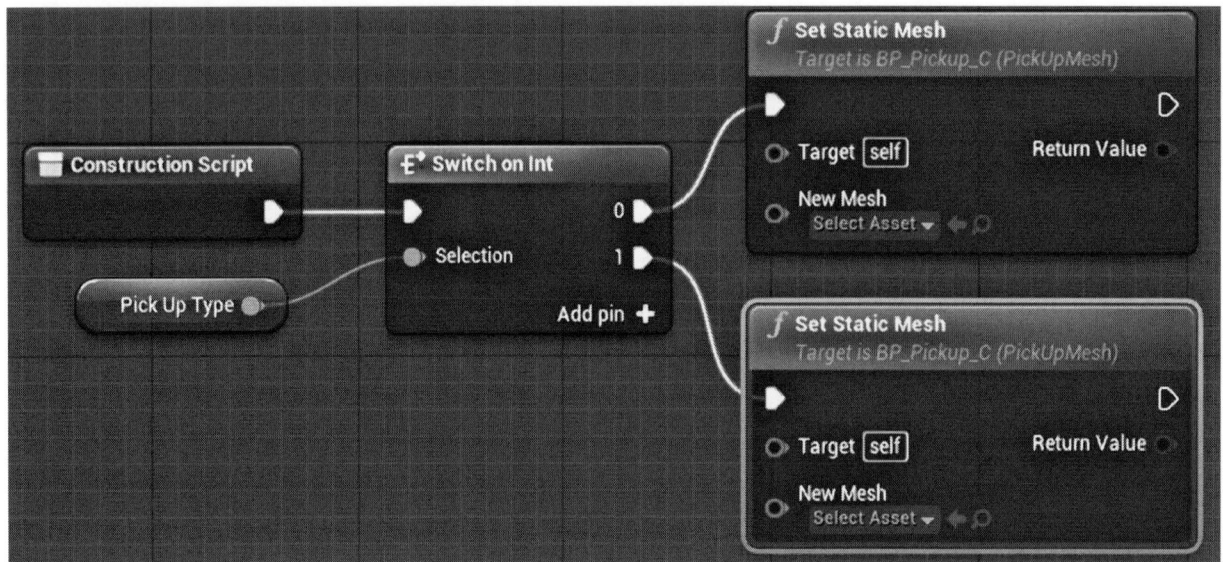

Now, within the "Set Static Mesh" nodes, select the "New Mesh"'s "Select Asset" dropdown menu and select the mesh you want to use.

Make sure that the mesh you use in the "Set Static Mesh" node is the one that corresponds with the output of the "Switch on Int" node that it's connected to.

For example, your first "Set Static Mesh" node should be setting the Static Mesh to the tin can mesh and the second "Set Static Mesh" node should be setting the mesh to the button!

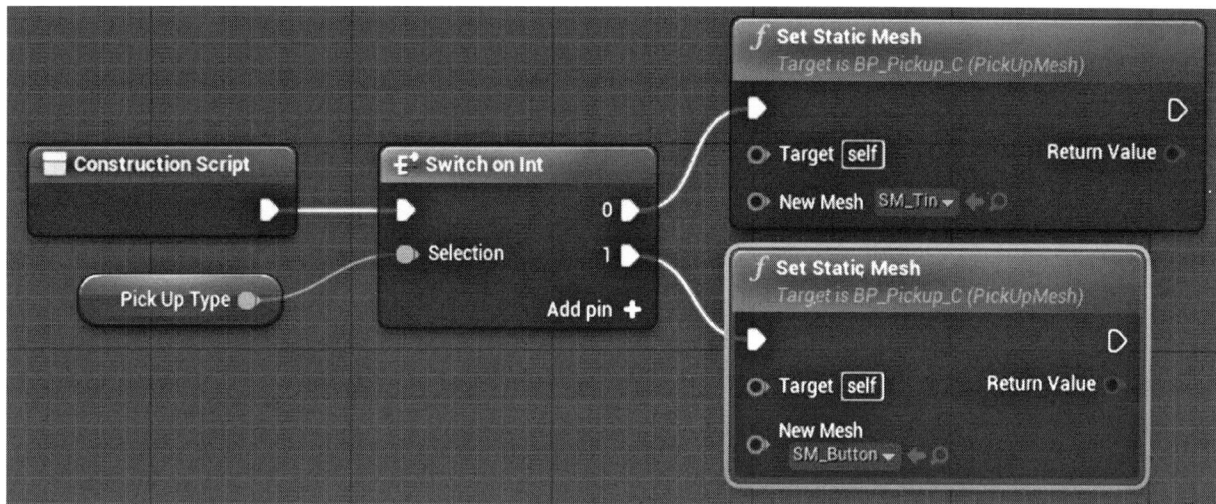

So your graph should currently look like this: **Construction Script** > **Switch on Int** (PickUpType) > **0** = Set Static Mesh (SM_Tin) / **1** = Set Static Mesh (SM_Button).

We're all done with this Construction Script, It's time to head into the Event Graph!

Event Graph... We meet again!

In this Event Graph, we need to state if the player is in the trigger volume we set up (The box we created in the components view). If the player is in the box, we need to "Add" the static mesh into the player "Backpack" and delete the "Static Mesh" from existence.

So let's get right to it! Head into your Event Graph of your BP_Pickup and let's add some code!

To add the collision event, head on into your variable library and give "Box1" a right-click (Or Ctrl + Click).

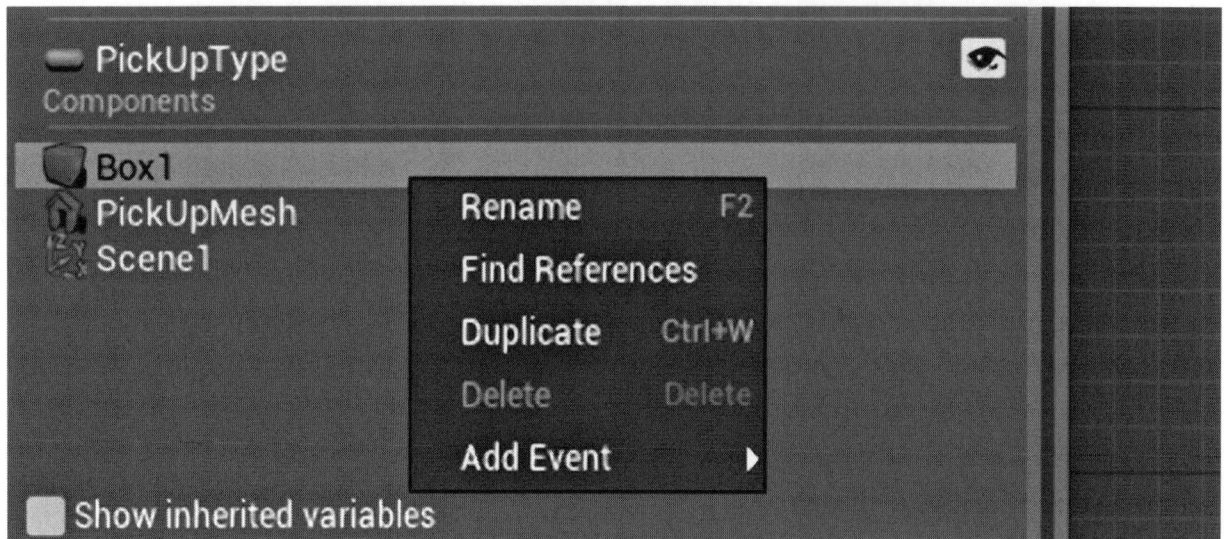

You'll notice in the drop-down menu that appears that there is a section called "Add Event". As we've explained before, and "Event" is the life-force of a Blueprint. Without the correct event firing, your code won't work. So let's go ahead and see what options this Add Event option gives us:

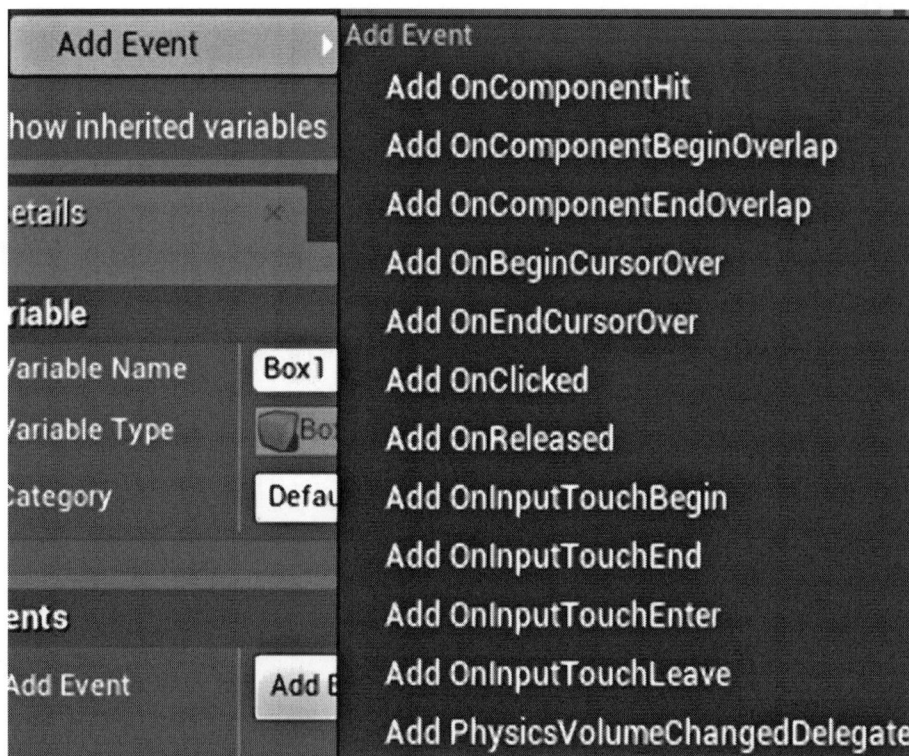

There's a whole boatload of choice here, so we'll quickly go over the options you'll MOST likely use on your adventures:

- AddOnComponentHit - This will fire if your collision volume gets "Hit" (Such as from a "Trace" [Which we covered before with the mouse cursor!])
- AddOnComponentBeginOverlap / End Overlap - We've covered these ones before. If a player or object (We decide!) enters (Or leaves!) the volume, we fire the code attached to these events!
- AddOnBeginCursorOver / EndOnCursorOver - These events fire when a cursor is highlighted over the trigger volume in question!; We'll cover this in detail later on!

For now, all we need is the "AddOnComponentBeginOverlap" event, so go ahead and click it now.

This will create the node in our Blueprint all ready for us to begin having fun with it!

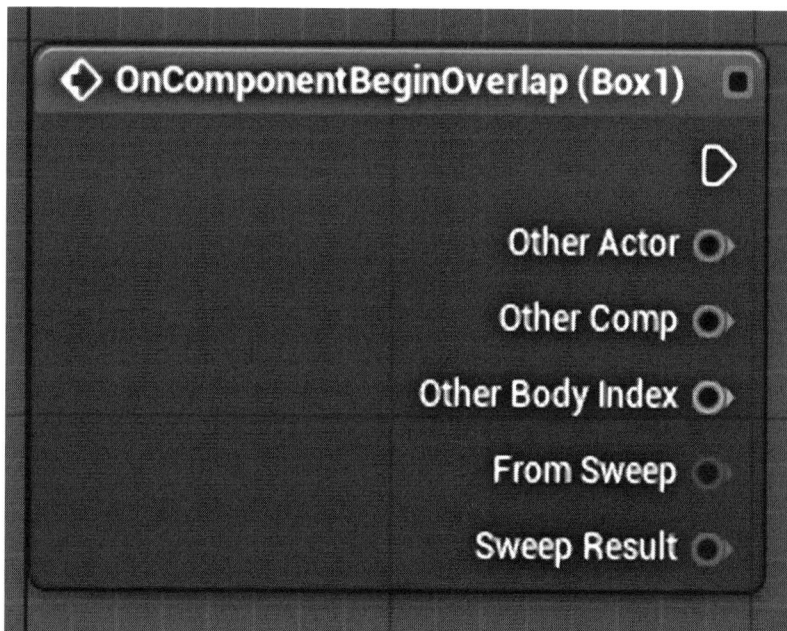

Just like we've already covered; We need to make sure that only the player can activate this code, so go ahead and grab the output pin of "Other Actor" and drag to the right to open up the Compact Blueprint Library. When it opens us, select "Equal(Object)" to create our "==" node.

Just like before, open the CBL once again and create a "Get Player Character" node and connect it to the bottom input of the "Equal(Object)" node.

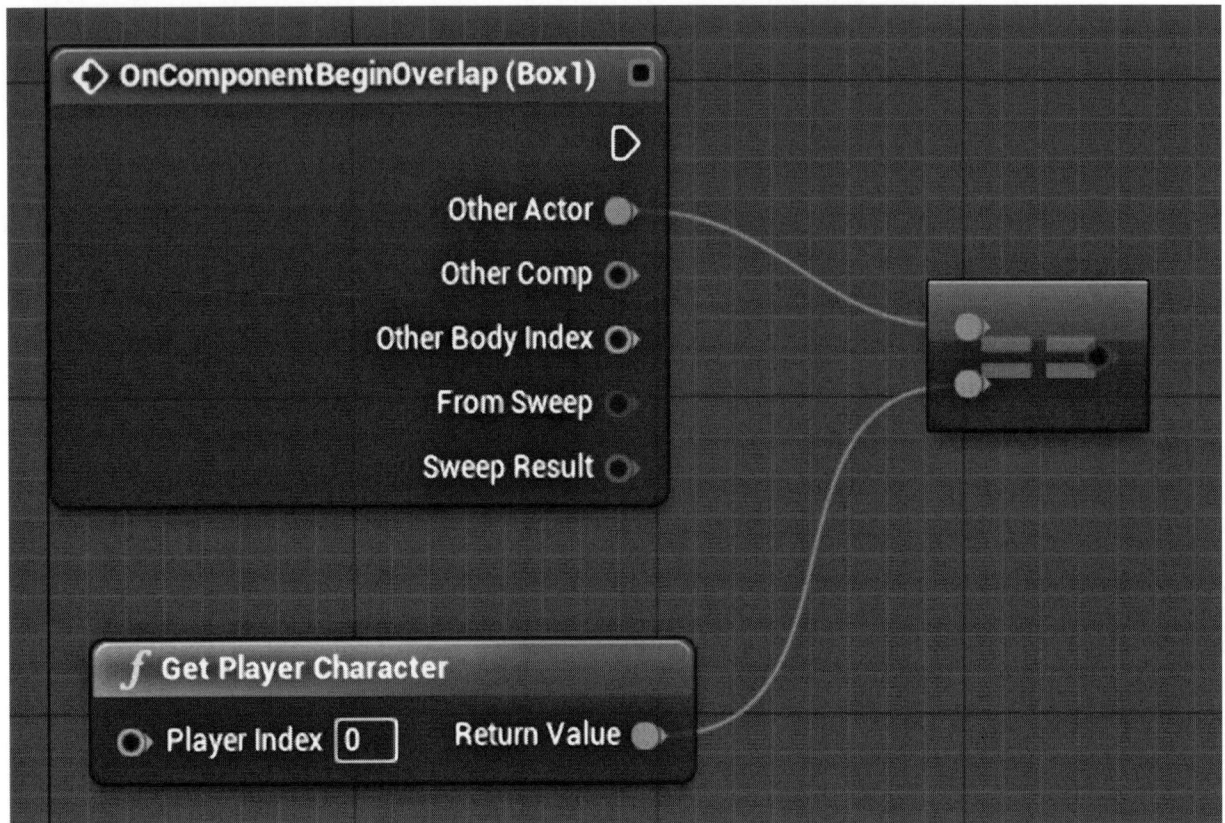

Before we continue, I quickly want to explain what the "Player Index" is and what it's used for. For our project, we don't need to touch it. It's left at zero because we only have a single player... But notice how it's a light green input? Do you remember what this stands for? That's right! - An Integer

If you were creating a multiplayer game, you'd use an integer to get the correct player and you'd use this input to fire this code for that player only; Useful if you want to kill / hurt a player or give them special powers via a powerup .etc!

Anyway, let's head back to OUR project!

You'll notice straight away that the "Equal(Object)" node has a red output pin, which stands for a true / false output. By now, you should be able to guess what needs to go here; But if not, don't worry! The answer is: Create a "Branch" node and hook up the "Condition" to the output of the "Equal(Object)" node. Once done, hook the input execution pin of the "Branch" to the output execution pin of the "Overlap" event node.

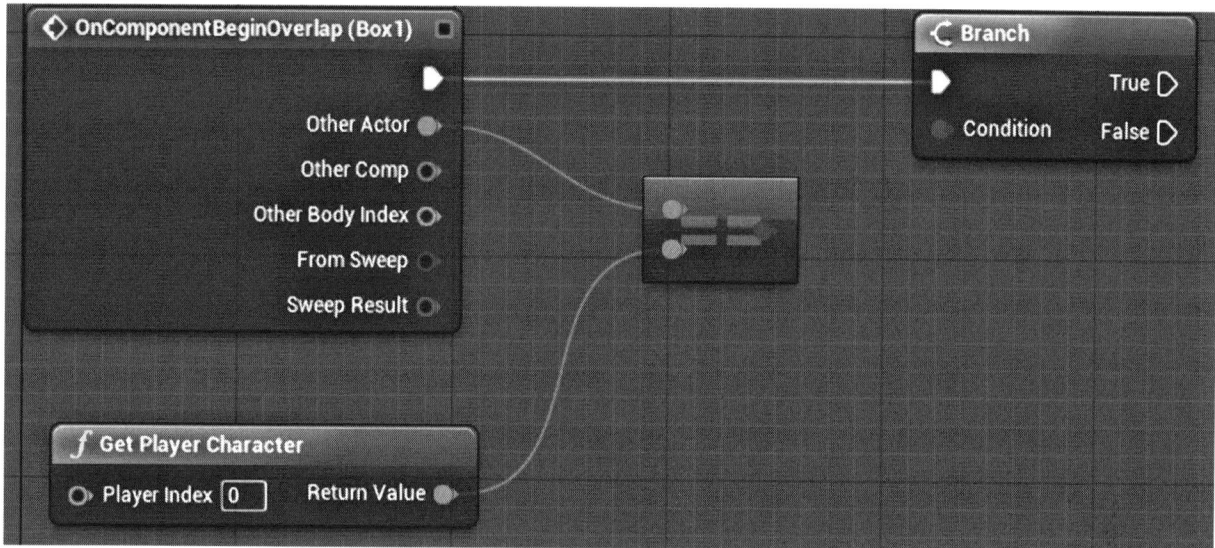

Excellent! So let's break down the code super-quickly: "If the player is touching this box then..."

Super! We're making great progress!

Now, we're going to do something which we have done before, create a "Switch on Int" node! Why? Because as you might have noticed, when creating this Blueprint, we set what type of object the Blueprint represents by the "PickupType" integer. As we have that information, we can use it to our advantage to make sure that the correct code fires, and the player doesn't end up with two tins or two buttons in their inventory!

This is where we're going to pick up the pace a little bit. I hate repeating myself and I'm sure by now you should be getting the hang of things. Don't worry - We'll go over the more confusing things still!

Just like we did in the construction script, create the "Switch on Int" node. Remove the default pin, add two pins (0 and 1) and hook "PickupType" into the "Selection" input.

271

Go ahead once you've done all of that and how it into the "True" from the "Branch" node!

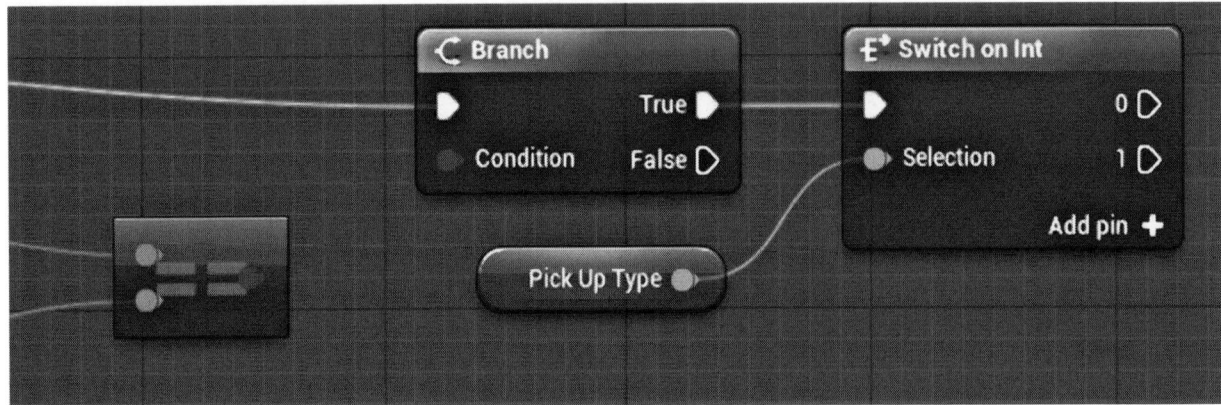

Before we can add what happens to this "Switch On Int", we need to quickly jump over to our "MyCharacter" blueprint and add a tiny amount of code!

Go with our "BP_Pickup" still open, head back into your main project view and open your "MyCharacter" blueprint up *(It's default location will be: "Game > Blueprints > MyCharacter" but Epic like to change it's location in every single update, so you might be better of using the "Search" feature)* via the "Content Browser".

MyCharacter? But I didn't make this!

You'll notice that there's some code in here already and if you check the "Components" tab, you'll notice that we already have a character, collision sphere and a camera. This was all created by Epic for the Third Person Template so we don't have to waste time creating it ourselves.

You'll notice immediately that it looks exactly the same as the character that spawns when we test our map; That's because it IS the same. This little dude/thing is our character in our game. If you wanted to (After this project is over), you could go back in and set the "Mesh" of your "Character" (And animation

Blueprint!") to your own character , with their own animations to give it a more personalised touch !

Why stop there? You can create extra characters and create an epic story spanning multiple characters ala Broken Age!

But that's for you to decide AFTER this book is done. For now, let's focus on getting the core mechanics out of the way!

We're going to create two custom events. One for if the tin can was picked up and one for the button. We'll be able to important parts of the code right now but we're limited into adding ALL of it as we haven't actually created the most important ingredient… More on that later!

Before we continue, make sure you're in the blueprint section of the "MyCharacter" blueprint. (I'm pretty sure I don't have to remind you how to get there / How to tell when you're there by now. If you DO need help getting there, just skim the past few chapters - We've mentioned it a bucketload of times now!)

We need to create two variables before we continue: "HasFiredTin" and "HasFiredButton". Make sure that they are Variable Type: Bool (Yes / No Variables!)

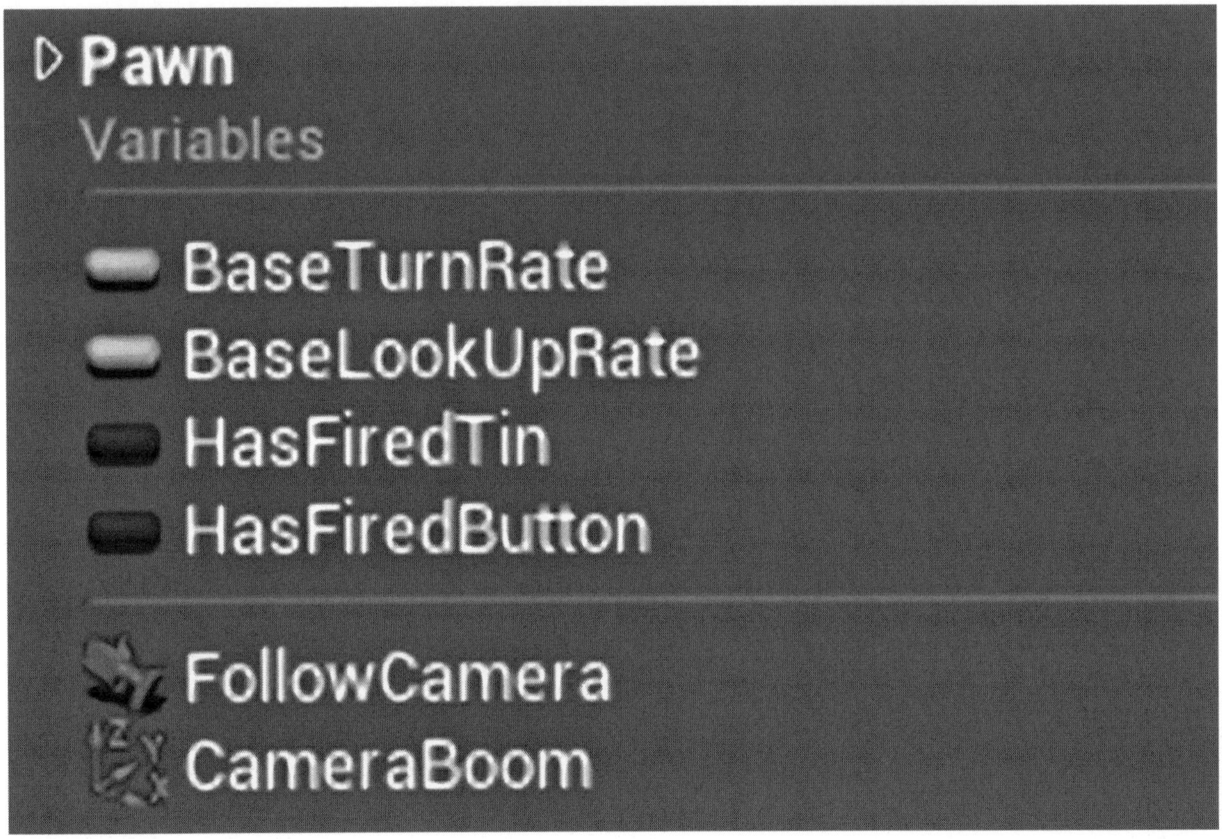

> ▷ **Pawn**
> Variables
>
> ⬤ BaseTurnRate
> ⬤ BaseLookUpRate
> ⬤ HasFiredTin
> ⬤ HasFiredButton
>
> 🌹 FollowCamera
> 📦 CameraBoom

We've created these two variables as we don't want the code we're about to create to fire multiple times; As I said before, we don't want 500 tins and 500 buttons in our Inventory - Just the one tin and one button would do fine!

Once you've created the two variables, go ahead and head into the actual Blueprint. Open up the CompactBlueprintLibrary and create two custom Events: One called: PickedUpTin and the other called: PickedUpButton.

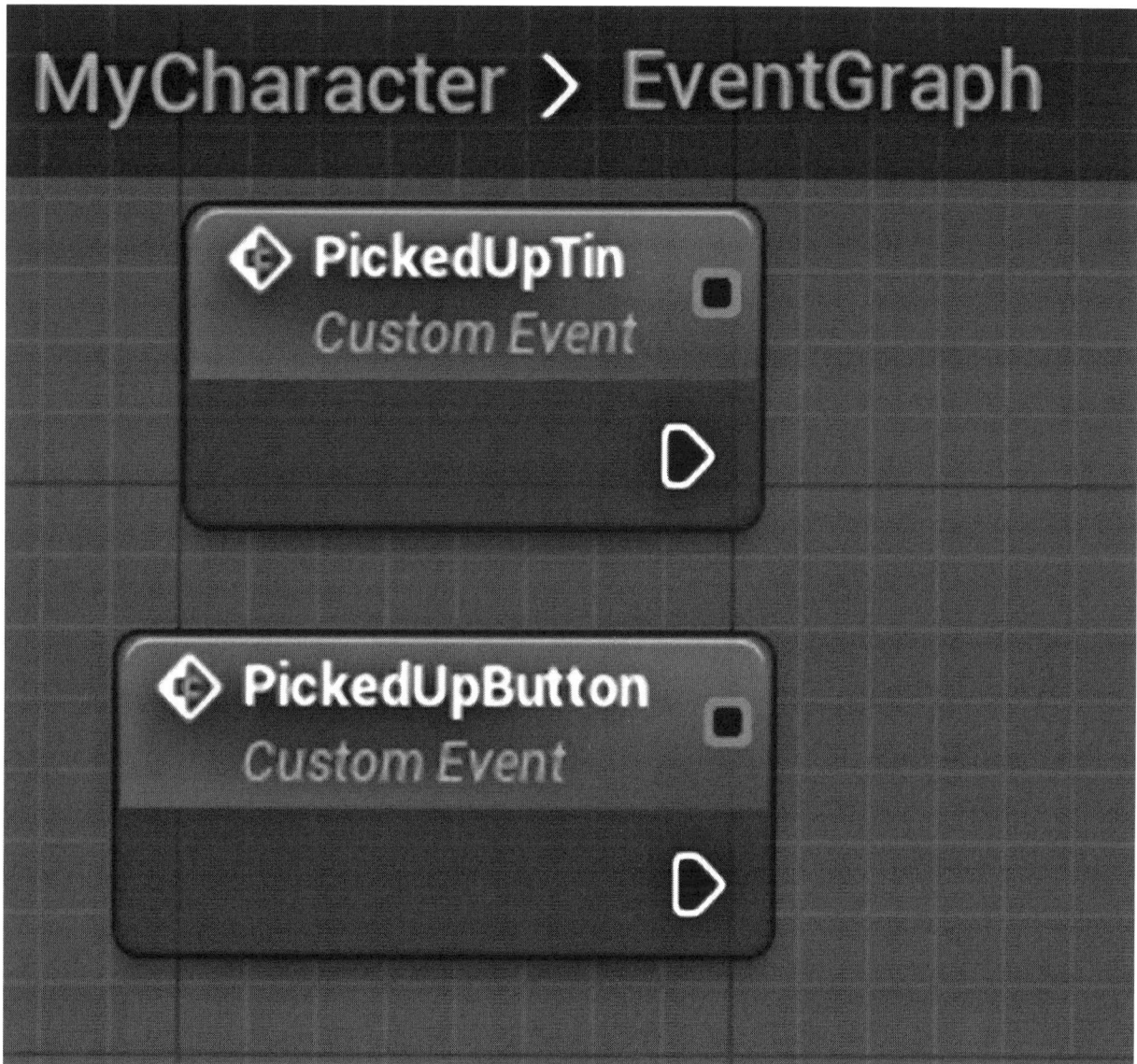

Now, from the Variable Library, drag in the two variables we created ("HasFiredTin" and "HasFiredButton"). When it asks, select "Get" and connect them both to Branches.

Go ahead and connect them to their corresponding events: PickedUpTin should be connected to the Branch that has "HasFiredTin" attached to it .etc

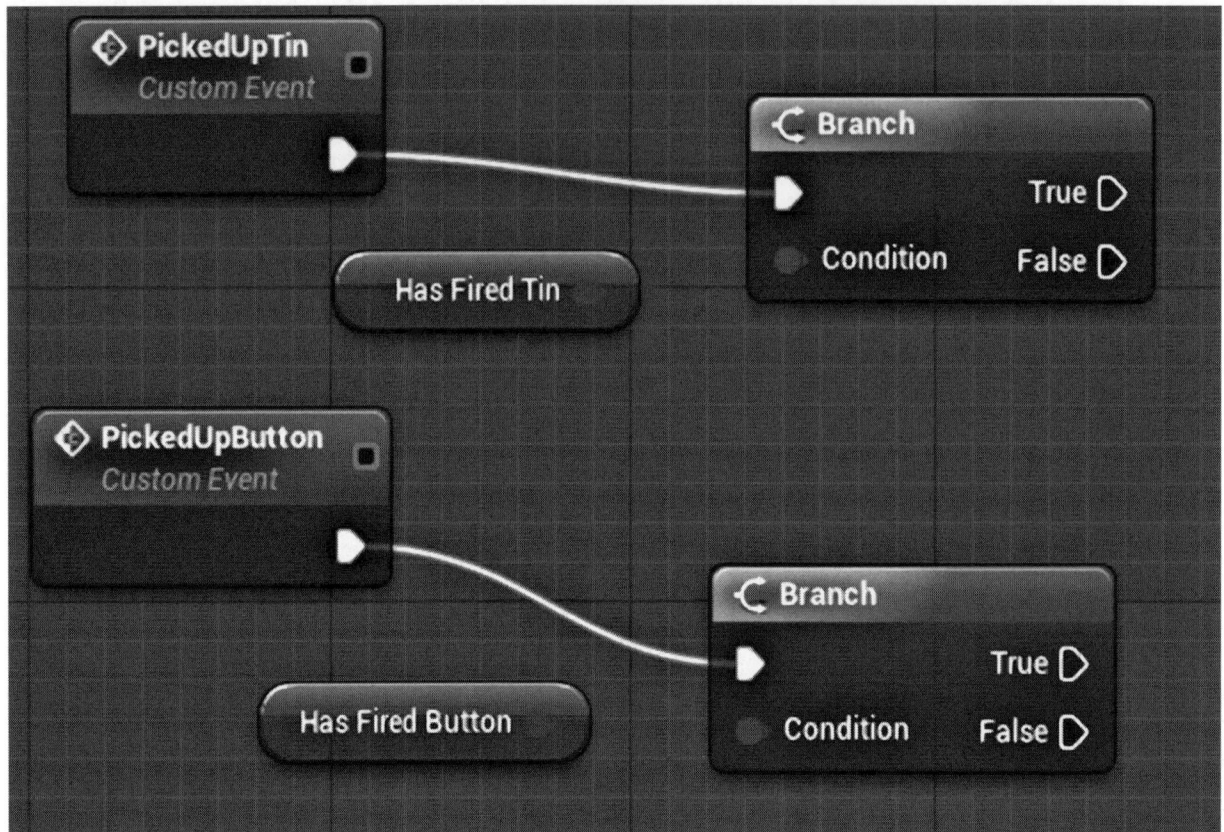

As we don't want to do anything if the button or tin has already been picked up, we'll leave the "True" output of the Branch blank (Not connected to anything).

What we're really going to focus on is what happens when the player has collided with either the tin of button. So let's focus on the "False" outputs of the "Branch" nodes.

First things first, when we're firing these custom events, we're checking to see if the code has already fired. As we are going "It has not fired yet", the first thing we'd better do is tell the Blueprint that the code is now firing.

We can do this very simply by just setting both "Has Fired Button" and "Has Fired Tin" to true, so let's do that now: From your "Variable Library", drag in "Has Fired Tin" and "Has Fired Button" again, into your Blueprint, this time selecting "Set" when it asks.

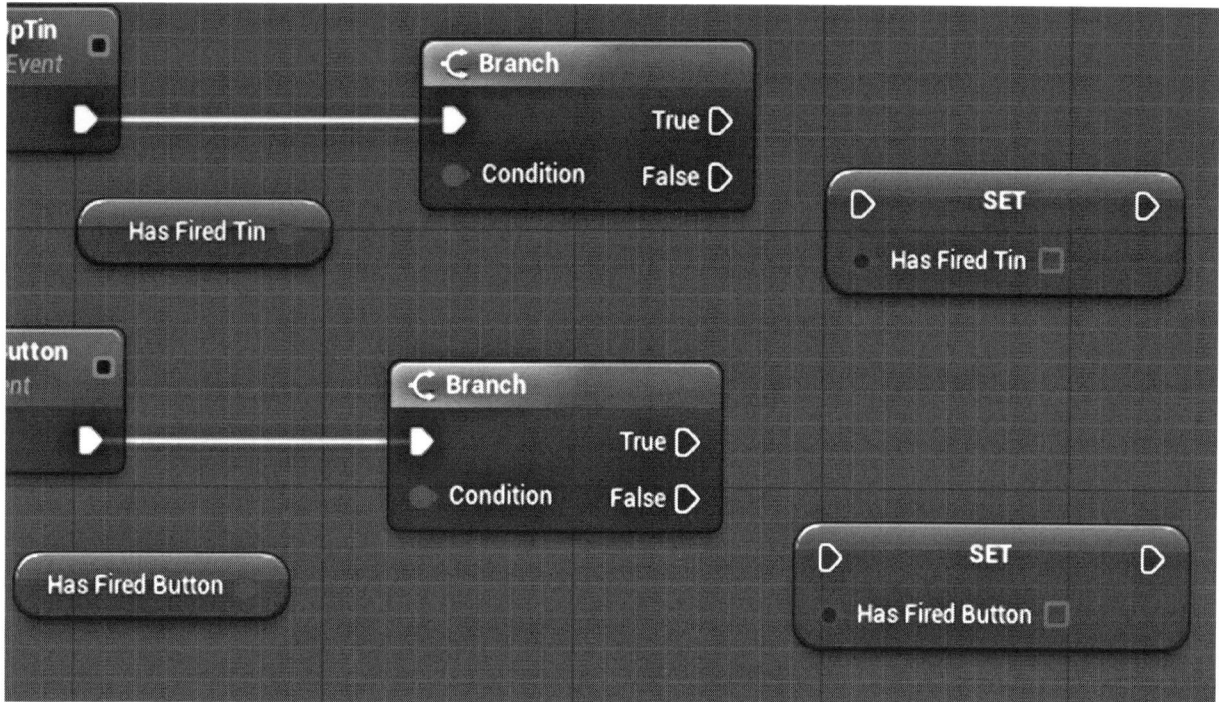

Go ahead and click the empty checkboxes in both of the nodes to set them to
"True" and connect them both to their respective "False" outputs.

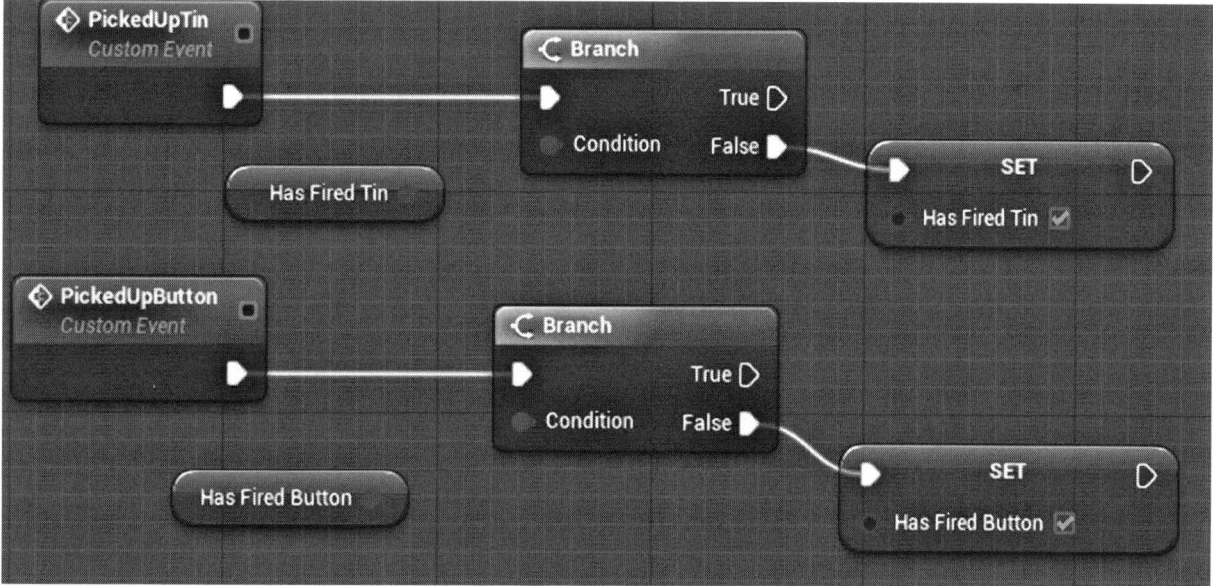

That's all we have to do for the "MyCharacter" blueprint for now. As always
Compile and Save and once saved, go ahead and close the window and re-open the
"BP_Pickup" one more.

277

Back to the BP_Pickup!

Remember where we left off in the BP_Pickup? We were about to add some code to the "SwitchOnInt", but we didn't. That's because the information we needed to have wasn't created... But now it has been!

Don't see what I mean? Well, you're about to!

Open up the CBL and search for "Get Player Character". Create the node. Once created, click the right-hand side output pin and drag to the right. This will open up the Compact Blueprint Library again. This time type in "Cast to MyCharacter" and you'll see "Cast to MyCharacter", go ahead and select that option to create the node.

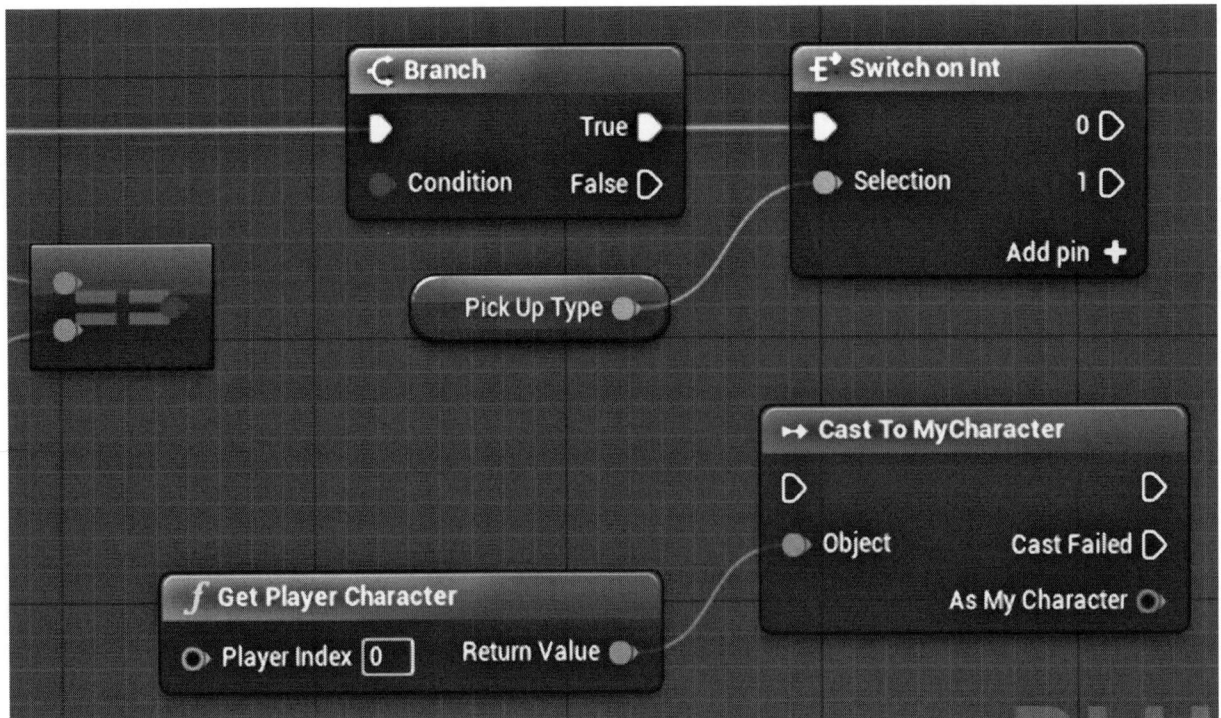

From the "As My Character" node, click and drag to the right. When the CBL opens again, search for "Picked Up" and select the "Picked Up Tin" node.

This node is the custom event we created earlier. When this node is activated, it fires the code in the "MyCharacter" blueprint that was attached to the custom event we created. How magical and mindblowing is that?!

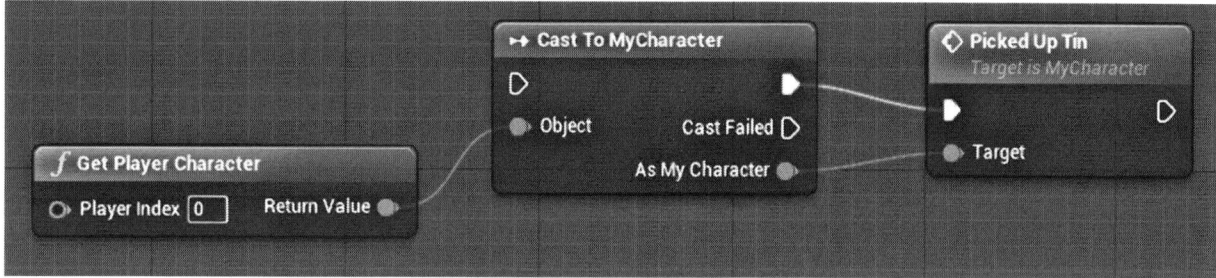

You'll notice that the code at the moment isn't going to fire because it isn't connected to the event ("OnComponcentBeginOverlap"). You can fix this by simply hooking the input execution pin of "Cast to MyCharacter" to the "0" output of "SwitchOnInt".

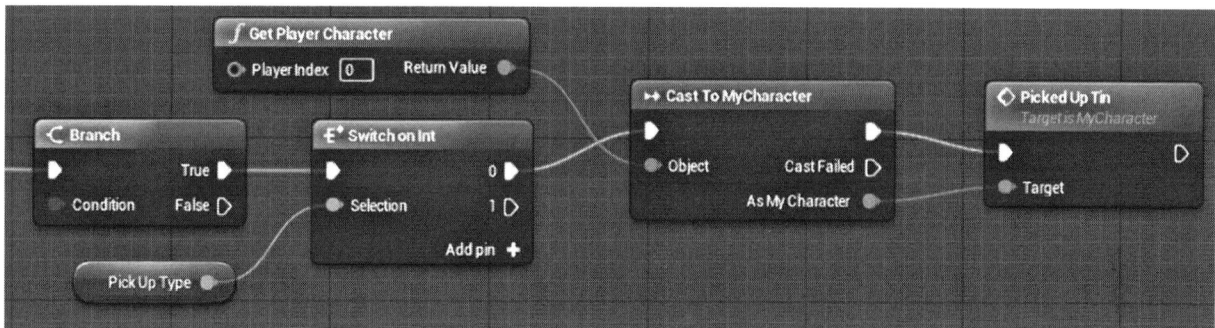

Now repeat the previous few steps but for "Picked Up Button" and connect it to the "1" output of "SwitchOnInt".

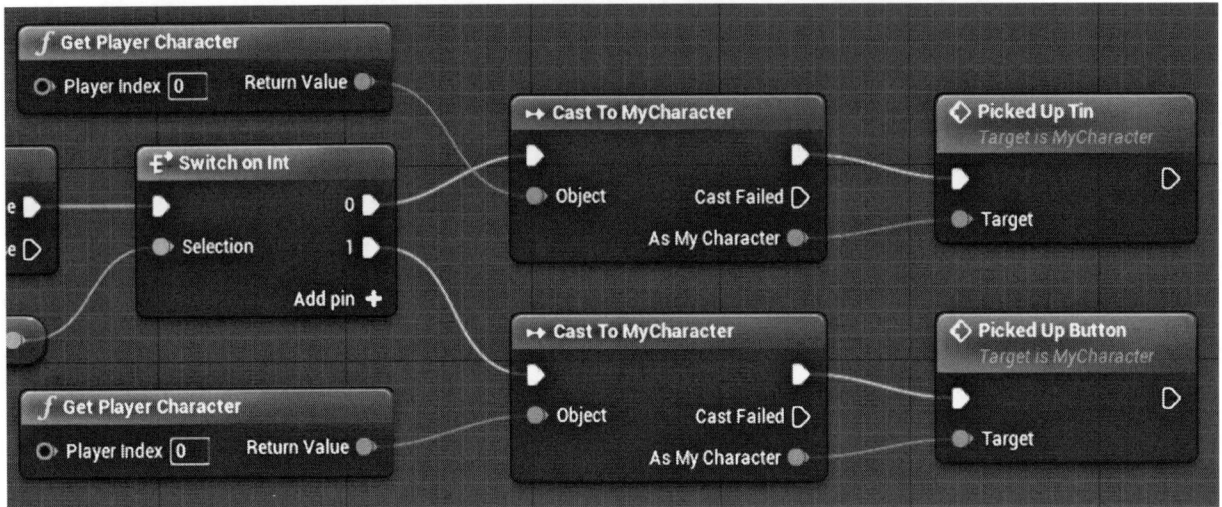

Excellent! Now all we need to do is set the "BP_Pickup" to self-destruct once the player has collided with it. I bet you're thinking that the whole Blueprint will fizzle and bang Mission Impossible style but we don't have enough pages for that; We're just going to make the Blueprint disappear; The fancy stuff will come later!

To destroy the Blueprint, all we have to do is open up the Compact Blueprint Library once more and type in "Destroy", selecting "Destroy Actor".

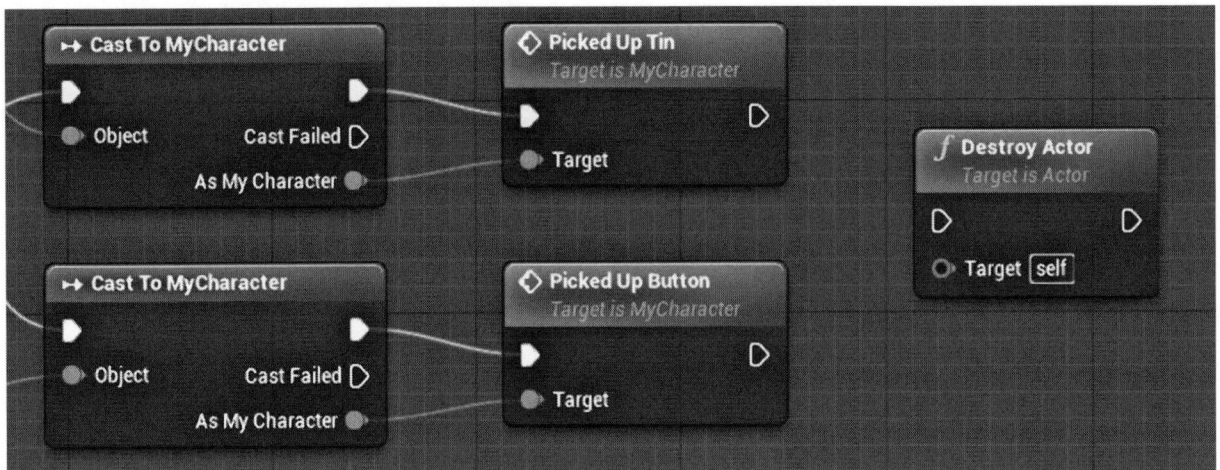

Simply connect both the output execution pins of the "Picked Up Tin" AND "Picked Up Button" and connect them both to the input of "Destroy Actor".

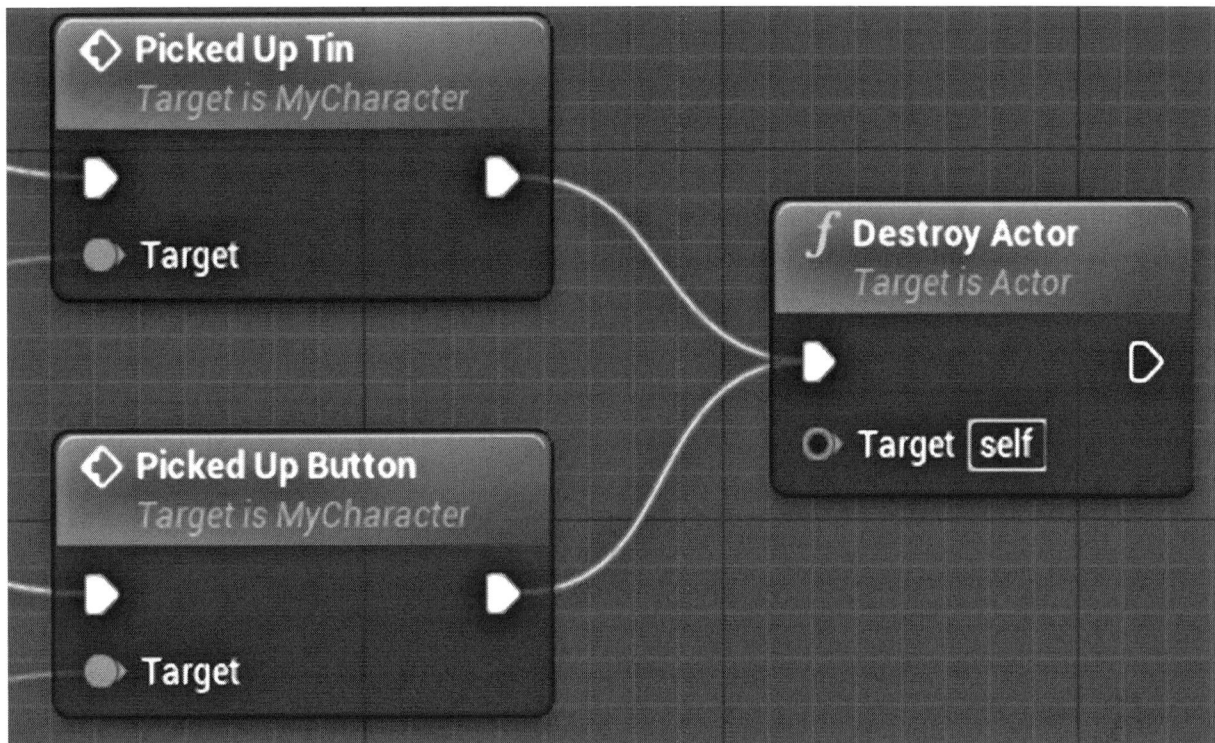

Excellent! Let's take a quick overview of what all this code means in plain english:

"If the player is touching this box, find out what type of object this is supposed to represent. If it's the tin, fire the code in the "MyCharacter" blueprint which tells it that it has picked up the "Tin" and if it's the button, do the same (But for the "Button"). Once you've told "MyCharacter" this information, destroy this Blueprint off the face of the virtual world."

Awesome! Go ahead and compile and save. We've got one place to head into before we can call this part of the mission complete... We need to head back to the Level Blueprint!

Return to the Level Blueprint!

Once you've compiled and saved the "BP_Pickup", head back into main Blueprint window and use the ribbon on the top to head back into the Level Blueprint. If you've forgotten how, simply go back a number of pages as we've talked about it a number of times now!

Once in your Level Blueprint, Head to your "Event Tick" event. Did you know if that you try to create another one (As you can only have one per blueprint!) it will jump to the already created node; Perfect for if you can't find it!

Now once you're back at your Event Tick, click your output pin (Which should already be connected to something). Click and drag to the right. When the CBL opens, type in Sequence and this will create a "Sequence" node with whatever was connected to the Event Tick before already connected to it.

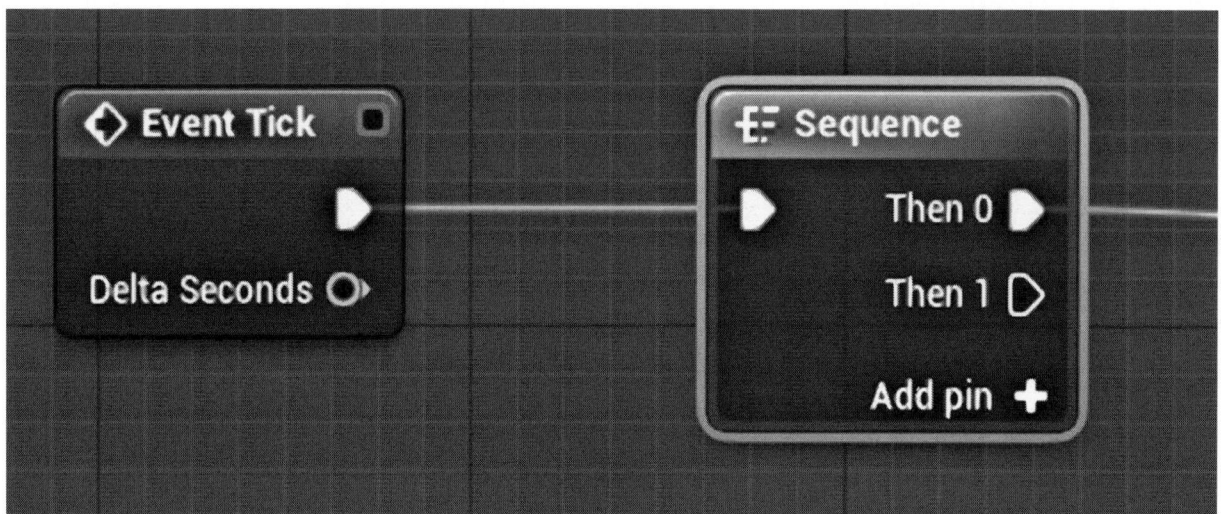

What is a "Sequence" node? - A sequence node is a node that fires multiple codes simultaneously. You normally create them when you need to fire multiple things at once or have only one output execution node when you need to (Our situation right now is a perfect example on how you use them!)

Before we continue, head back into your main scene view really quickly. Remember how we added the cameras and trigger boxes to the Level Blueprint? We're going to do a similar thing with one of the doors in our level. Pick any door in the level (Which the player can walk to) thats connected to the room where the Tin and Button will be. Found one?

Excellent! Now simply highlight the door by clicking it and head back into the Level Blueprint. If you open the Compact Blueprint Library again, You'll now see

"Add reference to BP_Door (Or whatever you called your door)". Click that to create the node we're after.

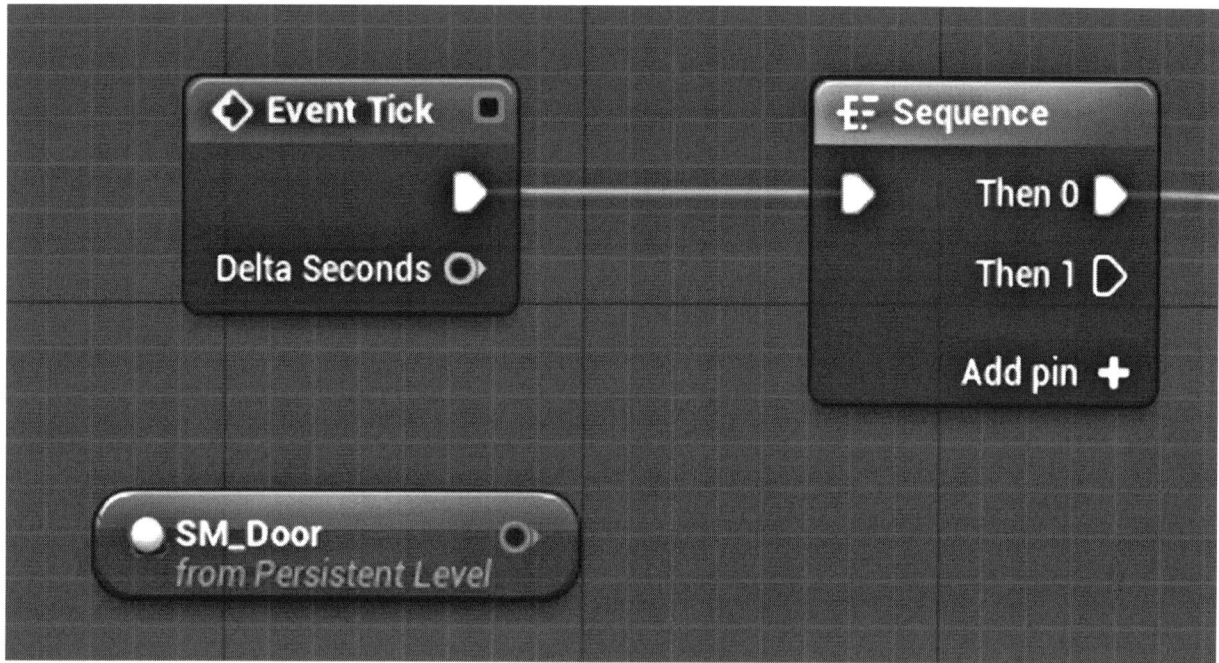

Excellent! Now let's pick up the pace a little bit; Create a new Variable in the Variable Library. Make it a variable type of "Bool" and called it "HasFired?".

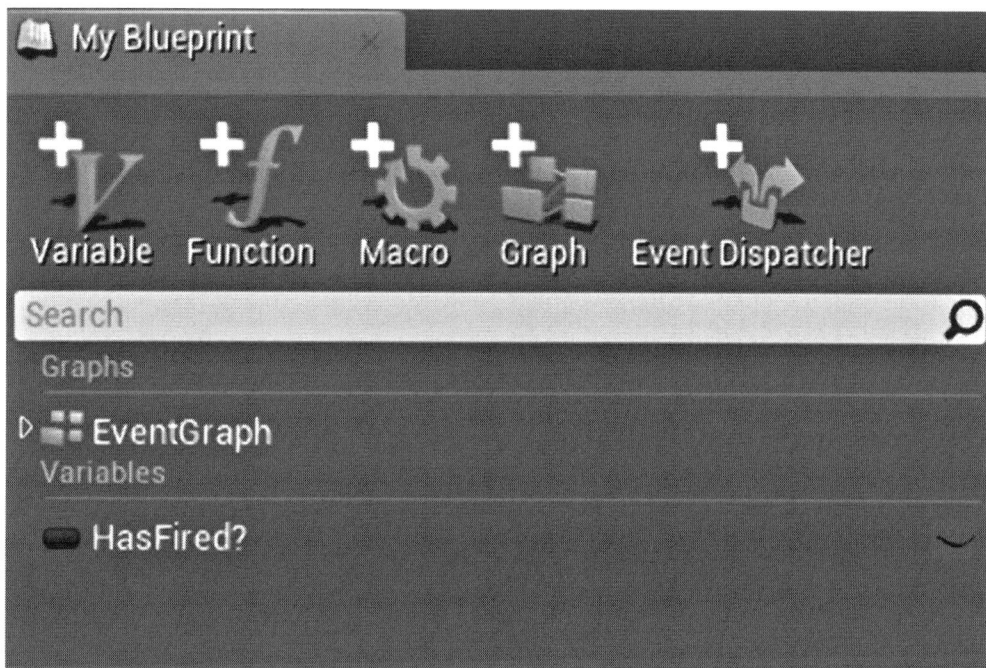

We don't need this now, but we will in the near future!

Now head back into your main Blueprint; Just like before, create a "Get Player Character" node and use it to create a "Cast to "MyCharacter"" node.

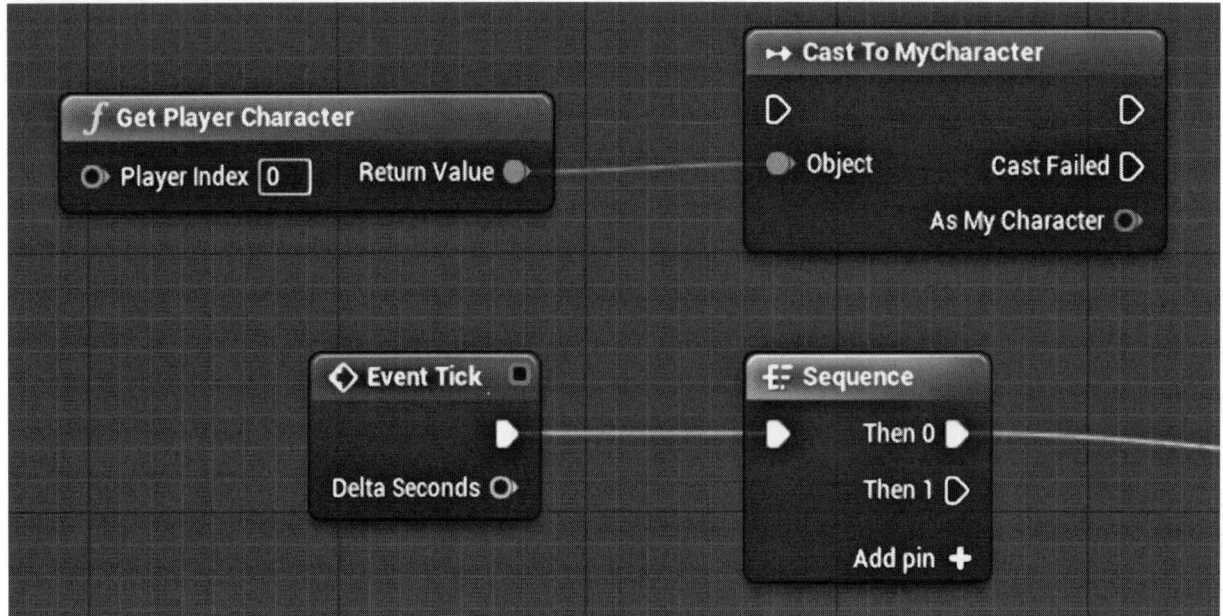

From the "AsMyCharacter" pin, click and drag to the right. If you type in "Has Fired Tin", it will show up.

IF IT DOESN'T, then you're using a certain engine version which randomly messed up casting. Don't worry, it's easy to fix. Simply head back into the "MyCharacter" blueprint and click the closed eye next to both of the "Has Fired Tin" and "Has Fired Button" variables in the variable library.

Simple compile, save and head back to the Level Blueprint. THEN Compile the Level Blueprint and repeat the "From the "AsMyCharacter" pin, click and drag to the right and type in "Has Fired Tin" - It will now show up!

Select "Get Has Fired Tin" and do it again for "Get Has Fired Button".

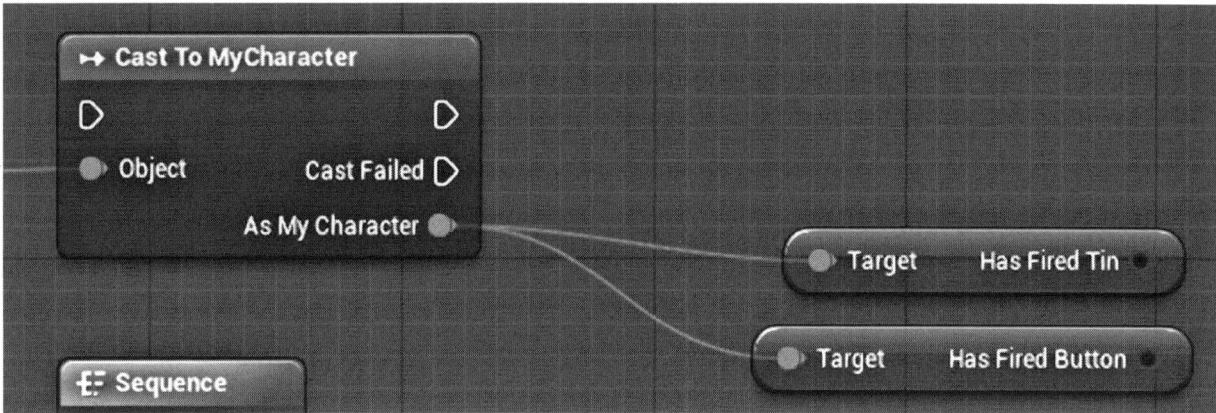

Now create two "Branch" nodes. Connect one of the "Has Fired Tin/Button" nodes to the condition of one of "Branch" and the other "Has Fired Tin/Button" node to the condition of the other "Branch" (The order doesn't really matter.

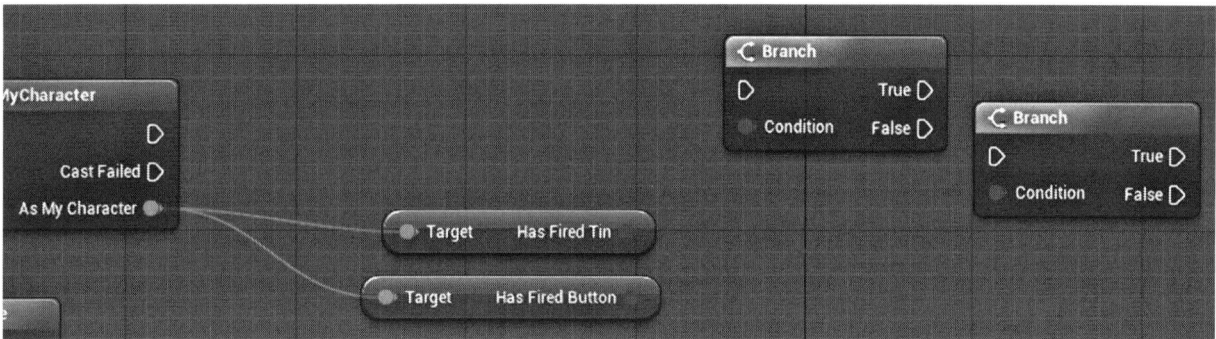

With the first "Branch", connect the output "True" to the input of the second "Branch".

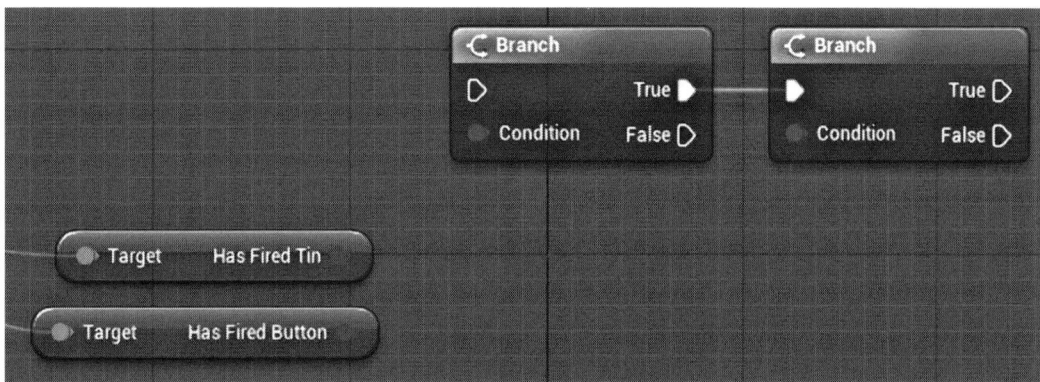

Now we're getting somewhere! Don't worry, I'll convert this code into plain English in a little while!

Remember the output execution pin from "Cast to MyCharacter" (Not the "Cast Failed" pin, but the other output execution pin)? Connect that for the first input of the "Branch".

Just before we continue, See the input execution pin of the "Cast To MyCharacter" - See how it's not connected to anything yet? Go ahead and link it to the "Then 1" pin of "Sequence" now.

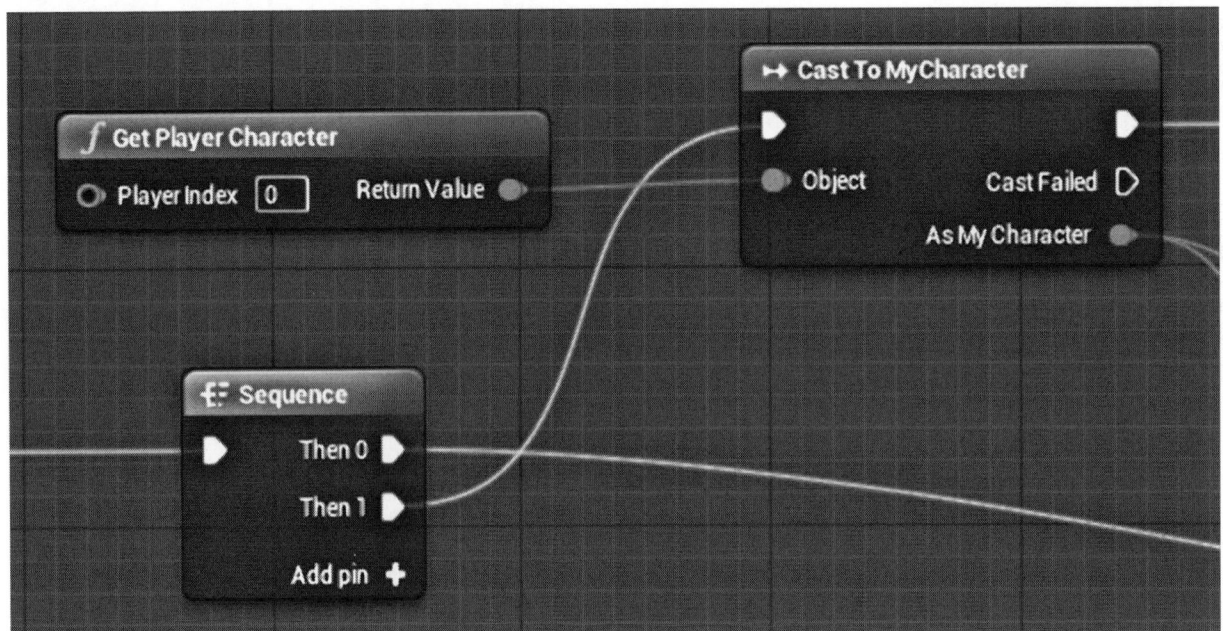

Awesome! We're almost done!

Now, create another "Branch" node and add it to the "True" output of the second "Branch". For the "Condition", drag in the "HasFired?" variable we created in the Variable Library a few steps ago.

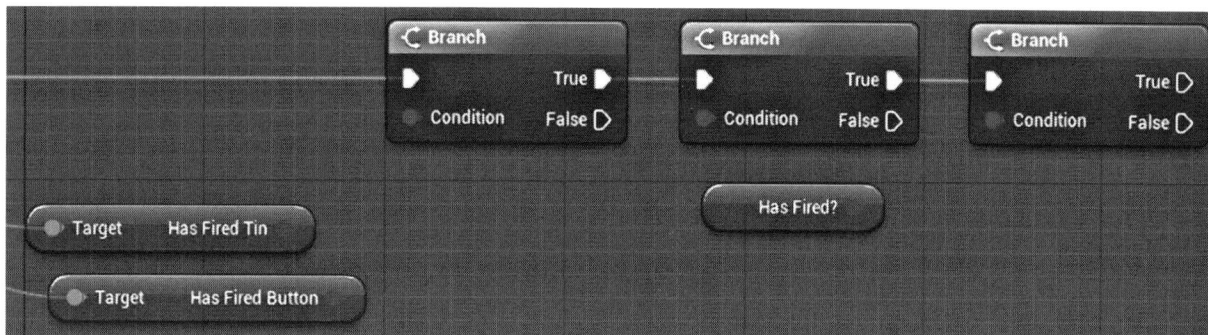

Now drag the variable in AGAIN but this time "Set" it. Connect this to the "False" output of the third "Branch" and make sure you tick the box in the "Set HasFired?" to True.

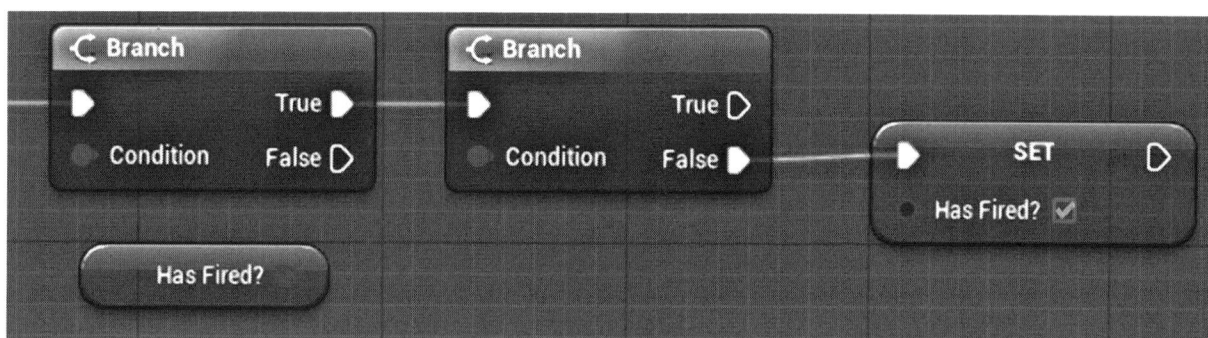

Remember the door you bought into the Blueprint a few steps ago? Now is it's time to shine! Bring it over and from the output pin of the "BP_Door" node (Or whatever you called it) and type in: OpenDoor (Or the name of the Custom Event in the BP_Door which we created AGES ago!)

Connect this node to after the "Set HasFired?".

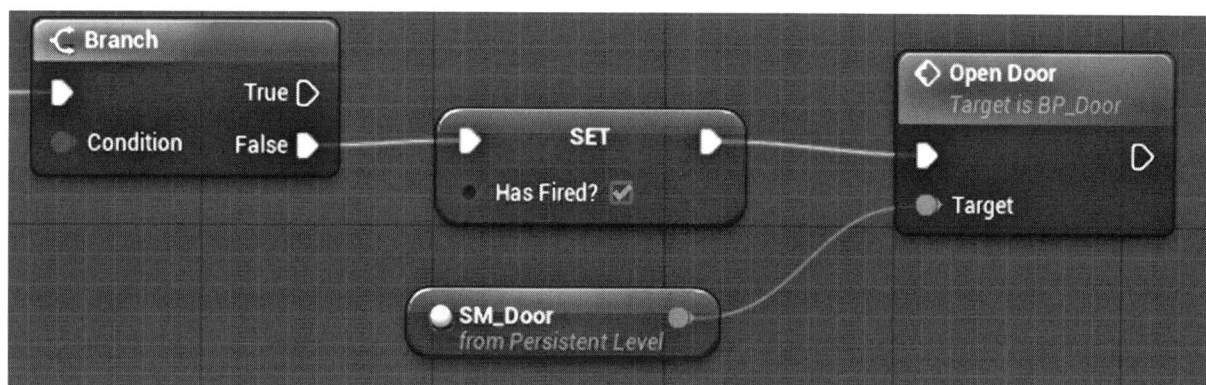

Epic! So what does all of this code mean? Let's translate!

"Find out if the Tin and Button have been picked up. If they have and this code hasn't fired yet, make sure the code doesn't fire again and open the door".

Brilliant! We're just missing ONE last thing from our project! Can you guess what it is…?

Placing our Creations into the World!

Find the room in which the player will start and where the door will open once both parts of the button and tin have been collect. In your Content Browser, drag in two "BP_Pickup"s.

Within the details panel of one of the two "BP_Pickup", set the default "PickUp Type" to 1 (Which will turn it into a button) and leave the other "BP_Pickup" at 0.

Now test out your project.

It works! Great stuff!

Now where do we go from here?...

Finale... For now!

Sadly, that's all from me for now. I know you're moaning and groaning. But this isn't the end!

This is just where Book #1 ends!

I didn't want to make this book TOO big, but I wanted to get the core information out of the way.

The next book will cover all the advanced stuff; As well as actually combining items to open doors, UMG (Heads up display), player choice (Talking to character to change events) as well as many other cool things!

We've just scratched the iceberg, but I recommend you tinker around and use everything you've learnt so far to expand on everything and create something awesome-er!

I originally wanted to cover everything in this one book, but the book grew in size quickly and thus everything that I've left out will be covered in Book #2. We've covered so much thus far that I didn't want overwhelm you with information!

When we return in Book #2, we've got a lot of ground to cover! So for now treat this as a break.

You've done a LOT and made some awesome stuff to build off!

Well done!

I hope you enjoyed this book; There's more to come, we've just scratched the surface!

Helpful Table of Variable Types

Variable Name	Variable Color	What does it used for?
Bool	Red	Yes / No (True or False)
Float	Green	Recording the time or a specific value (Such as speed: 15.10)
Integer	Turquoise	A number between 0 - infinity (That DOES NOT include decimals)
Vector	Yellow	X Y Z value of an object in the world (An object's location)
Rotator	Light Blue / Purple	X Y Z value of an object's rotation in the world (An object's location)

Printed in Great Britain
by Amazon.co.uk, Ltd.,
Marston Gate.